12.95

£5.95

©

Growth
Volume 2:
Energy, the Environment,
and Economic Growth

Library of Congress Cataloging-in-Publication Data

Jorgenson, Dale Weldeau, 1933–
  Growth / Dale W. Jorgenson.
    p.   cm.
  Includes bibliographical references and index.
  Contents: v. 1. Econometric general equilibrium modeling — v. 2. Energy, the environment, and economic growth.
  ISBN 0–262–10073–8 (v. 1: hc: alk. paper). — ISBN 0–262–10074–6 (v. 2: hc: alk. paper)
  1. Economic development — Econometric models. 2. Equilibrium (Economics).
  3. United States — Economic conditions — Econometric models. I. Title.
HD75.J67   1998   98–28689
338.9—dc21   CIP

Growth
Volume 2:
Energy, the Environment,
and Economic Growth

Dale W. Jorgenson

The MIT Press
Cambridge, Massachusetts
London, England

Contents

List of Tables   ix
Preface   xi
List of Sources   xxvii

1 Energy, the Environment, and Economic Growth   1
Dale W. Jorgenson and Peter J. Wilcoxen
    1.1   Introduction   1
    1.2   An Overview of the Model   14
    1.3   The Impact of Environmental Regulation   37
    1.4   The Impact of Higher Energy Prices   52
    1.5   The Impact of Carbon Taxes   65
    1.6   Conclusion   80

**2 Econometric Methods for Applied General Equilibrium
    Analysis   89**
Dale W. Jorgenson
    2.1   Introduction   89
    2.2   Producer Behavior   95
    2.3   Consumer Behavior   111
    2.4   Empirical Results   135

3 Environmental Regulation and U.S. Economic Growth   157
Dale W. Jorgenson and Peter J. Wilcoxen
    3.1   Introduction   157
    3.2   An Overview of the Model   159
    3.3   The Impact of Environmental Regulation   172
    3.4   Conclusions   188

**4 Reducing U.S. Carbon Dioxide Emissions: The Cost of
    Different Goals   195**
Dale W. Jorgenson and Peter J. Wilcoxen
    4.1   Introduction   195

4.2   An Overview of the Model   199
4.3   The Impact of Different Emissions Targets   208
4.4   Conclusion   222

5   The Economic Impact of the Clean Air Act Amendments
    of 1990   229
    Dale W. Jorgenson and Peter J. Wilcoxen
    5.1   Introduction   229
    5.2   An Overview of the Model   231
    5.3   The Impact of Environmental Regulation   239
    5.4   The Impact of the Clean Air Act Amendments of 1990   246

6   Reducing U.S. Carbon Dioxide Emissions: An
    Econometric General Equilibrium Assessment   253
    Dale W. Jorgenson and Peter J. Wilcoxen
    6.1   Introduction   253
    6.2   An Overview of the Model   254
    6.3   A Summary of Results   262
    6.4   Conclusion   272

7   Reducing U.S. Carbon Dioxide Emissions: An Assessment
    of Different Instruments   275
    Dale W. Jorgenson and Peter J. Wilcoxen
    7.1   Introduction   275
    7.2   An Overview of the Model   277
    7.3   An Assessment of Different Instruments   287
    7.4   Conclusion   299

8   Trade Policy and U.S. Economic Growth   303
    Mun S. Ho and Dale W. Jorgenson
    8.1   Introduction   303
    8.2   The Structure of the Model   305
    8.3   Effects of Trade Barriers   315
    8.4   Conclusion   329

9   Environmental Regulation and U.S. Trade   331
    Mun S. Ho and Dale W. Jorgenson
    9.1   Introduction   331
    9.2   A Dynamic Model of the U.S. Economy   333
    9.3   The Trade Impact of Environmental Legislations of
           1965–1977   344
    9.4   Conclusion   371

10 **Stabilization of Carbon Emissions and International
    Competitiveness of U.S. Industries**   **373**
    Mun S. Ho and Dale W. Jorgenson
    10.1   Introduction   373
    10.2   A Dynamic Model of the U.S. Economy   376
    10.3   Carbon Dioxide Emission Regulation and Trade   390
    10.4   Conclusion   408

11 **Fundamental Tax Reform and Energy Markets**   **413**
    Dale W. Jorgenson and Peter J. Wilcoxen
    11.1   Introduction   413
    11.2   An Overview of the Model   414
    11.3   Provisions of U.S. Tax Law   423
    11.4   Fundamental Tax Reform   425
    11.5   Conclusion   431
    Appendix   432

References   443
Index   465

List of Tables

1.2.1 Industry classification   15
1.2.2 Make and use table variables   18
1.3.1 The effects of removing environmental regulations   40
1.4.1 Long-run oil simulation results   57
1.4.2 Decomposition of effects on average growth over 1974–1985   64
1.5.1 Carbon emissions data for 1987   66
1.5.2 Summary of long-run carbon tax simulations   72
2.4.1 Parameter estimates: sectoral models of production and
        technical change   138
2.4.2 Classification of industries by biases of technical change   145
2.4.3 Pooled estimation results   147
3.1   Industry classifications   160
3.2   The effects of removing environmental regulations   176
3.3   Summary of the effects on growth over 1974–1985   191
4.1   Industry classifications   200
4.2   Carbon emissions data for 1987   206
4.3   Summary of long-run carbon tax simulations   216
5.1   Industry classifications   232
5.2   The effects of removing environmental regulations   241
6.1   Industry classifications   256
6.2   Domestic production and heat content of fossil fuels   260
6.3   Carbon emissions data for 1987   261
6.4   Selected results for scenarios 2–4 in 2020   267
6.5   Selected results revenue experiments in 2020   270
7.1   Industry classifications   278
7.2   Domestic production and heat content of fossil fuels   284
7.3   Carbon emissions data for 1987   285
7.4   Long-run effects of different tax instruments   292
7.5   Effects of carbon reduction policies on GNP growth (Differences
        from base case annual average growth rates over 1990–2020)   299

8.1	Import demand elasticities	306
8.2	Export price elasticities	312
8.3	Export demand functions—$\log X_{it} = \gamma_i + \lambda_i \log Y_i^*$	314
8.4	Tariff rates and quota equivalents in 1980	316
8.5	Tariff equivalents of selected quotas	317
8.6	Tariff equivalents of quotas on U.S. imports from Japan	317
8.7	Sectoral effects of eliminating all tariffs in 1980	321
8.8	Sectoral effects of tariff cuts in 2000	322
8.9	Elimination of all trade barriers versus tariffs only (% change)	327
8.10	Elimination of all trade barriers versus tariffs: effects on GNP	327
8.11	Sectoral effects of eliminating all tariffs and selected quotas*	328
9.2.1	Sectoral characteristics of model, 1985 ($billion)	335
9.2.2	Make and use table variables	338
9.2.3	Import demand elasticities—some comparisons	342
9.3.1	Industry environmental costs	347
9.3.2	Steady-state effects of removing environmental regulations	353
10.2.1	Sectoral characteristics of model, 1985 ($billion)	378
10.2.2	Make and use table variables	381
10.2.3	Import demand elasticities	386
10.2.4	Carbon emissions data for 1987	387
10.3.1	Steady-state effects of imposing carbon taxes. (% change from base case unless otherwise indicated)	398
11.1	Industry classifications	416
11.2	Make and use table variables	418

Preface

Dale W. Jorgenson

This is the second of two volumes containing my empirical studies of economic growth and presents an econometric model of the United States that captures the dynamic mechanisms underlying long-run trends. The first volume, *Econometric General Equilibrium Modeling*, introduces the econometric approach to modeling economic growth, using econometric representations of technology and preferences as basic building blocks. Earlier approaches to empirical modeling had "calibrated" the behavioral responses of producers and consumers to a single data point.

Calibration economizes radically on the use of data, but requires highly restrictive assumptions about technology and preferences, such as fixed input-output coefficients. This assumption is contradicted by the massive evidence of energy conservation in response to changes in world energy prices beginning in 1973. As a consequence of these changes and new environmental policies, a wealth of historical experience has accumulated on the price responsiveness of producers and consumers. This experience provides the empirical basis for estimating the impact of alternative economic policies.

This volume includes econometric studies of the impacts of energy, environmental, trade, and tax policies. The concept of an intertemporal price system provides the unifying framework. Such a price system balances demands and supplies for products and factors of production at each point of time. A forward-looking feature of the price system is that asset prices are linked to the present values of future capital services. This is combined with backward linkages among current capital services, the stock of capital, and past investments in modeling the long-run dynamics of economic growth.

The natural starting point for modeling economic growth is the neoclassical theory of economic growth originated by Robert M.

Solow (1956). In modeling the interrelationships between economic policies and economic growth we employ the form of this theory developed by David Cass (1965) and Tjalling C. Koopmans (1967). In the neoclassical model wage rates grow at the same rate as productivity in the long run, while rates of return depend on productivity growth and parameters describing saving behavior. However, these long-run characteristics of economic growth are independent of economic policies.

The neoclassical theory of economic growth also provides a basis for interpreting intermediate-run growth trends. In this context the intermediate run refers to the time needed for the capital-output ratio to converge to its long-run stationary value. Since this often requires several decades, intermediate-run trends are critical for policy evaluation. These have the same determinants as long-run trends, but also depend on economic policies through their effects on capital accumulation and rates of productivity growth over shorter periods.

In chapter 1, Peter J. Wilcoxen and I present an econometric model for analyzing the impacts of energy and environmental policies on the U.S. economy. We first introduce a distinction among industries and commodities. This makes it possible to model differences in the responses of producers to changes in energy prices and the imposition of pollution controls. We also distinguish among households by level of wealth and demographic characteristics. This facilitates modeling differences in responses of consumers to price changes and controls on pollution.

It is important to recognize at the outset that the dominant tradition in general equilibrium modeling does not employ econometric methods. This tradition originated with the seminal work of Wassily W. Leontief (1951, 1953) on input-output analysis. One important advantage of the "fixed-coefficients" assumption underlying input-output analysis is that the resulting general equilibrium model can be solved as a system of linear equations. In addition, the unknown parameters describing technology and preferences can be "calibrated" to match the data from a single inter-industry transactions table.

The obvious disadvantage of the assumption of fixed input-output coefficients is that energy and environmental policies induce changes in these coefficients. In fact, the objective of pollution control regulations is to induce producers and consumers to substitute less polluting inputs for more polluting ones. In addition, the fixed-coefficients assumption is directly contradicted by massive evidence of price-induced energy conservation in response to higher world energy prices beginning in 1973. Reductions in energy-output ratios induced by the successive energy crises of the 1970s and 1980s have averaged 15–20 percent.

In chapter 1, Wilcoxen and I have analyzed a "natural experiment" provided by variations in energy prices in the 1970s and 1980s. Over the period 1972–1987 U.S. emissions of carbon dioxide, an important by-product of the combustion of fossil fuels, were stabilized by price-induced energy conservation. We attempt to separate the long-run impact of higher energy prices from the intermediate-run impact of sharp increases in energy prices associated the energy crisis periods of 1973–1975 and 1978–1980. We find that "price shocks" account for almost two-thirds of the slowdown in economic growth during the period 1974–1985. Long-run increases in energy prices account for the remaining one-third.

The first successful implementation of an applied general equilibrium model without the fixed-coefficients assumption of input-output analysis is due to Leif Johansen (1960). Johansen retained the fixed-coefficients assumption in modeling demand for intermediate goods, including energy, but employed linear logarithmic or Cobb-Douglas production functions in modeling substitution between capital and labor services and technical change. He replaced the fixed-coefficients assumption for consumers by a system of demand functions originated by Ragnar Frisch (1959). These representations of technology and preferences make only minimal use of econometrics.

The essential features of Johansen's approach to applied general equilibrium modeling have been preserved in the models surveyed by Lars Bergman (1985) and John Shoven and John Whalley (1992). The unknown parameters describing technology and preferences in these models are determined by "calibration" to a Social Accounting Matrix (SAM) for a single point of time, supplemented by a small number of parameters estimated econometrically. Almost all general equilibrium models retain the fixed-coefficients assumption of Leontief and Johansen for energy and other intermediate goods, even in the face of widespread contradictory evidence.

Applied general equilibrium models calibrated to data for a single point of time have usually retained the assumption of constant returns to scale in production. As a consequence of this assumption, commodity prices can be expressed as a function of factor prices, using the nonsubstitution theorem of Paul Samuelson (1951). This greatly facilitates the solution of general equilibrium models by permitting a reduction in the dimensionality of the space of prices determined by the model. This feature of nonlinear general equilibrium models has been exploited in applications of "fixed point" methods for solution of these models pioneered by Herbert Scarf (1973, 1984).

To overcome the limitations of the Johansen approach, it is essential to employ econometric methods, like those I present in chapter 2. In order to implement econometric models of producer behavior I generate complete systems of demand functions, giving inputs of capital, labor, energy, and materials inputs (KLEM) in each industrial sector as functions of input prices and the level of output. Ernst R. Berndt and I (1973) originated this approach to modeling producer behavior and Edward A. Hudson and I (1974) employed the results in modeling energy policy and U.S. economic growth. Applications of this approach are presented in the accompanying volume, *Econometric General Equilibrium Modeling*.

Chapter 2 presents a more detailed econometric model of producer behavior that I have constructed with Barbara M. Fraumeni (1981). This includes separate econometric models for each of thirty-five industries that make up the U.S. economy. For each industry the model consists of a complete system of input demand functions, together with an equation that determines the rate of productivity growth. The rate of productivity growth and the input-output coefficients for capital, labor, energy, and materials inputs are functions of the prices of all four inputs as well as time trends. Estimation of these models requires data from a time series of interindustry transactions tables in current and constant prices. More details are provided in our paper in the volume, *Econometrics and Producer Behavior*.

Similarly, econometric models of consumer behavior can be used to overcome the limitations of the Frisch model employed by Johansen. Hudson and I employed a complete system of demand functions, giving quantities demanded as functions of prices and total expenditure. However, this model was based on the notion of a representative consumer. In chapter 2, I describe an alternative approach based on Lawrence Lau's (1982) theory of exact aggregation. One of the most remarkable features of models based on exact aggregation is that systems of demand functions for individuals can be recovered uniquely from the system of aggregate demand functions. This makes it possible to incorporate the implications of the theory of the individual consumer into a model of aggregate consumer behavior.

Chapter 2 presents an econometric model of aggregate consumer behavior based on the theory of exact aggregation that I have constructed with Lau and Thomas M. Stoker (1982). This approach requires time-series data on prices and aggregate quantities consumed, as well as cross-section data on individual quantities consumed, individual total expenditures, and attributes of individual households, such as demographic characteristics. Systems of aggregate demand functions depend on statistics of the joint distribution of individual total expenditures and attributes of individuals associated with differences in preferences. Additional details are given in our paper in the volume, *Aggregate Consumer Behavior*.

The starting point for construction of the econometric models presented in chapter 2 is a system of national accounts for the U.S. presented in my 1980 paper and implemented in my paper with Fraumeni (1980). This accounting system integrates production and income and expenditure accounts for the U.S. economy with a wealth account. The production account includes a complete interindustry transactions table for the thirty-five industrial sectors of the model in current and constant prices and is described in greater detail in chapter 1 in the volume, *International Comparisons of Economic Growth*. The income and expenditure and wealth accounts are also given in current and constant prices. These update and extend the accounts presented in my paper with Laurits Christensen, chapter 5 in the volume, *Postwar U.S. Economic Growth*.

In chapter 3, Wilcoxen and I present an intertemporal general equilibrium model for analyzing energy and environmental policies. This model incorporates the econometric representations of technology and preferences given in chapter 2 as basic building blocks. The production model includes systems of demand functions for capital, labor, energy, and materials inputs and a model of endogenous productivity growth for each of thirty-five sectors of the U.S. economy. The model of consumer behavior is based on exact aggregation and includes a systems of demand functions for five commodity groups—energy, food, nondurable goods, capital services, and other services for each of 672 household types.

In chapter 3, Wilcoxen and I analyze the impact of environmental regulations on U.S. economic growth. We have utilized detailed data on costs of compliance imposed on individual industries by these regulations. We first simulate future U.S. economic growth with the existing regulations in place in order to provide a base case for comparison with growth under alternative environmental policies. These policies correspond to different costs of pollution control for the industries and generate different time paths for U.S. economic growth. Removing environmental regulations produces an alternative growth path and we refer to this as the alternative case.

An intertemporal submodel incorporates backward-looking and forward-looking equations that determine the time paths of capital stock, consumption, and asset prices. Given the values of these variables in any time period, an intratemporal submodel determines prices that balance demands and supplies for the thirty-five commodity groups included in the model, capital and labor services, and non-competing imports. The two models must be solved simultaneously to obtain a complete intertemporal equilibrium. Additional details are given in chapter 1. Wilcoxen (1992) surveys alternative computational approaches for solving intertemporal general equilibrium models.

We decompose the overall effect of environmental regulations into components associated with pollution abatement in industry and controls on motor vehicle emissions. We measure the impact of the regulations by eliminating each type of control separately and then eliminating both. We compare growth in the base case with growth in these alternative cases. The growth path with pollution controls differs from the base case at the initial equlibrium, at steady state growth, and on the transition path that traces out the U.S. economy's adjustment to the alternative environmental policy.

Pollution controls have led to a reduction of 2.6 percent in the level of the national product, resulting from an even greater decline in capital accumulation. For many industries the most important impact of environmental regulation is through mandatory investment in costly pollution abatement equipment. The transition to long-run equilibrium of the capital-output ratio requires more than two decades. This illustrates the critical importance of the dynamics of adjustment to the long-run steady state. The industries most affected by these regulations are the motor vehicles and coal mining industries. Primary metals and petroleum refining have followed closely behind.

In chapter 5, Wilcoxen and I analyze the impact of the Clean Air Act Amendments of 1990. For this purpose we project the growth of the U.S. economy with and without this legislation. We begin with estimates of the cost of compliance with the legislation in the year 2005 prepared by the Environmental Protection Agency (1991), since the provisions of this legislation will be phased in gradually over a fifteen year period. The sectors affected by the new pollution controls are electric utilities and primary metals. There is a short-run surge of investment to take advantage of lower prices of investment goods before the full impact of the legislation works its way through the economy, but the long-run impact is to reduce capital accumulation and economic growth.

The Clean Air Act Amendments of 1990 included a provision, Section 812, that required the Environmental Protection Agency to conduct periodic studies of the impact of the Clean Air Act. The Agency submitted the first of these studies to the Congress in 1997. This study compared benefits and costs of the Clean Air Act during the period 1970 to 1990, prior to the Clean Air Act Amendments. The methodology for analyzing the impact of the Clean Air Act on the growth and structure of the U.S. economy is similar to that presented in chapters 3 and 5. For this purpose new data on costs of pollution controls have been constructed and inserted into the model that Wilcoxen and I have presented in chapter 3.

The 1997 study of the Clean Air Act by the Environmental Protection Agency combines costs of pollution controls with detailed estimates of environmental benefits. These estimates are based on emissions of pollutants covered by the Clean Air Act, effects of these emissions on air quality, and impacts of air quality on human health, natural ecosystems, and agriculture. Each of these impacts is evaluated economically to obtain the benefits of reductions in emissions and increases in air quality resulting from environmental regulations.

Emissions of greenhouse gases, such as carbon dioxide, gradually increase atmospheric concentrations. These gases trap heat reflected from the earth in the form of light and warm the atmosphere. The possibility that carbon dioxide emissions from fossil fuel combustion might lead to warming of the global climate through the "greenhouse effect" has emerged as a leading international concern. On December 10, 1997, 160 nations signed the Kyoto Agreement, calling for reductions in emissions of carbon dioxide and other greenhouse gases.

A policy often proposed for reducing emissions of carbon dioxide is a tax on fossil fuels in proportion to carbon content. This is known as a "carbon" tax and could lead to reductions in energy use, substitution of other forms of energy for fossil fuels, and substitution among fossil fuels to reduce carbon dioxide emissions. For example, substitution of natural gas for coal in electricity generation, holding the output of electricity constant, would reduce carbon dioxide emissions. In chapter 4 Wilcoxen and I employ the model presented in chapter 3 to analyze the economic impact of a carbon tax.

We assume that carbon dioxide emissions are proportional to fossil fuel use. We calculate the carbon content of each fuel by combining data from the Department of Energy on the heat content of the fuels with data from the Environmental Protection Agency on emissions of carbon dioxide per unit of heat produced by combustion. We consider three alternative goals:

1. Stabilizing carbon dioxide emissions at 1990 levels.

2. Decreasing carbon emissions gradually over the period 1990–2005 until they are twenty percent below 1990 levels.

3. Doing nothing until 2000, then gradually increasing the carbon tax over the period 2000–2010 to stabilize emissions at 2000 levels.

To simulate the impact of a carbon tax we constrain total carbon dioxide emissions and calculate the required level of the carbon tax. We hold the real value of government spending constant and allow the average tax on labor income to adjust in order to leave the government deficit unchanged. We hold the marginal tax rate on labor income constant, so that adjustments in the average tax rate reflect changes in the implicit zero-tax threshold. The principal impact of a carbon tax in all three simulations is to increase purchasers' prices of coal and crude oil. The rising price of fossil fuels results in a decline in primary energy use, as well as substitutions among fuels to reduce emissions.

The impact of a carbon tax is most severe for the coal mining industry. Even with the least stringent restrictions on emissions, coal production would fall by sixteen percent, relative to the base case. The most extreme restrictions could lead to a decline of more than fifty percent in coal mining and a fifteen percent reduction in electricity production. While the economy-wide effects of a carbon tax would be limited, the costs rise very rapidly with emission reductions. Since the benefits of a carbon tax depend on policies adopted by other countries, a cost-benefit comparison can be carried out only at the world level, as in the pioneering studies of Alan S. Manne and Richard Richels (1992) and William Nordhaus (1994), summarized in Chapter 1.

Daniel T. Slesnick, Wilcoxen, and I have evaluated the impact of a carbon tax on economic welfare in chapter 9 of the volume, *Measuring Social Welfare*. To estimate the impact of a carbon tax on individual welfare we consider a population of infinite-lived consumers or "dynasties." Households are classified by demographic characteristics, but each type is linked to similar types in the future through intergenerational altruism. We define social welfare on the distribution of individual welfare over the population of households. The welfare cost of a carbon tax is dominated by a loss in efficiency; the equity impact of the tax can be positive or negative, depending on the degree of aversion to inequality.

In chapter 7 Wilcoxen and I compare the effects of alternative tax instruments for reducing carbon dioxide emissions. We consider a Btu tax with tax rates proportional to the heat content of each fuel and an ad valorem tax with rates proportional to the value of the fuel. We constrain emissions at 1990 levels and calculate the rates required for each of the taxes. As in chapter 4, tax revenues are used to reduce the average tax on labor income, while holding marginal tax rates constant. As expected, the carbon tax achieves reductions with minimum impact on the U.S. economy and has the greatest impact on coal production. The energy tax is similar in its impact to a carbon tax. The ad valorem tax produces the most severe distortions in the economy, but has the least impact on coal mining.

In the tax simulations reported in chapters 4 and 7 the principal macroeconomic mechanism for adjusting to changes in tax policy is the alteration of rates of capital formation. A second mechanism is the pricing of capital assets through forward-looking expectations of future prices and discount rates. Both these mechanisms are captured by the intertemporal general equilibrium that Wilcoxen and I have presented in chapter 3. The most important impacts of the alternative tax policies are on the energy sector. The overall impact on the U.S. economy reflects the tax distortions introduced into energy markets.

In chapter 6 Wilcoxen and I summarize our contribution to Energy Modeling Forum 12, a comparison of the costs of limiting emissions of carbon dioxide organized by the Energy Modeling Forum at Stanford University. More than a dozen different models were compared in this study. Three features of our model are important in these comparisons. First, our model is highly disaggregated for both producers and consumers. Second, the model incorporates econometric models that reflect historical changes in energy prices. Third, productivity growth in each sector is an endogenous function of relative prices.

Even a modest carbon tax would raise substantial revenue. We first consider a lump-sum rebate of this revenue to households. This is, however, not the most likely use of the tax revenue, so we also consider lower marginal and average taxes on labor income. Finally, we consider lower average and marginal taxes on capital income. We find that methods for "recycling" the revenue have significant effects on the overall impact of a carbon tax. With a lump-sum rebate to households the aggregate output of the U.S. economy would decline by 1.70 percent in the long run, relative to the base case. When marginal as well as average tax rates on labor income are reduced, the decline in output is only 0.69 percent or less than half. Finally, a reduction in capital income taxes produces a gain in output of 1.10 percent.

The recycling of revenues from a carbon tax in order to reduce capital income illustrations the notion of a "double dividend." The first dividend is the improvement in environmental quality that results from lower carbon dioxide emission. The second is the stimulus to economic growth from greater investment and more rapid capital accumulation as a consequence of lower capital income taxes. This double dividend is the result of trading an existing tax distortion, namely, the distortion that results from capital income taxes, against a new distortion—the distortion of energy markets resulting from a carbon tax. Lawrence Goulder (1995) has surveyed the literature on the double dividend.

In chapter 8 Mun S. Ho and I present an intertemporal general equilibrium model for analyzing the impact of changes in trade policy on U.S. economic growth. This model preserves all of the features of the model summarized in chapter 1, including disaggregation into 35 industries and the corresponding commodities. The domestic supply of each commodity is the sum of the output of domestic industries and "competitive" imports, defined as imported commodities that are also produced in the U.S. At this level of disaggregation imports and domestically produced commodities are imperfect substitutes. We take the price of imports in foreign currency to be exogenous; the price in domestic currency depends on the terms of trade.

Domestic prices of imports include tariffs levied by the U.S. government. We model non-tariff barriers, such as quotas and "voluntary" export restrictions on foreign supplies in terms of tariff equivalent increases in prices of U.S. imports. Prices of imports reflect both tariff and non-tariff barriers. For each commodity group we model the share of imports in domestic supply econometrically. This share is a function of the ratio of the price of imports to the price of the domestically produced commodity, as well as a time trend. We model noncompetitive imports as inputs into the importing industries. Prices of these imports also reflect barriers to trade.

We express the demand for U.S. exports as a function of the rest of the world output and the price of U.S. exports. The price of U.S. exports in foreign currency depends on the U.S. domestic price, the terms of trade, and foreign tariffs. To complete the current account balance we include exogenous components, such as U.S. foreign aid. The foreign balance is exogenous and the terms of trade endogenous in our model. We provide a base case projection of U.S. economic growth with existing trade policies in place. We then simulate the impact of alternative trade policies, beginning with a multilateral reduction in tariffs with no changes in quantitative restrictions on trade.

The impact of a multilateral elimination of tariffs is to raise U.S. consumption of goods and services by 0.16 percent in the first year of the policy change. However, the impact on consumption rises over time to 0.82 percent in the long-run. The mechanism underlying the dynamics of the adjustment to tariff reductions is that a decline in the price of imports of capital goods stimulates investment and results in more rapid growth of the U.S. economy. Since the current account balance is exogenous, the terms of trade must fall in order to accommodate the higher level of imports, implying an increase in U.S. international competitiveness.

Commodities with the highest U.S. tariff levels—textiles, apparel, rubber, leather, and glass—have the largest gains in imports; chemicals, electrical machinery (including computers), and instruments face the highest tariff barriers in the rest of the world and benefit most from the increase in exports. The output and employment effects of tariff reductions largely parallel the shifts in imports and exports. Important penetration is so high in food, furniture, and leather industries that output falls, relative to the base case. Capital and labor shift to the U.S. industries that are the most competitive internationally.

We also consider elimination of quantitative restrictions on U.S. imports, as well as multilateral tariff reductions. The gains to the U.S. economy from removing these restrictions is considerably greater than the effects of tariff cuts alone. We compare the results of our simulations with those of Alan Deardorff and Robert Stern (1986) and Whalley (1985), using static multilateral general equilibrium models. Our estimates of the impact of multilateral tariff reductions for the first year are comparable with the results of these static simulations.

xxii   Preface

The effects of dynamic adjustments of businesses and households to changes in trade policy, excluded from static models, greatly predominate in the long run.

In chapter 9 Ho and I consider the impact of environmental regulation on U.S. trade. Specifically, we consider the effects of the environmental regulations described in chapter 3 on the competitiveness of U.S. industries and patterns of imports and exports. In chapter 3 Wilcoxen and I have found that the imposition of environmental regulations has a substantial cost in foregone domestic output. We have decomposed the impact of environmental regulation between pollution controls on industry and controls on motor vehicle emissions. The domestic output of coal mining and motor vehicles, the industries most affected by these controls, has been adversely affected by the imposition of these controls.

We construct a base case for analysis of the impact of environmental policy on U.S. trade by projecting the growth of output, imports, and exports with environmental regulations in place. We then consider the impact of alternative policies that eliminate these regulations. U.S. aggregate exports would rise by 0.27 percent in the long run, while U.S. imports would fall by 0.15 percent. Elimination of environmental regulations would produce a modest fall in the U.S. terms of trade, resulting in an increase in the competitiveness of U.S. industries.

Although the aggregate impact of pollution controls is relatively small, these controls have a substantial impact on the commodity composition of trade. Elimination of controls on motor vehicle emissions would increase imports and exports of vehicles by about ten percent. Exports of chemicals, petroleum products, and primary metals are adversely affected by pollution controls on industry, since controls increase the prices of U.S. exports of these commodity groups. These qualitative results are relatively insensitive to the magnitudes of our estimates of the elasticities of demand for imports and supply of exports.

In chapter 10, Ho and I consider the impact of restrictions on carbon dioxide emissions on U.S. trade. We first consider the imposition of carbon taxes that would achieve the three alternative goals Wilcoxen and I have examined in chapter 4. These taxes are levied on imports of crude oil and natural gas, as well as imports of refined petroleum products. Although coal exports are relatively modest, we assume that this coal is also subject to taxation. The main effect of stabilization of carbon dioxide emissions at 1990 levels would be to reduce oil imports by 3.6 percent, leading to a slight appreciation of the terms of trade and a fall in competitiveness of U.S. industries.

Coal exports would fall by 37 percent, while exports of refined petroleum products would decline by 10 percent. Other substantial losses of exports would be in the energy-intensive manufacturing industries—primary metals, rubber, and stone, clay, and glass. The slight deterioration in the terms of trade leads to increased imports of products other than crude petroleum and natural gas. All of these effects would be greatly magnified by adoption of a more stringent goal for reduction of carbon dioxide emissions, while a less stringent goal would diminish the policy impacts. Finally, we consider the substitution of an energy tax for a carbon tax; this provides a less efficient policy instrument for achieving the goal of reduced emissions.

Carbon taxes affect U.S. trade flows through three different channels. First, these taxes stimulate energy conservation and lead to reduced imports of fossil fuels. The composition of net exports is shifted away from energy-intensive commodities. Finally, capital accumulation and productivity growth are adversely affected by carbon taxes, reducing economic growth and changing the pattern of trade. Our model captures the difference between short-run and long-run impacts of carbon taxes through the dynamic mechanisms that affect economic growth. An important limitation of these results is that we do not consider international coordination of policies to reduce carbon dioxide emissions.

In chapter 11, Wilcoxen and I consider the impact of fundamental tax reform on energy markets. For this purpose we consider the effects of substituting a tax on consumption for corporate and individual income taxes at both federal and state and local levels. For this purpose we introduce models of the demand for different types of capital services for each of the thirty-five industrial sectors of the U.S. economy and the household sector. These models depend on tax policies through detailed measures of the cost of capital for each type of capital services presented in my book with Kun-Young Yun (1991), *Tax Reform and the Cost of Capital*.

Measures of the cost of capital incorporate the characteristic features of U.S. tax law and summarize information about the future consequences of investment decisions required for current decisions about the allocation of capital. The concept of the cost of capital makes it possible to represent the economically relevant features of tax statutes in a very succinct form. The model we present in chapter 11 is the ninth version of the model we originally presented in chapter 3. Successive versions of the model have incorporated more efficient solution algorithms and additional features, such as the disaggregation of capital services in chapter 11, that enhance the flexibility and usefulness of the model.

We consider substitution of a consumption tax for existing income taxes that would leave the government deficit unchanged. This substitution would have an immediate and powerful impact on the level of economic activity. Individuals would sharply curtail consumption of both goods and leisure and shift the composition of output toward investment. Real consumption would initially decline by five percent, but would grow rapidly and overtake the level of consumption under the current tax system within five years. Investment would jump sharply, generating much more rapid capital accumulation and a higher level of the national product.

Changes in relative prices would stimulate energy conservation, but this would be outweighed by the impact of increased economic growth, leading to an increase in energy consumption. This consumption would be somewhat more carbon intensive and emissions of carbon dioxide would increase. A recent report by the Alliance to Save Energy (1998), *Price It Right*, shows how fundamental tax reform could be combined with energy taxes that would reflect the costs of environmental damages. This study uses the same modeling framework as the one Wilcoxen and I present in chapter 11.

I conclude that an intertemporal price system provides the appropriate conceptual framework for modeling the impacts of energy, environmental, trade, and tax policies. The econometric approach presented in this volume makes it possible to preserve the features of aggregate growth models, while disaggregating the policy impacts. The studies presented in the volume distinguish among thirty-five sectors of the U.S. economy and also identify thirty-five commodity groups. In modeling consumer behavior we distinguish among 672 different household types, broken down by demographic characteristics. Aggregate demand functions are obtained by summing over individual demand functions.

The econometric method for modeling technology and preferences can be contrasted with the calibration approach employed in earlier general equilibrium models. The overwhelming advantage of the econometric method is that responses of production and consumption patterns to changes in energy prices, environmental controls, trade restrictions, and tax policies are derived from historical experience. The implementation of the econometric approach requires a system of national accounts that successfully integrates capital accounts with income and production accounts. The new accounting system incorporates an accumulation equation relating capital to past investments with an asset-pricing equation linking the price of assets to future prices and rates of return.

An important feature of the modeling framework for consumer behavior presented in this volume is that systems of individual demand functions can be recovered from the system of aggregate demand functions. The representation of consumer preferences underlying these individual demand functions can be used to generate measures of individual welfare that are useful in evaluating the distributional consequences of economic policies. These measures are cardinal and interpersonally comparable and can be combined into a measure of social welfare that captures both efficiency and equity impacts of policy changes.

Intertemporal general equilibrium modeling provides a very worthwhile addition to methodologies for evaluating the impact of energy, environmental, trade, and tax policies. The neoclassical theory of economic growth is essential for understanding the dynamic mechanisms that underlie long-run and intermediate-run growth trends. The econometric implementation of this theory is critical for exploiting the wealth of historical experience that has accumulated over the past several decades. This experience, interpreted within an intertemporal framework, provides valuable guidance in the formulation of future economic policies.

I would like to thank June Wynn of the Department of Economics at Harvard University for her excellent work in assembling the manuscripts for this volume in machine-readable form. Renate d'Arcangelo of the Editorial Office of the Division of Engineering and Applied Sciences at Harvard edited the manuscripts, proofread the machine-readable versions and prepared them for typesetting. Warren Hrung, then a senior at Harvard College, checked the references and proofread successive versions of the typescript. William Richardson and his associates provided the index. Gary Bisbee of Chiron Incorporated typeset the manuscript and provided camera-ready copy for publication. The staff of The MIT Press, especially Terry Vaughn, Victoria Richardson, Andrea Werblin, and Michael Sims, has been very helpful at every stage of the project. Financial support was provided by the Program on Technology and Economic Policy of the Kennedy School of Government at Harvard. As always, the author retains sole responsibility for any remaining deficiencies in the volume.

List of Sources

1. Dale W. Jorgenson and Peter J. Wilcoxen, "Energy, the Environment, and Economic Growth," in A. V. Kneese and J. L. Sweeney (eds.), *Handbook of Energy and Natural Resource Economics*, Vol. 3, 1993, pp. 1267–1349. Reprinted with kind permission of Elsevier Science-NL, Sara Burgerhartstraat 25, 1055 KV Amsterdam, The Netherlands.

2. Dale W. Jorgenson, "Econometric Methods for Applied General Equilibrium Analysis," in H. Scarf and J. Shoven (eds.), *Applied General Equilibrium Analysis*, Cambridge, Cambridge University Press, 1984, pp. 139–203. Reprinted with the permission of Cambridge University Press.

3. Dale W. Jorgenson and Peter J. Wilcoxen, "Environmental Regulation and U.S. Economic Growth," *The Rand Journal of Economics*, Vol. 21, No. 2, Summer 1990, pp. 314–340. Reprinted by permission.

4. Dale W. Jorgenson and Peter J. Wilcoxen, "Reducing U.S. Carbon Dioxide Emissions: The Cost of Different Goals," in J.R. Moroney (ed.), *Advances in the Economics of Energy and Resources*, Vol. 7, Greenwich, JAI Press, 1992, pp. 125–158. Reprinted by permission.

5. Dale W. Jorgenson and Peter J. Wilcoxen, "The Economic Impact of the Clean Air Act Amendments of 1990," *The Energy Journal*, Vol. 14, No. 1, January 1993, pp. 159–182. Reprinted by permission.

6. Dale W. Jorgenson and Peter J. Wilcoxen, "Reducing U.S. Carbon Dioxide Emissions: An Econometric General Equilibrium Assessment," *Resource and Energy Economics*, Vol. 15, No. 1, March 1993, pp. 7–26. Reprinted with kind permission of Elsevier Science-NL, Sara Burgerhartstraat 25, 1055 KV Amsterdam, The Netherlands.

7. Dale W. Jorgenson and Peter J. Wilcoxen, "Reducing U.S. Carbon Dioxide Emissions: An Assessment of Alternative Instruments," *Journal of Policy Modeling*, Vol. 15, Nos. 5 and 6, 1993, pp. 491–520. Reprinted with kind permission of Elsevier Science-NL, Sara Burgerhartstraat 25, 1055 KV Amsterdam, The Netherlands.

8. Mun S. Ho and Dale W. Jorgenson, "Trade Policy and U.S. Economic Growth," *Journal of Policy Modeling*, Vol. 16, No. 2, 1994, pp. 119–146. Reprinted with kind permission of Elsevier Science-NL, Sara Burgerhartstraat 25, 1055 KV Amsterdam, The Netherlands.

9. Mun S. Ho and Dale W. Jorgenson, "Environmental Regulation and U.S. Trade," not previously published.

10. Mun S. Ho and Dale W. Jorgenson, "Stabilization of Carbon Emissions and Competiveness of U.S. Industries," not previously published.

11. Dale W. Jorgenson and Peter J. Wilcoxen, "Fundamental Tax Reform and Energy Markets," *The Energy Journal*, Vol. 18, No. 3, July 1997, pp. 1–30. Reprinted by permission.

1

Energy, the Environment, and Economic Growth

*Dale W. Jorgenson and
Peter J. Wilcoxen*

1.1 Introduction

Economic growth is a critical determinant of demands for energy. Utilization of energy, especially combustion of fossil fuels, is an important source of environmental pollution. Growth projections are essential for estimates of future demands and supplies of energy and future requirements for pollution controls to maintain environmental quality. The natural point of departure for modeling economic growth is the neoclassical theory of growth originated by Solow (1956, 1988). This theory has been developed in the form used in modeling the interrelationships among energy, the environment, and economic growth by Cass (1965) and Koopmans (1967).[1]

Maler (1974, 1975) and Uzawa (1975, 1988) have presented neoclassical theories of economic growth with pollution abatement and Solow (1974a, 1974b) has provided a theory that includes supply and demand for an exhaustible resource. These theories have generated an extensive literature, surveyed by Dasgupta and Heal (1979). In the neoclassical theory of growth, wage rates grow at the same rate as productivity in the long run, while rates of return depend on productivity growth and parameters that describe saving behavior. These long-run properties of economic growth are independent of energy and environmental policies.

The neoclassical theory of economic growth also provides a framework for projecting intermediate-run growth trends. These trends depend on the same factors as long-run trends, but also depend on energy and environmental policies through their effects on capital accumulation and rates of productivity growth over shorter periods. In this context the intermediate run refers to the time needed for the capital-output ratio to converge to a long-run stationary value. This often requires several decades, so that intermediate-run trends are critical for policy evaluation.

A striking example of changes in growth trends is the sharp decline in rates of economic growth in the United States and other industrialized countries during the 1970s and 1980s. For example, Jorgenson (1990b) shows that U.S. real output grew at an annual rate of 3.7% during the period 1947–1973, while the annual growth rate for the period 1973–1985 was only 2.5%. Englander and Mittelstadt (1988) have shown that the slowdown has been even more severe in other industrialized countries. Two events coinciding with the slowdown—the advent of more restrictive environmental controls and the increase in world petroleum prices—have led to a vast outpouring of research directed at a fuller understanding of the interactions among energy supplies and prices, environmental quality and its cost, and the sources of economic growth.[2]

The neoclassical theory of economic growth has provided the framework for a number of important modeling studies of energy and environmental policies. Nordhaus (1994) has presented a Dynamic Integrated Climate-Economy (DICE) model for analyzing the economics of global warming. This is a one-sector neoclassical growth model for the world economy that integrates a production model for world output, a model of intertemporal choice based on utility maximization by a representative consumer, and a model of the impact of climate change on productivity. Nordhaus's model of climate change links climate change to the level of world output through a series of dynamic relationships based on the well-known greenhouse effect.[3]

Nordhaus considers the impact of a policy to control climate change by limiting the emissions of greenhouse gases, such as carbon dioxide. For this purpose he performs two simulations of world economic growth, first, with no controls on greenhouse gas emissions and, second, with optimal controls on these emissions. The optimization criterion is the intertemporal utility function of the representative consumer in the DICE model. The difference between the two simulations is very small for a half century after 1990. The optimal reduction in greenhouse gas emissions begins around 9% and rises gradually to 14% by the year 2100. The optimal policy can be implemented by means of a world carbon tax, which rises from $5 per ton of carbon in the 1990s to $20 per ton by the end of the twenty-first century.[4]

Nordhaus's model of world economic growth provides a dramatic illustration of the power of the neoclassical framework in analyzing the impact of energy and environmental policies. The parameters of this model are calibrated to extensive data on the growth of the world economy. Changes in the global climate are generated by economic activity, especially the combustion of fossil fuels. The physical model of climate change includes the principal features of simulation models for the global climate developed by climatologists. Climate change feeds back to economic activity by reducing productivity levels. These mechanisms provide the basis for the design of an optimal environmental policy by application of a sophisticated version of cost-benefit analysis.[5]

A carbon tax like that considered by Nordhaus would internalize the externality associated with carbon dioxide emissions. However, this externality affects the whole planet, while carbon taxes are the responsibility of individual governments. The design of an appropriate policy must involve international coordination. An important limitation of Nordhaus's approach is that it fails to capture differences among regions of the world economy and gains from international cooperation on policies for emissions control. These limitations have motivated the development of a number of multi-region models of the world economy and global climate change. The GLOBAL 2100 model developed by Manne and Richels (1992) is the one most similar in spirit to Nordhaus's model.

In the GLOBAL 2100 model the world economy is subdivided among five regions—the U.S.A., other OECD, the former Soviet Union, China, and the Rest of the World. Each region is represented by a one-sector neoclassical growth model patterned after Manne's (1981) MACRO model. Output of the region is a function of capital, labor, and energy inputs with exogenously given growth in productivity. Energy is allocated between electrical and non-electrical energy. Both forms of energy are supplied by a detailed energy technology assessment (ETA) model of the energy sector. The consumer sector in each region is modeled by means of a representative consumer who maximizes an intertemporal utility function. Environmental policy affects regional output through limitations on carbon dioxide emissions resulting from fossil fuel combustion. The model is employed by Manne and Richels for estimating costs of emissions controls.[6]

Manne and Richels consider the impact of restrictions on carbon dioxide emissions for each of the five regions individually. For this purpose they perform alternative simulations of regional economic growth, first, with no controls on carbon dioxide emissions to estimate the consequences of "Business-as-Usual" for energy utilization and emissions levels. The principal alternative simulation involves stabilizing these emissions at 1990 level through the year 2000, reducing them to twenty percent below this level by the year 2020, and stabilizing them at this level thereafter. The costs of this policy for the U.S.A. mounts to one percent of the gross domestic product (GDP) by the year 2000. These losses rise to two percent of the GDP by the year 2020 and eventually to 2.5%. This policy can be implemented by means of a carbon tax, which begins at $135 per ton in 1990 and rises sharply as emissions are reduced. The tax eventually reaches a level of $208 per ton.

Manne and Richels consider the sensitivity of their results to alternative assumptions about the availability of energy supplies and technologies and alternative carbon dioxide limits. They consider the economic impact of reducing U.S. emissions to fifty percent of 1990 levels by the year 2010 and stabilizing at that level thereafter. This produces much more substantial economic losses and requires considerably higher tax levels. Interaction among regions in the GLOBAL 2100 occurs through the world petroleum market and a hypothetical international market for emissions permits. Manne and Richels demonstrate that there would be sizeable gains from international trade in these permits. For example, the U.S.A. would find it worthwhile to import permits from China and the rest-of-the-world regions; in the year 2020 these imports would be valued at around $50 billion. The costs of restrictions on emissions would be reduced substantially by introducing international coordination of global climate policy through tradeable permits.

The GLOBAL 2100 model of Manne and Richels provides another excellent example of the potential of the neoclassical theory of economic growth for modeling the impact of energy and environmental policies. Their model is useful in assessing the costs of restrictions on carbon dioxide emissions and the potential benefits of international coordination. Through application of their energy technology assessment (ETA) model for each region, Manne and Richels also provide much valuable information on the potential pay-off from accelerated research and development on new energy sources and alternative energy technologies. However, the detail available for the individual regions is very limited, except for the energy sector. Their approach fails to capture important differences among industries and consumers that are critical to assessments of alternative energy and environmental policies at the national level. To overcome these limitations it is essential to employ an econometric approach for modeling the impacts of these policies. We next consider the application of this approach to the U.S.A., the region that has been studied most intensively.[7]

The framework for econometric analysis of the impact of energy and environmental policies is provided by intertemporal general equilibrium modeling.[8] The one-sector neoclassical growth models used by Nordhaus (1994) in modeling the world economy or Manne and Richels (1992) in modeling each region in their five-region model of the world economy provide illustrations of intertemporal general equilibrium models. The organizing mechanism of these models is an intertemporal price system balancing demand and supply for products and factors of production. In Nordhaus's DICE model there is only one product, world output, and two factors of production: capital and labor inputs. In the GLOBAL 2100 model of Manne and Richels there are three products in each region—regional output, electrical energy, and non-electrical energy—and two factors of production: capital and labor.

In addition, the intertemporal price system links the prices of assets in every time period to the discounted value of future capital services. This forward-looking feature is combined with backward linkages among investment, capital stock, and capital services in modeling the dynamics of economic growth. Neither Nordhaus (1992b) nor Manne and Richels (1992) have limited their considerations to characterization of economic growth in the long run. The alternative time paths of economic growth generated in their simulations depend on energy and environmental policies through their impact on capital accumulation. In Nordhaus's model productivity growth depends on these policies through the impact of greenhouse gas emissions on climate change and the effects of climate change on productivity. Productivity growth in the Manne-Richels model depends on the introduction of new sources of energy supplies and energy technologies in the ETA submodel of the energy sector.

In disaggregating the economic impacts of energy and environmental policies for the U.S.A., we preserve the key features of more highly aggregated intertemporal general equilibrium models. One important dimension for disaggregation is to introduce a distinction among industries and commodities in order to measure policy impacts for narrower segments of the economy. This also makes it possible to model differences among industries in responses to changes in energy prices and the imposition of pollution controls. A second dimension for disaggregation is to distinguish among households by level of wealth and demographic characteristics. This makes it possible to model differences in responses to price changes and environmental controls. It is also useful in examining the distributional effects of energy and environmental policies.[9] We begin our discussion of intertemporal general equilibrium modeling by focusing on the econometric methodology that is required.

At the outset of our discussion it is essential to recognize that the predominant tradition in general equilibrium modeling does not employ econometric methods. This tradition originated with the seminal work of Leontief (1951), beginning with implementations of the static input-output model over half a century ago. Leontief (1953) gave a further impetus to the development of general equilibrium modeling by introducing a dynamic input-output model. This model can be regarded as an important progenitor of the intertemporal general equilibrium models described below. Empirical work associated with input-output analysis is based on parameterizing technology and preferences from a single inter-industry transactions table.

The usefulness of the "fixed-coefficients" assumption that underlies input-output analysis is hardly subject to dispute. By linearizing technology and preferences Leontief solved at one stroke the two fundamental problems that arise in practical implementation of general equilibrium models. First, the resulting general equilibrium model can be solved as a system of linear equations with constant coefficients. Second, the unknown parameters describing technology and preferences can be estimated from a single data point. The data required are now available for all countries that have implemented the United Nations (1993) System of National Accounts.

The input-output approach was applied to modeling of environmental policy by Ayres and Kneese (1969) and Kneese, Ayres, and d'Arge (1970). Their work was especially notable for introducing a "materials balance" approach based on conservation of mass for all economic activities. Materials balances are useful in bringing out the fact that material not embodied in final products must be embodied in emissions of pollutants. These emissions accumulate as solid waste or enter the atmosphere or the hydrosphere and reduce air or water quality. In implementing the materials balance approach, the assumption that pollutants are generated in fixed proportions to output is a natural complement to the fixed-coefficients assumption of Leontief's input-output model.[10]

The most detailed implementation of the input-output approach to modeling energy and environmental policy is the United Nations Study presented by Leontief, Carter, and Petri (1977). In this study the world economy is divided among fifteen regions, including four regions representing industrialized countries—North America, Western Europe, Japan, and Oceania—and eleven regions representing countries at various stages of development. A fixed-coefficients input-output model with 45 industrial sectors and including resource requirements and pollution control activities is constructed for each region. The growth rate of GDP for each region is taken to be exogenously given. The regions are treated separately and also linked through international trade. One of the principal conclusions is that the availability of resources and requirements for pollution control do not pose insurmountable obstacles to growth of the developing countries.

One perspective on the United Nations Study is that it provides a response to the Meadows (1972) Report, *Limits to Growth*, for the Club of Rome. This report employs simulations based on systems dynamics to demonstrate the possibility of exhaustion of resources and inability to control pollution as barriers to growth of industrialized and developing countries. The viewpoint of the United Nations Study is reflected in the World Commission on Environment and Development Report (1987), *Our Common Future*, also known as the Brundtland Report. This report argues that economic development and maintenance of environmental quality are compatible through "sustainable development."[11]

The obvious objection to the fixed-coefficients approach to modeling energy and environmental policies is that these policies induce changes in the input-output coefficients. In fact, the objective of pollution control regulations is to induce producers and consumers to substitute less polluting inputs for more polluting ones. A prime example is the substitution of low-sulfur coal for high-sulfur coal by electric utilities and manufacturing firms to comply with regulations on sulfur dioxide emissions. Another important example is the shift from leaded to unleaded motor fuels in order to clean up motor vehicle emissions.

The first successful implementation of an applied general equilibrium model without the fixed-coefficients assumption of input-output analysis is due to Johansen (1960). Johansen retained the fixed-coefficients assumption in modeling demands for intermediate goods, but employed linear logarithmic or Cobb-Douglas production functions in modeling the substitution between capital and labor services and technical change. He replaced the fixed-coefficients assumption for household behavior by a system of demand functions originated by Frisch (1959). Finally, he developed a method for solving the resulting nonlinear general equilibrium model for growth rates of sectoral output levels and prices and implemented this model for Norway. Johansen's multi-sectoral growth (MSG) model is another important progenitor for the models of intertemporal general equilibrium we describe below.

Linear logarithmic production functions have the obvious advantage that the capital and labor input coefficients respond to price changes. Furthermore, the relative shares of these inputs in the value of output are fixed, so that the unknown parameters characterizing substitution between capital and labor inputs can be estimated from a single data point. In describing producer behavior, Johansen employed econometric methods only in estimating constant rates of technical change. Similarly, the unknown parameters of the demand system proposed by Frisch can be determined from a single data point, except for one parameter that must be determined econometrically.

The essential features of Johansen's approach have been preserved in the applied general equilibrium models surveyed by Bergman (1985) and Fullerton, Henderson, and Shoven (1984). The unknown parameters describing technology and preferences in these models are determined by "calibration" to a single data point. Data from a single inter-industry transactions table are supplemented by a small number of parameters estimated econometrically. The obvious disadvantage of this approach is that highly restrictive assumptions on technology and preferences are required to make calibration feasible.[12]

Almost all general equilibrium models retain the fixed-coefficients assumption of Leontief and Johansen for modeling demand for intermediate goods. However, this assumption is directly contradicted by massive evidence of price-induced energy conservation in response to higher world energy prices beginning in 1973.[13] Reductions in energy utilization induced by the successive energy crises of the 1970s and the higher level of energy prices prevailing in the 1980s has been documented in great detail by Schipper and Meyers (1992). This extensive survey covers nine OECD economies, including the U.S.A., for the period 1970–1989 and describes energy conservation in residential, manufacturing, other industry, services, passenger transport, and freight transport sectors. Reductions in energy-output ratios for these activities average 15–20%.[14]

Fixed coefficients for intermediate goods also rule out a very important response to environmental regulations by assumption. This is the introduction of special devices to treat wastes after they have been generated, substituting capital in the form of pollution control devices for other inputs such as energy or materials. This is commonly known as end-of-pipe abatement and is frequently the method of choice for retrofitting existing facilities to meet environmental standards. A typical example is the use of electrostatic precipitators to reduce the emissions of particulates from combustion. Regulations promulgated in the U.S. by the Environmental Protection Agency effectively encourage the use of this approach by setting standards for emissions on the basis of the "best available technology."

Another important limitation of the Johansen approach is that changes in technology are taken to be exogenous. This rules out another important method for pollution abatement by assumption. This is the introduction of changes in technology by redesigning production methods to reduce emissions. An important example is the introduction of fluidized bed technology for combustion, which results in reduced emissions. Gollop and Roberts (1983, 1985) have constructed a detailed econometric model of electric utility firms based on a cost function that incorporates the impact of environmental regulations on the cost of producing electricity and the rate of productivity growth. They conclude that the annual productivity growth of electric utilities impacted by more restrictive emissions controls declined by 0.59 percentage points over the period 1974–1979. This resulted from switching technologies to meet new standards for air quality.

To represent technologies and preferences that overcome the limitations of the Johansen approach, it is essential to employ econometric methods. A possible extension of Johansen's approach would be to estimate elasticities of substitution between capital and labor inputs along the lines suggested by Arrow, Chenery, Minhas, and Solow (1961). Unfortunately, constant elasticity of substitution (CES) production functions cannot easily encompass substitution among capital, labor, energy, and materials inputs. As Uzawa (1962) and

McFadden (1963) have shown, constant elasticities of substitution among more than two inputs imply, essentially, that elasticities of substitution among all inputs must be the same.

An alternative approach to the implementation of econometric models of producer behavior is to generate complete systems of demand functions for inputs of capital, labor, energy, and materials inputs in each industrial sector. Each system gives quantities of inputs demanded as functions of prices and output. This approach to modeling producer behavior was originated by Berndt and Jorgenson (1973) and employed in modeling energy policy and U.S. economic growth by Hudson and Jorgenson (1974). The approach was extended to incorporate endogenous technical change by Jorgenson and Fraumeni (1981).[15] A model combining substitution among capital, labor, energy and materials inputs and endogenous technical change is utilized in modeling environmental policy and U.S. economic growth by Jorgenson and Wilcoxen (1990b).

The econometric approach for modeling producer behavior has been implemented for Norway by Longva and Olsen (1983). The results are utilized in modeling energy policy and Norwegian economic growth by Longva, Lorentsen, and Olsen (1983). An updated and revised version of this model has been employed in assessing the impact of restrictions on carbon dioxide emissions on Norwegian economic growth by Glomsrod, Vennemo, and Johnsen (1992). Hazilla and Kopp (1986) have constructed an econometric model of producer behavior for the same thirty-five sectors of the U.S. economy analyzed by Jorgenson and Fraumeni (1981). Hazilla and Kopp (1990) use this model in measuring the costs of U.S. environmental regulations.[16]

As in the descriptions of technology by Leontief and Johansen, production in the econometric approach is characterized by constant returns to scale in each sector. As a consequence, commodity prices can be expressed as a function of factor prices, using the nonsubstitution theorem of Samuelson (1951). This greatly facilitates the solution of the econometric general equilibrium models constructed by Hudson and Jorgenson (1974) and Jorgenson and Wilcoxen (1990b), since the nonsubstitution theorem permits a substantial reduction in dimensionality of the space of prices to be determined by the model. The corresponding feature of the Johansen approach has been exploited in applications of the "fixed point" methods for solving nonlinear general equilibrium models pioneered by Scarf and Hansen (1973, 1984).

Similarly, econometric models of consumer behavior can be used to overcome the limitations of the Frisch (1959) model employed by Johansen. Models stemming from the path-breaking contributions of Schultz (1938), Stone (1954), and Wold (1953) consist of complete systems of demand functions, giving quantities demanded as functions of prices and total expenditure. These models incorporate the restrictions implied by the theory of consumer behavior by introducing the notion of a representative consumer. Aggregate demand functions are treated as if they could be generated by a single utilizing maximizing individual. Per capita quantities demanded can be expressed as functions of prices and per capita expenditure.

The obvious difficulty with the representative consumer approach is that aggregate demand functions can be expressed as the sum of individual demand functions. Aggregate demand functions depend on prices and total expenditures, as in the theory of individual consumer behavior. However, these demand functions depend on individual total expenditures rather than aggregate expenditure. If individual total expenditures are allowed to vary independently, models based on a representative consumer imply restrictions that severely limit the dependence of individual demand functions on individual expenditure.

The simplest form of restrictions required for the representative consumer approach is to require that preferences are identical and homothetic for all consumers. This set of restrictions is implicit in the linear logarithmic demand systems employed by Stone (1954a) and Wold (1953). Homothetic preferences are inconsistent with well-established empirical regularities in the behavior of individual consumers, such as Engel's Law, which states that the proportion of expenditure devoted to food is a declining proportion of total expenditure. Identical preferences for individual households are inconsistent with empirical findings that expenditure patterns depend on demographic characteristics of individual consumers.[17]

A weaker set of restrictions for the existence of a representative consumer has been presented by Gorman (1953), requiring that quantities consumed are linear in total expenditure with slopes that are identical for all consumers. Muellbauer (1975) and Lewbel (1989) have presented generalizations of these conditions, requiring that preferences are identical for all consumers, but that quantities consumed are not necessarily linear functions of expenditure.[18]

Econometric models of aggregate consumer behavior based on the theory of a representative consumer have been constructed by Berndt, Darrough, and Diewert (1977) and Deaton and Muellbauer (1980a,b). The econometric general equilibrium models of Glomsrud, Vennemo, and Johnsen (1992) and Hazilla and Kopp (1990) employ the representative consumer approach in modeling consumer behavior.

An alternative approach to econometric modeling of aggregate consumer behavior is provided by Lau's (1982) theory of exact aggregation. This approach makes it possible to dispense with the notion of a representative consumer. Systems of aggregate demand functions depend on statistics of the joint distribution of individual total expenditures and attributes of individuals associated with differences in preferences. One of the most remarkable features of models based on exact aggregation is that systems of demand functions for individuals can be recovered uniquely from the system of aggregate demand functions. This makes it possible to exploit all the implications of the economic theory of the individual consumer in constructing an econometric model of aggregate consumer behavior.

The implementation of an econometric model of aggregate consumer behavior based on the theory of exact aggregation has been carried out by Jorgenson, Lau, and Stoker (1982). Their approach requires time-series data on prices and aggregate quantities consumed. This approach also requires cross-section data on individual quantities consumed, individual total expenditures, and attributes of individual households, such as demographic characteristics.[19] By contrast the non-econometric approaches of Leontief and Johansen require only a single data point for prices, aggregate quantities consumed, and aggregate expenditure.

We continue our presentation of econometric modeling of the impact of energy and environmental policies by considering the intertemporal general equilibrium model of the U.S. economy constructed by Jorgenson and Wilcoxen (1990b). The general equilibrium model of production employed by Jorgenson and Wilcoxen is based on the model originated by Jorgenson and Fraumeni (1981). This model includes systems of demand functions for capital, labor, energy, and materials inputs and a model of endogenous productivity growth for each of thirty-five sectors of the U.S. economy. The Jorgenson-Wilcoxen model incorporates a model of aggregate consumer behavior based on the exact aggregation approach of Jorgenson, Lau, and Stoker (1982). This model dispenses with the notion of a representative consumer employed in previous econometric models of aggregate consumer behavior. The model includes a system of demand functions for five commodity groups—energy, food, nondurable goods, capital services, and other services. We outline the Jorgenson-Wilcoxen model in more detail in section 1.2 below.

Jorgenson and Wilcoxen (1990a) have presented a highly disaggregated model of the impact of environmental regulations on U.S. economic growth. Detailed data on costs of compliance imposed on individual industries by these regulations are utilized in modeling the impact of environmental policy. Alternative regulatory policies generate different costs of production for these industries and different time paths of economic growth for the U.S. economy. The industries most affected by environmental regulations are the motor vehicles and coal mining industries. These regulations have led to a substantial decline in the national product, amounting to a reduction of almost 2.6% in the long run. This reduction is produced by an even more severe decline in capital accumulation, illustrating the importance of the dynamics of adjustment of economic growth to its long-run trend. We outline the results of this study in section 1.3.

We have already summarized the studies of environmental policies for control of global warming by Nordhaus (1994) and Manne and Richels (1992). A very significant issue in modeling the impact of these policies is the price responsiveness of greenhouse gas emissions to changes in energy prices. In section 1.4 we present an analysis of a "natural experiment" provided by variations in energy prices during the 1970s and 1980s. Over the period 1972–1987 U.S. emissions of carbon dioxide were stabilized by price-induced energy conservation. A major portion of the corresponding reduction in the growth rate of national output—almost two-thirds—can be attributed to oil price surges that took place in 1973–1975 and 1978–1980. The change in the oil price levels between 1972 and 1987 accounted for about one-third of the slowdown in the growth of output. A more detailed analysis of the stabilization of carbon dioxide emissions is given by Jorgenson and Wilcoxen (1992b).

Finally, we turn our attention to the cost of controlling U.S. carbon dioxide emissions. For this purpose we summarize the results of a study of these costs by Jorgenson and Wilcoxen (1992a) in section 1.5. Jorgenson and Wilcoxen have considered three alternative sets of restrictions on carbon dioxide emissions—stabilizing these emissions at 1990 levels, curtailing emissions by twenty percent of 1990 levels of the period 1990–2005 and stabilizing thereafter, and allowing emissions to increase through the year 2000 and stabilizing at that level. The costs of stabilization at 1990 levels amount to a loss in the national product of half a percentage point. However, these costs rise at an increasing rate as emissions targets are made more restrictive. In section 1.6 we provide an overall evaluation of the econometric approach for modeling the impact of energy and environmental policies.

1.2 An Overview of the Model

Our analysis of the impact of energy and environmental policies is based on simulations of U.S. economic growth, using an intertemporal general equilibrium model of the U.S. economy. This model has been implemented econometrically by Jorgenson and Wilcoxen (1990b). In this section we outline the model, emphasizing features that are critical in assessing policy impacts. The starting point is a system of national accounts for the U.S. developed by Jorgenson (1980) and implemented by Fraumeni and Jorgenson (1980). This accounting system provides the time-series data needed for econometric modeling of producer and consumer behavior.[20]

The critical innovation in the accounting system implemented by Fraumeni and Jorgenson is the development of accounts for investment, capital stock, and capital services and the corresponding prices. These accounts incorporate a backward-looking accumulation equation for capital, linking the current flow of capital services to all past investments. They also include a forward-looking equation for the price of capital services, linking the price of investment goods to all future prices of capital services. Equations of this type are essential for modeling the dynamics of economic growth. The capital accounts employed by Jorgenson and Wilcoxen are described in detail by Jorgenson (1990b).

1.2.1 Producer Behavior

We have constructed submodels for each of four sectors of the U.S. economy: business, household, government, and the rest of the world. Since many of the most important features of our model are contained in our submodel of the business sector, we begin our presentation with this sector. Energy and environmental policies affect different

Table 1.2.1
Industry classifications

Number	Description
1	Agriculture, forestry, and fisheries
2	Metal mining
3	Coal mining
4	Crude petroleum and natural gas
5	Nonmetallic mineral mining
6	Construction
7	Food and kindred products
8	Tobacco manufacturers
9	Textile mill products
10	Apparel and other textile products
11	Lumber and wood products
12	Furniture and fixtures
13	Paper and allied products
14	Printing and publishing
15	Chemicals and allied products
16	Petroleum refining
17	Rubber and plastic products
18	Leather and leather products
19	Stone, clay, and glass products
20	Primary metals
21	Fabricated metal products
22	Machinery, except electrical
23	Electrical machinery
24	Motor vehicles
25	Other transportation equipment
26	Instruments
27	Miscellaneous manufacturing
28	Transportation and warehousing
29	Communication
30	Electric utilities
31	Gas utilities
32	Trade
33	Finance, insurance, and real estate
34	Other services
35	Government enterprises

industries in very different ways. For example, fossil fuel combustion results in emissions of pollutants, so that modeling the response to pollution control policies requires distinguishing among industries with different energy intensities. Accordingly, we have subdivided the business sector into the thirty-five industries shown in table 1.2.1. Each of these corresponds, roughly, to a two-digit industry in the Standard Industrial Classification. This level of industrial disaggregation makes it possible to measure the impact of alternative policies on relatively narrow segments of the U.S. economy.

We have also divided the output of the business sector into thirty-five commodities, each one the primary product of one of the industries. Many industries produce secondary products as well, for example, the textile industry produces both textiles and apparel, so that we have allowed for joint production. Each commodity is allocated between deliveries to intermediate demands by other industries and deliveries to final demands by households, governments, and the rest of the world.

We represent the technology of each industry by means of an econometric model of producer behavior. In order to estimate the unknown parameters of these production models we have constructed an annual time series of inter-industry transactions tables for the U.S. economy for the period 1947 through 1985.[21] The data for each year are divided between a *use* table and a *make* table. The use table shows the quantities of each commodity—intermediate inputs, primary factors of production, and noncompeting imports—used by each industry and final demand category.[22] The make table gives the amount of each commodity produced by each industry. In the absence of joint production this would be a diagonal array. The organization of the use and make tables is illustrated in figures 1.2.1 and 1.2.2; table 1.2.2 provides definitions of the variables appearing in these figures.

The econometric method for parameterizing our model stands in sharp contrast to the calibration method used in previous general equilibrium modeling. Calibration involves choosing parameters to replicate the data for a particular year.[23] Almost all general equilibrium models employ the assumption of fixed "input-output" coefficients for intermediate goods, following Johansen (1960). This allows the ratio of the input of each commodity to the output of an industry to be calculated from a single use table like the one presented in figure 1.2.1; however, it rules out substitution among intermediate goods, such as energy and materials, by assumption. It also ignores the distinction between industries and commodities and rules out joint production.

The econometric approach to parameterization has several advantages over the calibration approach. First, by using an extensive time series of data rather than a single data point, we can derive the response of production patterns to changes in prices from historical

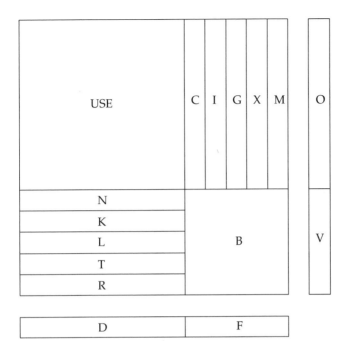

Figure 1.2.1
Organization of the *use* table.

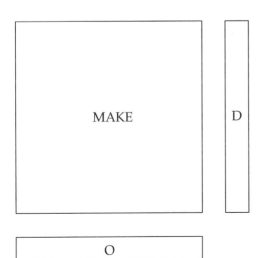

Figure 1.2.2
Organization of the *make* table.

Table 1.2.2
Make and use table variables

Category	Variable	Description
Industry-commodity flows:		
	USE	Commodities *used* by industries (use table)
	MAKE	Commodities *made* by industries (make table)
Final demand columns:		
	C	Personal consumption
	I	Gross private domestic investment
	G	Government spending
	X	Exports
	M	Imports
Value added rows:		
	N	Noncompeting imports
	K	Capital
	L	Labor
	T	Net taxes
	R	Rest of the world
Commodity and industry output:		
	O	Commodity output
	D	Industry output
Other variables:		
	B	Value added sold directly to final demand
	V	Total value added
	F	Total final demand

experience. This is particularly important for the analysis of energy and environmental policies, since energy prices have varied widely and environmental policies have changed substantially during our sample period. The calibration approach imposes responses to these changes through the choice of functional forms. For example, elasticities of substitution are set equal to zero by imposing the Leontief functional form used in input-output analysis or unity by imposing the Cobb-Douglas functional form employed by Johansen (1960). More generally, all elasticities of substitution are set equal to each other by imposing the constant elasticity of substitution functional form.[24]

A second advantage of the econometric approach is that parameters estimated from time series are much less likely to be affected by the peculiarities of the data for a particular time period. By construction, parameters obtained by calibration are forced to absorb all the random errors present in the data for a single benchmark year. This poses a severe problem when the benchmark year is unusual in some respect. For example, parameters calibrated to the year 1973 would incorporate into the model all the distortions in energy markets that resulted from price controls and the rationing of energy during the first oil crisis. Econometric parameterization greatly mitigates this problem by reducing the influence of disturbances for a particular time period.

Empirical evidence on substitutability among inputs is essential in analyzing the impact of environmental and energy policies. If it is easy for industries to substitute among inputs, the effects of these policies will be very different than if substitution were limited. Although calibration avoids the burden of data collection required by econometric estimation, it also specifies the substitutability among inputs by assumption rather than relying on empirical evidence. This can easily lead to substantial distortions in estimating the effects of energy and environmental policies.

An important feature of our production submodel is that an industry's productivity growth can be biased toward some inputs and away from others. Biased productivity growth is a common feature of historical data but is often excluded from models of production. By allowing for biased productivity growth, our model provides a separation between price-induced reductions in energy utilization and those resulting from changes in technology.[25] In addition, the rate of productivity growth for each industry in our model is determined endogenously as a function of input prices. Other econometric models for analyzing energy and environmental policies, for example, Hazilla and Kopp (1990), Hudson and Jorgenson (1974), and Longva, Lorentsen, and Olsen (1983) exclude biases in productivity growth and take the rate of productivity growth to be exogenous.

Another important feature of our production submodel is that we allow for joint production. Accordingly, the price of an industry's output may differ from the price of its primary product. Recall our example that the textile industry produces both textiles and apparel, so that the price of the industry's output is a function of the prices of both the textile and apparel commodities. To capture this, we include a price function for each commodity, giving the price of that commodity as a function of the prices of the outputs of all industries that produce it. We parameterize these commodity price functions econometrically, using data from the make table shown in figure 1.2.2.

Our models of producer behavior are based on two-stage allocation. At the first stage the value of each industry's output is allocated
among four commodity groups—capital, labor, energy, and materials.
We take the price of output to be a homothetically separable function
of the prices of commodities within each of these groups. This price
function must be homogeneous of degree one, nondecreasing, and
concave in the input prices. These restrictions are incorporated into
the system of input demand functions that we construct for each
industry.[26]

At the second stage of our production models the value of the
energy and materials aggregates is allocated among individual commodities. The price of energy is a function of the prices of coal, crude
petroleum, refined petroleum, electricity, and natural gas. In order to
limit the number of estimated parameters in the materials aggregate,
we employ a hierarchical tier structure of ten subaggregates.[27] We
derive demands for inputs of capital and labor services and the thirty-
five intermediate goods into each industry from the price function for
that industry.

To present our production model more formally, we first require
some notation. Let the thirty-five industries be indexed by i. We
denote the quantity of output from industry i by Z_i, and the quantities
of inputs of capital, labor, energy and materials by K_i, L_i, E_i and M_i.
Similarly, we denote the price of output from industry i by q_i, and the
prices of the four inputs by p_K^i, p_L^i, p_E^i and p_M^i. Further, we define the
shares of inputs in the value of output by:

$$v_K^i = \frac{p_K^i K_i}{q_i Z_i}, \quad v_L^i = \frac{p_L^i L_i}{q_i Z_i}, \quad v_E^i = \frac{p_E^i E_i}{q_i Z_i}, \quad v_M^i = \frac{p_M^i M_i}{q_i Z_i}.$$

We find it convenient to define the vector of input value shares for
industry i as follows:

$$v_i = (v_K^i, v_L^i, v_E^i, v_M^i).$$

Similarly, we define the vector of logarithms of input prices faced by
the industry as:

$$\ln p_i = (\ln p_K^i, \ln p_L^i, \ln p_E^i, \ln p_M^i)'.$$

We assume that industry i allocates the value of its output among
the four inputs in accord with the translog price function:

$$\ln q_i = \alpha_0^i + \ln p_i' \alpha_p^i + \alpha_t^i \, g_i(t)$$
$$+ \frac{1}{2} \ln p_i' B_{pp}^i \ln p_i + \ln p_i' \beta_{pt}^i \, g_i(t) + \frac{1}{2} \beta_{tt}^i g_i^2(t) . \tag{2.1}$$

The scalars α_0^i, α_t^i, β_{tt}^i, the vectors α_t^i, β_{pt}^i, and the matrix B_{pp}^i are unknown parameters that differ among industries, reflecting differences in technology. The function $g_i(t)$ contains additional unknown parameters and will be discussed in more detail below.

We can derive the value shares of inputs to industry i by differentiating the price function (2.1) with respect to logarithms of the input prices to obtain:

$$v_i = \alpha_p^i + \beta_{pp}^i \ln p_i + \beta_{pt}^i \, g_i(t) .$$

The elements of B_{pp}^i can be interpreted as *share elasticities* and represent the degree of substitutability among inputs. These parameters capture the price responsiveness of demands for energy and other inputs. The elements of β_{pt}^i are *biases of productivity growth* and represent the impact of changes in productivity on the value shares of the inputs.[28] These parameters incorporate "autonomous" improvements in the efficiency of utilization of energy and other inputs. By fitting both sets of parameters to historical data we are able to separate price-induced changes in input coefficients from those that result from changes in technology.

The limiting behavior of the function $g_i(t)$ presents a potential problem for long-run simulations. In order for the price function to be homogeneous of degree one, the elements of β_{pt}^i must sum to zero. If any of the elements is nonzero, there will be at least one negative element. Unless $g_i(t)$ remains bounded as t becomes large, the value share of the corresponding input will eventually become negative.[29] Accordingly, we take $g_i(t)$ to be logistic in form:

$$g_i(t) = \frac{1}{1 + \exp[-\mu_i(t - \tau_i)]} , \tag{2.2}$$

where the scalars μ_i and τ_i are unknown parameters which differ among industries. In the limit each of these functions goes to unity. Although this specification does not guarantee that the input value shares remain positive since extremely large elements of β_{pt}^i could still cause problems, we have found that it does so in practice.

Equation (2.2) also solves a second potential problem in long-run simulations. If productivity grows indefinitely, the existence of a balanced growth equilibrium requires that the rates of growth must eventually become the same for all industries. Otherwise, the industry with the highest rate of productivity growth would eventually come to dominate the economy. In our model, productivity growth is limited.

To show this we differentiate eq. (2.1) with respect to time to obtain the endogenous rate of productivity growth in industry i, say v_t^i:

$$-v_t^i = [\alpha_t^i + \beta_{pt}^i{}' \ln p_i + \beta_{tt}^i \, g_i(t)] \, \dot{g}_i(t) .$$

From the logistic formulation (2.2) it is clear that $\dot{g}_i(t)$ goes to zero in the limit, so that the level of productivity in each industry approaches a constant. This formulation has the advantages of representing productivity growth during the sample period in a flexible way, while producing long-run behavior of the economy consistent with balanced growth equilibrium.

The demand side of our model can be divided between intermediate and final demands for the thirty-five commodity groups, capital and labor services, and noncompeting imports presented in the use table (figure 1.2.1). Our models of producer behavior determine value shares for inputs of commodities, primary factors of production, and noncompeting imports into each industry. These value shares incorporate an income-expenditure identity for the industry, since the value of output must be equal to the value of all inputs. The value shares determine inputs per unit of output as functions of the input and output prices. The input-output coefficients are multiplied by the output of the industry to obtain the input quantities. These quantities are added over the thirty-five industries to obtain total intermediate demands for each commodity group, capital and labor services, and noncompeting imports.

In summary, our model of producer behavior consists of two parts. The first is a set of thirty-five industry price functions and the second is a set of thirty-five commodity price functions. We have described how the industry price functions determine input demands and output prices in detail. The commodity price functions link output prices to commodity prices and determine the allocation of the output of each commodity among industries. The industry price functions account for the industry columns in the use table (figure 1.2.1), and the commodity price functions for the commodity columns in the make table (figure 1.2.2). We turn next to modeling the final demand categories.

1.2.2   Consumer Behavior

Energy and environmental policies have different impacts on different households. For example, the imposition of a tax on energy would affect the relative prices faced by consumers. An increase in the price of energy resulting from the tax would adversely affect those consumers who devote a larger share of total expenditure to energy. To capture these differences among households, we have subdivided the household sector into demographic groups that differ by characteristics such as family size, age of head, region of residence, race, and urban versus rural location. We treat each household as a consuming unit, so that the household behaves like an individual maximizing a utility function.

We represent the preferences of each household by means of an econometric model of consumer behavior. Our models of consumer behavior incorporate time-series data on personal consumption expenditures from the annual inter-industry transactions tables for the U.S. economy represented in figure 1.2.1. The econometric approach for parameterization enables us to derive the response of household expenditure patterns to changes in prices from historical experience. Empirical evidence on substitutability among goods and services by households is essential in analyzing the impact of energy and environmental policies. If it is easy for households to substitute among commodities, the effects of these policies will be very different than if substitution were limited.

The econometric approach to modeling consumer behavior has the same advantages over the calibration approach as those we have described for modeling producer behavior. An additional feature of our models of consumer behavior is that they incorporate detailed cross-section data on the impact of demographic differences among households and levels of total expenditure on household expenditure patterns. We do not require that consumer demands are homothetic, so that patterns of individual expenditure change as total expenditure varies, even in the absence of price changes. This captures an important characteristic of cross-section observations on household expenditure patterns that is usually ignored in general equilibrium modeling. Finally, we aggregate over individual demand functions to obtain a system of aggregate demand functions. This makes it possible to dispense with the notion of a representative consumer.

Our econometric model of consumer behavior is based on two-stage allocation. We can summarize the representation of consumer behavior in terms of an indirect utility function for each household. At the first stage the household allocates total expenditure among five commodity groups—energy, food, nondurable goods, capital services, and other services. The indirect utility function must be homothetically separable in the prices of the commodities within each of these groups. This function must also be homogeneous of degree zero in prices faced by the household and total expenditure on all commodities. Finally, the function must be nonincreasing in the prices, nondecreasing in total expenditure, and quasi-convex in prices and expenditure. These restrictions are incorporated into the system of demand functions that we construct for each household.[30]

At the second stage of our model of consumer behavior, expenditure on each of the five commodity groups is allocated among labor and capital services and the individual commodities included in our model according to a hierarchical tier structure of demands. In order to keep the number of estimated parameters small we break up these commodity groups into a total of fifteen subaggregates.[31] As an example, the price of energy is a function of the prices of coal, refined petroleum, electricity, and natural gas. This results in a submodel of household energy consumption that is analogous to those employed in our econometric models of producer behavior.

To present the consumption model more formally, we require some additional notation. First, let the number of households be J, and the individual households be indexed by j.[32] Next, let the five commodity groups be indexed by n. We denote the price of commodity group n by p_n. Prices are assumed to be the same for all households. Similarly, we denote the quantity of commodity group n demanded by the household j by x_{nj}. In addition, if the total expenditure of consumer j is Y_j, the following budget constraint must hold:

$$Y_j = \sum_{n=1}^{5} p_n x_{nj} \ .$$

To allow for differences in preferences among households, we allow the indirect utility function to depend on a vector of attributes denoted A_j. Further, we define the expenditure share of consumer j on commodity n by:

$$w_{nj} = p_n \frac{x_{nj}}{Y_j}.$$

We find it convenient to define the vector of expenditure shares for consumer j as follows:

$$w_j = (w_{1j}, w_{2j}, \ldots, w_{5j})'.$$

Similarly, we define the vector of logarithms of prices faced by all consumers as:

$$\ln p = (\ln p_1, \ln p_2, \ldots, \ln p_5)'.$$

Finally, we define the ratios of these prices to total expenditures for consumer j as:

$$\ln \frac{p}{Y_j} = \left(\ln \frac{p_1}{Y_j}, \ln \frac{p_2}{Y_j}, \ldots, \ln \frac{p_5}{Y_j} \right)'.$$

We assume that household j allocates its total expenditure among the five commodity groups in accord with the translog indirect utility function:

$$\ln U_j = \ln \left(\frac{p}{Y_j} \right)' \alpha_p + \frac{1}{2} \ln \left(\frac{p}{Y_j} \right)' B_{pp} \ln \left(\frac{p}{Y_j} \right) + \ln \left(\frac{p}{Y_j} \right)' B_{pA} A_j. \tag{2.3}$$

The vector α_p and the matrices B_{pp} and B_{pA} are unknown parameters that are the same for all households. The vector of attributes A_j incorporates differences in preferences among households. The elements of this vector are one-zero dummy variables that classify households by the demographic characteristics—family size, age of head, region of residence, race, and urban versus rural location. Cross-classifying households by these characteristics, we distinguish among a total of 672 different household types.[33]

From the indirect utility (2.3), we can derive the expenditure shares of household j using the logarithmic form of Roy's identity. This produces the following:

$$w_j = \frac{1}{B_j}\left(\alpha_p + B_{pp} \ln \frac{p}{Y_j} + B_{pA} A_j\right),$$

where the denominator B_j takes the form:

$$B_j = \iota'\alpha_p + \iota'B_{pp} \ln \frac{p}{Y_j} + \iota'B_{pA} A_j ,$$

and ι is a vector of ones.

To derive a model of aggregate consumer behavior we assume that aggregate demand functions can be constructed from individual demand functions by exact aggregation. This requires that individual expenditure shares are linear in functions of the attributes A_j and total expenditure Y_j that vary among households. These conditions will be satisfied if and only if the terms involving the attributes and expenditures do not appear in the denominators of the individual expenditure shares. Thus, we require that:

$$\iota'B_{pp}\iota = 0, \quad \iota'B_{pA} = 0 .$$

In addition, we find it convenient to employ the normalization:

$$\iota'\alpha_p = -1.$$

The exact aggregation restrictions and the normalization given above imply that the denominators for individual households, B_j, each reduce to:

$$B = -1 + \iota'B_{pp} \ln p ,$$

where the subscript j is no longer needed, since the denominator is the same for all households. Under these restrictions the individual expenditure shares can be written:

$$w_j = \frac{1}{B}(\alpha_p + B_{pp} \ln p - B_{pp}\iota \ln Y_j + B_{pA} A_j) .$$

The individual expenditure shares are linear in the logarithm of expenditure $\ln Y_j$ and the attributes A_j, so we have satisfied the conditions for exact aggregation.

Aggregate expenditure shares, which we denote by w, are obtained by multiplying the individual expenditure shares by total expenditure for each household Y_j, adding over all households, and dividing by aggregate expenditure $\sum Y_j$ to give:

$$w = \frac{1}{B} \left(\alpha_p + B_{pp} \ln p - B_{pp}\iota \, \frac{\sum Y_j \ln Y_j}{\sum Y_j} + B_{pA} \, \frac{\sum Y_j A_j}{\sum Y_j} \right). \tag{2.4}$$

The parameters of this system are precisely the same as those of the household demand equations. The parameters B_{pp} represent the degree of substitutability among commodity groups within the household sector, while the parameters B_{pA} reflect the effect of changes in the demographic composition of the population and variations in relative expenditure levels for different demographic groups. Under homogeneity of degree zero, the vector $B_{pp}\iota$ captures the impact of changes in the level of aggregate expenditure and its distribution among households.

Unless preferences are homothetic, so that the elements of the vector $B_{pp}\iota$ are all zero, the composition of personal consumption expenditures varies with the level of aggregate expenditure and its distribution. Potentially, this could lead to a problem for long-run simulations similar to the one we encountered in modeling production. If aggregate expenditure were to increase indefinitely, eventually one of the expenditure shares would become negative. In practice, however, two other features of the model limit the growth of total expenditure. First, industry productivity levels eventually become constant, so that per capita total expenditure converges to a stationary limit. Second, our projection of the future U.S. population also converges to a stationary limit. This implies that aggregate expenditure eventually approaches a steady state value.[34]

The system of expenditure shares shown in eq. (2.4) allocates total expenditure to five broad groups of consumer goods. Expenditure on each of these groups is then broken down to the level of individual commodities, using a nested tier structure similar to that we have used for production. Given prices and total expenditure, this system allows us to calculate the elements of personal consumption column in the make table of figure 1.2.1. We employ the model to represent aggregate consumer behavior in simulations of the U.S. economy under alternative energy and environmental policies.

To determine the level of total expenditure we embed our model of personal consumption expenditures in a higher-level system that represents consumer preferences between goods and leisure and between saving and consumption. At the highest level each household allocates *full wealth*, defined as the sum of human and nonhuman wealth, across time periods. We formalize this decision by introducing a representative agent who maximizes an additive intertemporal utility function, subject to an intertemporal budget constraint. The allocation of full wealth is determined by the rate of time preference and the intertemporal elasticity of substitution.

The allocation of full wealth to the current time period is *full consumption*, defined as an aggregate of goods and leisure. Given this allocation, each household proceeds to a second stage of the optimization process—choosing the mix of leisure and goods. We represent household preferences at this stage by means of a representative agent with an indirect utility function that depends on the prices of leisure and goods. We derive demands for leisure and goods as functions of these prices and the wealth allocated to the current period. This implies an allocation of the household's exogenously given time endowment between leisure time and the labor market, so that this stage of the optimization process determines labor supply.

Our higher-level model of consumer behavior consists of two parts. At the highest level, we assume each household maximizes an additively separable intertemporal utility function:

$$U = \sum_{t=0}^{\infty} N_0 \prod_{s=1}^{t} \left(\frac{1+n_s}{1+\rho} \right) \ln F_t , \qquad (2.5)$$

where F_t is a per capita full consumption in period t, ρ is the rate of time preference, N_0 is the initial population, and n_s is the population growth rate in period s.

The household chooses the future path of full consumption F to maximize the intertemporal utility function U, subject to an intertemporal budget constraint. This requires that the present value of full consumption is no greater than household wealth. Wealth, in turn, is the present value of future earnings from the supply of capital and labor services, transfers from the government and the imputed value of leisure time. The conditions for optimality can be expressed in the form of an Euler equation. This equation gives the value of full consumption in one period in terms of the value of full consumption in the next period, the discount rate, and the rate of population growth.[35]

The Euler equation is forward-looking, so that the current level of full consumption incorporates expectations about all future prices and discount rates. The solution of our model includes this forward-looking relationship in every time period. The future prices and discount rates determined by the model enter full consumption for earlier periods through the assumption of perfect foresight or rational expectations. Under this assumption full consumption in every period is based on expectations about future prices and discount rates that are fulfilled by the solution of the model.

Once each period's full consumption has been found, we proceed to the second part of the representative agent household model. In this stage, the household divides the value of full consumption between personal consumption expenditures and leisure time. This has three effects. First, by determining the value of personal consumption expenditures it completes our model for household sector final demand. Second, the difference between the quantity of leisure consumed and the household's total time endowment determines the quantity of labor supplied.[36] Third, saving is determined by the difference between current income from the supply of capital and labor services and personal consumption expenditures.

Labor market time is allocated among the thirty-five industries represented in the model by equating labor supply with the sum of labor inputs demanded by these industries. In addition, labor services are included in demands for personal consumption expenditures and public consumption. We assume that labor is perfectly mobile among sectors, so that the price of labor services is proportional to a single wage rate for the economy as a whole. The supply price of labor is the numeraire for our price system.

We model the household allocation decision by assuming that full consumption is an aggregate of goods and leisure. The share of each in full consumption depends on the price of consumption goods, the price of leisure, and the household's share elasticity between the two. We take the price of consumption goods to be the cost of living index generated from the first stage of our model of consumer behavior by Jorgenson and Slesnick (1990). We take the price of leisure time to be the wage rate less the marginal tax rate on labor income.

Our model of consumer behavior allocates the value of full consumption between personal consumption expenditures and leisure time. Given aggregate expenditure on goods and services and its distribution among households, this model then allocates personal consumption expenditures among commodity groups, including capital and labor services and noncompeting imports. Finally, the income of the household sector is the sum of incomes from the supply of capital and labor services, interest payments from governments and the rest of the world, all net of taxes, and transfers from the government. Savings are equal to the difference between income and consumption, less personal transfers to foreigners and nontax payments to governments. This is the income-expenditure identity of the household sector.

In summary, our model of household behavior consists of three stages. First, it includes a system of expenditure share equations derived from maximization of a household utility function and satisfying conditions for exact aggregation. Second, it includes a higher-level representative-agent model that determines the intertemporal allocation of consumption through an Euler equation derived from maximization of an intertemporal utility function. Third, the representative agent model also allocates full consumption between goods and leisure, determining personal consumption expenditures, labor supply, and saving.

1.2.3   Investment and Capital Formation

Our investment model, like our model of saving, is based on perfect foresight or rational expectations. Under this assumption, the price of investment goods in every time period is based on expectations of future capital service prices and discount rates that are fulfilled by the solution of the model. In particular, we require that the price of new investment goods is always equal to the present value of future capital services.[37] The price of investment goods and the discounted value of future rental prices are brought into equilibrium by adjustments in future prices and rates of return. This incorporates the forward-looking dynamics of asset pricing into our model of intertemporal equilibrium.

For tractability we assume there is a single capital stock in the economy which is perfectly malleable and mobile among sectors, so that it can be reallocated among industries and final demand categories at zero cost. Under this assumption changes in energy and environmental policy can affect the distribution of capital and labor supplies among sectors, even in the short run. However, the total supply of capital in our model in each time period is perfectly inelastic, since the available stock of capital is determined by past investments. An accumulation equation relates capital stock to investments in all past time periods and incorporates the backward-looking dynamics of capital formation into our model of intertemporal equilibrium.

Since capital is perfectly malleable, the price of capital services in each sector is proportional to a single price of capital services for the economy as a whole. This rental price balances each period's supply with the sum of demands by all thirty-five industrial sectors together with the demand for personal consumption. Our model gives the price of capital services in terms of the price of investment goods at the beginning and end of each period, the rate of return to capital for the economy as a whole, the rate of depreciation, and variables describing the tax structure for income from capital. The income from capital in each period is equal to the value of capital services.

New capital goods are produced from the individual commodities included in our model. Each new unit of capital is an aggregate of commodities purchased for investment in producers' and consumers' durables, residential and nonresidential structures, and inventories. We have represented the technology for production of new capital goods by means of a price function for investment goods. We have estimated the unknown parameters of this investment submodel from time-series data on gross private domestic investment from the annual inter-industry tables for the U.S. economy represented in the use table (figure 1.2.1). As with our model of producer behavior, we use a nested tier structure of submodels to capture substitution among different inputs in the construction of new capital.[38]

The behavioral equations for our model include a system of demand functions for investment goods by business and household sectors. The business sector purchases goods for investments in producers' durables, residential and nonresidential structures, and inventories. The household sector purchases goods for investments in consumers' durables and residential structures. We generate value shares for all types of investment goods from the price function for new capital goods. We use these value shares to allocate the value of investment goods among commodity groups, resulting in the final demands for gross private domestic investment given in the use table (figure 1.2.1). Finally, we determine the quantity of each commodity by dividing the value of investment in that commodity by the corresponding price.

Our investment submodel allocates gross private domestic investment among commodity groups. The value of this investment must be equal to savings. The balance sheet identity of the household sector sets private wealth equal to the sum of the value of capital stock in the private sector, claims on governments, and claims on the rest of the world. The change in the value private wealth from period to period is the sum of private savings and the revaluation of wealth as the result of inflation.

In summary, capital formation in our model is the outcome of intertemporal optimization by producers. Optimization by producers is forward-looking and incorporates expectations about future prices and rates of return. Optimization by consumers is also forward-looking and depends on these same expectations. Both types of optimization are very important for modeling the impact of future energy and environmental policies. The effects of these policies will be anticipated by producers and consumers, so that future policies will have important consequences for current decisions.

1.2.4   Government and Foreign Trade

The two remaining final demand categories in our model are the government and rest-of-the-world sectors. We determine final demands for government consumption from the income-expenditure identity for the government sector.[39] The first step is to compute total tax revenue by applying exogenous tax rates to all taxable transactions in the economy. We then add the capital income of government enterprises, which is determined endogenously, and nontax receipts, determined exogenously, to tax receipts to obtain total government revenue.

The key assumption of our submodel of the government sector is that the government budget deficit can be specified exogenously. We add the deficit to total revenue to obtain total government spending. To arrive at government purchases of goods and services, we subtract interest paid to domestic and foreign holders of government bonds together with government transfer payments to domestic and foreign recipients. We allocate the remainder among commodity groups according to fixed shares constructed from historical data. Finally, we determine the quantity of each commodity by dividing the value of government spending on that commodity by its price.

Foreign trade has two quite different components—imports and exports. We assume that imports are imperfect substitutes for similar domestic commodities.[40] The goods actually purchased by households and firms reflect substitutions between domestic and imported products. The price responsiveness of these purchases is estimated from historical data taken from the import and export columns of the use table (figure 1.2.1), in our annual inter-industry transactions tables. In addition, the allocations of domestic supplies between domestic and imported commodities incorporate logistic time trends that capture determinants other than relative prices. The logistic functions approach unity in the limit, so that these trends eventually disappear. Since the prices of imports are given exogenously, the sum of intermediate and final demands implicitly determines quantities of imports of each commodity.

Exports, on the other hand, are modeled by a set of explicit foreign demand equations, one for each commodity, that depend on exogenously given foreign income and the foreign price of U.S. exports. Foreign prices are computed from domestic prices by adjusting for subsidies and the exchange rate. The demand elasticities in these equations are estimated from historical data. Our model incorporates the income-expenditure identity of the rest-of-the-world sector. The current account surplus is equal to the value of exports less the value of imports, plus interest received on domestic holdings of foreign bonds, less private and government transfers abroad, and less interest on government bonds paid to foreigners. The key assumption of our submodel of the rest-of-the-world sector is that the current account is exogenous and the exchange rate is endogenous.

In summary, final demands by governments are determined by first generating government revenues. Total expenditure is then determined from the income-expenditure identity of the government sector. The allocation of this expenditure among commodity groups is given exogenously. Final demands by the rest of the world are determined by modeling import demands and export supplies separately. The current account balance from the income-expenditure identity for the rest-of-the-world sector is taken to be exogenous, so that the exchange rate is determined by the equilibrium of the model.

1.2.5   Constructing the Base Case

In order to analyze the impact of changes in energy and environmental policies, we simulate the growth of the U.S. economy with and without changes in these policies.[41] Our first step is to generate a simulation with no changes in policy that we call the *base case*. The second step is to change the exogenous variables of the model to reflect a proposed policy change. We then produce a simulation that we refer to as the *alternative case*. Finally, we compare the two simulations to assess the effects of the change in policy. Obviously, the assumptions underlying the base case are of considerable importance in interpreting the results of our simulations.

We conclude this overview by outlining the solution of our model. An intertemporal submodel incorporates backward-looking and forward-looking equations that determine the time paths of capital stock, full consumption, and the price of assets. Given the values of these variables in any time period, an intratemporal submodel determines prices that balance demands and supplies for the thirty-five commodity groups included in the model, capital and labor services, and noncompeting imports. These two submodels must be solved simultaneously to obtain a complete intertemporal equilibrium.

To construct a simulation of U.S. economic growth, we first require the values of all exogenous variables in every time period. These variables are set equal to their historical values for the sample period, 1947 through 1985. We project the values for all exogenous variables for the post-sample period 1986 through 2050. After 2050, we assume that these variables remain constant at their values in 2050, which allows the model to converge to a steady state by the year 2100. The most important exogenous variables are those associated with U.S. population growth and the corresponding change in the time endowment of the U.S. economy. We project population by age, sex and educational attainment through the year 2050, using demographic assumptions consistent with Bureau of the Census projections.[42]

After 2050 we hold population constant, which is roughly consistent with Census Bureau projections. We project educational attainment by assuming that future demographic cohorts will have the same level of attainment as the cohort reaching age 35 in the year 1985. We then transform our population projection into a projection of the time endowment used in our model of the labor market by assuming that relative wages across all categories of workers are constant at 1985 levels. Since capital accumulation is endogenous, these population projections effectively determine the size of the economy in the more distant future.

Next, we consider exogenous components of our submodels of the government and rest-of-the-world sectors. We set all tax rates to their values in 1985, the last year in our sample period. We project a gradual decline in the government deficit through the year 2025, after which the deficit is held at four percent of the nominal value of the government debt. This has the effect of maintaining a constant ratio of the value of the government debt to the value of the national product when the inflation rate is four percent, as it is in our steady state. We assume that prices of imports in foreign currency and before tariffs remain constant in real terms at 1985 levels. Our projections of the current account deficit fall gradually to zero by the year 2000. After that we project a small current account surplus sufficient to produce a stock of net claims on foreigners by the year 2050 equal to the same proportion of national wealth as in 1982.

Given projections of the exogenous variables of our model of the U.S. economy, we can divide the simulation of U.S. economic growth into two steps. The first step is to construct a stationary solution corresponding to constant values of all exogenous variables. In the stationary solution both full consumption and capital stock are constant. We determine the stationary rate of return from the Euler equation from our model of consumer behavior. Similarly, we determine the stationary level of investment from our accumulation equation for capital stock. We take this stationary solution to be our projection of the U.S. economy for all years after 2100.

Our second step in the generation of a simulation is to construct a transition path to the steady state of our model, beginning with the initial level of capital stock. For this purpose we combine the solutions of our intertemporal and intratemporal models. Our intertemporal model determines time paths of full consumption, capital stock, and the price of new capital goods. These time paths are consistent with the forward-looking Euler equation from our model of consumer behavior and the asset pricing equation from our model of investment behavior. The model also determines the time path of capital stock consistent with the backward-looking accumulation equation for capital stock.

The solution of our intratemporal model determines prices for outputs of the thirty-five industries as functions of the prices of capital and labor services and noncompeting imports. These output prices are determined from the industry price functions included in our submodel of the business sector. Given these prices, the domestic supply prices for the thirty-five commodities included in this submodel are determined from the commodity price functions. Finally, the domestic supply price for each commodity is combined with the price of imports to determine the total supply price for each commodity. These prices enter the determination of intermediate demands by all industries and final demands by business, household, government, and rest-of-the-world sectors.

The prices of competing and noncompeting imports are given exogenously in every time period. The prices of capital and labor services are determined by balancing demands and supplies for these services. The supply of capital services is determined by previous investments and is taken as given in each period. The supply of labor services is determined endogenously within our model of consumer behavior. This model allocates full consumption in each period between personal consumption expenditures and leisure time. The model also allocates the exogenously given time endowment between the labor market and leisure time.

Our intratemporal model also guarantees that income-expenditure identities for all thirty-five industries and the household, government, and the rest-of-the-world sectors are satisfied. These identities imply that gross private domestic investment is equal to private savings plus the current account deficit less the government budget deficit. Since we take the government and current account deficits to be exogenous, changes in gross private domestic investment are driven by changes in private savings. Thus, changes in the rate of capital accumulation depend on changes in private savings and the price of investment goods.

It is interesting to contrast the behavior of our model with that of a one-sector neoclassical growth model. In the short run the supply of capital in our model is perfectly inelastic since it is completely determined by past investment. In the long run, however, the supply of capital is perfectly elastic, since the rate of return depends only on productivity growth and parameters that describe the intertemporal preferences of the household sector. Thus, in the long run the rate of return in our model is independent of energy and environmental policy, just as in a one-sector neoclassical growth model. Since our model has many sectors, however, different policies result in different levels of capital intensity, all corresponding to the same rate of return. This is impossible in a one-sector model.

In summary, we construct a simulation of U.S. economic growth by solving our model for given values of all exogenous variables in all time periods. First, we solve an intertemporal submodel that contains forward-looking equations determining the time paths of asset prices and full consumption. This submodel also includes a backward-looking equation determining the time path of capital stock from past investments. Given the values of these variables, our intratemporal or one-period submodel determines prices that balance demand and supply for the thirty-five commodity groups included in the model, capital and labor services, and noncompeting imports. We solve the two submodels simultaneously to obtain the full intertemporal equilibrium.

1.3   The Impact of Environmental Regulation

Our next objective is to assess the impact of environmental regulations introduced in the 1970s and early 1980s. Our approach will be to use the model of section 1.2 to simulate the growth of the U.S. economy with and without regulation. We begin by observing that our base case implicitly includes environmental regulation since it is based on historical data. Thus, to determine the effect of regulation we conduct counterfactual simulations in which regulation is removed from the economy. In addition, we decompose the overall effect of regulation into components associated with both pollution control in industry and controls on motor vehicle emissions. We conclude by estimating the overall impact of environmental regulation by eliminating both types of pollution control.

Removing environmental regulation produces simulations which differ from the base case at the steady state, at the initial (first year) equilibrium, and along the transition path between the two. The difference between the new steady state and the base case shows the long-run impact of environmental regulation after the capital stock has adjusted. The difference between the new initial equilibrium and the base case gives the short-run impact of a change in policy before the capital stock can adjust at all. However, since agents in the model have perfect foresight, this initial equilibrium reflects changes along the entire time path of future regulatory policy. Finally, the transition path between the initial equilibrium and the steady state traces out the economy's adjustment to the new environmental policy.

In presenting the results of our simulations, we begin by quantifying the impact of pollution controls on production costs. We then incorporate these cost changes into the model and run counterfactual simulations. In interpreting the simulation results, we first consider the impact of environmental regulation on the steady state of the economy, concentrating our analysis on a few key variables. Next, we analyze the transition path of economy from the initial equilibrium to the new steady state. We focus particular attention on the path of capital stock, since it is the most important overall measure of the effect of the change in policy. We also discuss a number of other important variables including the price of investment goods, the rental price of capital services and the level of the gross national product (GNP).

1.3.1   Operating Costs

We employ data collected by the Bureau of the Census to estimate
investment in pollution abatement equipment and operating costs of
pollution control activities for manufacturing industries.[43] The investment data give capital expenditures on pollution abatement equipment in current prices, while data on operating costs give current
outlays attributable to pollution control. These are the actual costs
reported by firms and do not include taxes levied as part of the Superfund program.[44] Figure 1.3.1 shows the share of pollution abatement
in industry costs. For most industries, pollution control accounts for
only a small part of total costs. The largest share is for the primary
metals industry and it amounts to slightly more than two percent.

Our first step in eliminating the operating costs of pollution control
is to estimate the share of pollution abatement in the total costs of each
industry. For years between 1973 and 1985, we have calculated the
actual share from historical data. After 1983, we assume that the share
remained constant at its 1983 value. Outside manufacturing, data
were only available for electric utilities and wastewater treatment
(wastewater treatment is part of the services industry). For both of
these industries, data on operating costs and investment expenditures
for pollution abatement are available from the Bureau of Economic
Analysis.[45]

For electric utilities, the Bureau of Economic Analysis also estimates
the extra cost of burning low-sulfur fuels to comply with sulfur
dioxide regulations. The principal low-sulfur fuel used by utilities is
low-sulfur coal. In terms of our model, switching from high-sulfur to
low-sulfur coal changes the relative proportions of the two products
in the output of the coal industry. Since low-sulfur coal is more
expensive when transportation costs are included, this increases the
price of coal. Eliminating regulations on sulfur emissions would
lower the price of coal by permitting substitution toward high-sulfur
grades. We model the impact of lifting these restrictions by subtracting the differential between high-cost and low-cost coal from the cost
of coal production.[46]

Twenty of the thirty-five industries in our model are subject to pollution abatement regulations. We use the share of abatement costs in
total costs for each industry to compute the share of total costs excluding pollution abatement. Let the share for industry i be denoted λ_i.
Since our data set on pollution abatement ends in 1983, we assume the

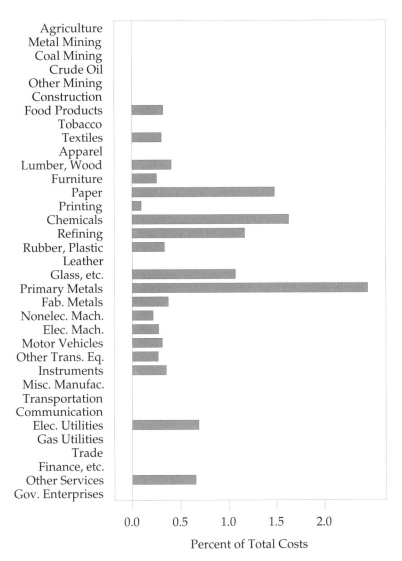

Figure 1.3.1
Abatement costs by industry.

shares for later years are constant at their 1983 values. To simulate the effect of eliminating the operating costs associated with pollution abatement we insert the cost shares λ_i into the cost function for each industry. More precisely, we modify the translog price functions as follows:

$$\ln q_i = \ln \lambda_i + \alpha_0^i + \ln p_i' \alpha_p^i + \alpha_t^i g_i(t)$$

$$+ \frac{1}{2} \ln p_i' B_{pp}^i \ln p_i + \ln p_i' \beta_{pt}^i g_i(t) + \frac{1}{2} \beta_{tt}^i g_i(t) \ .$$

This has the effect of excluding operating costs associated with pollution control from total costs in each industry.

The long-run impact of eliminating the operating costs of pollution abatement is summarized in the column labeled ENV in table 1.3.1.

The output of the economy, as measured by the gross national product, rises by 0.728%. Much of this comes from an increase in the capital stock which rises by 0.544%. Since the model has a perfectly elastic supply of savings in the long run, the rate of return is unaffected by regulation. However, the price of new investment goods falls by 0.897%. This increases capital accumulation and reduces the price of capital services. Cheaper capital services lead to a fall in the prices of goods and services and a rise in full consumption by 0.278%. This increase is less than that of gross national product, since full consumption includes leisure time as well as personal consumption expenditures. Finally, the exchange rate, which gives the domestic cost of foreign goods, falls slightly, indicating an increase in the international competitiveness of the U.S. economy.[47]

The long-run effects of eliminating operating costs associated with pollution abatement on the prices and outputs of individual industries are shown in figure 1.3.2. Figure 1.3.2(a) shows the percentage change in the steady-state purchaser's price of each commodity while figure 1.3.2(b) gives percentage changes in industry output levels. Not

Table 1.3.1
The effects of removing environmental regulations

| Variable | Percentage change in steady state | | | |
	ENV	INV	MV	ALL
Capital stock	0.544	2.266	1.118	3.792
Price of investment goods	−0.897	−2.652	−1.323	−4.520
Full consumption	0.278	0.489	0.282	0.975
Real GNP	0.728	1.290	0.752	2.592
Rental price of capital	−0.907	−2.730	−1.358	−4.635
Exchange rate	−0.703	−0.462	−0.392	−1.298

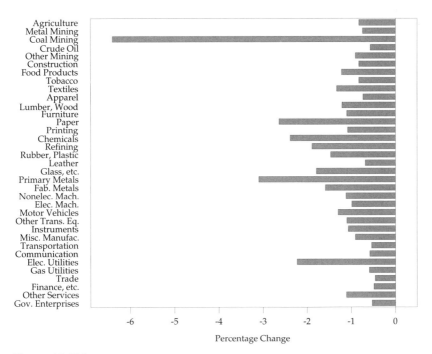

Figure 1.3.2(a)
Effect of ENV on prices.

surprisingly, the principal beneficiaries of eliminating operating costs are the most heavily regulated industries. The greatest expansion of output occurs in coal production, since the fuel cost differential between low-sulfur and high-sulfur coal is large relative to the total costs of the coal industry. Turning to manufacturing industries, primary metals, paper, and chemicals have the largest gains in output from the elimination of operating costs for pollution abatement. Several other sectors benefit from the removal of operating costs of pollution abatement, but the impact is fairly modest.

We now turn from the long-run impact of eliminating operating costs to its dynamic effects. Figure 1.3.3 shows the effects of removing operating costs on the time paths of full consumption, the price of new capital goods, the capital stock and the level of gross national product. After 1973, the price of investment goods falls slowly, reflecting the gradual price decline brought about by the elimination of operating costs associated with increasingly stringent regulations.

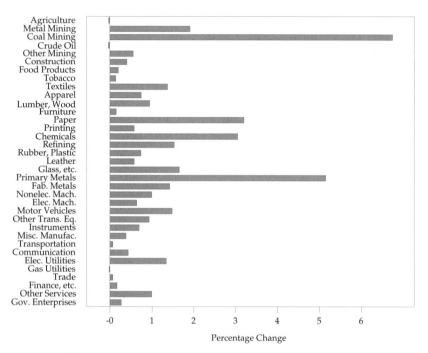

Figure 1.3.2(b)
Effect of ENV on output.

Lower costs of investment goods tend to increase the rate of return, stimulate savings, and produce more rapid capital accumulation. Additional capital eventually brings down the rental price of capital, lowering costs still further. This, in turn, raises the level of GNP.

The transition from the short run to the steady state is relatively slow, requiring almost three decades for the capital stock to adjust to the change in environmental policy. Figure 1.3.3(c) shows that the adjustment process is not complete until the year 2000. In part this reflects the nature of the experiment: the actual regulations were imposed gradually, so their removal is also gradual. On the other hand, full consumption attains its final value fairly quickly as a consequence of intertemporal optimization by households. Since income is permanently higher in the future, consumption rises in anticipation. However, the rise of consumption is dampened by an increase in the rate of return that produces greater investment.

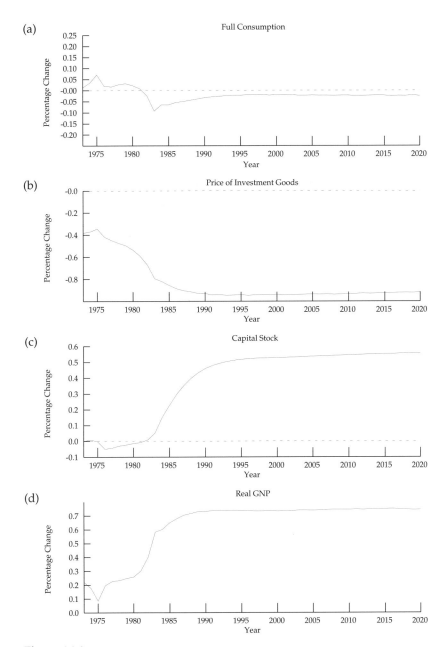

Figure 1.3.3
(a) Full consumption; (b) price of investment goods; (c) capital stock; (d) real GNP.

1.3.2   Investment in Pollution Control Equipment

For some industries, the most important impact of environmental regulation is through mandatory investment in costly pollution abatement equipment. Investment in pollution control devices crowds out
investment for ordinary capital accumulation, reducing the rate of
economic growth. Our second simulation is designed to assess the
impact of this investment.

The share of pollution control in total investment rose to a peak in
the early 1970s and then declined substantially. This can be attributed
to the fact that much of the early effort in pollution control was
directed at reducing emissions from existing sources by retrofitting
equipment already in place. Later, restrictions on emissions from new
sources became more important. New source regulations increase the
cost of new investments because producers are required to purchase
pollution abatement equipment whenever they acquire new investment goods. The economic effects of retrofitting are quite different
from investment in new source control, so we distinguish between the
two in constructing our counterfactual simulation.

We begin by assuming that investment in pollution control equipment provides no benefits to producers other than satisfying environmental regulations. Accordingly, we simulate mandated investment
as an increase in the price of investment goods. Unfortunately, our
data set does not distinguish between investments required for new
and existing facilities. To separate the two, we assume the backlog of
investment for retrofitting old sources was eliminated by 1983. This
allows us to infer that the 1983 share of pollution abatement devices in
total investment was due entirely to new investment. Thus, we can
simulate the impact of removing environmental regulations on new
investment by reducing the price of investment goods by that proportion. This captures the effect of requirements for pollution abatement
on investment in new capital goods, but does not include the effect of
windfall losses to owners of the capital associated with old sources of
emissions.

This approach has certain limitations that should be pointed out.
First, it relies on the assumption that capital is completely malleable
and mobile between sectors. An alternative technique would be to
incorporate costs of adjustment into our models of producer behavior.
However, this approach would lead to considerable additional complexity in modeling and simulating producer behavior. Moreover, the

long-run impact of environmental regulations would be unaffected by costs of adjustment, since these costs would be zero in the steady state of our model.

Column INV of table 1.3.1 gives the steady-state effects of removing mandated investment in pollution control devices. The largest change is in the capital stock, which rises by 2.266% as a direct result of the drop in the price of investment goods. In the short run, this price decline pushes up the rate of return, raising the level of investment. Higher capital accumulation leads to a fall in the rental price of capital services, decreasing the overall price level. The long-run level of full consumption rises by 0.489%, almost double the increase resulting from eliminating operating costs of pollution abatement. The 1.290% rise in GNP is also nearly twice as large. The exchange rate appreciates by 0.462%, indicating an increase in the international competitiveness of the U.S. economy.

Figure 1.3.4 shows the long-run effect of eliminating pollution abatement investment on commodity prices and industry output.

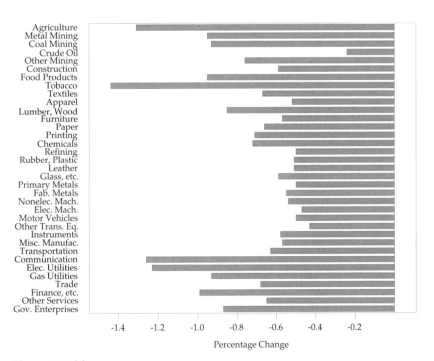

Figure 1.3.4(a)
Effect of INV on prices.

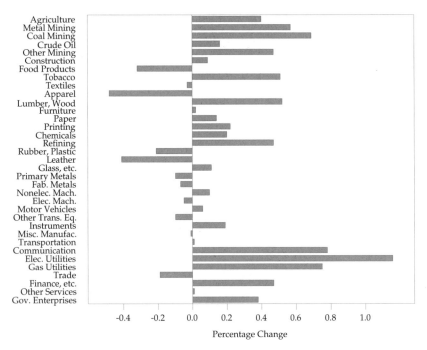

Figure 1.3.4(b)
Effect of INV on output.

These effects stem from the drop in the rental price of capital services. The largest gains in output are for communications, electric utilities, and gas utilities, since these are the most capital intensive industries. While most sectors gain from eliminating investment for pollution control, a few sectors are hurt by the change. Outputs of food, apparel, rubber and plastic, and leather decline. These sectors are among the least capital intensive, so that the fall in the rental price of capital services has little effect on the prices of outputs. This leads both intermediate and final demand sectors to substitute away from those commodities. Moreover, nonhomotheticity in consumption leads to a relative drop in the output of less income-elastic goods such as food.

The transition path of the U.S. economy after investment requirements for pollution control have been eliminated is summarized in figure 1.3.5. The process of adjustment is markedly different from that of the previous simulation. Capital stock grows immediately and

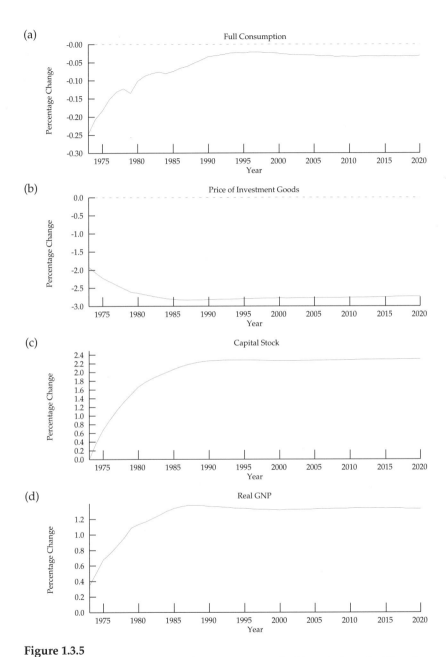

Figure 1.3.5
(a) Full consumption; (b) price of investment goods; (c) capital stock; (d) real
GNP.

rapidly to its new equilibrium value. This comes about as a consequence of the fall in the price of investment goods. As new capital
goods become cheaper, beginning in 1973, the rate of return rises,
driving up investment and producing a sharp increase in the capital
stock. The initial surge in investment is financed by an increase in
savings brought about by a temporary drop in consumption. Later,
consumption rises as the capital stock grows.

1.3.3   Motor Vehicle Emissions Control

Environmental regulation is not limited to controlling pollution by
industries in the business sector. Restrictions on motor vehicle emissions affect both businesses and households. Like pollution control in
industry, the reduction of motor vehicle exhaust emissions requires
both capital expenditures and operating costs. A catalytic converter is
a typical piece of pollution abatement equipment requiring capital
expenditure, and the premium paid for unleaded gasoline is an example of an increase in operating costs.

Kappler and Rutledge (1985) present data on the capital costs associated with motor vehicle regulation and three types of operating
cost—increased fuel consumption, increased fuel prices, and increased
vehicle maintenance. We first divide the total cost of pollution abatement equipment between imported and domestic vehicles in proportion to their shares in total supply. We then exclude the cost of this
equipment from the total cost of domestic motor vehicle production,
while reducing the price of imported motor vehicles in proportion to
the cost of pollution control devices.

Given the industries in our model, the price premium for unleaded
motor fuels can best be modeled as a change in the cost of output of
the petroleum refining sector. This is similar to the treatment of the
fuel cost differential between high-sulfur and low-sulfur coal. Only
the operating costs associated with higher fuel prices were removed in
this simulation; fuel consumption and vehicle maintenance were held
constant. Consequently, our results understate the overall impact of
emission controls.

As shown in column MV of table 1.3.1, the long-run economic
impact of imposing emissions controls on motor vehicles is similar in
magnitude to the impact of pollution controls in industry (column
ENV). The capital stock rises by 1.118%, full consumption increases
by 0.282%, real GNP increases by 0.752% and the exchange rate

appreciates by 0.392%. Almost all of the impact is due to the drop in motor vehicle prices resulting from the elimination of required pollution control equipment. Motor vehicles are one of the principal inputs into the production of investment goods, so that changes in their price have a significant effect on the overall price of investment goods. As with our investment simulation, a drop in the price of investment goods raises the rate of return and leads to large changes in the capital stock.

The long-run effects of eliminating motor vehicle emissions controls on commodity prices and industry outputs are shown in figure 1.3.6. The principal beneficiary of the elimination of these regulations is the motor vehicles industry itself. This is due in part to the fact that the demand for motor vehicles is price elastic: a price change of seven percent produces an output change of fourteen percent. Thus, a small drop in price produces a large change in output. Two other industries also benefit significantly from the change in policy—petroleum

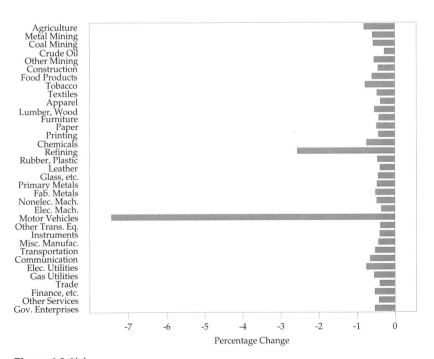

Figure 1.3.6(a)
Effect of MV on prices.

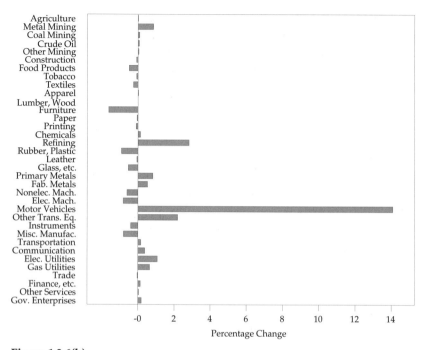

Figure 1.3.6(b)
Effect of MV on output.

refining and electric utilities. Both gain from the reduction in fuel prices associated with elimination of the fuel price premium.

The dynamic response of the economy to an elimination of vehicle regulations is so similar to the response for the investment simulation that we omit the graphs. The differences can be attributed to the fact that vehicle regulation began in earnest somewhat later and the imposed significantly smaller changes on the price of investment goods.

1.3.4 The Overall Impact of Environmental Regulation

To measure the total impact of eliminating all three costs of environmental regulation—operating costs resulting from pollution abatement in industry, mandated investments to meet environmental standards in particular industries and cost of emission controls on motor vehicles—we performed a final simulation. However, this experiment was not a simple combination of the three components.

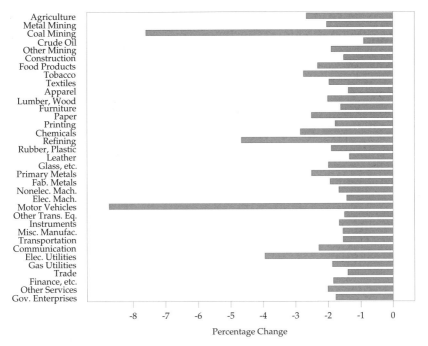

Figure 1.3.7(a)
Effect of ALL on prices.

Operating costs include capital costs, so combining the reductions in operating costs with the elimination of mandated investment would count the cost reductions associated with capital twice. To solve this problem, the capital component was removed from operating costs in the combined simulation. The results of removing all forms of environmental regulation are summarized in column ALL of table 1.3.1.

The long-run consequences of pollution control for different commodities and industries are presented in figure 1.3.7. The sectors hit hardest by environmental regulations were the motor vehicles and coal mining industries. Primary metals and petroleum refining followed close behind. About half the remaining industries have increases in output of one to five percent after pollution controls are removed. The rest are largely unaffected by environmental regulations. The economy follows the transition path to the new steady state shown in figure 1.3.8. Driven by large changes in the price of investment goods, the capital stock rises sharply. The quantity of full consumption rises at a similar rate, as does real GNP. The adjustment

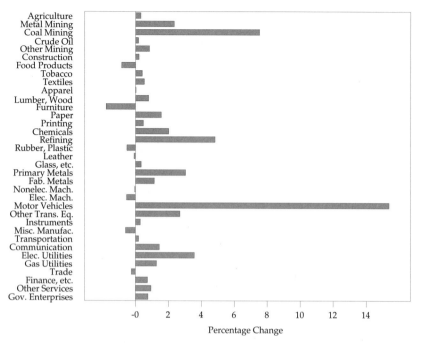

Figure 1.3.7(b)
Effect of ALL on output.

process is dominated by the rapid accumulation of capital and is largely completed within two decades.

1.4   The Impact of Higher Energy Prices

The possibility that carbon dioxide emissions from fossil fuel use might lead to global warming has become a leading environmental concern. Many scientific and environmental organizations have called for immediate action to limit these emissions. To the extend that the emissions are a global externality, one possible policy would be to introduce a Pigouvian tax on fossil fuel use. In particular, it would be possible to introduce a tax on the carbon content of fossil fuels. A carbon tax would reduce the use of fossil fuels by inducing substitution of energy sources such as solar, nuclear, and hydroelectric power for coal, petroleum, and natural gas. In addition, a carbon tax would raise the cost of using energy and induce the substitution of capital, labor, and materials inputs for energy.

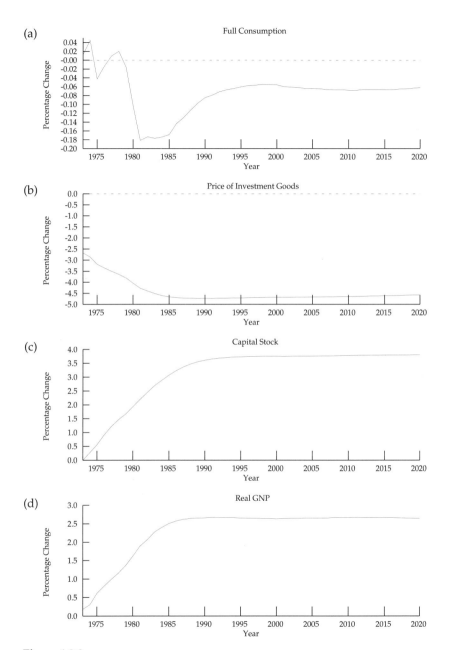

Figure 1.3.8
(a) Full consumption; (b) price of investment goods; (c) capital stock; (d) real GNP.

A carbon tax employs higher energy prices, especially higher prices of fossil fuels, to reduce carbon dioxide emissions. The past two decades of U.S. historical experience have provided a natural experiment that is useful in assessing the economic impact of this strategy. Between 1973 and 1975 the price of imported petroleum increased by a factor of three as a consequence of supply disruptions associated with the Arab Oil Embargo. Between 1978 and 1980 oil prices doubled as a result of disruptions in supply that followed the Iranian Revolution. The historical time path of petroleum prices between 1965 and 1990 in real terms is presented in figure 1.4.1.

The dramatic increases in world petroleum prices during the 1970s were followed by a gradual decline in prices between 1980 and 1985 that gave way to a precipitous drop in 1986. By 1987 real petroleum prices had stabilized at levels that were more than double those prevailing in 1972. The increase in world petroleum prices raised the real cost of energy in the U.S.A. for all forms of energy. This increase in energy prices resulted in substantial energy conservation and stabilized carbon dioxide emissions for a period of fifteen years between 1972 and 1987. In figure 1.4.2 we present historical data on carbon dioxide emissions for the period 1965 to 1987. In 1972, carbon dioxide emissions released 1224 million tons of carbon into the atmosphere.[48] Fifteen years later, in 1987, the emissions were identical.

In order to analyze the natural experiment that resulted from higher world petroleum prices since 1973, we have simulated the growth of the U.S. economy with and without these price increases. We take the actual path of world petroleum prices over the period 1973–1987 as our base case and extrapolate real petroleum prices forward from 1987 at the level of prices prevailing in 1987. As alternatives to the base case we have considered the following scenarios:

OIL72: The real price of imported petroleum is held constant at its 1972 level. Thus, this scenario omits both the long-term increase in the level of world petroleum prices between 1972 and 1987 and the price shocks associated with supply disruptions in 1973–1975 and 1978–1980.

OIL81: The real price of imported petroleum follows its historical path through the peak level in 1981, but after that it remains constant at the 1981 level. This scenario is the same as the base case through the year 1981, but omits the decline in world petroleum prices from 1981 to 1987.

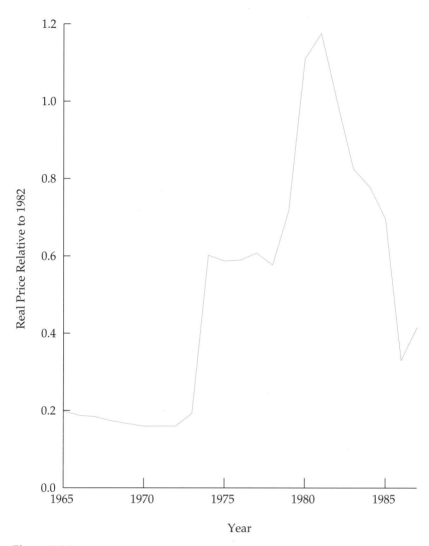

Figure 1.4.1
Real price of oil.

OIL87: The real price of imported petroleum rises linearly from its
1972 level to its level in 1987, after which it remains constant. This
scenario omits the price shocks of 1973–1975 and 1978–1980, but captures the long-term rise in world petroleum prices over the fifteen
year period between 1972 and 1987.

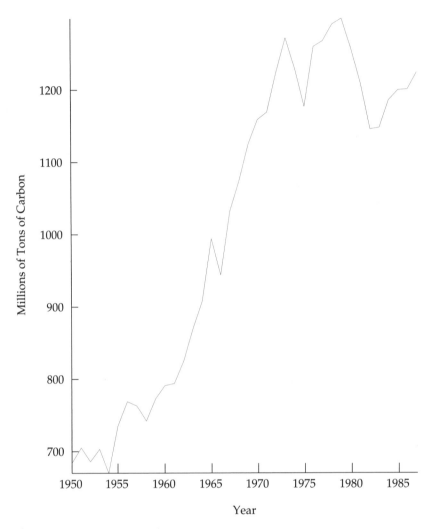

Figure 1.4.2
Total carbon emissions.

By comparing the results for each of these simulations to our base case (in which world oil prices follow their historical course) we can assess the cost of stabilizing carbon dioxide emissions through high oil prices. Moreover, by analyzing all three of the alternative scenarios we can decompose the impact of the increase in world petroleum prices into separate components associated with the sharp price increases of the 1970s and the overall rise in the price level between 1972 and 1987.

1.4.1   Effects on the Steady State

Since the long-run price of petroleum is the same in the base case and the OIL87 scenario, there are only three distinct long-run equilibrium paths for our four scenarios. The base case associated with the historical path of oil prices and the revised OIL87 scenario result in the same long-run behavior of the economy. However, the OIL81 scenario is associated with higher oil prices while the OIL72 scenario captures the effects of lower oil prices. The aggregate impacts of these scenarios are presented in table 1.4.1.

Under OIL72, the price of imported oil is 61% lower than the base case while under OIL81 it is 183% higher. Apart from important differences in the magnitudes, the long-run impacts of OIL72 and OIL81 are close to mirror images of each other. With lower oil prices real gross national product is 1.186% higher in the long run, while higher prices result in a 1.339% decrease in real GNP. Also, it is clear that the level of world oil prices has an important long-run impact on the U.S. economy. Lower prices increase GNP while higher prices decrease it. The real exchange rate, defined as the price of U.S. imports relative to the price of U.S. exports, is 1.098% lower under OIL72 than in the base case, and it is 1.254% higher under OIL81.

More rapid economic growth under the OIL72 petroleum price scenario leads to a capital stock that is 0.790% above the base case level and a capital rental price that is 0.713% lower. This is brought about in part by a 0.886% fall in the price of investment goods. In the long run the rate of return in the U.S. economy is the same under all three scenarios—the base case, OIL72, and OIL81. As before, OIL81 is close

Table 1.4.1
Long-run oil simulation results

Variable	Scenario	
	OIL72	OIL81
Price of imported oil	−61.419	183.128
Capital stock	0.790	−0.912
Price of investment goods	−0.886	1.059
Real GNP	1.186	−1.339
Full consumption	0.432	−0.494
Rental price of capital	−0.713	0.857
Exchange rate	−1.098	1.254

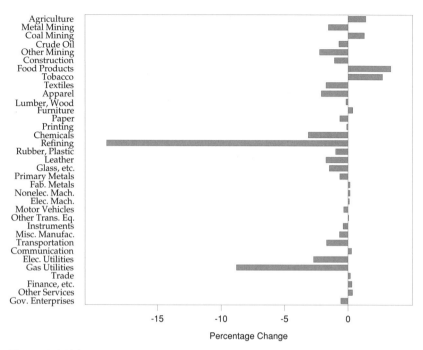

Figure 1.4.3(a)
Effect of OIL81 on output.

to a mirror image of OIL72, having a higher price of investment goods, a lower capital stock and a higher rental price of capital.

The final indicator of aggregate U.S. economic activity given in table 1.4.1 is full consumption. This is an important indicator of the change in consumer welfare associated with variations in the world oil price. Since leisure time is closely tied to the exogenous time endowment of the U.S. economy, we find that full consumption is only 0.432% higher with lower oil prices in the OIL72 scenario and 0.494% lower with higher oil prices in the OIL81 scenario.

Finally, we present changes in industry output levels from the base case for OIL81 and OIL72 in figure 1.4.3. Higher oil prices result in a drastic fall in the output of the petroleum refining sector illustrated graphically in figure 1.4.3. The output of electric utilities is also substantially lower. The output of chemical manufacturing and gas utilities are also reduced by higher oil prices, while food and tobacco experience a modest increase in output as a consequence of substitution away from energy-intensive commodities by businesses and

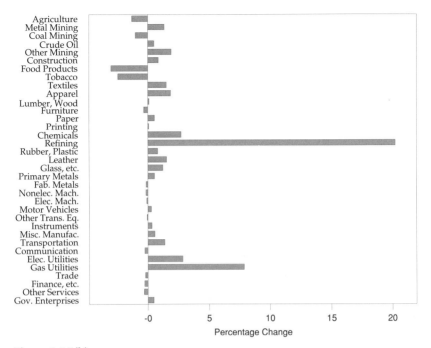

Figure 1.4.3(b)
Effect of OIL72 on output.

households. As before, the OIL72 scenario, corresponding to lower oil prices, is almost a mirror image of the high oil price scenario.

1.4.2 Dynamic Effects

In section 1.2 we showed that the dynamics of our model are determined by the backward-looking capital accumulation equation and the forward-looking asset pricing and Euler equations. We can illustrate these mechanisms by first considering the OIL87 scenario, which has the same long-run world petroleum price as the base case, but omits the price shocks of the 1970s. Figure 1.4.4 gives a comparison between this scenario and the base case.

In figure 1.4.4, we see that the long-run behavior of the U.S. economy is identical in the base case and the OIL87 scenario. However, the transition path toward long-run equilibrium is very different in the two scenarios. Between 1973 and 1987, oil prices are higher in the base case than in OIL87. Thus, during that period real income is

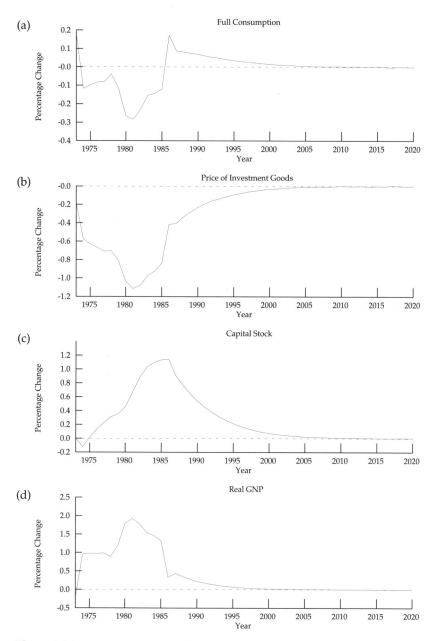

Figure 1.4.4
(a) Full consumption; (b) price of investment goods; (c) capital stock; (d) real
GNP.

higher under OIL87. However, this increase in income is only temporary because prices become the same after 1987. Since households
have perfect foresight, they know the change is temporary, so consumption increases very little and most of the extra income is saved.
This leads to the pattern of capital accumulation shown in figure
1.4.4(c).

By the year 2005, differences between the base case and the OIL87
scenario are negligible. However, the impact of differences in world
petroleum prices through 1987 is still substantial after ten years have
elapsed. The model captures the effects of changes in world oil prices
along the transition path toward long-run equilibrium of the U.S.
economy. However, the dynamics represented in the model are too
highly simplified to capture the short-run impact of higher world oil
prices.

In the OIL81 scenario, world oil prices are above their historical values after 1981. A comparison between this scenario and the base case
is given in figure 1.4.5. Reflecting the long-run increase in oil prices,
levels of full consumption decrease from the beginning of our simulations in 1973. This decrease facilitates the accumulation of capital in
anticipation of future consumption needs. The sharp drop in the capital stock after 1987 reflects the permanent decline in real income after
that time.

In the OIL72 scenario, world petroleum prices are below those of
the base case after 1972. We have already seen that the long-run
impact of lower oil prices is a kind of mirror image of the effects of the
higher oil prices in the OIL81 scenario. In figure 1.4.6 we present the
dynamics the economy's adjustment to lower oil prices. In this case,
the path of full consumption shown in figure 1.4.6(a) is somewhat
misleading. Figure 1.4.6(a) shows the value of full consumption
falling during the early years of the simulation. During that period,
however, the price of consumption falls by more than enough to
compensate, so the quantity of full consumption actually rises.
This reaches a peak in 1987, when world petroleum prices reach their
long-run level under the base case. After that, it gradually sub-
sides to a long-run level that is substantially above the base case.
While this long-run level is the reverse of that in OIL81 (the high price
scenario) the transition path followed by the economy is very different. Under OIL72, the economy undergoes a boom (relative to the
base case) in both investment and consumption. Capital is accumulated very rapidly through 1987 and then declines slowly to a

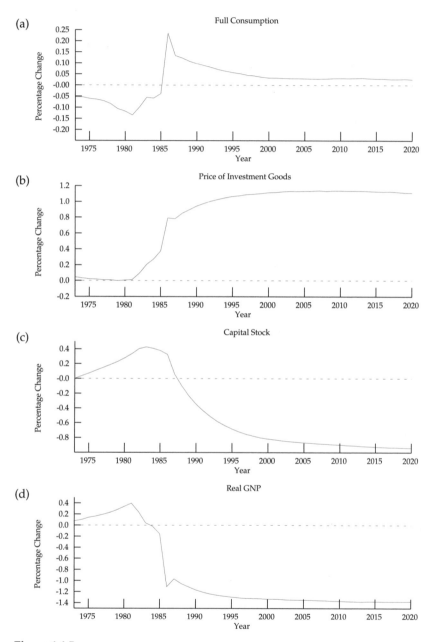

Figure 1.4.5
(a) Full consumption; (b) price of investment goods; (c) capital stock; (d) real GNP.

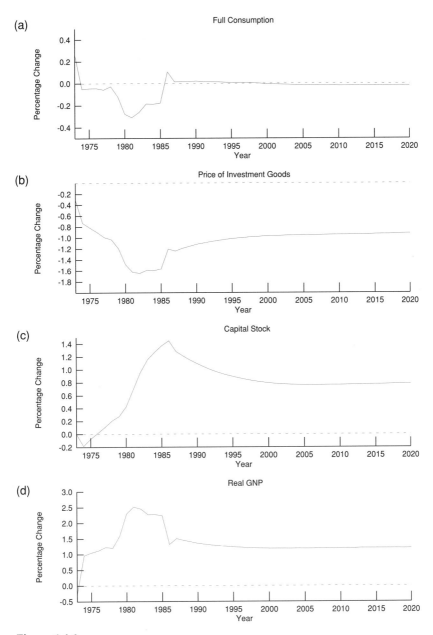

Figure 1.4.6
(a) Full consumption; (b) price of investment goods; (c) capital stock; (d) real GNP.

long-term equilibrium which sustains higher consumption after 1987. The difference between real GNP in the OIL72 scenario and the base case peaks in 1981, when the difference in petroleum prices is most pronounced; the long-run difference in real GNP is considerably lower.

1.4.3   Summary

By comparing the OIL72 and the OIL87 simulations we can separate the impact of higher long-term world oil prices from the effects of the oil price surges that took place in 1973–1975 and 1978–1980. Recall that the OIL72 scenario corresponds to permanently lower oil prices at levels that prevailed before 1973, while OIL87 represents a gradual increase in world oil prices to the level of 1987. In table 1.4.2 we summarize the impact of higher oil prices and decompose it into effects attributable to the long-run increase and those attributable to the price shocks of the 1970s. As shown in the table, the growth rate of real GNP was 0.216% per year lower over the period 1974–1985 in the base case than the OIL72 scenario. Thus, the rise in oil prices accounts for a substantial portion of the slowdown in U.S. economic growth after 1973.

The portion of the slowdown that can be attributed to the price shocks of the 1970s is captured by the OIL87 scenario. OIL87 has the same long-run price trend as the base case, but it omits the sharp rise and fall of oil prices during the 1970s and early 1980s. Under this scenario the growth of real gross national product over the period 1974–1985 was 0.136% per year higher than in the base case. Thus, the price shocks account for almost two-thirds of the overall 0.216% drop in growth. The remainder, given by the difference between OIL72 and OIL87, shows the effect of a gradual increase in oil prices. This difference accounts for a slowdown of 0.080% per year in the average annual growth rate of real GNP over the period 1974–1985.

Table 1.4.2
Decomposition of effects on average growth over 1974–1985

Description	Change in growth rate
Total change (OIL72)	0.216
Change due to price surge (OIL87)	0.136
Change due to price level (OIL72–OIL87)	0.080

1.5   The Impact of Carbon Taxes

In the preceding section, we have calculated the implicit cost of stabilizing carbon dioxide emissions through high world oil prices. Clearly, however, this is not a policy that the U.S. government would choose voluntarily. A more likely policy would be a broad-based tax on the carbon content of all fossil fuels. Such a tax could be applied to primary production of coal, oil and natural gas, and would have the advantage of taxing emissions directly. In this section, we examine the carbon taxes that would be needed to attain various carbon dioxide emission targets, and discuss how those taxes would affect the economy.

1.5.1   Computing Carbon Emissions

The first step in simulating different carbon tax policies is to calculate carbon dioxide emissions. For tractability, we have assumed that these emissions are proportional to fossil fuel use. This implies that the carbon dioxide produced by a given combustion process cannot be reduced. In practice this is largely the case.[49] We then calculate the carbon content of each fossil fuel in the following way. From the U.S. Department of Energy we obtain the average heat content of each fuel in millions of Btu per unit of quantity (U.S. Department of Energy, 1990). Next, we obtain data from the Environmental Protection Agency (EPA) on the amount of carbon emitted per million Btu produced from each fuel.[50] Multiplying EPA's figures by the heating value of the different fuels gives the carbon content of each fuel. Carbon emissions can then be calculated from total fuel production. Table 1.5.1 gives the data for for each fuel in 1987.

Our simulation model is normalized so that all prices are equal to unity in 1982. The quantities do not correspond directly to physical units. Moreover, the model has a single aggregate sector for oil and gas. To convert the figures above into a form appropriate for the model's quantity units, we sum carbon production for oil and gas and divide by the model's base case output of oil and gas in 1987. This gives the carbon coefficient for the industry. Similarly, the coefficient for coal is computed by dividing total carbon production from coal by the model's 1987 value for coal output. These coefficients are then used to compute carbon emissions in each simulation.

Table 1.5.1
Carbon emissions data for 1987

Item	Fuel		
	Coal	Oil	Gas
Unit of measure	ton	bbl	kcf
Heat content (10^6 Btu per unit)	21.94	5.80	1.03
Emissions rate			
(kg per 10^6 Btu)	26.9	21.4	14.5
(kg per unit)	590.2	124.1	14.9
Total domestic output 10^6 units	0.9169	0.3033	17.8
Total carbon emissions 10^6 tons	595.3	414.1	268.6

1.5.2   Carbon Dioxide Emissions Policies

We now turn to the consequences of using a carbon tax to achieve different carbon dioxide emissions levels. We have run three simulations in addition to the base case, one for each of the following policies:

(1) Stabilizing carbon emissions at the 1990 base level beginning immediately.

(2) Decreasing carbon emissions gradually over 1990–2005 until they are 20% below the 1990 base level.

(3) Doing nothing until 2000, then gradually increasing the carbon tax over 2000–2010 to stabilize emissions at the year-2000 base level.

These policies vary considerably in stringency. In 1990, base case fossil fuel use produced 1576 million tons of carbon. Policy 1 would keep that level constant forever, even in the face of rapid GNP growth. Policy 2, however, is even more restrictive: it requires emissions to drop to 1261 million tons by 2005 and remain at that level forever. Policy 3, on the other hand, is the least restrictive: it allows emissions to rise to the base case year 2000 level of 1675 million tons.

In each simulation, we constrain total carbon emissions and allow the level of the carbon tax to be determined endogenously. The tax is applied to primary fuels in proportion to carbon content. Since even the least stringent policy produces substantial tax revenue, it is necessary to make an assumption about how the revenue would be used.

In these simulations, we hold the real value of government spending constant at its base case level. We then allow the average tax on labor to adjust to keep the difference between government spending and government revenue equal to the exogenous budget deficit. At the same time, we hold the marginal tax on labor constant, so that adjustments in the average rate reflect changes in the implicit zero-tax threshold.

1.5.3   Long-Run Effects

The principal direct consequence of all three carbon control strategies is to increase purchasers' prices of coal and crude oil. This can be seen most clearly by examining the model's results for each simulation at a particular point in time, so in this section we present detailed results for the year 2020. We begin with results for the first experiment: holding emissions at 1990 levels. By the year 2020, maintaining 1990 emissions will require a tax of $16.96 per ton of carbon contained in primary fuels.[51] Using the data in table 1.5.1, it can be shown that this amounts to a tax of about $11.01 per ton of coal, $2.32 per barrel of oil or $0.28 per thousand cubic feet of gas. The tax would generate revenue of $26.7 billion annually.

The rising price of fossil fuels results in substitution toward other energy sources and away from energy in general. Total Btu consumption falls by 12% to about 68 quadrillion Btu (quads). This substitution away from energy, and hence toward more expensive production techniques, results in a drop of 0.7% in the capital stock and 0.5% in real GNP. These figures are fairly small because they measure, in a loose sense, the welfare losses from introducing a small distortionary tax. Since revenue from the tax is returned to households through lump-sum adjustments in the income tax, social welfare falls due to the inefficiency of the tax.

At the commodity, level the impact of the tax varies considerably. Figure 1.5.1(a) shows changes in the supply price of the 35 commodities measured as percentage changes relative to the base case. The largest change occurs in the price of coal, which rises by 40%. This, in turn, increases the price of electricity by about 5%. Electricity prices rise considerably less than coal prices because coal accounts for only about 13% of total utility costs. Other prices showing significant effects are those for crude and refined petroleum and gas utilities. These rise, directly or indirectly, because of the tax on oil.

These changes in prices affect demands for the commodities, which in turn determine how industry outputs are affected. Figure 1.5.1(b) shows percentage changes in quantities produced by the 35 industries. Most of the sectors show only small changes in output. Coal mining is the exception; its output falls by 26%. Coal is affected strongly because the demand for it is somewhat elastic. Most coal is purchased by electric utilities, which in our model can substitute toward other fuels when the price of coal rises. Moreover, the utilities also have some ability to substitute other inputs, such as labor and capital, for energy, further reducing the demand for coal. Since electric utilities play such an important role in determining how a carbon tax affects coal mining, we now digress briefly to discuss how the utilities are represented in the model.

Electric utilities, like all other sectors, are represented by a nested translog unit cost function. The top tier of the function gives cost in terms of the prices of four inputs: capital, labor, an energy aggregate, and a materials aggregate. Substitution between energy and other

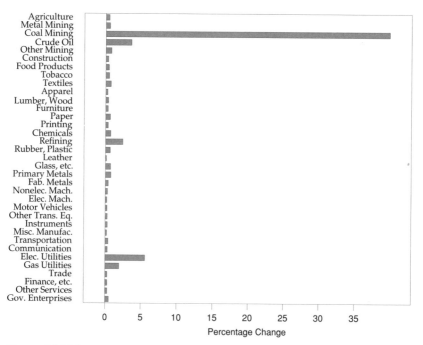

Figure 1.5.1(a)
Effect of CONST on prices.

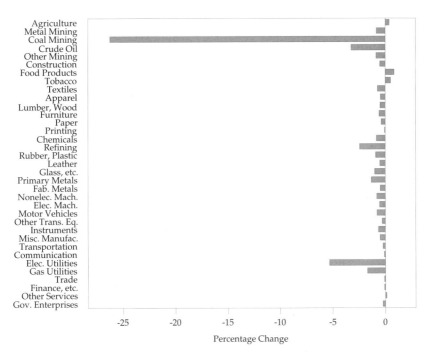

Figure 1.5.1(b)
Effect on CONST on output.

inputs takes place at this level. The price of the energy aggregate itself is formed at a lower tier by translog aggregation of the prices of five inputs: coal, crude petroleum, refined petroleum, electricity, and natural gas from gas utilities. Substitution among fuels takes place at that level.

Estimated parameters govern the ease of substitution at both the top tier and the energy tier of the cost function. At the top level, substitution between energy and capital is very inelastic (an elasticity of −0.15), substitution between energy and labor is moderately inelastic (−0.64), and substitution between energy and materials is slightly elastic (−1.16). Thus, increases in the relative price of energy will, for the most part, induce substitution toward materials. In addition, substitution possibilities exist at the energy tier. The elasticity of substitution between coal and refined petroleum is −0.7, although between coal and natural gas it is only −0.1. Thus, an increase in the relative price of coal will produce some substitution toward other fuels. Overall, the parameters appearing in the cost function for electric utilities imply that an increase in the relative price of coal will lead to substitution toward other fuels and toward non-energy inputs.

The second policy we consider is a 20% reduction below 1990 emission rates, to be phased in gradually over 15 years. By 2020, this would amount to a drop of 32% below base case emissions, and would require a tax of $60.09 per ton of carbon. Using the data in table 1.5.1, this is equivalent to a tax of $39.01 per ton of coal, $8.20 per barrel of oil, or $0.98 per thousand cubic feet of gas. The tax would produce $75.8 billion in revenues. Comparing these results to those for maintaining 1990 emissions shows that the tax would more than triple, from $17 to $60. At equilibrium, the tax gives the marginal cost of reducing emissions by an additional ton of carbon, so that further reductions are becoming significantly more difficult.

Tighter carbon regulations also lead to a reduction in total fossil fuel Btu production to 57 quads, a drop of 27% from the base case. This, in turn, reduces the capital stock by 2.2% and real GNP by 1.6%. These figures are about triple the values obtained for holding emissions at 1990 levels. Although the changes in capital and GNP appear small, recall that they are measures of deadweight loss associated with fairly large marginal changes in the energy sector.

At the commodity and industry level, results for this experiment are qualitatively similar to those for maintaining 1990 emissions, although they are numerically somewhat different. Figure 1.5.2(a) shows percentage changes in commodity prices relative to the base case. The price of coal more than doubles, rising by 137% from its base case value. The price of oil rises by 13%, while that of electricity rises by about 18%. The prices of refined petroleum and natural gas also rise, but by somewhat less. Comparing figures 1.5.2(a) and 1.5.1(a) shows how this simulation compares with the previous one. In particular, commodity prices rise roughly in proportion to the increase in the carbon tax. The tax rises by a factor of 3.5, and so do most of the percentage changes in commodity prices.

The quantity results, shown in figure 1.5.2(b), display a similar pattern except that they scale up in proportion to the change in carbon reductions rather than the change in taxes. That is, reducing emissions to 20% below 1990 levels requires a cut of about twice the size needed to reach 1990 levels. Thus, percentage changes in quantities from the base case are about twice those of the previous experiment. The most important results are the 53% drop in coal production and the 15% drop in electricity produced.

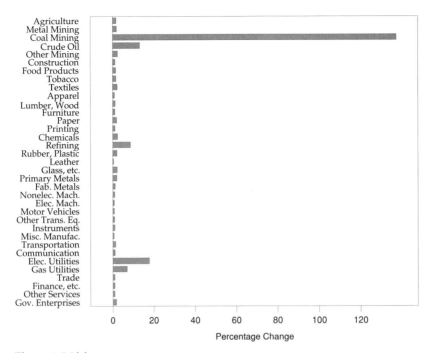

Figure 1.5.2(a)
Effect of CUT20 on prices.

By contrast, the looser restrictions implied by maintaining emissions at year-2000 levels produce much smaller effects on the economy. The tax required is only $8.55 per ton of carbon, which implies charges of $5.55 per ton of coal, $1.17 per barrel of oil, or $0.14 per thousand cubic feet of gas. The tax would produce $14.4 billion annually in revenue. Aggregate effects are also considerably smaller than in the two previous scenarios. The capital stock falls by 0.4%, and GNP drops by 0.3%, about half the value obtained in the 1990 simulation. This is quite reasonable since the cut in emissions is about half as deep. The industry results look qualitatively so similar to those of the previous experiments that we omit the graphs. The principal numerical result is that coal prices rise by 20% while coal output shrinks by about 16%.

The results of all three carbon tax simulations are summarized in table 1.5.2, in which the policies are listed in order of increasing stringency. From these results, it appears that stabilizing emissions at the base-case level in the year 2000 can be accomplished with a very low

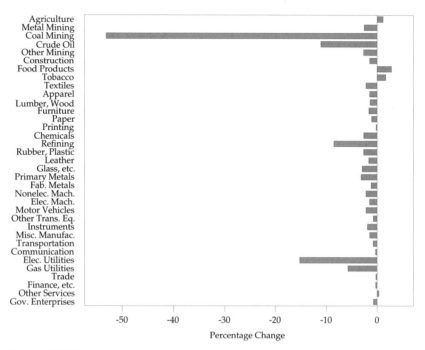

Figure 1.5.2(b)
Effect of CUT20 on output.

Table 1.5.2
Summary of long-run carbon tax simulations

		Emissions target		
Variable	Unit	2000 Level	1990 Level	80% of 1990
Carbon emission	%Δ	−8.4	−14.4	−31.6
Carbon tax	$/ton	8.55	16.96	60.09
Tax on coal	$/ton	5.55	11.01	39.01
Tax on oil	$/bbl	1.17	2.32	8.20
Tax on gas	$/kfc	0.14	0.28	0.98
Labor tax rate	Δ	−0.25	−0.45	−1.22
Tax revenue	10⁹$	14.4	26.7	75.8
Btu production	%Δ	−7.1	−12.2	−27.4
Capital stock	%Δ	−0.4	−0.7	−2.2
Real GNP	%Δ	−0.3	−0.5	−1.6
Price of coal	%Δ	20.3	40.0	137.4
Quantity of coal	%Δ	−15.6	−26.3	−53.2
Price of electricity	%Δ	2.9	5.6	17.9
Quantity of electricity	%Δ	−2.9	−5.3	−15.3
Price of oil	%Δ	1.8	3.6	13.3

carbon tax and a minimal disturbance of the economy. The strongest effect would be felt by the coal mining industry, which sees its demand fall as electric utilities substitute toward other fuels. More stringent regulations would lead to markedly higher energy prices and greater disruption of the economy. Coal mining would bear the brunt of the changes brought about by the tax under any scenario. Of the remaining sectors, electric utilities would be affected most strongly.

1.5.4 Intertemporal Results

Carbon restrictions adopted today will have effects far into the future. At the same time, anticipated future restrictions will have effects today. To assess the intertemporal consequences of carbon taxes, we now turn to the model's dynamic results. As with the long-run results, we begin by discussing a carbon tax designed to maintain emissions at 1990 levels. Following that, we examine the dynamic behavior of other experiments.

The path of the carbon tax needed to maintain 1990 emissions is shown in figure 1.5.3(a). Base case emissions increase over time, so the tax grows gradually, about $0.70 per year, over the next few decades. It reaches a peak around the year 2020 when our forecast of the U.S. population crests.[52] The tax produces significant reductions in carbon emissions which are shown in figure 1.5.3(b) as percentage changes from the base case. Emissions begin dropping immediately and by 2020 are about 14% below their unconstrained level.

As suggested by the long-run results, the principal effect of the tax is to reduce coal mining. This is shown clearly in figure 1.5.4(a), which gives percentage changes in coal output from the base case. Production gradually slows as the tax is introduced. It does not, however, fall all the way back to its 1990 level—some of the reduction in emissions comes about through reductions in oil consumption. This can be seen in figure 1.5.4(b), which gives percentages changes in crude petroleum and natural gas extraction over time.

The increasing price of energy raises costs and reduces household income. This, in turn, changes the rate of capital accumulation. The outcome is shown in figure 1.5.5(a), which gives percentage changes in the capital stock from the base case. Unlike variables in the preceding graphs, the capital stock does not start declining immediately; instead, it tends to remain near its base case level for the first few

(a)

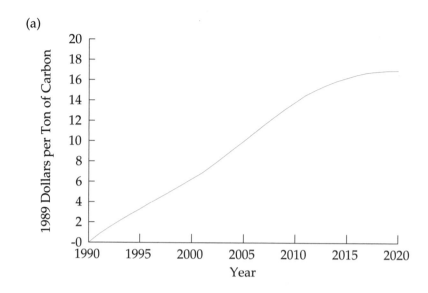

(b)

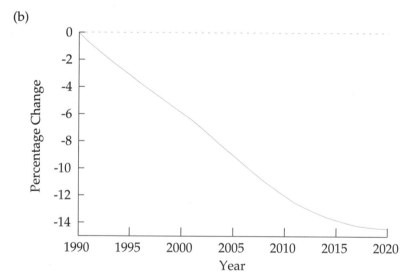

Figure 1.5.3
(a) Carbon tax under CONST; (b) carbon emissions under CONST.

(a)

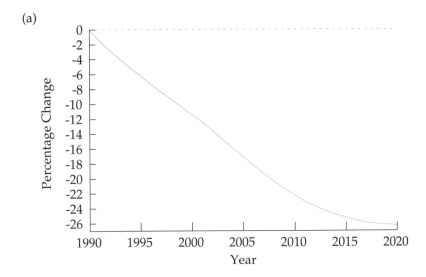

(b)

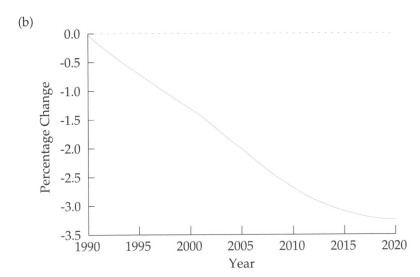

Figure 1.5.4
(a) Coal production under CONST; (b) oil and gas extraction under CONST.

(a)

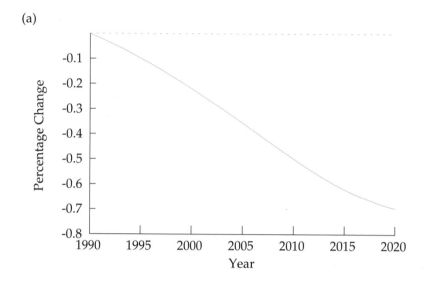

(b)

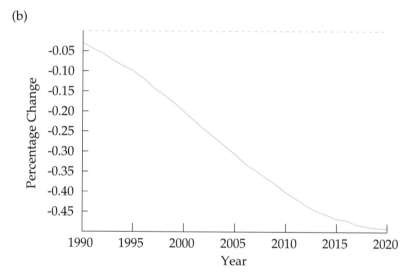

Figure 1.5.5
(a) Capital stock under CONST; (b) real GNP under CONST.

years. This is the consequence of intertemporal optimization by households. From a household's point of view, the effect of the tax is to decrease its real income by an amount related to the tax's dead-weight loss.[53] Thus, the household regards carbon taxes as reductions in future earnings, so it reacts by lowering consumption in all periods. In the early years, however, the carbon tax is minimal and household income is largely unaffected. During that period, therefore, the drop in consumption leads to an increase in saving. This helps maintain investment—and thus the capital stock—in the early years of the simulation. Eventually, the income effect of the tax begins to be felt and the capital stock finally starts to decline relative to the base case.

The decline in growth of the capital stock leads to a drop in GNP growth, as shown in figure 1.5.5(b). Over time GNP gradually falls by about half a percent relative to the base case. The capital stock, however, is not the only factor contributing to the decline. In addition, higher energy prices reduce the rate of technical change in industries which are energy-using. This leads to slower income growth and helps keep GNP below its base case level. In fact, under the carbon tax simulation average annual GNP growth over the period 1990–2020 is 0.02 percentage points lower than in the base case.[54] About half of this is due to slowing productivity growth and half to slower capital accumulation.

The two alternative carbon control targets we examined showed dynamic behavior qualitatively similar to that we have described above. These results can best be displayed by plotting each variable's values for all three simulations on a single graph.[55] Figure 1.5.6(a), for example, shows the paths of the carbon tax needed to achieve each of the targets. The highest path is the tax required to reduce emissions to 20% below their 1990 levels; the central path is that for maintaining 1990 emissions; and the lowest path is the tax needed to stabilize emissions at year-2000 levels. Similarly, figure 1.5.6(b) shows the carbon reductions achieved under each of the policies.[56] Plotting three curves on each figure makes it easy to compare different targets. For example, many of the figures show that as the target becomes more stringent, the variable of interest is pushed further away from the base case. However, some of the figures show much more interesting behavior, and we will focus on these for the remainder of this section.

The first feature apparent from figure 1.5.6(b) is that the three targets require carbon reductions of roughly 8, 14 and 32%. Keeping these reductions in mind, figure 1.5.7(a) shows that coal production

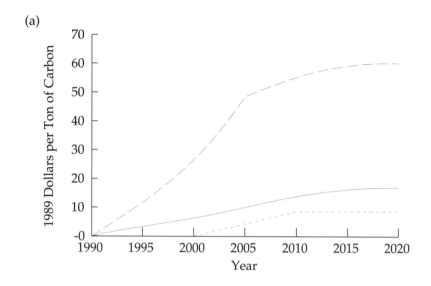

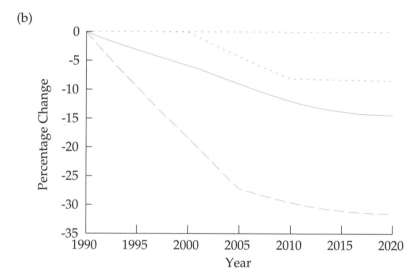

Figure 1.5.6
(a) Carbon tax; (b) carbon emissions.

(a)

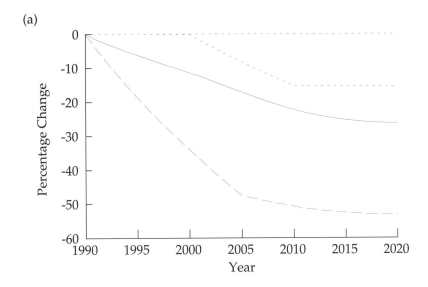

(b)

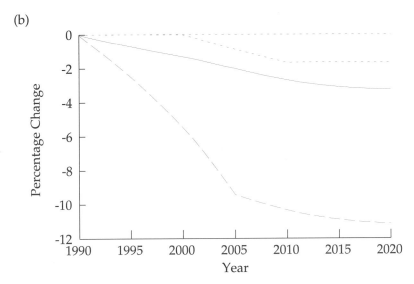

Figure 1.5.7
(a) Coal production; (b) oil and gas extraction.

does not fall in proportion to the drop in emissions. This occurs because it becomes increasingly costly to drive coal production. Coal users, notably electric utilities, find it increasingly difficult to substitute away from coal as the amount they use of it decreases. This is reflected in figure 1.5.7(b), which shows that oil extraction increases more sharply as regulations become more stringent.

One of the most interesting results of our study is shown in figure 1.5.8(a), a graph of the capital stock under the three policies. Figure 1.5.8(a) is a very clear example of the effects of intertemporal optimization by households. For the policy which has least effect and occurs farthest in the future—maintaining emissions at year-2000 levels—the early reduction in consumption actually leads to a temporary increase in the capital stock. This comes about because households reduce consumption in anticipation of lower future earnings. Only under the most stringent policy—reducing emissions by 20% from 1990 levels—does the capital stock begin to fall immediately. Finally, the results for GNP, shown in figure 1.5.8(b), echo those for the capital stock. As mentioned above, GNP falls because of the drop in capital accumulation and the reduction in productivity growth resulting from higher energy prices.

1.6   Conclusion

The purpose of this section is to evaluate the usefulness of intertemporal general equilibrium modeling as a practical guide to assessment of the impacts of energy and environmental policies. The neoclassical theory of economic growth has been applied to the evaluation of policies to control global climate change by Nordhaus (1994), Manne and Richels (1992), and Jorgenson and Wilcoxen (1992a). Nordhaus's model of the world economy includes a physical model of climate change. This provides the basis for designing an optimal environmental policy that can be implemented by means of a carbon tax. The policy results from a sophisticated application of cost-benefit analysis.

The GLOBAL 2100 model of Manne and Richels (1992) disaggregates the world economy into five regions—each represented by a one-sector neoclassical growth model. Environmental policy affects the output of each region through restrictions on carbon dioxide emissions resulting from fossil fuel combustion. This approach is useful in assessing the costs of these restrictions and the benefits from international cooperation in controlling global climate change through

(a)

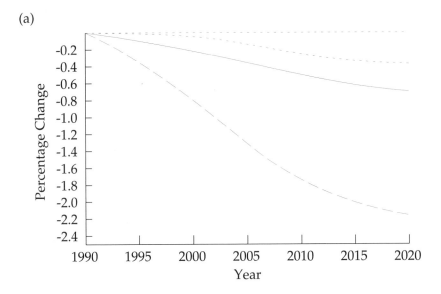

(b)

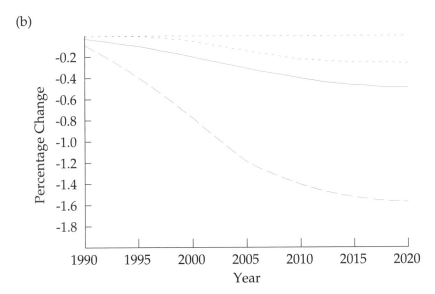

Figure 1.5.8
(a) Capital stock; (b) real GNP.

tradeable permits. Finally, the energy technology assessment (ETA) submodel provides valuable information on the payoff from accelerated research and development on new energy sources and alternative energy technologies.

The framework for the econometric approach to modeling the impact of energy and environmental policies is also provided by intertemporal general equilibrium theory. This makes it possible to preserve the features of the aggregate growth models employed by Nordhaus (1994) and Manne and Richels (1992), while disaggregating the impacts of these policies. We have distinguished among thirty-five industrial sectors of the U.S. economy and have also identified thirty-five commodity groups, each one the primary product of one of the industries. In modeling consumer behavior we have distinguished among 672 different household types, broken down by demographic characteristics. Aggregate demand functions for components of consumer expenditure are constructed by summing over individual demand functions.

The econometric method for parameterization used in modeling technology and preferences can be contrasted with the calibration approach employed in earlier general equilibrium models. The main advantage of the econometric approach is that the responses of production and consumption patterns to changes in energy prices and environmental controls can be derived from historical experience. The implementation of the econometric approach requires a system of national accounts that successfully integrates capital with the income and production. The new accounting system incorporates an accumulation equation relating capital to past investments and an asset-pricing equation linking the price of assets to future prices and rates of return.

Jorgenson and Wilcoxen (1990b) have provided a highly disaggregated model of the impact of environmental regulations on U.S. economic growth. This model incorporates detailed data on costs of compliance with environmental regulations by individual industries. An important mechanism for adjusting to changes in environmental policy is altering rates of capital formation. A second mechanism is the pricing of capital assets through forward-looking expectations of future prices and discount rates. This illustrates the significance of intertemporal general equilibrium modeling for obtaining insights into dynamic effects of energy and environmental policies on U.S. economic growth.

Jorgenson and Wilcoxen (1992a) have analyzed a "natural experiment" in stabilization of carbon dioxide emissions for the U.S. during the period 1972–1987. This is the result of price-induced energy conservation that has important feedbacks to the rate of economic growth through capital asset pricing and capital formation. By combining forward-looking features of the model with the backward-looking capital accumulation equation, the decline in economic growth can be separated into two components. The first is the impact of the rise in energy prices from 1972–1987. The second is the effect of the energy price shocks of 1973–1975 and 1978–1980. The slowdown in economic growth during the period is largely attributable to the price shocks.

Finally, Jorgenson and Wilcoxen (1992b) have modeled the impact on U.S. economic growth of a carbon tax that would stabilize emissions of carbon dioxide at 1990 levels. Since the tax would be phased in gradually, this has a relatively modest impact on growth. Both consumers and producers anticipate the steady increase in carbon tax rates and plan accordingly. This brings about a gradual re-orientation of the economy to reduce dependence on coal, the most carbon intensive fuel, and conserve energy more generally. An important qualification is that the cost of controlling carbon dioxide emissions rises at an increasing rate as restrictions on these emissions become more stringent.

Although the intertemporal general equilibrium approach has proved to be useful in modeling the impact of energy and environmental policies, much remains to be done to exploit the full potential of this approach. As an illustration, the model of consumer behavior employed by Jorgenson and Wilcoxen (1990b) successfully dispenses with the notion of a representative consumer. An important feature of this model is that systems of individual demand functions can be recovered from the system of aggregate demand functions. The consumer preferences underlying these individual demand systems can be used to generate measures of individual welfare that are useful in evaluating the distributional consequences of energy and environmental policies.

For example, Jorgenson and Slesnick (1985) have separated the impacts of changes in U.S. petroleum taxes into equity and efficiency components. Similarly, Jorgenson and Slesnick (1987b) have considered the equity and efficiency impacts of natural gas price deregulation in the U.S. Finally, Jorgenson, Slesnick, and Wilcoxen (1992) have analyzed the progressiveness or regressiveness of carbon taxes that would stabilize emissions of carbon dioxide at 1990 levels. Although the size of the equity impact depends on normative considerations, the efficiency impact greatly dominates in all three applications.

Our conclusion is that intertemporal general equilibrium modeling provides a very worthwhile addition to methodologies for modeling the economic impact of energy and environmental policies. The neoclassical theory of economic growth is essential for understanding the dynamic mechanisms that underly long-run and intermediate-run growth trends. The econometric implementation of this theory is critical for capitalizing on the drastic changes in energy prices and substantial alterations in environmental policies of the past two decades. This wealth of historical experience, interpreted within an intertemporal framework, can provide valuable guidance in future policy formulation.

Notes

1. The Cass-Koopmans theory of economic growth has been discussed by Lucas (1988) and Romer (1989).

2. This literature has been surveyed by Christiansen, Gollop, and Haveman (1980) and Christiansen and Tietenberg (1985).

3. Overviews of the greenhouse warming problem are presented by Cline (1992), Manne and Richels (1992), Chapter 1, Nordhaus (1991a), and Schelling (1992). We discuss the greenhouse effect and control of global climate change in section 1.5.

4. A carbon tax was first analyzed by Nordhaus (1979) and has been discussed by the Congressional Budget Office (1990). Alternative policy options for stabilizing the global climate are described in detail by EPA (1989).

5. Optimal policies for controlling global climate change have also been analyzed by Peck and Teisberg (1990, 1992). Cline (1992) provides a detailed cost-benefit analysis of policies for climate control.

6. Many estimates of costs of emissions controls on carbon dioxide are now available. Detailed surveys are given by Cline (1992), Hoeller, Dean, and Nicolaisen (1991) and Nordhaus (1991b). Dean (1992) present a survey of estimates of costs of controlling carbon dioxide emissions from six multi-region models of the world economy, including the GLOBAL 2100 model of Manne and Richels (1992). These estimates are based on comparable assumptions about future world economic growth and world petroleum prices.

7. Beaver (1993) presents a detailed survey of models of the U.S. economy that have been used in modeling the impacts of energy and environmental policies in EMF-12, a project of the Energy Modeling Forum at Stanford University.

8. The classic formulation of intertemporal general equilibrium theory is by Lindahl (1929). A detailed survey of intertemporal general equilibrium theory is presented by Stokey, Lucas, and Prescott (1989).

9. We describe possible approaches to calculation of distributional effects in section 1.6.

10. Detailed surveys of fixed-coefficient input-output models applied to environmental policy, including those of Leontief (1970) and Leontief and Ford (1972), are presented

by Forsund (1985) and James, Jansen, and Opschoor (1978). The "materials balance" approach is considered in the context of the Arrow-Debreu theory of general equilibrium by Maler (1974, 1985).

11. The concept of sustainable development is discussed by the World Bank (1992). Meadows (1992) provides an update of the earlier Club of Rome Report.

12. Johansen's approach has been used in modeling environmental policies for Norway by Forsund and Strom (1976). We discuss the calibration method for parameterization in more detail below.

13. We describe reductions in energy utilization after 1973 for U.S. industries in section 1.4. Long-run trends in U.S. energy utilization have been analyzed by Schurr and Netschert (1960) and Schurr, Burwell, Devine, and Sonenblum (1990).

14. Price-induced energy conservation in the U.S. has been analyzed in greater detail by Hogan and Jorgenson (1991), Jorgenson (1981, 1984b), Jorgenson and Fraumeni (1981), and Jorgenson and Stoker (1984).

15. Alternative models of endogenous productivity growth are surveyed by Jorgenson (1984a, 1990b). A comprehensive survey of models of producer behavior constructed along the lines of Berndt and Jorgenson (1973) is presented by Jorgenson (1986).

16. The same sectoral disaggregation has been used by the Congressional Budget Office (1990) in analyzing the effects of a carbon tax on U.S. economic growth. Surveys of the literature on the econometric approach to general equilibrium modeling are given by Bergman (1990), Hazilla and Kopp (1990), and Jorgenson (1982). Bergman provides detailed comparisons with alternative approaches to general equilibrium modeling.

17. Reviews of the literature are presented by Deaton and Muellbauer (1980b) and Jorgenson (1990a).

18. The implications of these restrictions have been discussed by Jorgenson (1984a, 1990a) and Kirman (1992).

19. The theory of exact aggregation is discussed by Jorgenson, Lau, and Stoker (1982) and Lau (1982). Econometric models based on the theory of exact aggregation are surveyed by Jorgenson (1990a) and Stoker (1993).

20. Conventional systems of national accounts, such as the United Nations (1968) System of National Accounts and the U.S. National Income and Product Accounts are unsatisfactory for modeling purposes, since they do not successfully integrate capital accounts with income and production accounts. The system of U.S. national accounts presented by Fraumeni and Jorgenson (1980) disaggregates the accounts constructed by Christensen and Jorgenson (1973) to the industry level. The Christensen-Jorgenson system is used in modeling the U.S. economy by Jorgenson and Yun (1990).

21. Inter-industry transactions tables for the U.S. are derived from those of the Bureau of Economic Analysis (1984). Income data are from the U.S. national income and product accounts, also developed by the Bureau of Economic Analysis (1986). The data on capital and labor services are based on those of Jorgenson, Gollop, and Fraumeni (1987). Our data integrate the capital accounts described by Jorgenson (1990b) with an accounting system based on the United Nations (1968) System of National Accounts. Details are given by Wilcoxen (1988), Appendix C.

22. Noncompeting imports are imported commodities that are not produced domestically.

23. See Mansur and Whalley (1984) for more detail on the calibration approach. An example of this approach is Borges and Goulder (1984), who present a model of energy policy calibrated to data for the year 1973. A more recent example is given by Whalley and Wigle (1991), who present a multi-region model of the world economy and analyze the consequences of imposing an international carbon tax.

24. Surveys of functional forms employed in modeling producer behavior have been presented by Fuss, McFadden, and Mundlak (1978), Jorgenson (1986), and Lau (1986).

25. Dean (1992) has drawn attention to the fact that this separation is the key to differences in estimates of the costs of reducing carbon dioxide emissions among alternative models of the world economy.

26. A more detailed discussion of our econometric methodology is presented by Jorgenson (1984a, 1986).

27. Two-stage allocation in the context of producer behavior is discussed in more detail by Jorgenson (1986) and Blackorby, Primont, and Russell (1978). The tier structure for our models of producer behavior is described by Wilcoxen (1988), Appendix A.

28. The translog price function was introduced by Christensen, Jorgenson, and Lau (1971, 1973). For further discussion of share elasticities and biases of productivity growth, see Jorgenson (1986).

29. This is often overlooked in modeling producer behavior, where it is customary to take these functions to be linear in time: $g_i(t) = t$. See, for example, Jorgenson (1984a).

30. The particular form of our model follows Jorgenson and Slesnick (1987a). For further discussion of our econometric methodology, see Jorgenson (1984a, 1990a).

31. Two-stage allocation in the context of consumer behavior is discussed in more detail by Jorgenson, Slesnick, and Stoker (1987, 1988) and Blackorby, Primont, and Russell (1978). The tier structure for our model of consumer behavior is described by Wilcoxen (1988), Appendix A.

32. The number of households varies over the sample period 1947 through 1985, but is approximately one hundred million at the end of the period.

33. There are seven categories for family size, six categories for age of head, four categories for region of residence, two categories for race, and two categories for urban versus rural location. For further details, see Jorgenson and Slesnick (1987a). The translog indirect utility function was introduced by Christensen, Jorgenson, and Lau (1975). Surveys of functional forms employed in modeling consumer behavior have been presented by Blundell (1986), Deaton (1986), and Lau (1986).

34. Projections of population and the long-run behavior of the economy are discussed in greater detail below.

35. The Euler equation approach to modeling intertemporal consumer behavior was originated by Hall (1978). Our application of this approach to full consumption follows Jorgenson and Yun (1990).

36. We assume the household has a single exogenous endowment of time which can be used for either labor or leisure. During the sample period, 1947 through 1985, we calculate the endowment by adjusting the population for educational attainment; for later periods, we employ the population projections of the Bureau of the Census and our own projections of future educational attainment.

37. The relationship between the price of investment goods and the rental price of capital services is discussed in greater detail by Jorgenson (1989).

38. The tier structure for our model of production for new capital goods is presented by Wilcoxen (1988), Appendix A.

39. Our treatment of government spending differs from the U.S. national accounts in that we have assigned government enterprises to the corresponding industry wherever possible. We include the remaining purchases by the government sector in final demands by governments.

40. This approach was originated by Armington (1969). See Wilcoxen (1988) and Ho (1989) for further details on the implementation of this approach.

41. Our solution method is described in Wilcoxen (1988), Appendix E. Methods for solving intertemporal general equilibrium models are surveyed in detail by Wilcoxen (1992).

42. Our breakdown of the U.S. population by age, educational attainment, and sex is based on the system of demographic accounts compiled by Jorgenson and Fraumeni (1989). The population projections are discussed in detail by Wilcoxen (1988), Appendix B.

43. The Census data come from various issues of the annual publication, *Pollution Abatement Cost and Expenditure*. A detailed description of our data is given by Wilcoxen (1988), Appendix D.

44. Superfund taxes amounting to more than a billion dollars a year were placed on the petroleum refining and chemicals industries in 1981 and on the primary metals industry in 1986. These may have had a substantial impact on U.S. economic growth, but we do not examine their consequences in this chapter.

45. Further details are given by Wilcoxen (1988), Appendix D.

46. Details of our methodology for estimating cost differentials between high-sulfur and low-sulfur coal are given by Wilcoxen (1988), Appendix D.

47. An alternative analysis of the impact of environmental regulation on U.S. international competitiveness is given by Kalt (1988).

48. Carbon dioxide emissions are conventionally measured by amount of carbon they contain.

49. Unlike ordinary pollutants, carbon dioxide is one of the natural products of combustion. Little can be done to change the amount of it produced when burning any particular fuel.

50. Environmental Protection Agency (1990) internal memoranda.

51. All dollar amounts are in 1989 prices.

52. As noted in section 1.2, our population projections are based on those of the Bureau of the Census (1989).

53. Since revenue earned by the tax is given back to households through a horizontal shift in the labor tax schedule, the simulation is essentially the replacement of a lump sum tax (the labor tax) by a distorting one (the carbon tax).

54. The difference in two variables growing at rates differing by 0.02 percentage points is about 2% after a hundred years.

55. Recall that the targets were (1) maintaining 1990 emissions, (2) reducing emissions by 20% below 1990 levels, and (3) gradually introducing taxes to stabilize at year-2000 emissions.

56. Notice that target policies are drawn using the same line type in each graph. Maintaining 1990 emissions is always a solid line, reducing emissions to 20% below 1990 is always dashed, and maintaining emissions at year-2000 levels is dash-dotted. Also, variables are plotted on the same scale across different tax instruments for easier comparison.

2   Econometric Methods for Applied General Equilibrium Analysis

Dale W. Jorgenson

2.1 Introduction

The development of computational methods for solving nonlinear general equilibrium models along the lines pioneered by Scarf (1973; chapter 1) has been the focus of much recent research. By comparison, the development of econometric methods for estimating the unknown parameters describing technology and preferences in such models has been neglected. The purpose of this chapter is to summarize the results of recent research on econometric methods for estimating the parameters of nonlinear general equilibrium models. For this purpose, we present econometric models of producer and consumer behavior suitable for incorporation into a general equilibrium model of the U.S. economy. The most important feature of these models is that they encompass all of the restrictions implied by economic theories of producer and consumer behavior.

At the outset of our discussion it is essential to recognize that the predominant tradition in applied general equilibrium modeling does not employ econometric methods. This tradition originated with the seminal work of Leontief (1951, 1953), beginning with the implementations of the static input-output model half a century ago. Leontief gave a further impetus to the development of general equilibrium modeling by introducing a dynamic input-output model. Empirical work associated with input-output analysis is based on estimating the unknown parameters of a general equilibrium model from a single inter-industry transactions table.

The usefulness of the "fixed-coefficients" assumption that underlies input-output analysis is hardly subject to dispute. By linearizing technology and preferences, it is possible to solve at one stroke the two fundamental problems that arise in the practical implementation of general equilibrium models. First, the resulting general equilibrium model can be solved as a system of linear equations with constant coefficients. Second, the unknown parameters describing technology and preferences can be estimated from a single data point.

The first successful implementation of an applied general equilibrium model without the fixed-coefficients assumption of input-output analysis is due to Johansen (1960). Johansen retained the fixed-coefficients assumption in modeling demands for intermediate goods, but employed linear-logarithmic or Cobb-Douglas production functions in modeling the substitution between capital and labor services and technical change. He replaced the fixed-coefficients assumption for household behavior by a system of demand functions originated by Frisch (1959).

Linear-logarithmic production functions imply that relative shares of inputs in the value of output are fixed, so that the unknown parameters characterizing substitution between capital and labor inputs can be estimated from a single data point. In describing producer behavior, Johansen employed econometric methods only in estimating constant rates of technical change. Similarly, the unknown parameters of the demand system proposed by Frisch can be determined from a single data point, except for one parameter that must be estimated econometrically.

The essential features of Johansen's approach have been preserved in the applied general equilibrium models surveyed by Fullerton, Henderson, and Shoven (1984) and by Mansur and Whalley (1984). The unknown parameters describing technology and preferences in these models are determined by "calibration" to a single data point. Data from a single inter-industry transactions table are supplemented by a small number of parameters estimated econometrically. The obvious disadvantage of this approach is that highly restrictive assumptions on technology and preferences are required in order to make calibration feasible.

As an example of the restrictive assumptions on technology employed in the calibration approach, we first observe that almost all applied general equilibrium models retain the fixed-coefficients assumption of Leontief and Johansen for modeling demand for intermediate goods. This assumption is directly contradicted by recent evidence of changes in energy utilization in response to the higher energy prices that have prevailed since 1973. As an example of restrictive assumption on preferences employed in the calibration approach, we observe that preferences are commonly assumed to be homothetic, which is contradicted by empirical evidence on consumer behavior going back more than a century.

To implement models of producer and consumer behavior that are less restrictive than those of Johansen, it is essential to employ econometric methods. A possible econometric extension of Johansen's approach would be to estimate elasticities of substitution between capital and labor inputs along the lines suggested by Arrow, Chenery, Minhas, and Solow (1961). Unfortunately, constant elasticity of substitution (CES) production functions cannot easily be extended to encompass substitution among capital, labor, and intermediate inputs or among intermediate inputs. As Uzawa (1962) and McFadden (1963) have shown, constant elasticities of substitution among more than two inputs imply, essentially, that elasticities of substitution among all inputs must be the same.

An alternative approach to the implementation of econometric models of producer behavior is to generate complete systems of demand function for inputs in each industrial sector. Each system gives quantities of inputs demanded as functions of prices and output. This approach to modeling producer behavior was first implemented by Berndt and Jorgenson (1973). As in the descriptions of technology by Leontief and Johansen, production is characterized by constant returns to scale in each sector. As a consequence, commodity prices can be expressed as function-of-factor prices, using the nonsubstitution theorem of Samuelson (1951). This greatly facilitates the solution of the econometric general equilibrium model constructed by Hudson and Jorgenson (1974) by permitting a substantial reduction in dimensionality of the space of prices to be determined by the model.

The implementation of econometric models of producer behavior is very demanding in terms of data requirements. These models require the construction of a consistent time series of inter-industry transactions tables. By comparison, the non-econometric approaches of Leontief and Johansen require only a single inter-industry transactions table. Second, the implementation of systems of input demand function requires methods for the estimation of parameters in systems of nonlinear simultaneous equations. Finally, the restrictions implied by the economic theory of producer behavior require estimation under both equality and inequality constraints.

Similarly, econometric models of consumer behavior can be employed in applied general equilibrium models. Econometric models stemming from the pathbreaking contributions of Schultz (1938),

Stone (1954b), and Wold (1953) consist of complete systems of demand functions giving quantities demanded as functions of prices and total expenditure. A possible approach to incorporating the restrictions implied by the theory of consumer behavior is to treat aggregate demand functions as if they could be generated by a single representative consumer. Per capita quantities demanded can be expressed as functions of prices and per capita expenditure.

The obvious difficulty with the representative consumer approach is that aggregate demand functions can be expressed as the sum of individual demand function. Aggregate demand functions depend on prices and total expenditures, as in the theory of individual consumer behavior. However, aggregate demand functions depend on individual total expenditures rather than aggregate expenditure. If individual expenditures are allowed to vary independently, models of aggregate consumer behavior based on a single representative consumer imply restrictions that severely limit the dependence of individual demand functions on individual expenditure.

An alternative approach to the construction of econometric models of aggregate consumer behavior is provided by Lau's (1977b, 1982) theory of exact aggregation. In this approach, systems of aggregate demand functions depend on statistics of the joint distribution of individual total expenditures and attributes of individuals associated with differences in preferences. One of the most remarkable features of models based on exact aggregation is that systems of demand functions for individuals can be recovered uniquely from the system of aggregate demand functions. This feature makes it possible to exploit all the implications of the economic theory of the individual consumer in constructing an econometric model of aggregate consumer behavior.

The implementation of an econometric model of aggregate consumer behavior based on the theory of exact aggregation has been carried out by Jorgenson, Lau, and Stoker (1980, 1981, 1982). Their approach requires time series data on prices and aggregate quantities consumed. This approach also requires cross-section data on individual quantities consumed, individual total expenditures, and attributes of individual households, such as demographic characteristics. By comparison, the non-econometric approaches of Leontief and Johansen require only a single data point for prices and aggregate quantities consumed. The implementation of a system of aggregate demand functions requires methods for combining time series and cross-section data for the estimation of parameters in systems of nonlinear simultaneous equations.

In section 2.2, we present an econometric model of producer behavior, originally implemented for 35 industrial sectors of the U.S. economy by Jorgenson and Fraumeni (1981). This model is based on a production function for each sector, giving output as a function of inputs of intermediate goods produced by other sectors and inputs of the primary factors of production, capital, and labor services. Output also depends on time as an index of the level of technology. Producer equilibrium under constant returns to scale implies the existence of a sectoral price function, giving the price of output as a function of the input prices and time. To incorporate the restrictions implied by the economic theory of producer behavior, we generate our econometric model from a price function for each sector.

Sectoral price functions must be homogeneous of degree one, nondecreasing, and concave in input prices. In addition, we assume that these price functions are homothetically separable in the prices of capital, labor, energy, and materials input. Under homothetic separability our model of producer behavior is based on a two-stage allocation process. In the first stage, the value of sectoral output is allocated among capital, labor, energy, and materials inputs. In the second stage, the value of each of the inputs is allocated among individual types of that input. Two-stage allocation makes is possible to determine the rate of technical change and the shares of 35 intermediate goods and two primary factors of production in the value of output as functions of input prices.

Our model of producer behavior consists of a system of equations giving the shares of all inputs in the value of output and the rate of technical change as functions of relative prices and time. To formulate an econometric model, we add a stochastic component to these equations. Since the rate of technical change is not directly observable, we consider a form of the model with autocorrelated disturbances. We can transform the data to eliminate the autocorrelation. We treat the prices as endogenous variables and estimate the unknown parameters by means of econometric methods appropriate for systems of nonlinear simultaneous equations. Finally, we impose restrictions on the parameters that assure that the underlying sectoral price functions are homogeneous, nondecreasing, and concave in input prices.

In section 2.3, we present an econometric model of aggregate consumer behavior that has been implemented for the U.S. economy by

Jorgenson, Lau, and Stoker (1980, 1981, 1982). This model is based on a utility function for each consumer, giving utility as a function of quantities of individual commodities. Consumer equilibrium implies the existence of an indirect utility function for each consumer. The indirect utility function gives the level of utility as a function of prices of individual commodities, total expenditure, and attributes of the consumer associated with differences in preferences among consumers. To incorporate the restrictions implied by the economic theory of consumer behavior we generate our econometric model from an indirect utility function for each consumer.

Indirect utility functions must be homogeneous of degree zero in prices and expenditure, nonincreasing in prices and increasing in expenditure, and quasi-convex in prices and expenditure. In addition, we assume that these indirect utility functions are homothetically separable in the prices of five commodity groups—energy, food and clothing, consumer services, capital services, and other nondurable expenditures. Under homothetic separability, our model of consumer behavior is based on a two-stage allocation process. In this first stage, total expenditure is allocated among commodity groups. In the second stage, the expenditure on each commodity group is allocated among individual commodities within the group. Two-stage allocation makes is possible to determine the shares of 35 commodities in total expenditure as functions of prices, total expenditure, and consumer attributes.

Our model of individual consumer behavior consists of a system of equations giving the shares of all commodities in total expenditure as functions of relative prices, total expenditure, and consumer attributes. To obtain a model of aggregate consumer behavior, we multiply individual expenditures shares by expenditure for each consuming unit, add over all consuming units, and divide by aggregate expenditure. Our model of aggregate consumer behavior consists of equations giving the shares of all commodities in aggregate expenditure as functions of relative prices. The aggregate expenditure shares also depend on the joint distribution of total expenditure and attributes of individual consumers, such as demographic characteristics. The impact of changes in this distribution is summarized by means of certain statistics of the joint distribution.

To formulate an econometric model of individual consumer behavior, we add a stochastic component to the equations for the individual expenditure shares. Aggregation over individuals results in disturbances that are heteroscedastic. We can transform the data on aggregate expenditure shares to eliminate the heteroscedasticity. We estimate the unknown parameters by means of econometric methods for combining cross-section data on patterns of individual expenditures with time series data on patterns of aggregate expenditures. As before, we treat the prices as endogenous variables and employ methods appropriate for systems of nonlinear simultaneous equations. Finally, we impose restrictions on the parameters that assure that the underlying indirect utility functions are homogeneous, nonincreasing in prices and increasing in expenditures, and quasi-convex in prices and expenditure.

In section 2.4 we present the empirical results of implementing our econometric models of producer and consumer behavior for the U.S. economy. We give empirical results of implementing the model of producer behavior described in section 2.2 for 35 industrial sectors. We limit our presentation to the first stage of the two-stage process for the allocation of the value of sectoral output. Similarly, we give empirical results of implementing the model of consumer behavior described in section 2.3, limiting our presentation to the first stage of the two-stage process for the allocation of total expenditure. We employ family size, age of head, region of residence, race, and urban versus rural residence as attributes of individual households associated with differences in preferences.

2.2   Producer Behavior

In this section, our objective is to analyze technical change and the distribution of the value of output for 35 industrial sectors of the U.S. economy. Our most important conceptual innovation is to determine the rate of technical change and the distributive shares of productive inputs simultaneously as functions of relative prices. We show that the effects of technical change on the distributive shares are precisely the same as the effects of relative prices on the rate of technical change.

Our methodology is based on a model of production treating substitution among inputs and changes in technology symmetrically. The model is based on a production function for each industrial sector, giving output as a function of time and of capital, labor, energy, and materials inputs. Necessary conditions for producer equilibrium in each sector are given by equalities between the distributive shares of the four productive inputs and the corresponding elasticities of output with respect to each of these inputs.

Producer equilibrium under constant returns to scale implies that the value of output is equal to the sum of the value of capital, labor, energy, and materials inputs into each sector. Given this identity and equalities between the distributive shares and the elasticities of output with respect to each of the inputs, we can express the price of output as a function of the prices of capital, labor, energy, and materials inputs and of time. We refer to this function as the sectoral price function.

Given sectoral price functions for all 35 industrial sectors, we can generate econometric models that determine the rate of technical change and the distributive shares of the four productivity inputs endogenously for each sector. The distributive shares and the rate of technical change, like the price of sectoral output, are functions of relative prices and time. We assume that the prices of sectoral outputs are transcendental-logarithmic or, more simply, translog functions of the prices of the four inputs and time.

Although technical change is endogenous in our models of production, and technical change, these models must be carefully distinguished from models of induced technical change, such as those analyzed by Hicks (1932), Kennedy (1964), Samuelson (1965), von Weizsäcker (1962), and many others.[1] In those models, the biases of technical change are endogenous and depend on relative prices. In our models, the biases of technical change are fixed, whereas the rate of technical change is endogenous and depends on relative prices.

As Samuelson (1965) has pointed out, models of induced technical change require intertemporal optimization, since technical change at any point of time affects future production possibilities. In our models myopic decision rules are appropriate, even though the rate of technical change is endogenous, provided that the price of capital input is treated as a rental price for capital services.[2] The rate of technical change at any point of time is a function of relative prices, but does not affect future production possibilities. This vastly simplifies the modeling of producer behavior and greatly facilitates the implementation of our econometric models.

2.2.1 Translog Model of Producer Behavior

Given myopic decision rules for producers in each industrial sector, we can describe all of the implications of the theory of production in terms of the sectoral price functions.[3] The sectoral price functions must be homogeneous of degree one, nondecreasing, and concave in the prices of the four inputs. A novel feature of our econometric methodology is to fit econometric models of sectoral production and technical change that incorporate all of these implications of the theory of production.

To represent our models of producer behavior, we first require some notation. There are I industrial sectors, indexed by $i = 1, 2, \ldots, I$. We denote the quantities of sectoral outputs by $\{Z_i\}$ and the quantities of sectoral capital, labor, energy, and materials inputs by $\{K_i, L_i, E_i, M_i\}$. Similarly, we denote the prices of sectoral outputs by $\{q_i\}$ and the prices of the four sectoral inputs by $\{p_K^i, p_L^i, p_E^i, p_M^i\}$. We can define the shares of inputs in the value of output for each of the sector by:

$$v_K^i = \frac{p_K^i K_i}{q_i Z_i}, \quad v_L^i = \frac{p_L^i L_i}{q_i Z_i}, \quad v_E^i = \frac{p_E^i E_i}{q_i Z_i},$$

$$V_M^i = \frac{p_M^i M_i}{q_i Z_i} \quad (i = 1, 2, \ldots, I).$$

Outputs are valued in producers' prices, while inputs are valued in purchasers' prices. In addition, we require the following notation:

$v_i = (v_K^i, v_L^i, v_E^i, v_M^i)$—vector of value shares of the ith industry $(i = 1, 2, \ldots, I)$

$\ln p_i = (\ln p_K^i, \ln p_L^i, \ln p_E^i, \ln p_M^i)$—vector of logarithms of prices of sectoral inputs of the ith industry $(i = 1, 2, \ldots, I)$

$t =$ time as an index of technology.

We assume that the ith industry allocates the value of its output among the four inputs in accord with the price function:

$$\ln q_i = \alpha_0^i + \ln p_i' \alpha_p^i + \alpha_t^i \cdot t + \frac{1}{2} \ln p_i' \beta_{pp}^i \ln p_i$$

$$+ \ln p_i' \beta_{pt}^i \cdot t + \frac{1}{2} \beta_{tt}^i \cdot t^2 \quad (i = 1, 2, \ldots, I). \tag{2.1}$$

For these price functions, the prices of outputs are transcendental or, more specifically, exponential functions of the logarithms of the prices of inputs. We refer to these forms as *transcendental-logarithmic* price functions or, more simply, translog price functions,[4] indicating the role of the variables that enter the price functions. In this reorientation, the scalars $\{\alpha_0^i, \alpha_t^i, \beta_{tt}^i\}$, the vectors $\{\alpha_p^i, \beta_{pt}^i\}$, and the matrices $\{\beta_{pp}^i\}$ are constant parameters that differ among industries, reflecting differences among sectoral technologies. Differences in technology among time periods within an industry are represented by time as an index of technology.

The value shares of the ith industry can be expressed in terms of the logarithmic derivatives of the sectoral price function with respect to the logarithms of the prices of the corresponding inputs:

$$v_i = \frac{\partial \ln q_i}{\partial \ln p_i} \quad (i = 1, 2, \ldots, I). \tag{2.2}$$

Applying this relationship to the translog price function, we obtain the system of sectoral value shares:

$$v_i = \alpha_p^i + \beta_{pp}^i \ln p_i + \beta_{pt}^i \cdot t \quad (i = 1, 2, \ldots, I). \tag{2.3}$$

We can define the *rate of technical change* for each of the sectors, say $\{v_t^i\}$, as the negative of the rate of growth of the price of sectoral output with respect to time, holding the prices of sectoral capital, labor, energy, and materials inputs constant:

$$v_t^i = -\frac{\partial \ln q_i}{\partial t} \quad (i = 1, 2, \ldots, I). \tag{2.4}$$

For the translog price function this relationship takes the form:

$$- v_t^i = \alpha_t^i + \beta_{pt}^{i'} \ln p_i + \beta_{tt}^i \cdot t \quad (i = 1, 2, \ldots, I). \tag{2.5}$$

Given the sectoral price functions, we can define the *share elasticities with respect to price*[5] as the derivatives of the value shares with respect to the logarithms of the prices of capital, labor, energy, and materials inputs. For the translog price functions, the matrices of share elasticities with respect to price $\{\beta_{pp}^i\}$ are constant. We can also characterize these functions as *constant share elasticity* or CSE price functions, indicating the role of fixed parameters that enter the sectoral price functions.[6] Similarly, we can define the *biases of technical change with respect to price* as derivatives of the value shares with respect to time.[7] Alternatively, we can define the biases of technical change with respect to price as derivatives of the rate of technical change with respect to the logarithms of the prices of capital, labor, energy, and materials inputs.[8] These two definitions of biases of technical change are equivalent. For the translog price functions, the vectors of biases of technical change with respect to price $\{\beta_{pt}^i\}$ are constant. Finally, we can define the *rate of change of the negative of the rate of technical change* as the derivative of the rate of technical change with respect to time.[9] For the translog price functions, these rates of change $\{\beta_{tt}^i\}$ are constant.

The negative of the average rates of technical change in any two points of time, say t and $t-1$, can be expressed as the difference between successive logarithms of the price of output, less a weighted average of the differences between successive logarithms of the prices given by the average value shares:

$$-\bar{v}_t^i = \ln q_i(t) - \ln q_i(t-1) - \bar{v}_K^i[\ln p_K^i(t) - \ln p_K^i(t-1)]$$
$$- \bar{v}_L^i[\ln p_L^i(t) - \ln p_L^i(t-1)] - \bar{v}_E^i[\ln p_E^i(t) - \ln p_E^i(t-1)]$$
$$- \bar{v}_M^i[\ln p_M^i(t) - \ln p_M^i(t-1)] \quad (i = 1, 2, \ldots, I) \quad (2.6)$$

where

$$\bar{v}_t^i = \frac{1}{2}[v_t^i(t) + v_t^i(t-1)] \quad (i = 1, 2, \ldots, I)$$

and the average value shares in the two periods are given by:

$$\bar{v}_K^i = \frac{1}{2}[v_K^i(t) + v_K^i(t-1)]$$

$$\bar{v}_L^i = \frac{1}{2}[v_L^i(t) + v_L^i(t-1)]$$

$$\bar{v}_E^i = \frac{1}{2}[v_E^i(t) + v_E^i(t-1)]$$

$$\bar{v}_M^i = \frac{1}{2}[v_M^i(t) + v_M^i(t-1)] \quad (i = 1, 2, \ldots, I).$$

We refer to the expressions for the average rates of technical change $\{\bar{v}_t^i\}$ as the *translog price indexes of the sectoral rates of technical change.*

Our model of producer behavior is based on two-stage allocation. In the first stage, the value of sectoral output is allocated among sectoral capital, labor, energy, and materials inputs. In the second stage, the value of each of the four inputs is allocated among individual types of that input. We have characterized the behavior of the ith industry $(i = 1, 2, \ldots, I)$ in terms of the price function that underlies the two-stage allocation process. In addition to homogeneity, monotonicity, and concavity, this price function has the property of homothetic separability in prices of individual types of capital, labor, energy, and materials inputs.

We can regard each of the input prices $\{p_K^i, p_L^i, p_E^i, p_M^i\}$ as a function of its components. These functions must be homogeneous of degree one, nondecreasing, and concave in the prices of the individual inputs. We can consider specific forms for price indexes of each of the four inputs as functions of the individual types of that input. If each of these prices is a translog function of its components, we can express the differences between successive logarithms of the prices as a weighted average of differences between successive logarithms of prices of individual types of that input with weights given by the average value shares. We can refer to the resulting expressions as *translog indexes of the prices of capital, labor, energy and materials inputs.*[10]

2.2.2   Integrability

Our next step in representing our models of producer behavior is to employ the implications of the theory of production in specifying econometric models of technical change and the distribution of the value of output. If a system of equations, consisting of sectoral value shares and the rate of technical change, can be generated from a sectoral price function, we say that the system is *integrable*. A complete set of conditions for integrability expressed in terms of the system of equations is the following:

1. *Homogeneity.* The sectoral value shares and the rate of technical change are homogeneous of degree zero in the input prices.

We can write the sectoral value shares and the rate of technical change in the form:

$$v_i = \alpha_p^i + \beta_{pp}^i \ln p_i + \beta_{pt}^i \cdot t$$
$$- v_t = \alpha_t^i + \beta_{pt}^{i'} \ln p_i + \beta_{tt}^i \cdot t \quad (i = 1, 2, \ldots, I) \tag{2.7}$$

where the parameters $\{\alpha_p^i, \alpha_t^i, \beta_{pp}^i, \beta_{pt}^i, \beta_{tt}^i\}$ are constant. Homogeneity implies that these parameters must satisfy:

$$\beta_{pp}^i \iota = 0$$
$$\beta_{pt}^{i'} \iota = 0 \ I \ (i = 1, 2, \ldots, I). \tag{2.8}$$

For four sectoral inputs there are five restrictions implied by homogeneity.

2. *Product exhaustion.* The sum of the sectoral value shares is equal to unity:

$$v_i' \iota = 1 \quad (i = 1, 2, \ldots, I).$$

Product exhaustion implies that the value of the four sectoral inputs exhausts the value of the product. Product exhaustion implies that the parameters must satisfy the restrictions:

$$\alpha_p^{i'} \iota = 1$$
$$\beta_{pp}^{i'} \iota = 0$$
$$\beta_{pt}^{i'} \iota = 0 \quad (i = 1, 2, \ldots, I). \tag{2.9}$$

For four sectoral inputs there are six restrictions implied by product exhaustion.

3. *Symmetry.* The matrix of share elasticities and biases and rate of change of technical change must be symmetric.

Imposing homogeneity and product exhaustion restrictions, we can write the system of sectoral value shares and the rate of technical change without imposing symmetry in the form:

$$v_i = \alpha_p^i + \beta_{pp}^i \ln p_i + \beta_{pt}^i \cdot t$$
$$- v_t^i = \alpha_t^i + \beta_{tp}^{i'} \ln p_i + \beta_{tt}^i \cdot t \quad (i = 1, 2, \ldots, I). \tag{2.10}$$

A necessary and sufficient condition for symmetry is that the matrix of parameters must satisfy the restrictions

$$\begin{bmatrix} \beta_{pp}^i & \beta_{pt}^i \\ \beta_{tp}^{i'} & \beta_{tt}^i \end{bmatrix} = \begin{bmatrix} \beta_{pp}^i & \beta_{pt}^i \\ \beta_{pt}^{i'} & \beta_{tt}^i \end{bmatrix}' \tag{2.11}$$

For four sectoral inputs the total number of symmetry restrictions is 10.

4. *Nonnegativity.* The sectoral value shares must be nonnegative:

$$v_i \geqq 0 \quad (i = 1, 2, \ldots, I).$$

By product exhaustion the sectoral value shares sum to unity, so that we can write

$$v_i \geq 0 \quad (i = 1, 2, \ldots, I)$$

where $v_i \geq 0$ implies $v_i \geq 0$ and $v_i \neq 0$.

Nonnegativity of the sectoral value shares is implied by monotonicity of the sectoral price functions:

$$\frac{\partial \ln q_t}{\partial \ln p_i} \geqq 0 \quad (i = 1, 2, \ldots, I).$$

For the translog price function the conditions for monotonicity take the form:

$$\frac{\partial \ln q_i}{\partial \ln p_i} = \alpha_p^i + \beta_{pp}^i \ln p_i + \beta_{pt}^i \cdot t \geqq 0 \quad (i = 1, 2, \ldots, I). \tag{2.12}$$

Since the translog price functions are quadratic in the logarithms of sectoral input prices $\ln p_i$ $(i = 1, 2, \ldots, I)$, we can always choose prices so that the monotonicity of the sectoral price functions is violated. Accordingly, we cannot impose restrictions on the parameters of the translog price functions that would imply nonnegativity of the sectoral value shares for all prices and time. Instead we consider restrictions on the parameters that imply concavity of the sectoral price functions or monotonicity of the sectoral value shares for all nonnegative value shares.

5. *Monotonicity.* The matrix of share elasticities must be nonpositive-definite.

Concavity of the sectoral price functions implies that the matrices of second-order partial derivatives, say $\{H_i\}$, are nonpositive-definite,[11] so that the matrices $\{\beta_{pp}^i + v_i v_i' - V_i\}$ are nonpositive-definite:[12]

$$\frac{1}{q_i} \cdot N_i \cdot H_i \cdot N_i = \beta_{pp}^i + v_i v_i' - V_i \quad (i = 1, 2, \ldots, I) \tag{2.13}$$

where the sectoral price functions are positive and:

$$
N_i = \begin{bmatrix} p_K^i & 0 & 0 & 0 \\ 0 & p_L^i & 0 & 0 \\ 0 & 0 & p_E^i & 0 \\ 0 & 0 & 0 & p_M^i \end{bmatrix}, \quad V_i = \begin{bmatrix} v_K^i & 0 & 0 & 0 \\ 0 & v_L^i & 0 & 0 \\ 0 & 0 & v_E^i & 0 \\ 0 & 0 & 0 & v_M^i \end{bmatrix} \quad (i = 1, 2, \ldots, I)
$$

and $\{\beta_{pp}^i\}$ are matrices of constant share elasticities as defined above.

Without violating the product exhaustion and nonnegativity restrictions on the sectoral value shares, we can set the matrices $\{v_i v_i' - V_i\}$ equal to zero, for example, by choosing one of the value shares to be equal to unity and the other value shares equal to zero. Necessary conditions for the matrices $\{\beta_{pp}^i + v_i v_i' - V_i\}$ to be nonpositive-definite are that the matrices of constant share elasticities $\{\beta_{pp}^i\}$ must be nonpositive-definite. These conditions are also sufficient, since the matrices $\{v_i v_i' - V_I\}$ are nonpositive-definite for all nonnegative value shares summing to unity and the sum of two nonpositive-definite matrices is nonpositive-definite.

To impose concavity in the translog price functions, the matrices of constant shares elasticities $\{\beta_{pp}^i\}$ can be represented in terms of their Cholesky factorizations:

$$
\beta_{pp}^i = T_i D_i T_i' \quad (i = 1, 2, \ldots, I)
$$

where $\{T_i\}$ are unit lower triangular matrices and $\{D_i\}$ are diagonal matrices. For four inputs we can write the matrices $\{\beta_{pp}^i\}$ in terms of their Cholesky factorizations as follows:

$$
\beta_{pp}^i = \begin{bmatrix}
\delta_1^i & \lambda_{21}^i \delta_1^i & \lambda_{31}^i \delta_1^i \\
\lambda_{21}^i \delta_1^i & \lambda_{21}^i \lambda_{21}^i \delta_1^i + \delta_2^i & \lambda_{21}^i \lambda_{31}^i \delta_1^i + \lambda_{32}^i \delta_2^i \\
\lambda_{31}^i \delta_1^i & \lambda_{31}^i \lambda_{21}^i \delta_1^i + \lambda_{32}^i \delta_2^i & \lambda_{31}^i \lambda_{31}^i \delta_1^i + \lambda_{32}^i \lambda_{32}^i \delta_2^i + \delta_3^i \\
\lambda_{41}^i \delta_1^i & \lambda_{41}^i \lambda_{21}^i \delta_1^i + \lambda_{42}^i \delta_2^i & \lambda_{41}^i \lambda_{31}^i \delta_1^i + \lambda_{42}^i \lambda_{32}^i \delta_2^i + \lambda_{43}^i \delta_3^i
\end{bmatrix}
$$

$$
\begin{bmatrix}
\lambda_{41}^i \delta_1^i \\
\lambda_{41}^i \lambda_{21}^i \delta_1^i + \lambda_{42}^i \delta_2^i \\
\lambda_{41}^i \lambda_{31}^i \delta_1^i + \lambda_{42}^i \lambda_{32}^i \delta_2^i + \lambda_{43}^i \delta_3^i \\
\lambda_{41}^i \lambda_{41}^i \delta_1^i + \lambda_{42}^i \lambda_{42}^i \delta_2^i + \lambda_{43}^i \lambda_{43}^i \delta_3^i + \delta_4^i
\end{bmatrix} \quad (i = 1, 2, \ldots, I)
$$

where

$$
T_i = \begin{bmatrix} 1 & 0 & 0 & 0 \\ \lambda_{21}^i & 1 & 0 & 0 \\ \lambda_{31}^i & \lambda_{32}^i & 1 & 0 \\ \lambda_{41}^i & \lambda_{42}^i & \lambda_{43}^i & 1 \end{bmatrix}, \quad
D_i = \begin{bmatrix} \delta_1^i & 0 & 0 & 0 \\ 0 & \delta_2^i & 0 & 0 \\ 0 & 0 & \delta_3^i & 0 \\ 0 & 0 & 0 & \delta_4^i \end{bmatrix} \quad (i = 1, 2, \ldots, I) .
$$

The matrices of constant share elasticities $\{\beta_{pp}^i\}$ must satisfy symmetry restrictions and restriction implied by product exhaustion. These restrictions imply that the parameters of the Cholesky factorizations must satisfy the following conditions:

$$
\begin{aligned}
1 + \lambda_{21}^i + \lambda_{31}^i + \lambda_{41}^i &= 0 \\
1 + \lambda_{32}^i + \lambda_{42}^i &= 0 \\
1 + \lambda_{43}^i &= 0 \\
\delta_4^i &= 0 \quad (i = 1, 2, \ldots, I).
\end{aligned}
$$

Under these conditions, there is a one-to-one transformation between the matrices of constant share elasticities $\{\beta_{pp}^i\}$ and the parameters of the Cholesky factorizations $\{T_i, D_i\}$. The matrices of share elasticities are nonpositive-definite, if and only if the diagonal elements of the matrices $\{D_i\}$, the so-called Cholesky values, are nonpositive.

Similarly, we can provide a complete set of conditions for integrability of the systems of sectoral value shares for individual inputs for the second stage of the two-stage allocation process. For example, the sectoral value shares for individual capital inputs are homogeneous of degree zero in the prices of these inputs, the sum of the sectoral value shares is equal to unity, and the matrix of share elasticities with respect to prices of individual capital inputs must be symmetric. These conditions can be used to generate restrictions on the parameters of the translog price indexes for capital input. The restrictions are analogous to those for the first stage of the two-stage allocation process, except that restrictions on the equation for the rate of technical change are omitted.

The sectoral value shares for individual capital inputs must be nonnegative; as before, we cannot impose conditions on the parameters of the translog price indexes for capital input that would imply nonnegativity of the sectoral value shares for all prices and time. Instead, we can consider restrictions on the parameters that imply concavity of the sectoral price functions for capital input for all nonnegative value shares. These restrictions are precisely analogous to those for concavity of the sectoral price functions. These restrictions can be imposed by representing the matrices of constant share elasticities in terms of their Cholesky factorizations and requiring that the corresponding Cholesky values are nonpositive. Similar restrictions can be imposed on the parameters of translog price functions for labor, energy, and materials inputs.

2.2.3   Stochastic Specifications

Our models of producer behavior are generated from translog price functions for each industrial sector. To formulate an econometric model of production and technical change, we add a stochastic component to the equations for the value shares and the rate of technical change. We associate this component with unobservable random disturbances at the level of the individual industry. The industry maximizes profits for given prices of inputs, but the value shares of inputs are chosen with a random disturbance. This disturbance may result from errors in implementation of production plans, random elements in sectoral technologies not reflected in the models of producer behavior, or errors of measurements in the value shares. We assume that each of the equations for the value shares and the rate of technical change have two additive components.[13] The first is a nonrandom function of the prices of capital, labor, energy, and materials inputs and time; the second is an unobservable random disturbance that is functionally independent of these variables.

To represent an econometric model of production and technical change, we require some additional notation. We consider observations on expenditure patterns by I industries, indexed by $i = 1, 2, \ldots, I$, for T time periods, indexed by $t = 1, 2, \ldots, T$. The vector of value shares of the ith industry in the tth time period is denoted v_{it}, $(i = 1, 2, \ldots, I; t = 1, 2, \ldots, T)$. Similarly, the rate of technical change of the ith industry in the tth time period is denoted v_{it}^t $(i = 1, 2, \ldots, I; t = 1, 2, \ldots, T)$. The vector of price indexes for capital, labor, energy, and materials inputs for the ith industry in the tth time period is denoted p_{it}, $(i = 1, 2, \ldots, I; t = 1, 2, \ldots, T)$. Similarly, the vector of logarithms of input price indexes is denoted $\ln p_{it}$ $(i = 1, 2, \ldots, I; t = 1, 2, \ldots, T)$. As before, time as an index of technology is denoted by t.

We obtain econometric models of production and technical change corresponding to translog price functions by adding random disturbances to the equations for the value shares and the rate of technical change in each industry:

$$v_{it} = \alpha_p^i + \beta_{pp}^i \ln p_{it} + \beta_{pt}^i \cdot t + \varepsilon_{it}$$

$$-v_{it}^t = \alpha_t^i + \beta_{pt}^{i'} \ln p_{it} + \beta_{tt}^i \cdot t + \varepsilon_{it}^t \quad (i = 1, 2, \ldots, I; t = 1, 2, \ldots, T) \qquad (2.14)$$

where $\{\varepsilon_{it}\}$ is the vector of unobservable random disturbances for the value shares of the ith industry and the tth time period and $\{\varepsilon_{it}^t\}$ is the corresponding disturbance for the rate of technical change. Since the value shares for all inputs sum to unity for each industry in each time period, the random disturbances corresponding to the four value shares sum to zero in each time period:

$$\iota'\varepsilon_{it} = 0 \quad (i = 1, 2, \ldots, I; t = 1, 2, \ldots, T) \qquad (2.15)$$

so that these disturbances are not distributed independently.

We assume that the unobservable random disturbances for all five equations have expected value equal to zero for all observations:

$$E\begin{pmatrix} \varepsilon_{it} \\ \varepsilon_{it}^t \end{pmatrix} = 0 \quad (i = 1, 2, \ldots, I; t = 1, 2, \ldots, T). \qquad (2.16)$$

We also assume that these disturbances have a covariance matrix that is the same for all observations; since the random disturbances corresponding to the four value shares sum to zero, this matrix is nonnegative-definite with rank at most equal to four. We assume that the covariance matrix of the random disturbances, say $\{\Sigma^i\}$, for instance, has rank four, where:

$$V\begin{pmatrix} \varepsilon_{it} \\ \varepsilon_{it}^t \end{pmatrix} = \Sigma^i \quad (i = 1, 2, \ldots, I; t = 1, 2, \ldots, T).$$

Finally, we assume that the random disturbances corresponding to distinct observations in the same or distinct equations are uncorrelated.[14] Under this assumption, the covariance matrix of random disturbances for all observations has the Kronecker product form:

$$V \begin{pmatrix} \varepsilon^i_{K1} \\ \varepsilon^i_{K2} \\ \vdots \\ \varepsilon^i_{KT} \\ \varepsilon^i_{L1} \\ \vdots \\ \varepsilon^t_{tT} \end{pmatrix} = \Sigma^i \otimes i = 1, 2, \ldots, I; t = 1, 2, \ldots, T). \tag{2.17}$$

The sectoral rates of technical change $\{v^t_{it}\}$ are not directly observable; however, the equation for the translog price indexes of the sectoral rates of technical change can be written:

$$-\bar{v}^t_{it} = \alpha^i_t + \beta^{i'}_{pt} \overline{\ln p_{it}} + \beta^i_{tt} \cdot \bar{t} + \bar{\varepsilon}^t_{tt} \quad (i = 1, 2, \ldots, I; t = 2, 3, \ldots, T) \tag{2.18}$$

where $\bar{\varepsilon}^t_{it}$ is the average disturbance in the two periods:

$$\bar{\varepsilon}^t_{it} = \frac{1}{2} [\varepsilon^t_{it} + \varepsilon^t_{i,t-1}] \quad (i = 1, 2, \ldots, I; t = 2, 3, \ldots, T).$$

Similarly, $\overline{\ln p_{it}}$ is a vector of averages of the logarithms of the prices of the four inputs and $\bar{t}$ is the average of time as an index of technology in the two periods.

Using our new notation, the equations for the value shares of capital, labor, energy, and materials inputs can be written:

$$\bar{v}_{it} = \alpha^i_p + \beta^i_{pp} \overline{\ln p_{it}} + \beta^i_{pt} \cdot \bar{t} + \bar{\varepsilon}_{it} \quad (i = 1, 2, \ldots, I; t = 2, 3, \ldots, T) \tag{2.19}$$

where $\bar{\varepsilon}_{it}$ is a vector of averages of the disturbances in the two periods. As before, the average value shares sum to unity, so that the average disturbances for the equations corresponding to value shares sum to zero:

$$\iota' \bar{\varepsilon}_{it} = 0 \quad (i = 1, 2, \ldots, I; t = 2, 3, \ldots, T). \tag{2.20}$$

The covariance matrix of the average disturbances corresponding to the equation for the rate of technical change for all observations, say Ω, is proportional to a Laurent matrix:

$$V \begin{pmatrix} \bar{\varepsilon}^i_{t2} \\ \bar{\varepsilon}^i_{t3} \\ \vdots \\ \bar{\varepsilon}^i_{tT} \end{pmatrix} \sim \Omega \quad (i = 1, 2, \ldots, I) \tag{2.21}$$

where

$$\Omega = \begin{bmatrix} \frac{1}{2} & \frac{1}{4} & 0 & \cdots & 0 \\ \frac{1}{4} & \frac{1}{2} & \frac{1}{4} & \cdots & 0 \\ 0 & \frac{1}{4} & \frac{1}{2} & \cdots & 0 \\ \vdots & \vdots & \vdots & & \vdots \\ 0 & 0 & 0 & \cdots & \frac{1}{2} \end{bmatrix}.$$

The covariance matrix of the average disturbance corresponding to each equation for the four value shares is the same, so that the covariance matrix of the average disturbances for all observations has the Kronecker product form:

$$V \begin{pmatrix} \bar{\varepsilon}^i_{K2} \\ \bar{\varepsilon}^i_{K3} \\ \vdots \\ \bar{\varepsilon}^i_{KT} \\ \bar{\varepsilon}^i_{L2} \\ \vdots \\ \bar{\varepsilon}^i_{tT} \end{pmatrix} = \Sigma^i \otimes \Omega \quad (i = 1, 2, \ldots, I). \tag{2.22}$$

Although disturbances in equations for the average rate of technical change and the average value shares are autocorrelated, the data can be transformed to eliminate the autocorrelation. The matrix Ω is positive-definite, so that there is a matrix P such that:

$$P\Omega P' = I$$
$$P'P = \Omega^{-1}.$$

To construct the matrix P we can first invert the matrix Ω to obtain the inverse matrix Ω^{-1}, a positive-definite matrix. We then calculate the Cholesky factorization of the inverse matrix Ω^{-1},

$\Omega^{-1} = TDT'$

where T is a unit lower triangular matrix and D is a diagonal matrix with positive elements along the main diagonal. Finally, we can write the matrix P in the form:

$P = D^{1/2}T'$

where $D^{1/2}$ is a diagonal matrix with elements along the main diagonal equal to the square roots of the corresponding elements of D.

We can transform equations for the average rates of technical change by the matrix $P = D^{1/2}T'$ to obtain equations with uncorrelated random disturbances

$$
D^{1/2}T'
\begin{pmatrix}
\bar{v}^i_{t2} \\
\bar{v}^i_{t3} \\
\vdots \\
\bar{v}^i_{tT}
\end{pmatrix}
= D^{1/2}T'
\begin{pmatrix}
1 \, \overline{\ln p^i_{K2}} & \cdots & 2 - \dfrac{1}{2} \\
1 \, \overline{\ln p^i_{K3}} & \cdots & 3 - \dfrac{1}{2} \\
\vdots & & \vdots \\
1 \, \overline{\ln p^i_{KT}} & \cdots & T - \dfrac{1}{2}
\end{pmatrix}
\begin{pmatrix}
\alpha^i_t \\
\beta^i_{Kt} \\
\vdots \\
\beta^i_{tt}
\end{pmatrix}
+ D^{1/2}T'
\begin{pmatrix}
\bar{\varepsilon}^i_{t2} \\
\bar{\varepsilon}^i_{t3} \\
\vdots \\
\bar{\varepsilon}^i_{tT}
\end{pmatrix}
$$

$$(i = 1, 2, \ldots, I). \qquad (2.23)$$

since

$P\Omega P' = (D^{1/2}T')\Omega(D^{1/2}T')' = I.$

The transformation $P = D^{1/2}T'$ is applied to data on the average rates of technical change $\{\bar{v}^i_t\}$ and data on the average values of the variables that appear on the right-hand side of the corresponding equation.

We can apply the transformation $P = D^{1/2}T'$ to the equations for average value shares to obtain equations with uncorrelated disturbances. As before, the transformation is applied to data on the average value shares and the average values of variables that appear in the corresponding equations. The covariance matrix of the transformed disturbances from the equations for the average value shares and the equation for the average rate of technical change has the Kronecker product form:

$$(I \otimes D^{1/2}T')(\Sigma^i \otimes \Omega)(I \otimes D^{1/2}T')' = \Sigma^i \otimes I \qquad (i = 1, 2, \ldots, I). \qquad (2.24)$$

To estimate the unknown parameters of the translog price function, we combine the first three equations for the average value shares with the equation for the average rate of technical change to obtain a complete econometric model of production and technical change. We estimate the parameters of the equations for the remaining average value share, using the restrictions on these parameters given above. The complete model involves fourteen unknown parameters. A total of sixteen additional parameters can be estimated as functions of these parameters, given the restrictions. Our estimate of the unknown parameters of the econometric model of production and technical change is based on the nonlinear three-stage least-squares estimator introduced by Jorgenson and Laffont (1974).

2.2.4   Summary and Conclusion

In this section, we have presented a model of producer behavior based on transcendental-logarithmic or translog price functions for all industrial sectors. These price functions incorporate restrictions on producer behavior that result from maximization of profit subject to a production function. Our model of producer behavior is based on a two-stage allocation process. For each stage of the allocation process, the behavior of the industry is generated by sectoral price functions that are homogeneous of degree one, nondecreasing, and concave in prices.

For all industrial sectors, we have employed conditions for producer equilibrium under perfect competition. We have assumed constant returns to scale at the industry level. Finally, we have employed a description of technology that leads to myopic decision rules. To incorporate differences in technology among industrial sectors into our model of producer behavior, we allow the parameters of the translog price functions to differ among sectors. Similarly, to permit differences in technology among time periods for a given sector, we introduce time as an index of technology into the sectoral price functions.

Given translog price functions for each industrial sector, we derive value shares of inputs and the rate of technical change for that sector by logarithmic differentiation. For the first stage of the two-stage allocation process, this results in value shares for inputs and a rate of technical change that are linear in the logarithms of input prices and in time. Since the translog price functions for the second stage of the two-stage allocation process depend only on prices of individual inputs, the value shares for inputs are linear in the logarithms of input prices.

The value shares of inputs and the rate of technical change at the first stage of the two-stage allocation process are homogeneous of degree zero in input prices. For four sectoral inputs, homogeneity implies five restrictions on the parameters of the translog price functions. Second, the sum of the sectoral value shares is equal to unity, so that the value of the four sectoral inputs exhausts the value of the product. Product exhaustion implies six restrictions on the parameters for four inputs. Third, the matrix of share elasticities and biases and the rate of change of technical change must be symmetric, implying 10 restrictions on the parameters.

Monotonicity of the sectoral price function implies that sectoral value shares must be nonnegative. Similarly, concavity of the price function implies that the matrix of share elasticities must be nonpositive-definite. Since it is always possible to choose prices so that monotonicity of the price function or nonnegativity of the value shares is violated, we consider restrictions that imply monotonicity of the value shares wherever they are nonnegative.

2.3 Consumer Behavior

We now turn to models of aggregate consumer behavior. Before proceeding with the presentation, we first set down some notation. There are J consumers, indexed by $j = 1, 2, \ldots, J$. There are N commodity groups in the economy, indexed by $n = 1, 2, \ldots, N$; p_n is the price of the nth commodity group, assumed to be the same for all consumers. We denote by $p = (p_1, p_2, \ldots, p_N)$ the vector of prices of all commodity groups. The quantity of the nth commodity group demanded by the jth consumer is x_{nj} and total expenditure of the jth consumer is $Y_j = \sum_{n=1}^{N} p_n x_{nj}$. Finally, A_j is a vector of individual attributes of the jth consumer.[15]

We assume that the demand for the nth commodity group by the jth consumer x_{nj} can be expressed as a function f_{nj} of the price vector p, total expenditure Y_j, and the vector of attributes A_j:

$$x_{nj} = f_{nj}(p, Y_j, A_j). \tag{3.1}$$

Aggregate demand for the nth commodity group is given by:

$$\sum_{j=1}^{J} x_{nj} = \sum_{j=1}^{J} f_{nj}(p, Y_j, A_j).$$

In models of consumer behavior based on aggregate quantities consumed, the aggregate demand function depends on the price vector p, aggregate expenditure $\sum_{j=1}^{J} Y_j$, and possibly some index of aggregate attributes, say $\sum_{j=1}^{J} A_j$. Thus, we may write:

$$\sum_{j=1}^{J} f_j(p, Y_j, A_j) = F\left(p, \sum_{j=1}^{J} Y_j, \sum_{j=1}^{J} A_j \right) \tag{3.2}$$

where f_j is a vector-valued individual demand function:

$$f_j = \begin{bmatrix} f_{1j} \\ f_{2j} \\ \vdots \\ f_{Nj} \end{bmatrix} \quad (j = 1, 2, \ldots, J)$$

giving the vector of demands for all N commodities by the jth consumer, and F is a vector-valued aggregate demand function, giving the vector of demands for all N commodities by all J consumers.

The conditions under which equation (3.2) holds for all expenditures $\{Y_j\}$, all prices, and all possible attributes have been derived by Gorman (1953) under the assumption of utility maximization by individual consumers. Gorman's conditions imply

1. $f_j(p, Y_j, A_j) = h_1(p)Y_j + h_2(p)A_j + C_j(p) \quad (j = 1, 2, \ldots, J)$

2. $F\left(p, \sum_{j=1}^{j} Y_j, \sum_{j=1}^{J} A_j \right) = h_1(p) \sum_{j=1}^{J} Y_j + h_2(p) \sum_{j=1}^{J} A_j + \sum_{j=1}^{J} C_j(p)$

where the vector-valued function $h_1(p)$ is homogeneous of degree -1 and the vector-valued functions $\{h_2(p), C_j(p)\}$ are homogeneous of degree 0. In other words, the individual demand functions are linear in expenditure and attributes. They are identical up to the addition of a function that is independent of expenditure and attributes. Furthermore, if aggregate demands are equal to zero when aggregate expenditure is equal to zero, individuals must have identical homothetic preferences.[16]

Homothetic preferences are inconsistent with well-established empirical regularities in the behavior of individual consumers, such as

Engel's law, which states that the proportion of expenditure devoted to food is a decreasing function of total expenditure.[17] Identical preferences for individual households are inconsistent with empirical findings that expenditure patterns depend on demographic characteristics of individual households.[18] Even the weaker form of Gorman's results, that quantities consumed are linear functions of expenditure with identical slopes for all individuals, is inconsistent with empirical evidence from budget studies.[19]

Despite the conflict between Gorman's characterization of individual consumer behavior and the empirical evidence from cross-section data, this characterization has provided an important stimulus to empirical research based on aggregate time series data. The line expenditure system, proposed by Klein and Rubin (1947) and implemented by Stone (1954b), has the property that individual demand functions are linear in total expenditure. The resulting system of aggregate demand functions has been used widely as the basis for econometric models of aggregate consumer behavior. Generalizations of the linear expenditure system that retain the critical property of linearity of individual demand functions in total expenditure have also been employed in empirical research.[20]

Muellbauer (1975, 1976a, 1976b) has substantially generalized Gorman's characterization of the representative consumer model. Aggregate expenditure shares, interpreted as the expenditure shares of a representative consumer, may depend on prices and on a function of individual expenditure not restricted to aggregate or per capita expenditure. In Muellbauer's model of the representative consumer, individual preferences are identical but not necessarily homothetic. Furthermore, quantities consumed may be nonlinear functions of expenditure rather than linear functions, as in Forman's characterization. An important consequence of this nonlinearity is that aggregate demand functions depend on the distribution of expenditure among individuals. Berndt, Darrough, and Diewert (1977), and Deaton and Muellbauer (1980a, 1980b), have implemented aggregate models of consumer behavior that conform to Muellbauer's characterization of the representative consumer model, retaining the assumption that preferences are identical among individuals.

Lau (1977b, 1982) has developed a theory of exact aggregation that makes it possible to incorporate differences in individual preferences. We first generalize the concept of an aggregate demand functions to that of a function that depends on general symmetric functions of individual expenditures and attributes:

$$\sum_{j=1}^{J} f_j(p, Y_j, A_j) = F(p, g_1(Y_1, Y_2, \ldots, Y_J, A_1, A_2, \ldots, A_J), g_2(Y_1, Y_2, \ldots,$$

$$Y_J, A_1, A_2, \ldots, A_J), \ldots, g_1(Y_1, Y_2, \ldots, Y_J, A_1, A_2, \ldots, A_J)) \quad (3.3)$$

where each function $g_i(i = 1, 2, \ldots, I)$ is symmetric in individual expenditures and attributes, so that the value of this function is independent of the ordering of the individuals. We refer to the functions $\{g_i\}$ as index functions. These functions can be interpreted as statistics describing the population. To avoid triviality we assume also that the function $\{g_i\}$ is functionally independent.

The fundamental theorem of exact aggregation establishes conditions for equation (3.3) to hold for all prices, individual expenditures, and individual attributes. These conditions are the following:

1. All the individual demand functions for the same commodity are identical up to the addition of a function independent of individual attributes and expenditure.

2. All the individual demand functions must be sums of products of separate functions of the prices and of the individual attributes and expenditure.

3. The aggregate demand functions depend on certain index functions of individual attributes and expenditures. The only admissible index functions are additive in functions of individual attributes and expenditures.

4. The aggregate demand functions can be written as linear functions of the index functions.[21]

Specialization of the fundamental theorem of exact aggregation have appeared earlier in the literature. For example, if there is only one index function and we take $g_1 = \sum_{j=1}^{J} Y_j$, aggregate expenditure for the economy, then this theorem implies that for given prices, all consumers must have parallel linear Engel curves. Restricting demands to be nonnegative for all prices and expenditures implies that for given prices, all consumers have identical linear Engel curves. Restricting demands to be nonnegative for all prices and expenditures implies that for given prices, all consumers have identical linear Engel curves. These are the results of Gorman (1953). Muellbauer's condition for the existence of a representative consumer,

$$\sum_{j=1}^{j} f_{nj}(p, Y_j) - F_n(g_2(Y_{1,2}, \ldots, Y_j), p)\left(\sum_{j=1}^{J} y_j\right) \quad (n = 1, 2, \ldots, N)$$

can be viewed as a special case of equation (3.3) with the number of indexes I equal to 2 and the first index function $g_1(Y_1, Y_2, \ldots, Y_j) = \sum_{j=1}^{J} Y_j$ equal to aggregate expenditure. The representative consumer interpretation fails for the case of more than two index functions.

2.3.1 Translog Model of Consumer Behavior

We next present individual and aggregate models of consumer behavior based on the theory of exact aggregation. The theory of exact aggregation requires that the individual demand functions must be linear in a number of functions of individual attributes and expenditure. Representing aggregate demand functions as the sum of individual demand functions, we find that the aggregate demand functions depend on the distribution of expenditure among individuals as well as the level of per capita expenditure and prices. The aggregate demand functions also depend on the joint distribution of expenditures and demographic characteristics among individuals.

In our model of consumer behavior, the individual consuming units are households. We assume that household expenditures on commodity groups are allocated so as to maximize a household welfare function. As a consequence, the household behaves in the same way as an individual maximizing a utility function.[22] We require that the individual demand functions are integrable, so that these demand functions can be generated by Roy's (1943) identity from an indirect utility function for each consuming unit.[23] We assume that these indirect utility functions are homogeneous of degree zero in prices and expenditure, nonincreasing in prices and nondecreasing in expenditure, and quasi-convex in prices and expenditure.

To allow for differences in preferences among consuming units, we allow the indirect utility functions for the jth unit to depend on a vector of attributes A_j; each attribute is represented by a dummy variable equal to unity when the consuming unit has the corresponding characteristic and zero otherwise. In our model of consumer behavior, there are several groups of attributes. Each consuming unit is assigned one of the attributes in each of the groups.

To represent our model of consumer behavior we require the following additional notation:

$w_{nj} = p_n x_{nj}/Y_j$: Expenditure shares of the nth commodity group in the budget of the jth consuming unit ($j = 1, 2, \ldots, J$).

$w_j = (w_{1j}, w_{2j}, \ldots, 2_{Nj})$: Vector of expenditure shares for the jth consuming unit ($j = 1, 2, \ldots, J$).

$\ln(p/Y_j) = (ln(p_{1/Y_j)}, ln(p\_2/Y_j), \ldots, ln(p_{N/Y_j)}$: Vector of logarithms of ratios of prices to expenditure by the j consuming unit ($j = 1, 2, \ldots, J$).

$\ln p = (\ln p_1, \ln p_2, \ldots, \ln p_N)$: Vector of logarithms of prices.

We assume that the jth consuming unit allocates its expenditures in accord with the transcendental logarithmic or translog indirect utility function,[24] say U_j, where:

$$\ln U_j = G(A_j) + \ln\left(\frac{p}{Y_j}\right)' \alpha_p + \frac{1}{2} \ln\left(\frac{p}{Y_j}\right)' \beta_{pp} \ln \frac{p}{Y_j}$$

$$+ \ln\left(\frac{p}{Y_j}\right)' \beta_{pA} A_j \quad (j = 1, 2, \ldots, J). \tag{3.4}$$

In this representation the function G depends on the attribute vector A_j but is independent of the prices p and expenditure Y_j. The vector α_p and the matrices β_{pp} and β_{pA} are constant parameters that are the same for all consuming units.

The expenditure shares of the jth consuming unit can be derived by the logarithmic form of Roy's identity:

$$w_{nj} = \frac{\partial \ln U_j}{\partial \ln(p_n/Y_j)} + \sum \frac{\partial \ln U_j}{\partial \ln(p_n/Y_j)} \quad (n = 1, 2, \ldots, N; j = 1, 2, \ldots, J). \tag{3.5}$$

Applying this identity to the translog indirect utility function, we obtain the system of individual expenditure shares:

$$w_j = \frac{1}{B_j}\left(\alpha_p + \beta_{pp} \ln \frac{p}{Y_j} + \beta_{pA} A_j\right) \quad (j = 1, 2, \ldots, J) \tag{3.6}$$

where the denominators $\{B_j\}$ take the form:

$$B_j = \iota'\alpha_p + \iota'\beta_{pp} \ln \frac{p}{Y_j} + \iota'\beta_{pA} A_j \quad (j = 1, 2, \ldots, J) \tag{3.7}$$

and ι is a vector of ones.

We first observe that the function G that appears in the translog indirect utility function does not enter into the determination of the individual expenditure shares. This function is not identifiable from observed patterns of individual expenditure allocation. Second, since the individual expenditure shares can be expressed as ratios of functions that are homogeneous and linear in the unknown parameters—$(\alpha_p, \beta_{pp}, \beta_{pA})$, these shares are homogeneous of degree zero in the parameters. By multiplying a given set of the unknown parameters by a constant, we obtain another set of parameters that generates the same system of individual budget shares. Accordingly, we can choose a normalization for the parameters without affecting observed patterns of individual expenditure allocation. We find it convenient to employ the normalization

$$\iota'\alpha_p = -1.$$

Under this restriction any change in the set of unknown parameters will be reflected in changes in individual expenditure patterns.

   The conditions for exact aggregation are that the individual expenditure shares are linear in functions of the attributes $\{A_j\}$ and total expenditures $\{Y_j\}$ for all consuming units.[25] These conditions will be satisfied if and only if the terms involving the attributes and expenditures do not appear in the denominators of the expressions given above for the individual expenditure shares, so that

$$\iota'\beta_{pp}\iota = 0$$
$$\iota'\beta_{pA} = 0.$$

These restrictions imply that the denominators $\{B_j\}$ reduce to

$$B = -1 + \iota'\beta_{pp} \ln p$$

where the subscript j is no longer required, since the denominator is the same for all consuming units. Under these restrictions the individual expenditure shares can be written:

$$w_j = \frac{1}{B} (\alpha_p + \beta_{pp} \ln p - \beta_{pp}\iota \cdot \ln Y_j + \beta_{pA}A_j) \quad (j = 1, 2, \ldots, J). \qquad (3.8)$$

The individual expenditure shares are linear in the logarithms of expenditures $\{\ln Y_j\}$ and the attributes $\{A_j\}$, as required by exact aggregation.

   Aggregate expenditure shares, say w, are obtained by multiplying individual expenditure shares by expenditure for each consuming unit, adding over all consuming units, and dividing by aggregate expenditure

$$W = \frac{\sum Y_j w_j}{\sum Y_j}.$$ (3.9)

The aggregate expenditure shares can be written:

$$w = \frac{1}{B}\left(\alpha_p + \beta_{pp}\ln p - \beta_{pp}\iota\frac{\sum Y_j \ln Y_j}{\sum Y_j} + \beta_{pA}\frac{\sum Y_j A_j}{\sum Y_j}\right)$$ (3.10)

Aggregate expenditure shares depend on prices p. They also depend on the distribution of expenditures over all consuming units through the function $(\sum Y_j \ln Y_j)/\sum Y_j$, which may be regarded as a statistic of the distribution. This single statistic summarizes the impact of changes in the distribution of expenditures among individual consuming units on aggregate expenditure allocation. Finally, aggregate expenditure shares depend on the distribution of expenditures among demographic groups through the functions $\{\sum Y_j A_j / \sum Y_j\}$, which may be regarded as statistics of the joint distribution of expenditures and attributes. Since the attributes are represented as dummy variables, equal to one for a consuming unit with that characteristic and zero otherwise, these functions are equal to the shares of the corresponding demographic groups in aggregate expenditure. We conclude that aggregate expenditure patterns depend on the distribution of expenditure over all consuming units through the statistic $(\sum Y_j \ln Y_j)/\sum Y_j$ and the distribution among demographic groups through the statistics $\{\sum Y_j A_j / \sum Y_j\}$.

Our model of individual consumer behavior is based on two-stage allocation. In the first stage, total expenditure is allocated among N commodity groups. In the second stage, total expenditure on each commodity group is allocated among the individual commodities within each group.[26] We have characterized the behavior of the individual consumer in terms of properties of the indirect utility function. In addition to the properties of homogeneity, monotonicity, and quasi-convexity, the indirect utility function that underlies the two-stage allocation process is homothetically separable in prices of the individual commodities.

We can regard each of the prices of commodity groups $\{p_n\}$ as a function of the prices of individual commodities within the group. These functions must be homogeneous of degree one, nondecreasing, and concave in the prices of the individual commodities. We can consider specific forms for price indexes for each commodity group. If each of these prices is a translog function of its components, we can express the difference between successive logarithms of the price of each commodity group as a weighted average of the differences between successive logarithms of prices of individual commodities within the group with weights given by the average value shares. We refer to these expressions for the prices of the N commodity groups $\{p_n\}$ as *translog prices indexes* for these groups.[27]

2.3.2   Integrability

Systems of individual expenditure shares for consuming units with identical demographic characteristics can be recovered in one and only one way from the system of aggregate expenditure shares under exact aggregation. This makes it possible to employ all the implications of the theory of individual consumer behavior in specifying an econometric model of aggregate expenditure allocation. If a system of individual expenditure shares can be generated from an indirect utility function by means of the logarithmic form of Roy's identity, we say that the system is integrable. A complete set of conditions for integrability, expressed in terms of the system of individual expenditure shares, is the following:

   1. *Homogeneity.* The individual expenditure shares are homogeneous of degree zero in prices and expenditure.

   We can write the individual expenditure shares in the form:

$$w_j = \frac{1}{B} \left(\alpha_p + \beta_{pp} \ln p - \beta_{pY} \ln Y_j + \beta_{pA} A_j \right) \quad (j = 1, 2, \dots, J)$$

where the parameters $\{\beta_{pY}\}$ are constant and the same for all consuming units. Homogeneity implies that this vector must satisfy the restrictions:

$$\beta_{pY} = \beta_{pp} \iota. \tag{3.11}$$

Given the exact aggregation restriction, there are $N - 1$ restrictions implied by homogeneity.

   2. *Summability.* The sum of the individual expenditure shares over all commodity groups is equal to unity:

$\sum w_{nj} = 1 \quad (j = 1, 2, \ldots, J)$.

We can write the denominator B in the form:

$B = -1 + \beta_{Yp} \ln p$

where the parameters $\{\beta_{Yp}\}$ are constant and the same for all commodity groups and all consuming units. Summability implies that these parameters must satisfy the restrictions

$\beta_{Yp} = \iota' \beta_{pp}$.   (3.12)

Given the exact aggregation restrictions, there are $N - 1$ restrictions implied by summability.

3. *Symmetry.* The matrix of compensated own- and cross-price effects must be symmetric.

Imposing homogeneity and summability restrictions, we can write the individual expenditure shares in the form:

$$w_j = \frac{1}{B}\left(\alpha_p + \beta_{pp} \ln \frac{p}{Y_j} + \beta_{pA} A_j\right) \quad (j = 1, 2, \ldots, J)$$

where the denominator B can be written:

$B = -1 + \iota' \beta_{pp} \ln p$.

The typical element of the matrix of uncompensated own- and cross-price effects takes the form:

$$\frac{\partial x_{nj}}{\partial(p_m/Y_j)} = \frac{1}{(p_n/Y_j)(p_m/Y_j)}\left[\frac{1}{B}(\beta_{nm} - w_{nj}\beta_{Ym}) - \delta_{nm}w_{nj}\right]$$

$(n, m = 1, 2, \ldots, N; \; j = 1, 2, \ldots, J)$

where

$\beta_{Ym} = \sum \beta_{nm} \qquad (m = 1, 2, \ldots, N)$

$\delta_{nm} = 0 \quad$ if $\; n \neq m$

$\qquad = 1 \quad$ if $\; n = m \; (n, m = 1, 2, \ldots, N)$.

The corresponding element of the matrix of compensated own- and cross-price effects takes the form:

$$\frac{\partial x_{nj}}{\partial(p_m/Y_j)} - x_{mj} \sum \frac{\partial x_{nj}}{\partial(p_1/Y_j)} \cdot \frac{p_1}{Y_j}$$

$$= \frac{1}{(p_n/Y_j)(p_m/Y_j)} \left[\frac{1}{B}(\beta_{nm} - w_{nj}\beta_{Ym}) - \delta_{nm}w_{nj} \right]$$

$$- x_{mj} \sum \frac{1}{(p_{n/Y_j})(p_{l/Y_j})} \left[\frac{1}{B}(\beta_{nl} - w_{nj}\beta_{Yl}) - \delta_{nl}w_{nj} \right] \frac{p_l}{Y_j}$$

$$(n, m = 1, 2, \ldots, N; \; j = 1, 2, \ldots, J).$$

The full matrix of compensated own- and cross-price effects, say S_j, becomes

$$S_j = P_j^{-1} \left[\frac{1}{B}(\beta_{pp} - w_j\iota'\beta_{pp} - \beta_{pp}\iota w_j' + w_j\iota'\beta_{pp}\iota w_j') + w_jw_j' - W_j \right] P_j^{-1}$$

$$(j = 1, 2, \ldots, J) \qquad\qquad (3.13)$$

where

$$P_j^{-1} = \begin{bmatrix} \dfrac{1}{p_{1/Y_j}} & 0 & \cdots & 0 \\ 0 & \dfrac{1}{p_2/Y_j} & \cdots & 0 \\ \vdots & \vdots & & \vdots \\ 0 & 0 & \cdots & \dfrac{1}{p_{N/Y_j}} \end{bmatrix}, \quad W_j = \begin{bmatrix} w_{1j} & 0 & \cdots & 0 \\ 0 & w_{2j} & \cdots & 0 \\ \vdots & \vdots & & \vdots \\ 0 & 0 & \cdots & w_{Nj} \end{bmatrix}$$

$$(j = 1, 2, \ldots, J).$$

The matrices $\{S_j\}$ must be symmetric for all consuming units.

If the system of individual expenditure shares is to be generated from a translog indirect utility function, a necessary and sufficient condition for symmetry is that the matrix β_{pp} must be symmetric. Without imposing the condition that this matrix is symmetric we can write the individual expenditure shares in the form:

$$w_j = \frac{1}{B}\left(\alpha_p + \beta_{pp}\ln\frac{p}{Y_j} + \beta_{pA}A_j\right) \; (j = 1, 2, \ldots, J).$$

Symmetry implies that the matrix of parameters β_{pp} must satisfy the restrictions

$$\beta_{pp} = \beta'_{pp} \, . \tag{3.14}$$

The total number of symmetry restrictions is $\dfrac{1}{2} N(N - 1)$.

4. *Nonnegativity.* The individual expenditure shares must be non-negative

$$w_{nj} \geqq 0 \quad (N = 1, 2, \ldots, N; \, j = 1, 2, \ldots, J) \, .$$

By summability the individual expenditure shares sum to unity, so that we can write

$$w_j \geq 0 \quad (J = 1, 2, \ldots, J)$$

where $w_j \geqq 0$ implies $w_{nj} \geq 0$, $(n = 1, 2, \ldots, N)$ and $w_j \neq 0$.

Nonnegativity of the individual expenditure shares is implied by monotonicity of the indirect utility function

$$\frac{\partial \ln U_j}{\partial \ln (p/Y_j)} \leqq 0 \quad (j = 1, 2, \ldots, J).$$

For the translog indirect utility function the conditions for monotonicity take the form:

$$\frac{\partial \ln U_j}{\partial \ln (p/Y_j)} = \alpha_p + \beta_{pp} \ln \frac{p}{Y_j} + \beta_{pA} A_j \leqq 0 \quad (j = 1, 2, \ldots, J) \, . \tag{3.15}$$

Summability implies that not all the expenditure shares are zero, so that

$$B = -1 + \iota' \beta_{pp} \ln p < 0 \, . \tag{3.16}$$

Since the translog indirect utility function is quadratic in the logarithms of prices in $\ln p$, we can always choose the prices so that the individual expenditure shares violate the nonnegativity conditions. Alternatively, we can say that it is possible to choose the prices so the monotonicity of the indirect utility function is violated. Accordingly, we cannot impose restrictions on the parameters of the translog indirect utility function that would imply nonnegativity of the individual expenditure shares or monotonicity of the indirect utility function for all prices and expenditure. Instead, we consider restrictions on the parameters that imply quasi-convexity of the indirect utility function or monotonicity of the system of individual demand functions for all nonnegative expenditure shares.

5. *Monotonicity.* The matrix of compensated own-and cross-price effects must be nonpositive-definite.

We first impose homogeneity, summability, and symmetry restrictions on the expenditure shares. We restrict consideration to values of the prices p, expenditures $\{Y_j\}$, and attributes $\{A_j\}$ for which the individual expenditure shares satisfy the nonnegativity restrictions, so that $w_j \geqq 0$, $(j = 1, 2, \ldots, J)$. The summability restrictions imply that $\iota' w_j = 1$, $(j = 1, 2, \ldots, J)$. We can write the matrix of price effects in the form:

$$S_j = P_j^{-1} \left[\frac{1}{B} (I - \iota w_j')' \beta_{pp}(I - \iota w_j') + w_j w_j' - W_j \right] P_j^{-1} \quad (j = 1, 2, \ldots, J).$$

A necessary and sufficient condition for monotonicity of the systems of individual expenditure shares is that the matrices

$$\left\{ \frac{1}{B} (I - \iota w_j') \beta_{pp}(I - \iota w_j') + w_j w_j' - W_j \right\}$$

are nonpositive-definite for all expenditure shares satisfying the non-negativity and summability conditions.

We next consider restrictions on the parameters of the translog indirect utility function implied by monotonicity of the individual expenditure shares. If $\iota' \beta_{pp} = 0$, the denominator B is independent of prices and the translog indirect utility function is homothetic; otherwise, for a given value of the individual expenditure shares we can make the denominator B as large or as small as we wish by a suitable choice of prices p. A necessary and sufficient condition for monotonicity of the systems of individual expenditure shares is that the matrices

$$\left\{ \frac{1}{B} (I - \iota w')' \beta_{pp}(I - \iota w_j') \right\} \quad \text{and} \quad \{w_j w_j' - W_j\}$$

are both nonpositive-definite.

The matrices $\{w_j w_j' - W_j\}$ are nonpositive-definite for all expenditure shares satisfying the nonnegativity and summability restrictions. A sufficient condition for nonpositive definiteness of the matrices

$$\left\{ \frac{1}{B}(I - \iota w_j')' \beta_{pp}(I - \iota w_j') \right\}$$

is that the matrix β_{pp} is nonnegative-definite. However, if the quadratic form $z' \beta_{pp} z$ achieves the value zero, which must be a minimum, for any vector z not equal to zero, then z is a characteristic vector of β_{pp} corresponding to a zero characteristic value if β_{pp} is nonnegative-definite. Hence, $\beta_{pp} \iota = 0$ and the translog indirect utility function is homothetic.

Next, we introduce the definition due to Martos (1969) of a *merely positive-subdefinite matrix*. A merely positive-subdefinite matrix, say P, is a real symmetric matrix such that

$$x' P x < 0$$

implies $Px \geq 0$ or $Px \leq 0$ and P is not nonnegative-definite. Similarly, a *strictly merely positive-subdefinite* matrix is a real symmetric matrix such that

$$x' P x < 0$$

implies $Px > 0$ or $Px < 0$. A complete characterization of merely positive-subdefinite matrices has been provided by Cottle and Ferland (1972), who have shown that such matrices must satisfy the conditions:

1. P consists of only nonpositive elements; and
2. P has exactly one negative characteristic value.

A complete characterization of strictly merely positive-subdefinite matrices has been provided by Martos (1969), who has shown that a strictly merely positive-subdefinite matrix must satisfy the additional condition:

3. P does not contain a row (or column) of zeros.

We observe that this condition does not imply in itself that a strictly merely positive-subdefinite matrix is nonsingular.

A necessary and sufficient condition for monotonicity is either that the translog indirect utility function is homothetic or that β_{pp}^{-1} exists and is strictly merely positive-subdefinite. To impose restrictions on the matrix β_{pp} implied by monotonicity of the systems of individual expenditure shares, we first provide a Cholesky factorization of this matrix

$$\beta_{pp} = TDT'$$

where T is a unit lower triangular matrix and D is a diagonal matrix.

Since the matrix β_{pp}^{-1} is strictly merely positive-subdefinite, all the elements of this matrix are nonpositive. We can express the nonpositivity constraints on these elements in terms of the elements of the Cholesky factorization of the matrix β_{pp}, where:

$$\beta_{pp} = TDT'\ .$$

Finally, we include restrictions on the Cholesky values; the matrix β_{pp} has exactly one negative Cholesky value, the last in order, and $N - 1$ positive Cholesky values. Combining these restrictions with nonpositivity restrictions on the elements of β_{pp}^{-1}, we obtain a complete set of restrictions implied by the monotonicity of the system of individual expenditure shares.

Similarly, we can provide a complete set of conditions for integrability of the system of individual expenditure shares for the second stage of the two-stage allocation process. For example, the individual expenditure shares for commodities within each group are homogeneous of degree zero in commodity prices, the sum of these shares is equal to unity, and the matrix of compensated own- and cross-price effects must be symmetric for each group. The restrictions are analogous to those for price indexes we have employed in models of producer behavior.

The individual expenditure shares must be nonnegative for each commodity group; as before, we can always choose prices so that the monotonicity of the indirect utility function for each commodity group is violated. We can consider restrictions on the parameters that imply quasi-convexity of the homothetic translog indirect utility function or monotonicity of the system of individual demand functions for all nonnegative expenditure shares for each commodity group. Again, the conditons for monotonicity for expenditure shares that satisfy the nonnegativity restrictions are precisely analogous to those we have employed for models of producer behavior.

2.3.3   Stochastic Specifications

The model of consumer behavior presented in section 2.3.2 is generated from a translog indirect utility function for each consuming unit. To formulate an econometric model of consumer behavior, we add a stochastic component to the equations for the individual expenditure shares. We associate this component with unobservable random disturbances at the level of the individual consuming unit. The consuming unit maximizes utility, but the expenditure shares are chosen with a random disturbance. This disturbance may result from errors in implementation of consumption plans, random elements in the determination of consumer preferences not reflected in our list of attributes of consuming units, or errors of measurement of the individual expenditure shares. We assume that each of the equations for the individual shares has two additive components. The first is a nonrandom function of prices, expenditure, and demographic characteristics. The second is an unobservable random disturbance that is functionally independent of these variables.

To represent our econometric model of consumer behavior we introduce some additional notation. We consider observations on expenditure patterns by J consuming units, indexed by $j = 1, 2, \ldots, J$, for T time periods, indexes by $t = 1, 2, \ldots, T$. The vector of expenditure shares for the jth consuming unit in the tth time period is denoted w_{jt}, $(j = 1, 2, \ldots, J; t = 1, 2, \ldots, T)$. Similarly, expenditure for the jth unit on all commodity groups in the tth time period is denoted Y_{jt}, $(j = 1, 2, \ldots, J; t = 1, 2, \ldots, T)$. The vector of prices faced by all consuming units in the tth time period is denoted p_t $(t = 1, 2, \ldots, T)$. Similarly, the vector of logarithms of prices in the tth time period is denoted in $\ln p_t$ $(t = 1, 2, \ldots, T)$. The vector of logarithms of ratios of prices to expenditure for the jth consuming unit in the t time period is denoted $\ln(p_t/Y_{jt})$, $(j = 1, 2, \ldots, J; t = 1, 2, \ldots, T)$.

Using our notation, the individual expenditure shares can be written:

$$w_{jt} = \frac{1}{B_t}\left(\alpha_p + \beta_{pp} \ln \frac{p_t}{Y_{jt}} + \beta_{pA} A_j\right) + \varepsilon_{jt} \ (j = 1, 2, \ldots, J; t = 1, 2, \ldots, T) \quad (3.17)$$

where

$$B_t = -1 + \iota'\beta_{pp} \ln p_t \quad (t = 1, 2, \ldots, T)$$

and $\{\varepsilon_{jt}\}$ are the vectors of unobservable random disturbances for all J consuming units and all T time periods. Since the individual expenditure shares for all commodities sum to unity for each consuming unit in each time period, the unobservable random disturbances for all commodities sum to zero for each unit in each time period:

$$\iota' \varepsilon_{jt} = 0 \quad (j = 1, 2, \ldots, J; t = 1, 2, \ldots, T). \tag{3.18}$$

These disturbances are not distributed independently.

We assume that the unobservable random disturbances for all commodities have expected value equal to zero for all observations:

$$E(\varepsilon_{jt}) = 0 \quad (j = 1, 2, \ldots, J; t = 1, 2, \ldots, T). \tag{3.19}$$

We also assume that these disturbances have the same covariance matrix for all observations:

$$V(\varepsilon_{jt}) = \Omega^{\varepsilon}, \quad (j = 1, 2, \ldots, J; t, = 1, 2, \ldots, T).$$

Since the disturbances sum to zero for each observation, this matrix is nonnegative-definite with rank at most equal to $N - 1$, where N is the number of commodities. We assume that the covariance matrix has rank equal to $N - 1$.

Finally, we assume that disturbances corresponding to distinct observations are uncorrelated. Under this assumption the covariance matrix of the disturbances for all consuming units at a given point of time has the Kronecker product form:

$$V \begin{pmatrix} \varepsilon_{1t} \\ \varepsilon_{2t} \\ \vdots \\ \varepsilon_{jt} \end{pmatrix} = \Omega_t \otimes I. \tag{3.20}$$

The covariance matrix of the disturbances for all time periods for a given individual has an analogous form. The unknown parameters of the system of equations determining the individual expenditure shares can be estimated from time series data on individual expenditure shares, prices, total expenditure, and demographic characteristics.

At any point of time, the aggregate expenditure shares are equal to the individual expenditure shares multiplied by the ratio of individual expenditure to aggregate expenditure. Although the data for individual consuming units and for the aggregate of all consuming units are based on the same definitions, the aggregate data are not obtained by summing over the data for individuals. Observations on individual consuming units are based on a random sample from the population of all consuming units. Observations for the aggregate of all consuming units are constructed from data on production of commodities and on consumption of these commodities by households and by other consuming units such as businesses, governments, and the rest of the world. Accordingly, we must introduce an additional source of random error in the equations for the aggregate expenditure shares, corresponding to unobservable errors of measurement in the observations that underlie the aggregate expenditure shares.

We assume that each of the equations for the aggregate expenditure shares has three additive components. The first is a weighted average of the nonrandom functions of prices, expenditure, and demographic characteristics that determine the individual expenditure shares. The second is a weighted average of the unobservable random disturbances in equations for the individual expenditure shares. The third is a weighted average of the unobservable random errors of measurement in the observations on the aggregate expenditure shares.

Denoting the vector of aggregate expenditure shares at time t by w_t $(t = 1, 2, \ldots, T)$, we can express these shares in the form:

$$
w_t = \frac{1}{B_t} \left(\alpha_p + \beta_{pp} \ln p_t \right) - \frac{1}{B_t} \beta_{pp} \iota \frac{\sum_{j=1}^{J} Y_{jt} \ln Y_{jt}}{\sum_{j=1}^{J} Y_{jt}}
$$

$$
+ \frac{1}{B_t} \beta_{pA} \frac{\sum_{j=1}^{J} Y_{jt} A_j}{\sum_{j=1}^{J} Y_{jt}} + \varepsilon_t \quad (t = 1, 2, \ldots, T) \tag{3.21}
$$

where

$$
B_1 = -1 + \iota' \beta_{pp} \ln p_t \quad (t = 1, 2, \ldots, T)
$$

as before, and $\{\varepsilon_t\}$ are the vectors of unobservable random disturbances for the tth time period.

The aggregate disturbances ε_t can be expressed in the form:

$$
\varepsilon_t = \frac{\sum_{j=1}^{J} Y_{jt} \varepsilon_{jt}}{\sum_{j=1}^{J} Y_{jt}} + \frac{\sum_{j=1}^{J} Y_{jt} v_{jt}}{\sum_{j=1}^{J} Y_{jt}} \quad (t = 1, 2, \ldots, T) \tag{3.22}
$$

where $\{v_{jt}\}$ are the vectors of errors of measurement that underlie the data on the aggregate expenditure shares. Since the random disturbances for all commodities sum to zero in each time period,

$$
\iota' \varepsilon_t = 0 \quad (j = 1, 2, \ldots, J; t = 1, 2, \ldots, T) \tag{3.23}
$$

these disturbances are not distributed independently.

We assume that the errors of measurement that underlie the data on the aggregate expenditure shares have expected value equal to zero for all observations:

$$E(\nu_{jt}) = 0 \quad (j = 1, 2, \ldots, J; t = 1, 2, \ldots, T).$$

We also assume that these errors have the same covariance matrix for all observations:

$$V(\nu_{jt}) = \Omega_\nu \quad (j = 1, 2, \ldots, J; t = 1, 2, \ldots, T)$$

and that the rank of this matrix is equal to $N - 1$.

If the errors of measurement are distributed independently of expenditure and of the disturbances in the equations for the individual expenditure shares, the aggregate disturbances have expected value equal to zero for all time periods:

$$E(\varepsilon_t) = 0 \quad (t = 1, 2, \ldots, T) \tag{3.24}$$

and have a covariance matrix given by

$$V(\varepsilon_t) = \frac{\sum_{j=1}^{J} Y_{jt}^2}{(\sum_{j=1}^{J} Y_{jt})^2} \Omega_\varepsilon + \frac{\sum_{j=1}^{J} Y_{jt}^2}{(\sum_{j=1}^{J} Y_{jt})^2} \Omega_\nu \quad (t = 1, 2, \ldots, T)$$

so that the aggregate disturbances for different time periods are heteroscedastic.

We can correct for heteroscedasticity of the aggregate disturbances by transforming the observations on the aggregate expenditure shares as follows:

$$\rho_t w_t = \frac{\rho_t}{B_t} (\alpha_p + \beta_{pp} \ln p_t) - \frac{\rho_t}{B_t} \beta_{pp} \iota \frac{\sum_{j=1}^{J} Y_{jt} \ln Y_{jt}}{\sum_{j=1}^{J} Y_{jt}}$$

$$+ \frac{\rho_t}{B_t} \beta_{pA} \frac{\sum_{j=1}^{J} Y_{jt} A_j}{\sum_{j=1}^{J} Y_{jt}} + \rho_t \varepsilon_t \quad (t = 1, 2, \ldots, T)$$

where

$$\rho_t^2 = \frac{(\sum_{j=1}^{J} Y_{jt})^2}{\sum_{j=1}^{J} Y_{jt}^2} \quad (t = 1, 2, \ldots, T).$$

The covariance matrix of the transformed disturbances, say Ω, becomes

$$V(\rho_t \varepsilon_t) = \Omega_\varepsilon + \Omega_\nu = \Omega.$$

This matrix is nonnegative-definite with rank equal to $N - 1$. Finally, we assume that the errors of measurement corresponding to distinct observations are uncorrelated. Under this assumption the covariance matrix of the transformed disturbances at all points of time has the Kronecker product form

$$
V \begin{pmatrix} \rho_1 \varepsilon_1 \\ \rho_2 \varepsilon_2 \\ \vdots \\ \rho_T \varepsilon_T \end{pmatrix} = \Omega \otimes I .
\tag{3.25}
$$

We next discuss the estimation of the translog model of aggregate consumer behavior, combining a single cross section of observations on individual expenditure patterns with several time series observations on aggregate expenditure patterns. Suppose first that we have a random sample of observations on individual expenditure patterns at a given point of time. Prices for all consumers are the same. The translog model (3.17) takes the form

$$
w_j = \gamma_1 + \gamma_2 \ln Y_j + \Gamma_3 A_j + \varepsilon_j \quad (j = 1, 2, \ldots, J)
\tag{3.26}
$$

where we drop the time subscript. In this model γ_1 and γ_2 are vectors of unknown parameters and Γ_3 is a matrix of unknown parameters. Random sampling implies that disturbances for difference individuals are uncorrelated. We assume that the data matrix with $(1, \ln Y_j, A_j)$ as its jth row is of full rank.

The parameters of γ_1, γ_2, and Γ_3 are identified in the cross section. Moreover, the model (3.26) is a multivariate regression model, except that the vector of disturbances ε_j has a singular distribution. A model where one equation has been dropped is a multivariate regression model so that the unique, minimum-variance, unbiased estimator of the unknown parameters γ_1, γ_2, and Γ_3 is obtained by applying ordinary least squares to each equation separately.

To link the parameters γ_1, γ_2, and Γ_3 to the parameters of the translog model of aggregate consumer behavior, we first observe that the parameters of the translog model can be identified only up to a normalization, since multiplying all of the parameters by the same nonzero constant leaves the expenditure shares unchanged. The usual normalization is $\iota' \alpha_p = -1$, giving the unknown parameters the same sign as those in the translog indirect utility function. Second, without loss of generality we can take the prices of all goods to be equal to unity for a particular period of time. In the application to a single cross section, we take all prices at the date of the survey to be equal to unity. The prices for all other time periods are expressed relative to prices of this base period.

Given the normalization of the parameters and the choice of base period for measurement of the prices, we obtain the following correspondence between the unknown parameters of the cross-section model and the parameters of the translog model of aggregate consumer behavior:

$$\gamma_1 = -\alpha_p$$
$$\gamma_2 = \beta_{pp}\iota$$
$$\Gamma_3 = -\beta_{pA} \tag{3.27}$$

The constants α_p and the parameters associated with demographic characteristics of individual households β_{pA} can be estimated from a single cross section. The parameters associated with total expenditure $\beta_{pp}\iota$ can also be estimated from a single cross section. The remaining parameters, those associated with prices, can be estimated from time series data on aggregate expenditure patterns. Since the model is linear in parameters for a cross section, we can use ordinary least-squares regression to estimate the impact of the demographic structure on aggregate expenditure patterns.

After correction for heteroscedasticity the translog model of aggregate consumer behavior is given by:

$$\rho_t w_t = \frac{\rho_t}{B_t}(\alpha_p + \beta_{pp}\ln p_t) - \frac{\rho_t}{B_t}\beta_{pp}\iota\frac{\sum_{j=1}^{J}Y_{jt}\ln Y_{jt}}{\sum_{j=1}^{J}Y_{jt}}$$
$$+ \frac{\rho_t}{B_t}\beta_{pA}\frac{\sum_{j=1}^{J}Y_{jt}A_j}{\sum_{j=1}^{J}Y_{jt}} + \rho_1\varepsilon_t \quad (t = 1, 2, \ldots, T) \tag{3.28}$$

where

$$B_t = -1 + \iota'\beta_{pp}\ln p_t \quad (t = 1, 2, \ldots, T)$$

and ε_t is a vector of unobservable random disturbances. We have time series observations on prices p_t, the expenditure statistic $\sum Y_{jt} \ln Y_{jt} / \sum Y_{jt}$, the vector of attribute-expenditure statistics $\{\sum Y_{jt} A_j / \sum Y_{jt}\}$, and the heteroscedasticity correction ρ_t $(t = 1, 2, \ldots, T)$.

The translog model in (3.28) might appear to be a nonlinear regression model with additive errors, so that nonlinear regression techniques could be employed.[28] However, the existence of supply functions for all commodities makes it more appropriate to treat some of the right-side variables as endogenous. For example, shifts in prices due to demand-supply interactions may cause significant shifts in the distribution of expenditure. To obtain a consistent estimator for this model, we could specify supply functions for all commodities and estimate the complete model by full-information maximum likelihood.

Alternatively, to estimate the model in (3.28) we can consider limited information techniques utilizing instrumental variables. In particular, we can introduce a sufficient number of instrumental variables to identify all parameters. We estimate the model by nonlinear three-stage least squares (NL3SLS).[29] Application of NL3SLS to our model would be straightforward except for the fact that the covariance matrix of the disturbances is singular. We obtain NL3SLS estimators of the complete system by dropping one equation and estimating the resulting system of $N - 1$ equations by NL3SLS; we derive an estimator for parameters of the remaining equation from the conditions for summability. The parameter estimates are invariant to the choice of the equation omitted in the model for aggregate time series data and the model for individual cross-section data.

In the analysis of the model to be applied to cross-section data on individual expenditure patterns, we have assumed that individual disturbances and individual total expenditure are uncorrelated. If aggregate demand-supply interactions induce shifts in the distribution of expenditure, the zero correlation assumption cannot be strictly valid for all consumers at the individual level. However, the cross section is a random sample that includes a minute percentage of the total population, so that it is reasonable to assume that the correlations between total expenditure and disturbances at the individual level are negligible.

The NL3SLS estimator can be employed to estimate all parameters of the model of aggregate expenditures, provided that these parameters are identified. Since we wish to obtain a detailed characterization of the impact of changes in the demographic structure of the population, the model (3.28) contains a large number of parameters and requires a large number of time series observations for identification. The technical conditions for identification are quite complicated. A sufficient condition for under identification is that the number of instruments is less than the number of parameters. For the translog model of aggregate consumer behavior, this occurs if:

$$(N-1)(1+S) = \frac{(N+1)N}{2} - 1 > (N-1) - (V,T) \qquad (3.29)$$

where N is the number of commodities, S is the number of components of A_{jt}, and V is the number of instruments. The left-hand side of (3.29) is the number of free parameters of the translog model under symmetry of the matrix β_{pp} and the right-hand side is the number of instruments, assuming that no collinearity exists among the instruments.

Condition (3.29) is met in our application, so that not all parameters are identified in the model for aggregate time series data. We next consider methods utilizing individual cross-section data together with aggregate time series data to obtain identification. As we have seen, cross-section data can be used to identify the constant α_p, the coefficients of total expenditure $-\beta_{pp}\iota$, and the demographic coefficients β_{pA}. Only the price coefficients β_{pp} must be identified from aggregate time series data. A necessary condition for identification of these parameters is:

$$\frac{(N-1)N}{2} < (N-1) - (V,T) \qquad (3.30)$$

or

$$\frac{N}{2} < -(V,T) . \qquad (3.31)$$

This condition is met in our application. Sufficient conditions amount to the nonlinear analog of the absence of multicollinearity. These conditions are quite weak and hold in our application.

In order to pool cross-section and time series data, we combine the model for individual expenditures and the model for aggregate expenditure and apply the method of NL3SLS to the whole system. The instruments for the cross-section model are the micro data themselves; for the aggregate model, the instruments are variables that can be taken to be distributed independently of the aggregate disturbances. The data sets are pooled statistically, where estimates of the covariance matrix of the aggregate disturbances from time series data and the covariance matrix of the individual disturbances from cross-section data are used to weight aggregate and cross-section data, respectively. The resulting estimator is consistent and asymptotically efficient in the class of instrumental variable estimators utilizing the instruments we have chosen.

2.3.4   Summary and Conclusion

In this section, we have presented a model of aggregate consumer behavior based on transcendental logarithmic or translog indirect utility functions for all consuming units. These indirect utility functions incorporate restrictions on individual behavior that result from maximization of a utility function subject to a budget constraint. Our model of individual consumer behavior is based on a two-stage allocation process. For each stage of the allocation process, the individual consuming unit has indirect utility functions that are homogeneous of degree zero in prices and expenditure, nonincreasing in prices and nondecreasing in expenditure, and quasi-convex in prices and expenditure.

To incorporate differences in individual preferences into our model of aggregate consumer behavior, we allow the indirect utility functions for all consuming units to depend on attributes, such as demographic characteristics that vary among individuals. Each attribute is represented by a dummy variable equal to unity when the consuming unit has the corresponding characteristic and zero otherwise.

Given translog indirect utility functions for each consuming unit, we derive the expenditure shares for that unit by means of Roy's Identity. For the first stage of the two-stage allocation process, this results in expenditure shares for commodity groups that can be expressed as ratios of two functions that are linear in the logarithms of ratios of price indexes to total expenditure and in attributes. The denominators for these ratios are functions that are the same for all commodity groups.

Under exact aggregation, the individual expenditure shares are linear in function of attributes and total expenditure. The denominators are independent of total expenditure and attributes and are the same for all individuals. The translog indirect utility functions for the second stage of the two-stage allocation process correspond to homothetic preferences. This results in expenditure shares for individual commodities that are linear in the logarithms of prices; these shares satisfy the conditions required for exact aggregation.

To derive aggregate expenditure shares for commodity groups, we multiply the individual expenditure shares by total expenditure for each consuming unit, sum over all consuming units, and divide by aggregate expenditure. The aggregate expenditure shares, like the individual shares, can be expressed as ratios of two functions. The denominators are the same as for individual expenditure shares. The numerators are linear in the logarithms of price indexes of all commodity groups, in a statistic of the distribution of expenditure over all consuming units $\{\sum Y_j \ln Y_j / \sum Y_j\}$, and in the shares of all demographic groups in aggregate expenditure $\{\sum Y_j A_j / \sum Y_j\}$.

The individual expenditure shares are homogeneous of degree zero in prices and expenditure. Given the restrictions implied by exact aggregation, this implies an additional $N-2$ restrictions on the parameters of the translog indirect utility functions, where N is the number of commodities. Second, the sum of individual expenditure shares over all commodity groups is equal to unity. Again, given the exact aggregation restrictions, there are $N-2$ additional restrictions implied by summability. Third, the matrix of compensated own- and cross-price effects must be symmetric. This implies $\frac{1}{2} N(N-1) - 1$ additional restrictions on the parameters of the translog indirect utility functions.

Monotonicity of the indirect utility functions implies that the individual expenditure shares must be nonnegative. Similarly, quasi-convexity of the indirect utility functions implies that the individual expenditure shares must be monotonic or, equivalently, that the matrix of compensated own- and cross-price substitution effects must be nonpositive-definite. It is always possible to choose prices so that monotonicity of the indirect utility functions or nonnegativity of the individual expenditure shares is violated. Accordingly, we consider restrictions that imply monotonicity of the expenditure shares whenever they are nonnegative.

2.4   Empirical Results

In sections 2.2.2 and 2.2.3 we have presented econometric models of producer and consumer behavior suitable for incorporation into general equilibrium models of the U.S. economy. The most important innovation in these econometric models is that they encompass all restrictions on the parameters implied by the economic theories of producer and consumer behavior. These restrictions take the form of equalities required for monotonicity subject to nonnegativity restrictions.

Our model of producer behavior is based on industries as producing units. Each industry behaves like an individual producer, maximizing profit subject to a production function characterized by constant returns to scale. The allocation of the value of output among inputs can be generated from a translog price function for each industry. In addition, our model of producer behavior determines the rate of technical change endogenously for each industry. Time is included in the price function for each sector as an index of technology.

Our model of consumer behavior is based on households as consuming units. Expenditures within the household are allocated so as to maximize a household welfare function. Each household behaves in the same way as an individual maximizing a utility function subject to a budget constraint. All consuming units are classified by demographic characteristics associated with differences in preferences among households. For each of these characteristics, households are divided among mutually exclusive and exhaustive groups. Each demographic characteristic is represented by a qualitative or dummy variable, equal to unity when the household is in the group and zero otherwise.

2.4.1   Producer Behavior

Our first objective is to present the empirical results of implementing the model of producer behavior described in section 2.2 for 35 industrial sectors of the U.S. This model is based on a two-stage process for the allocation of the value of output in each sector among capital, labor, energy, and materials inputs. The value of inputs from these four commodity groups exhausts the value of the output for each of the 35 sectors. We limit our presentation of empirical results to the first stage of the two-stage process.

To implement our econometric models of production and technical change we have assembled a time series data base for 35 industrial sectors of the U.S. For capital and labor inputs, we have first compiled data by sector on the basis of the classification of economic activities employed in the U.S. Census Bureau's National Income and Product Accounts. We have then transformed these data into a format appropriate for the classification of activities employed in the U.S. Census Bureau's Interindustry Transactions Accounts. For energy and materials inputs, we have compiled data by sector on inter-industry transactions on the basis of the classification of activities employed in the U.S. Interindustry Transactions Accounts.[30]

The endogenous variables in our models of producer behavior are value shares of sectoral inputs for four commodity groups and the sectoral rate of technical change. We can estimate four equations for each industry, corresponding to three of the value shares and the rate of technical change. As unknown parameters we have three elements of the vector $\{\alpha_p^i\}$, the scalar $\{\alpha_t^i\}$, six share elasticities in the matrix $\{\beta_{pp}^i\}$, which is constrained to be symmetric, three biases of technical change in the vector $\{\beta_{pt}^i\}$, and the scalar $\{\beta_{tt}^i\}$, so that we have a total of fourteen unknown parameters for each industry. We estimate these parameters from time series data for the period 1958–74 for each industry, subject to the inequality restrictions implied by monotonicity of the sectoral input value shares. The results are given in table 2.4.1.

Our interpretations of the empirical results reported in table 2.4.1 begins with an analysis of the estimates of the parameters $\{\alpha_p^i, \alpha_t^i\}$. If all other parameters were set equal to zero, the sectoral price functions would be linear-logarithmic in prices and linear in time. The parameters $\{\alpha_p^i\}$ would correspond to constant-value shares of inputs and the negative of the parameters $\{\alpha_t^i\}$ to constant rates of technical change. The parameters $\{\alpha_p^i\}$ are nonnegative for all 35 sectors included in our study and are estimated very precisely. The parameters $\{\alpha_t^i\}$ are estimated less precisely and are negative in fifteen sectors and are positive in twenty sectors.

The estimated share elasticities with respect to price, $\{\beta_{pp}^i\}$, describe the implications of patterns of substitution for the distribution of the value of output among capital, labor, energy, and materials inputs. Positive share elasticities imply that the corresponding value shares increase with an increase in price; negative share elasticities imply that the value shares decrease with price; zero share elasticities correspond to value shares that are independent of price. The concavity constraints on the sectoral price functions contribute substantially to the precision of our estimates, but require that the share of each input be nonincreasing in the price of the input itself.

By imposing monotonicity on the sectoral input value shares or concavity of the sectoral price functions, we have reduced the number of share elasticities to be fitted from 350, or ten for each of our 35 industrial sectors, to 132, or an average of less than five per sector. All share elasticities are constrained to be zero for eleven of the 35

Table 2.4.1

Parameter estimates: sectoral models of production and technical change

Parameter	Agriculture, forestry, and fisheries	Metal mining	Coal mining	Crude petroleum and natural gas	Nonmetallic mining	Construction
AK	.170(.00445)	.216(.0108)	.237(.00643)	.449(.00559)	.270(.00346)	.0686(.000640)
AL	.254(.00475)	.313(.0226)	.469(.0121)	.103(.00272)	.310(.00963)	.439(.00310)
AE	.0243(.000580)	.0393(.00251)	.121(.00279)	.0565(.000676)	.0746(.000921)	.0254(.000393)
AM	.551(.00430)	.432(.0242)	.173(.0102)	.391(.00736)	.345(.00882)	
AT	−.0329(.0546)	.0151(.0602)	.00643(.0757)	.0246(.0759)	.0767(.0271)	.0471(.00565)
BKK						
BKL						
BKE						
BKM						
BKT	−.00247(.000603)	.000775(.00147)	.00868(.000873)	−.0795(.000759)	.00187(.0470)	.000295(.00008680)
BLL	−.220(.0356a)	−.405(.265)	−.433(.0420)			
BLE	−.00158(.00427)	.0255(.0224)	−.0526(.00385)			
BLM	.222(.0342)	.379(.244)	.485(.0459)			
BLT	.00530(.00147)	.0154(.00671)	.00472(.00165)	−.000914(.000369)	−.00189(.00131)	−.00923(.00158)
BEE	−.0000114(.0000620)	−.00161(.00181)	−.00639(.00113)			
BEM	.00159(.00433)	−.0239(.0206)	.0590(.00689)			
BET	.000210(.000175)	−.000104(.000607)	−.00731(.000378)	.000814(.0000916)	.00172(.000125)	−.00159(.000222)
BMM	−.223(.0333)	−.356(.224)	−.544(.0507)			
BMT	−.00798(.00139)	−.0160(.00639)	−.00609(.00138)	.000895(.000998)	−.00170(.00120)	.0105(.00174)
BTT	−.00966(.00741)	.000849(.00815)	.00180(.0103)	.00291(.0103)	.00781(.00364)	.00343(.000771)

Table 2.4.1 (continued)

Parameter	Food and kindred products	Tobacco manufacturers	Textile mill products	Apparel and other fabrics; textile production	Lumber and wood products	Furniture and fixtures
AK	.0548(.000404)	.162(.00238)	.0698(.00158)	.0405(.000285)	.151(.00192)	.0635(.000857)
AL	.146(.00267)	.136(.00345)	.200(.00476)	.306(.00225)	.267(.00583)	.360(.00516)
AE	.0114(.000457)	.00347(.000345)	.0150(.000216)	.00628(.0000910)	.0178(.000828)	.00912(.000217)
AM	.788(.00290)	.699(.00495)	.715(.00634)	.647(.00634)	.647(.00229)	.564(.00530)
AT	.0188(.0115)	.0850(.119)	−.0183(.0126)	−.0126(.0299)	−.00477(.0357)	−.00306(.0203)
BKK						
BKL						
BKE						
BKM						
BKT	−.00130(.0000548)	.000955(.000322)	−.000395(.000214)	.000240(.0000386)	.00456(.000260)	−.000677(.000116)
BLL	−.132(.0205)	−.0269(.0158)	−1.022(.0830)			
BLE	.00631(.00352)	.00126(.00154)	−.0687(.00393)			
BLM	.126(.0214)	.0256(.0157)	1.090(.0814)			
BLT	.00104(.000569)	.00456(.000953)	−.000195(.000646)	−.00232(.0006)	−.00120(.000791)	.0189(.00170)
BEE	−.000301(.000348)	−.0000588(.000143)	−.00185(.000651)	−.00462(.000768)		
BEM	−.00601(.00318)	−.00120(.00140)	.00185(.000651)	.0733(.00463)		
BET	−.0000788(.0000977)	.0000296(.0000914)	.000291(.0000293)	.000267(.00005)	.000625(.000112)	.00144(.0000744)
BMM	−.120(.0226)	−.0244(.0157)	−.00185(.000651)	−1.164(.0794)		
BMT	.000332(.000603)	−.00555(.00107)	.000299(.000860)	.00181(.0000)	−.00399(.000719)	−.01(.00169)
BTT	.00230(.00156)	.0157(.0161)	−.000871(.00168)	−.00203(.00405)	.000383(.00483)	.00110(.00276)

Table 2.4.1 (continued)

Parameter	Paper and allied products	Printing publishing, and allied industries	Chemicals and allied products	Petroleum refining	Rubber and miscellaneous plastic products	Leather and leather products
AK	.111(.000562)	.103(.000741)	.128(.00135)	.105(.00582)	.0982(.00151)	.0467(.00143)
AL	.242(.00292)	.362(.00450)	.201(.00311)	.0670(.00199)	.271(.00334)	.342(.00469)
AE	.0322(.000333)	.00822(.000218)	.0885(.00165)	.599(.00373)	.0261(.000279)	.0795(.000188)
ANI	.615(.00290)	.526(.00494)	.582(.00412)	.229(.00268)	.605(.00431)	.604(.00469)
AT	.0372(.0301)	-.0129(.0233)	.0130(.0206)	.00582(.0375)	.0318(.0291)	-.00105(.0239)
BKK						
BKL						
BKE						
BKM						
BKT	-.00208(.0000762)	.000400(.000101)	-.00545(.000183)	.0001333(.00789)	-.00356(.000204)	-.000401(.000193)
BLL	-.316(.0393)	-.327(.0704)	-.0237(.0449)	-.280(.0208)		
BLE	-.0196(.00578)	-.00875(.00384)	-.000362(.0164)	.0346(.00870)		
BLM	.336(.0382)	.335(.0726)	.0240(.0520)	.246(.0272)		
BLT	.00708(.00107)	.00948(.00234)	-.00241(.00160)	-.00130(.000291)	-.00238(.000453)	-.00141(.000636)
BEE	-.00122(.000772)	-.00339(.00100)	-.00000555(.000499)	-.00428(.00237)		
BEM	.0208(.00654)	.0121(.00436)	.000368(.0169)	-.0304(.00635)		
BET	.00109(.000156)	.000493(.000129)	.00177(.000610)	.000948(.000508)	.0059(.0000378)	.000225(.0000255)
BMM	-.357(.0378)	-.347(.0751)	-.0244(.0631)	-.215(.0325)		
BMT	-.00610(.00104)	-.0104(.00242)	.00608(.00186)	.000217(.000407)	.00535(.000584)	.00159(.000637)
BTT	.00916(.00409)	-.00181(.00316)	.00440(.00281)	.00135(.00509)	.0651(.00395)	-.000777(.00326)

Table 2.4.1 (continued)

Parameter	Stone, clay, and glass products	Primary metal industries	Fabricated metal	Machinery (except electrical)	Electrical machinery	Motor vehicles and motor vehicle equipment
AK	.119(.00139)	.0893(.00110)	.0874(.000893)	.0966(.00211)	.0923(.00187)	.108(.00185)
AL	.371(.00189)	.277(.00302)	.337(.00253)	.311(.00193)	.343(.00342)	.188(.00029)
AE	.0432(.00100)	.0407(.000492)	.0115(.000194)	.0115(.000158)	.0104(.000215)	.00737(.0000757)
AM	.467(.00281)	.593(.00361)	.564(.00293)	.581(.00343)	.554(.00278)	.697(.00429)
AT	.0132(.0180)	−.00898(.0257)	.0312(.0199)	.00187(.0133)	−.00690(.0178)	.0208(.0327)
BKK						
BKL						
BKE						
BKM						
BKT	−.00405(.000189)	−.00226(.000149)	.000220(.000121)	−.00156(.000286)	−.000289(.000254)	−.000485(.000251)
BLL	−.738(.0696)		−.174(.0229)	.455(.0488)		−.174(.0510)
BLE	−.114(.0119)		−.0302(.00276)	−.0280(.00596)		−.174(.0510)
BLM	.852(.0778)		.204(.0221)	.483(.0524)		.174(.0509)
BLT	.0209(.00169)	.00176(.000409)	.00505(.000554)	.0746(.00104)	−.00252(.000464)	.00959(.00186)
BEE	−.0176(.00288)		−.00526(.00137)	−.00173(.000646)		−.0000126(.0000977)
BEM	.132(.0145)		.0355(.00402)	.0298(.00659)		.000470(.00182)
BET	.00262(.000317)	−.000389(.0000667)	.000634(.0000489)	.000854(.000125)	.000195(.0000292)	.000150(.0000652)
BMM	−.983(.0883)		−.239(.0208)	−.513(.0567)		−.175(.0509)
BMT	−.0194(.00191)	.000893(.000490)	−.00590(.000582)	−.00675(.00118)	.00262(.000378)	−.00926(.00190)
BTT	.00273(.00243)	−.00121(.00348)	.00537(.00271)	.00119(.00181)	.00226(.00241)	.00428(.00444)

Table 2.4.1 (continued)

Parameter	Transportation equipment and ordinance	Instruments	Miscellaneous manufacturing industries	Transportation	Communications	Electric utilities
AK	.0371(.00160)	.123(.00276)	.0905(.00242)	.169(.00126)	.364(.00275)	.324(.00249)
AL	.371(.00497)	.325 (.00391)	.329(.00295)	.425(.00174)	.388(.00252)	.229(.00187)
AE	.00933(.000148)	.00676(.000162)	.0112(.000198)	.0550(.0009)	.0125(.000821)	.247(.00513)
AM	.583(.00482)	.545(.00627)	.569(.00253)	.351(.00226)	.236(.00329)	.201(.00480)
AT	-.0259(.0235)	.0348(.0382)	.0273(.0182)	-.0367(.0112)	-.0449(.0299)	.0303(.0203)
BKK						
BKL						
BKE						
BKM						
BKT	-.00173(.000217)	-.00145(.0000375)	.000132(.000328)	-.000768(.0017)	-.00280(.000373)	-.00604(.000338)
BLL	-.327(.0771)	-.645 (.0298)				
BLE	.00982(.00247)	-.00159(.00194)				
BLM	.317(.0778)	.646(.0298)				
BLT	.00389(.00164)	.00974(.000661)	-.000581(.000400)	-.00131(.000236)	.0000186(.000342)	-.00681(.000254)
BEE	-.000295(.000181)	-.00000392(.00000956)		-.00481(.00258)	-.0905(.0183)	
BEM	-.00953(.00230)	.00159(.00195)		.00481(.00258)	.0905(.0183)	
BET	-.0000433(.0000533)	.0000853(.0000338)	.000316(.0000269)	.000712(.000119)	-.000272(.000115)	.0079(.000679)
BMM	-.308(.0785)	-.648 (.0299)		-.00481(.00258)	-.0905(.0183)	
BMT	-.00212(.00165)	-.00837(.000937)	.000134(.000344)	.00136(.000307)	.00306(.00044)	.00488(.000631)
BTT	-.00263(.00319)	.00569(.00518)	.00264(.00247)	-.00257(.00151)	.00188(.00406)	.00754(.00275)

Table 2.4.1 (continued)

Parameter	Gas utilities	Trade	Finance, insurance, and real estate	Services	Government enterprises
AK	.219(.00410)	.148(.00144)	.244(.00784)	.0984(.000536)	.0954(.00669)
AL	.180(.00188)	.560(.00460)	.238(.00196)	.509(.00356)	.567(.0112)
AE	.548(.00485)	.0230(.00128)	.0175(.000357)	.0204(.000435)	.0336(.00166)
AM	.0527(.00137)	.270(.00466)	.501(.00852)	.372(.00346)	.304(.00723)
AT	.0153(.0201)	.00327(.0148)	-.0429(.0567)	-.0136(.00797)	-.0166 (.0519)
BKK					
BKL					
BKE					
BKM					
BKT	-.00609(.000556)	.000106(.000195)	-.00429(.00106)	.00066(.0000727)	.00437(.000908)
BLL		-1.023(.0905)	-.0414(.0491)	-.335(.102)	-.194(.184)
BLE		.0303(.0106)	-.00109(.00797)	.00444(.0108)	.0306(.0308)
BLM		.992(.0929)	.0425(.0492)	.330(.0978)	.164(.156)
BLT	.00779(.000255)	.0320(.00261)	.00140(.00102)	.0121(.00256)	.0215(.00972)
BEE	-.0767(.00705)	-.000900(.000646)	-.0000289(.000425)	-.0000590(.000279)	-.00481(.00572)
BEM	.0767(.00705)	-.0294(.00993)	.00112(.00839)	-.00439(.0105)	-.0258(.0254)
BET	.00155(.000659)	-.00150(.000353)	.0000309(.000160)	.00000105(.000270)	-.00222(.00163)
BMM	-.0767(.00705)	-.963(.0961)	-.0436(.0506)	-.326(.0949)	-.138(.133)
BMT	-.00325(.000190)	-.0306(.00266)	.00286(.00151)	-.0128(.00245)	-.0237(.00818)
BTT	.00213(.00272)	.240(.00200)	.000351(.00764)	-.00142(.00108)	-.00157(.00706)

Notation:

Text	Table 2.4.1	Text	Table 2.4.1	Text	Table 2.4.1
$\alpha_p^i =$	AK AL AE AM	$\beta_{pp}^i =$	BKK BKL BKE BKM . BLL BLE BLM . . BEE BEM BKT . . BMM BLT	$\beta_{pt}^i =$	BET BMT
$\alpha_t^i =$	AT			$\beta_{tt}^i =$	BTT

industries, so that our representation of technology reduces to a price function that is linear-logarithmic in the input prices at any given time for these industries. For fifteen of the 35 industries the share elasticities with respect to the price of labor input, are set to equal zero. Finally, for all 35 industries the share elasticities with respect to the price of capital input, are set to equal zero.

We continue the interpretation of the parameters estimates given in table 2.4.1 with estimated biases of technical change, with respect to price $\{\beta^i_{pt}\}$. These parameters can be interpreted as the change in the share of each input with respect to time, holding price constant. Alternatively, they can be interpreted as the change in the negative of the rate of technical change with respect to the price of the corresponding input. For example, if the bias of technical change with respect to the price of capital input is positive, we say that technical change is capital-using; if the bias is negative, we say that technical change is capital-saving.

A classification of industries by patterns of the biases of technical change is given in table 2.4.2. The patterns that occur with greatest frequency are capital-saving, labor-saving, energy-using, and materials-saving technical change. Each of these patterns occurs for eight of the 35 industries for which we have fitted biases. We find that technical change is capital-saving for 21 of the 35 industries, labor-using for 21 industries, energy-using for 26 industries, and materials-saving for 24 industries.

The final parameter in our models of producer behavior is the rate of change of the negative of the rate of technical change $\{\beta^i_{tt}\}$. We find that the rate of technical change is decreasing with time for 24 of the 35 industries and increasing for the remaining ten. Whereas the biases of technical change with respect to the prices of capital, labor, energy, and materials inputs are estimated very precisely, we find that the rate of change is estimated with much less precision. Overall, our empirical results suggest a considerable degree of similarity across the industries, especially in the qualitative character of the distribution of the value of output among inputs and of changes in technology.

2.4.2   Consumer Behavior

We next present the empirical results of implementing the model of consumer behavior described in section 2.3. This model is based on a two-stage process for the allocation of consumer expenditures among

Table 2.4.2
Classification of industries by biases of technical change

Pattern of biases	Industries
Capital-using Labor-using Energy-using Materials-saving	Tobacco; printing and publishing; fabricated metal; services
Capital-using Labor-using Energy-saving Materials-saving	Metal mining; coal mining; trade; government enterprises
Capital-using Labor-saving Energy-using Materials-using	Apparel; petroleum refining; miscellaneous manufacturing
Capital-using Labor-saving Energy-using Materials-saving	Nonmetallic mining; lumber and wood
Capital-using Labor-saving Energy-saving Materials-using	Construction
Capital-saving Labor-using Energy-using Materials-using	Finance, insurance, and real estate
Capital-saving Labor-using Energy-using Materials-saving	Agriculture; furniture; paper; stone, clay, and glass; nonelectrical machinery; motor vehicles; instruments; gas utilities
Capital-saving Labor-using Energy-saving Materials-using	Food; primary metal; communications
Capital-saving Labor-saving Energy-using Materials-using	Crude petroleum and natural gas; textiles; chemicals; rubber and plastic; leather; electric machinery; transportation; electric utilites
Capital-saving Labor-using Energy-saving Materials-saving	Transportation equipment

commodities. As for producer behavior, we limit our presentation of empirical results to the first stage of the two-stage allocation process. At the first stage we divide consumer expenditures among five commodity groups:

1. *Energy*: Expenditure on electricity, gas, heating oil, and gasoline.

2. *Food and Clothing*: Expenditures on food, beverages, and tobacco; clothing expenditures; and other related expenditures.

3. *Other Nondurable Expenditure*: The remainder of the budget, which includes some transportation and trade margins from other expenditures.

4. *Capital Services*: The service flow from consumer durables as well as a service flow from housing.

5. *Consumer Services*: Expenditures on services, such as entertainment, maintenance and repairs of automobiles and housing, tailoring, cleaning, and insurance.

We employ the following demographic characteristics as attributes of individual households:

1. *Family Size*: 1, 2, 3, 4, 5, 6, and 7 or more persons.

2. *Age of Head*: 15–24, 25–34, 35–44, 45–54, 55–65, 65 and over.

3. *Region of Residence*: Northeast, North-Central, South, and West.

4. *Race*: White, nonwhite.

5. *Type of Residence*: Urban, rural.

Our cross-section observations on individual expenditures for each commodity group and demographic characteristics are for the year 1972 from the 1972–73 Survey of Consumer Expenditures.[31] Our time series observations of prices and aggregate expenditures for each commodity group are based on data on personal consumption expenditures from the U.S. Interindustry Transactions Accounts for the period 1958–74.[32] We employ time series data on the distribution of expenditures over all households and among demographic groups based on *Current Population Reports*. To complete our time-series data set we compile data for our heteroscedasticity adjustment from the *Current Population Reports*.[33]

In our application, we have expenditure shares for five commodity groups as endogenous variables at the first stage, so that we estimate four equations. As unknown parameters, we have four elements of the vector α_p, four expenditure coefficients of the vector $\beta_{pp}\iota$, sixteen attribute coefficients for each of the four equations in the matrix β_{pA}, and ten price coefficients in the matrix β_{pp}, which is constrained to be symmetric. The expenditure coefficients are sums of price coefficients in the corresponding equation, so that we have a total of 82 unknown parameters. We estimate the complete model, subject to inequality restrictions implied by monotonicity of the individual expenditure shares, by pooling time series and cross-section data. The results are given in table 2.4.3.

Table 2.4.3
Pooled estimation results

Variable	Numerator coefficient	Standard error
For equation W_{EN}		
Constant	−0.17874	0.005363
$\ln p_{EN}$	0.01805	0.003505
$\ln p_{FC}$	−0.08745	0.014618
$\ln p_O$	0.02325	0.011342
$\ln p_{CAP}$	−0.02996	0.009905
$\ln p_{SERV}$	0.05898	0.015862
$\ln M$	0.01712	0.000614
$F2$	−0.01784	0.000971
$F3$	−0.02281	0.001140
$F4$	−0.02675	0.001243
$F5$	−0.02677	0.001424
$F6$	−0.02861	0.001723
$F7$	−0.02669	0.001908
$A30$	−0.00269	0.001349
$A40$	−0.00981	0.001440
$A50$	−0.00844	0.001378
$A60$	−0.01103	0.001374
$A70$	−0.00971	0.001336
RNC	−0.00727	0.000909
RS	−0.00481	0.000906
RW	0.00621	0.000974
RLK	0.00602	0.001157
RUR	−0.01463	0.000890
For equation $W_{rm}FC$		
Constant	−0.56700	0.011760
$\ln p_{EN}$	−0.08745	0.014618
$\ln p_{FC}$	0.58972	0.094926
$\ln p_O$	−0.11121	0.064126

Table 2.4.3 (continued)

Variable	Numerator coefficient	Standard error
$\ln p_{CAP}$	0.00158	0.057450
$\ln p_{SERV}$	−0.44384	0.101201
$\ln M$	0.05120	0.001357
$F2$	−0.03502	0.002030
$F3$	−0.05350	0.002390
$F4$	−0.07016	0.002605
$F5$	−0.08486	0.002987
$F6$	−0.08947	0.003613
$F7$	−0.11520	0.003799
$A30$	−0.02189	0.002813
$A40$	−0.04961	0.003015
$A50$	−0.05067	0.002878
$A60$	−0.05142	0.002870
$A70$	−0.03929	0.002791
RNC	0.01993	0.001897
RS	0.01511	0.001893
RW	0.01854	0.002039
BLK	−0.01026	0.002419
RUR	0.01547	0.001878
For equation W_O		
Constant	−0.32664	0.010446
$\ln p_{EN}$	0.02325	0.011342
$\ln p_{FC}$	−0.11121	0.064126
$\ln p_O$	0.19236	0.083095
$\ln p_{CAP}$	−0.16232	0.023397
$\ln p_{SERV}$	0.03887	0.028097
$\ln M$	0.01903	0.001203
$F2$	−0.01616	0.001921
$F3$	−0.02748	0.002143
$F4$	−0.03584	0.002336
$F5$	−0.03882	0.002678
$F6$	−0.04298	0.003239
$F7$	−0.05581	0.003406
$A30$	−0.01293	0.002524
$A40$	−0.02584	0.002703
$A50$	−0.02220	0.002582
$A60$	−0.02199	0.002574
$A70$	−0.00826	0.002503
RNC	0.01160	0.001702
RS	0.00278	0.001698
RW	0.01375	0.001827
BLK	−0.00320	0.002169
RUR	0.00783	0.001680

Table 2.4.3 (continued)

Variable	Numerator coefficient	Standard error
For equation W_{CAP}		
Constant	0.85630	0.026022
$\ln p_{EN}$	−0.02996	0.009905
$\ln p_{FC}$	0.00158	0.057450
$\ln p_O$	−0.16232	0.023397
$\ln p_{CAP}$	0.51464	0.053931
$\ln p_{SERV}$	−0.20176	0.079587
$\ln M$	−0.12217	0.002995
$F2$	0.00161	0.004557
$F3$	0.01074	0.005361
$F4$	0.01928	0.005843
$F5$	0.02094	0.006700
$F6$	0.02976	0.008106
$F7$	0.05885	0.008522
$A30$	0.03385	0.006320
$A40$	0.05225	0.006761
$A50$	0.04761	0.006463
$A60$	0.03685	0.006444
$A70$	0.00492	0.006267
RNC	−0.04438	0.004261
RS	−0.03193	0.004250
RW	−0.02574	0.004574
BLK	0.02338	0.005431
RUR	−0.05752	0.004198
For equation W_{SERV}		
Constant	−0.78391	0.024099
$\ln p_{EN}$	0.05898	0.015862
$\ln p_{FC}$	−0.44384	0.101201
$\ln p_O$	0.03887	0.028097
$\ln p_{CAP}$	−0.20176	0.079587
$\ln p_{SERV}$	0.51293	0.143707
$\ln M$	0.03481	0.002772
$F2$	0.06742	0.004242
$F3$	0.09306	0.004989
$F4$	0.11348	0.005437
$F5$	0.12952	0.006234
$F6$	0.13130	0.007543
$F7$	0.13886	0.007928
$A30$	0.00367	0.005885
$A40$	0.03301	0.006292
$A50$	0.03371	0.006018
$A60$	0.04758	0.006001
$A70$	0.05233	0.005836

Table 2.4.3 (continued)

Variable	Numerator coefficient	Standard error
RNC	0.02011	0.003968
RS	0.01884	0.003957
RW	−0.01277	0.004258
BLK	−0.01592	0.005055
RUR	0.04885	0.003907

Notation:

W = budget share $\ln p$ = log price

In order to designate the proper good to which W or $\ln p$ refers, we append the following subscripts where appropriate:

EN	=	energy	CAP	=	capital services
FC	=	food and closing	SERV	=	consumer services
O	=	other nondurable goods			

Further notation is given as

$\ln M$	=	log total expenditure
$F2$	=	dummy for family size 2
$F3$	=	dummy for family size 3
$F4$	=	dummy for family size 4
$F5$	=	dummy for family size 5
$F6$	=	dummy for family size 6
$F7$	=	dummy for family size 7
	or more	
$A30$	=	dummy for age class 25–34
$A40$	=	dummy for age class 35–44
$A50$	=	dummy for age class 45–54
$A60$	=	dummy for age class 55–64
$A70$	=	dummy for age class 65 and older
RNC	=	dummy for region North-Central
RS	=	dummy for region South
RW	=	dummy for region West
BLK	=	dummy for nonwhite head
RUR	=	dummy for rural residence

The impacts of changes in total expenditures and in demographic characteristics of the individual household are estimated very precisely. This reflects the fact that estimates of the expenditure and demographic effects incorporate a relatively large number of cross-section observations. The impacts of prices enter through the denominator of the equations for expenditure shares; these price coefficients are estimated very precisely since they also incorporate cross-section data. Finally, the price impacts also enter through the numerators of equations for the expenditure shares. These parameters are estimated less precisely, since they are based on a much smaller number of time series observations on prices.

Individual expenditure shares for capital services increase with total expenditure, whereas all other shares decrease with total expenditure. As family size increases, the shares of energy, food and clothing, and other nondurable expenditures increase, whereas the shares of capital services and consumer services decrease. The energy share increases with age of head of household, whereas the consumer services decrease. The shares of food and clothing and other nondurables increase with age of head, whereas the share of capital services decreases.

The effects of region of residence on patterns of individual expenditures is small for energy and other nondurables. Households living in the North-Central and South regions use relatively more capital services and slightly more energy; these households use less consumer services. The only difference between whites and nonwhites is a smaller share of capital services and a larger share of consumer services for nonwhites. Finally, shares of food and clothing, consumer services, and other nondurables are smaller for rural families, whereas the shares of capital services and energy are much larger. Our overall conclusion is that differences in preferences among consuming units are very significant empirically and must be incorporated into models of aggregate consumer behavior.

2.4.3   Conclusion

Our empirical results for sector patterns of production and technical change are very striking and suggest a considerable degree of similarity across industries. However, it is important to emphasize that these results have been obtained under strong simplifying assumptions. First, for all industries, we have employed conditions for producer equilibrium under perfect competition; we have assumed constant returns to scale at the industry level; finally, we have employed a description of technology that lead to myopic decision rules. These assumptions must be justified primarily by their usefulness in implementing production models that are uniform for all 35 industrial sectors of the U.S. economy.

Although it might be worthwhile to weaken each of the assumptions, we have enumerated above, a more promising direction for further research appears to lie within the framework provided by these assumptions. First, we can provide a more detailed model for allocation among productive inputs. We have disaggregated energy and materials into 35 groups—five types of energy and 30 types of materials—by constructing a hierarchy of models for allocation within the energy and materials aggregates. The second research objective suggested by our results is to incorporate the production models for all 35 industrial sectors into a general equilibrium model of production in the U.S. economy. An econometric general equilibrium model of the U.S. economy has been constructed for nine industrial sectors by Hudson and Jorgenson (1974). This model is currently being disaggregated to the level of the 35 industrial sectors included in our study.

In this chapter, we have presented an econometric model of aggregate consumer behavior and implemented this model for households in the United States. The model incorporates aggregate time series data on quantities consumed, prices, the level and distribution of total expenditures, and demographic characteristics of the population. It also incorporates individual cross-section data on the allocation of consumer expenditures among commodities for households with different demographic characteristics. We have obtained evidence of very significant differences in preferences among households that differ in demographic characteristics in the United States.

Our next research objective is to provide a more detailed model for allocation of consumer expenditures among commodity groups. For this purpose, we have disaggregated the five commodity groups into 36 individual commodities by constructing a hierarchy of models for allocation within each of the five groups—energy, food and clothing, other nondurable goods, capital services, and consumer services. Our final research objective is to incorporate our model of aggregate consumer behavior into the 35-sector general equilibrium model of the U.S. economy now under development. The resulting model can be employed in assessing the impacts of alternative economic policies on the welfare of individuals with different levels of income and different demographic characteristics, including family size, age of head, region, type of residence, and race.[34]

Notes

1. A review of the literature on induced technical change is given by Binswanger (1978a). Binswanger distinguishes between models, like ours and those of Ben-Zion and Ruttan (1978), Lucas (1967), and Schmookler (1966), with an endogenous rate of technical change, and models, like those of Hicks (1932), Kennedy (1964), Samuelson (1965), von Weizsäcker (1962), and others, with an endogenous bias of technical change. Additional references are given by Binswanger (1978a).
2. For further discussion of myopic decision rules, see Jorgenson (1973).
3. The price function was introduced by Samuelson (1953).
4. The translog price function was introduced by Christensen, Jorgenson, and Lau (1971, 1973). The translog price function was first applied at the sectoral level by Berndt and Jorgenson (1973) and Berndt and Wood (1975). References to sectoral production studies incorporating energy and materials inputs are given by Berndt and Wood (1979).
5. The share elasticity with respect to price was introduced by Christensen, Jorgenson, and Lau (1971, 1973) as a fixed parameter of the translog price function. An analogous concept was employed by Samuelson (1973). The terminology is due to Jorgenson and Lau (1983).
6. The terminology *constant share elasticity price function* is due to Jorgenson and Lau (1983), who have shown that constancy of share elasticities with respect to price, biases of technical change with respect to price, and the rate of change of the negative of the rate of technical change are necessary and sufficient for representation of the price function in translog form.
7. The bias of technical change was introduced by Hicks (1932). An alternative definition of the bias of technical change is analyzed by Burmeister and Dobell (1969). Binswanger (1974) has introduced a translog cost function with fixed biases of technical change. Alternative definitions of biases of technical change are compared by Binswanger (1978b).
8. This definition of the bias of technical change with respect to price is due to Jorgenson and Lau (1983).
9. The rate of change of the negative of the rate of technical change was introduced by Jorgenson and Lau (1983).
10. The price indexes were introduced by Fisher (1922) and have been discussed by Tornquist (1936), Theil (1965), and Kloek (1966). These indexes were first derived from the translog price function by Diewert (1976). The corresponding index of technical change was introduced by Christensen and Jorgenson (1973). The translog index of technical change was first derived from the translog price function by Diewert (1980) and by Jorgenson and Lau (1983). Earlier, Diewert (1976) had interpreted the ratio of translog indexes of the prices of input and output as an index of productivity under the assumption of Hicks neutrality.
11. The following discussion of share elasticities with respect to price and concavity follows that of Jorgenson and Lau (1983). Representation of conditions for concavity in terms of the Cholesky factorization is due to Lau (1978).
12. The following discussion of concavity for the translog price function is based on that of Jorgenson and Lau (1983).

13. The following formulation of an econometric model of production and technical change is based on that of Jorgenson and Lau (1983).

14. The Cholesky factorization is used to obtain an equation with uncorrelated random disturbances by Jorgenson and Lau (1983).

15. Note that when we consider only a single commodity or a single consumer, we can suppress the corresponding commodity or individual subscript. This is done to keep the notation as simple as possible; any omission of subscripts will be clear from the context.

16. If aggregate demands are zero when aggregate expenditure is equal to zero, $C_j(p) = 0$.

17. See, for example, Houthakker (1957) and the references given there.

18. Alternative approaches to the representation of the effects of household characteristics on expenditure allocation are presented by Barten (1964), Gorman (1976), and Prais and Houthakker (1955). Empirical evidence on the impact of variations in demographic charateristics on expenditure allocation is given by Lau, Lin, and Yotopoulos (1978), Muellbauer (1977), Parks and Barten (1973), and Pollak and Wales (1980). A review of the literature is presented by Deaton and Muellbauer (1980b, pp. 191–213).

19. Alternative approaches to the representation of the effects of total expenditure on expenditure allocation are reviewed by Deaton and Muellbauer (1980b, pp. 148–60). Gorman (1981) shows that Engel curves for an individual consumer that are linear in certain functions of total expenditure, as required in the theory of exact aggregation considered below, involve at most three linearly independent functions of total expenditure. Evidence from budget studies on the nonlinearity of Engel curves is presented by Leser (1963), Muellbauer (1976b), Pollak and Wales (1978), and Prais and Houthakker (1955).

20. See, for example, Blackorby, Boyce, and Russell (1978), and the references given there.

21. We omit the proof of this theorem, referring the interested reader to Lau (1977b, 1982).

22. See Samuelson (1956) for details.

23. The specification of a system of individual demand functions by means of Roy's Identity was first implemented empirically in a path-breaking study by Houthakker (1960). A detailed review of econometric models of consumer behavior based on Roy's Identity is given by Lau (1977a).

24. Alternative approaches to the representation of the effects of prices on expenditure allocation are reviewed by Barten (1977), Deaton and Muellbauer (1980b, pp. 60–85), and Lau (1977a). The indirect translog utility function was introduced by Christensen, Jorgenson, and Lau (1975) and was extended to encompass changes in preferences over time by Jorgenson and Lau (1975).

25. These conditions are implied by the fundamental theorem of exact aggregation presented in section 2.1, above.

26. Two-stage allocation is discussed by Blackorby, Primont, and Russell (1978, especially pp. 103–216); they give detailed references to the literature.

27. See Diewert (1976) for a detailed justification of this approach to price index numbers.

28. See Malinvaud (1980, chapter 9) for a discussion of these techniques.

29. Nonlinear two-stage least-squares estimators were introduced by Amemiya (1974). Subsequently, nonlinear three-stage least-squares estimators were introduced by Jorgenson and Laffont (1974). For detailed discussion of nonlinear three-stage least-squares estimators, see Amemiya (1977), Gallant (1977), Gallant and Jorgenson (1979), and Malinvaud (1980, chapter 20).

30. Data on energy and materials are based on annual inter-industry transactions tables for the United States, 1958–1974, compiled by Jack Faucett and Associates (1977) for the Federal Preparedness Agency. Data on labor and capital are based on estimates by Fraumeni and Jorgenson (1980).

31. The cross-section data are described by Carlson (1974).

32. The preparation of these data is described in detail in Jack Faucett and Associates (1977).

33. This series is published annually by the U.S. Bureau of the Census. For our study, numbers 33, 35, 37, 39, 41, 43, 47, 51, 53, 59, 60, 62, 66, 72, 75, 79, 80, 84, 85, 90, 96, 97, and 101 were employed together with technical report numbers 8 and 17.

34. See, for example, Jorgenson, Lau, and Stoker (1980, 1981).

3   Environmental Regulation and U.S. Economic Growth

Dale W. Jorgenson and
Peter J. Wilcoxen

3.1   Introduction

The most striking economic development in the United States during the postwar period has been the sharp decline in the rate of economic growth during the 1970s and 1980s. Real output grew at an average annual rate of 3.7 percent during the period 1947–1973. By contrast the growth rate from 1973 to 1985 was only 2.5 percent, fully 1.2 percentage points lower. Two events coincided with the slowdown—the advent of environmental regulation and the increase of world petroleum prices. In this study, we focus on the relationship of pollution abatement costs and economic growth.

We begin with the usual disclaimer in economic studies of the costs of environmental regulation. In this article, we quantify the costs of environmental regulation and compare these costs with those of governmentally mandated activities that are financed directly through the government budget. We have not attempted to assess the benefits resulting from a cleaner environment.[1] We have not accounted for consumption benefits resulting from environmental cleanup or production benefits associated with pollution abatement. The conclusions of this study cannot be taken to imply that pollution control is too burdensome or, for that matter, insufficiently restrictive.

Pollution control legislation began in earnest in the United States in 1965, when amendments to the Clean Air Act set national automobile emissions standards for the first time. The extent of regulation increased dramatically in 1970 with the passage of the National Environmental Policy Act and amendments to the Clean Air Act. In 1972, the Clean Water Act was passed and revisions to this Act and the Clean Air Act were adopted in 1977.[2] The consequence of this legislation was a large and abrupt shift of economic resources toward pollution abatement.

The possible responses of producers to new environmental regulations fall into three categories—substitution of less polluting inputs for more polluting ones, investment in pollution abatement devices to clean up waste, and changes in production processes to reduce emissions. Switching toward cleaner inputs is the least disruptive of these responses, since it does not require a reorganization of the production process. A prime example is the substitution of low-sulfur coal for high-sulfur coal by electric utilities during the 1970s to comply with restrictions on sulfur dioxide emissions. Another important example is the shift from leaded to unleaded fuels for the purpose of cleaning up motor vehicle emissions.

The second response to emissions controls is the use of special devices to treat wastes after they have been generated. This is commonly known as end-of-pipe abatement and is frequently the method of choice for retrofitting existing facilities to meet newly imposed environmental standards. A typical example is the use of electrostatic precipitators to reduce the emission of particulates from combustion. Regulations promulgated in the United States by the Environmental Protection Agency effectively encourage the use of this approach by setting standards for emissions on the basis of "best available technology."

Process changes involve redesigning production methods to reduce emissions. An example is the introduction of fluidized bed technology for combustion, which results in reduced emissions. Gollop and Roberts (1983) constructed a detailed econometric model of electric utility firms that is based on a cost function that incorporates the impact of environmental regulation on the cost of producing electricity and the rate of productivity growth. They concluded that annual productivity growth of electric utilities impacted by more restrictive emissions controls declined by 0.59 percentage points over the period 1974–1979. This was the result of switching technologies to meet new standards for sulfur dioxide emissions.

We analyze the impact of environmental regulation by simulating the long-term growth of the U.S. economy with and without regulation. For this purpose, we have constructed a detailed model of the economy that includes the determinants of long-run growth. Before considering the impact of specific pollution controls we present an overview of the model in section 3.2. We focus attention on features that facilitate the incorporation of changes in environmental policy. We also discuss the dynamics of the response of the economy to new pollution abatement requirements.

In section 3.3 we show that pollution abatement has emerged as a major claimant on the resources of the U.S. economy. The long-run cost of environmental regulation is a reduction of 2.59 percent in the level of the U.S. gross national product. This is more than ten percent of the share of total government purchases of goods and services in the national product during the period 1973–1985. Over this period the annual growth rate of the U.S. economy has been reduced by 0.191 percent. This is several times the reduction in growth estimated in previous studies.

Since the stringency of pollution control differs substantially among industries, our model also assesses the impact of environmental regulations on individual industries. We have analyzed the interactions between industries in order to quantify the full repercussions of these regulations. We find that pollution controls have had their most pronounced effects on the chemicals, coal mining, motor vehicles, and primary processing industries—such as petroleum refining, primary metals, and pulp and paper. For example, we find that the long-run output of the automobile industry has been reduced by fifteen percent, mainly as a consequence of motor vehicle emissions controls.

3.2   An Overview of the Model

The purpose of our model of the U.S. economy is to analyze the impact of changes in environmental policy by simulating the long-term growth of the economy with and without regulation. We began by dividing the U.S. economy into business, household, government, and rest-of-the-world sectors. Since environmental regulations differ substantially among industries, we subdivided the business sector into the thirty-five industries listed in table 3.1. Each industry produces a primary product, and many industries also produce one or more secondary products. Thirty-five commodity groups are represented in our model, each corresponding to the primary product of one of the industries listed in table 3.1.

The total supply of each commodity group is provided by domestic production and imports from the rest of the world. This supply is divided between intermediate and final demands. Intermediate demands are the inputs of the commodity into all thirty-five industries.

Table 3.1
Industry classifications

Number	Description
1	Agriculture, forestry, and fisheries
2	Metal mining
3	Coal mining
4	Crude petroleum and natural gas
5	Nonmetallic mineral mining
6	Construction
7	Food and kindred products
8	Tobacco manufacturers
9	Textile mill products
10	Apparel and other textile products
11	Lumber and wood products
12	Furniture and fixtures
13	Paper and allied products
14	Printing and publishing
15	Chemicals and allied products
16	Petroleum refining
17	Rubber and plastic products
18	Leather and leather products
19	Stone, clay, and glass products
20	Primary metals
21	Fabricated metal products
22	Machinery, except electrical
23	Electrical machinery
24	Motor vehicles
25	Other transportation equipment
26	Instruments
27	Miscellaneous manufacturing
28	Transportation and warehousing
29	Communication
30	Electric utilities
31	Gas utilities
32	Trade
33	Finance, insurance, and real estate
34	Other services
35	Government enterprises

Final demands include expenditures by the household and government sectors for consumption, purchases by the business and household sectors for investment, and exports to the rest of the world. Each industry utilizes inputs of capital and labor services, and these services are also allocated to final demands. Noncompeting imports and commodities that are not produced domestically are allocated in the same way as capital and labor services.

To implement our model we have constructed a consistent time series of inter-industry transactions tables for the U.S. economy, covering the period 1947–1985.[3] These tables provide detailed information on production by each of the thirty-five industries in current and constant prices. The quantities of each commodity, including primary factors of production and noncompeting imports, have been allocated to intermediate and final demands in using a use table. The quantities of all commodities made by each industry are presented in a make table. The use and make tables are presented diagrammatically in figure 3.1. Figure 3.2 provides definitions of the variables that occur in both tables.

3.2.1   Producer Behavior

The first problem in modeling producer behavior is to represent substitution among inputs. For this purpose we have constructed econometric models of the demands of each industry for all inputs. We have identified inputs of capital and energy separately, since environmental regulations often require the use of specific types of equipment or restrict the combustion of certain types of fuels. For example, a restriction on sulfur dioxide emissions may require the substitution of low-sulfur for high-sulfur fuel. Similarly, regulations on particulate emissions may necessitate the use of an electrostatic precipitator, which requires additional capital inputs.

The econometric approach to modeling producer behavior is very demanding in terms of data requirements. An alternative approach is to characterize substitution among inputs by calibration from a single data point.[4] For example, almost all applied general equilibrium models employ the assumption of fixed "input-output" coefficients for intermediate goods, following the specification originated by Johansen (1960).[5] The ratio of the input of each commodity to the output of an industry is calculated from a single use table, like the one presented in figure 3.1. However, the possibility of substitution among intermediate goods, such as energy and materials, is ruled out by assumption.

A high degree of substitutability among inputs implies that the cost of environmental regulation is low, while a low degree of substitutability implies high costs of environmental regulation. Although a calibration approach avoids the burden of estimation, it also specifies the nature of substitutability among inputs by assumption rather than

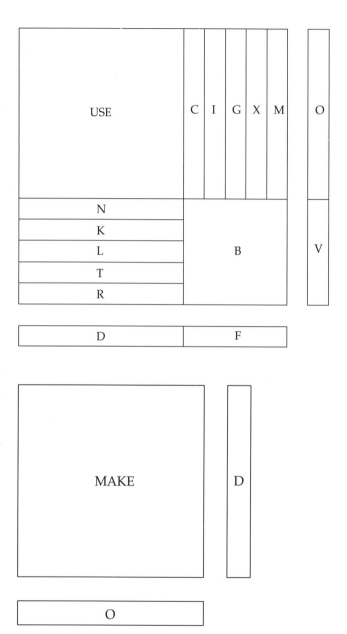

Figure 3.1
Organization of the *use* and *make* tables.

Category	Variable	Description
Industry-Commodity Flows:		
	USE	Commodities *used* by industries (use table)
	MAKE	Commodities *made* by industries (make table)
Final Demand Columns:		
	C	Personal consumption
	I	Gross private domestic investment
	G	Government spending
	X	Exports
	M	Imports
Value Added Rows:		
	N	Noncompeting imports
	K	Capital
	L	Labor
	T	Net taxes
	R	Rest of the world
Commodity and Industry Output:		
	O	Commodity output
	D	Industry output
Other Variables:		
	B	Value added sold directly to final demand
	V	Total value added
	F	Total final demand

Figure 3.2
Use and make table variables.

relying on empirical evidence. This defeats the main purpose of modeling the impact of environmental policy. We conclude that empirical evidence on substitutability among inputs is essential in analyzing the impact of environmental regulations.

The most important mechanisms for control of environmental pollution are to induce substitution away from polluting inputs and require pollution abatement. These measures can affect the rate of productivity growth in an industry. If the level of productivity in an industry increases, the price of the output of the industry will fall relative to the prices of its inputs, while a decrease in the industry's productivity level will result in a rise in the price of its output relative to its input prices. Our models of producer behavior endogenize productivity growth by representing the rate of productivity growth in each industry as a function of the prices of all its inputs.[6]

Our econometric models of producer behavior allocate the value of the output of each industry among the inputs of the thirty-five commodity groups, capital services, labor services, and noncompeting imports. Inputs of the thirty-five commodities into each industry are given in the columns labeled U in the use table presented in figure 3.1. Inputs of capital services, labor services, and noncompeting imports into all industries are given in the rows labeled K, L, and N, respectively. The remaining rows of this table give indirect taxes paid by all industries and inputs of factor services from the rest of the world into these industries.

The sum of all entries in each column of the use table is the value of the output of the corresponding industry. This output includes a primary product and, possibly, one or more secondary products. We have modeled the shares of all industries that produce a given commodity in the value of the total domestic production of that commodity as functions of the output prices of these industries. The model uses these shares to allocate the domestic supply of each commodity among the industries that produce it. This allocation is given in the columns of the make table in figure 3.1. Similarly, we have modeled the value shares of imports and domestic production of each commodity and employed these shares in generating the imports of each commodity in the column labeled M in the use table, figure 3.1.[7]

In our model of the U.S. economy, there is a single stock of capital that is allocated among all sectors, including the household sector. The supply of capital available in each period is the result of past investment. This relationship is represented by an accumulation equation that gives capital at the end of each period as a function of investment during the period and capital at the beginning of the period. This equation is backward-looking and captures the impact of investments in all past periods on the capital available in the current period. We have assumed that capital is perfectly malleable and mobile among sectors, so that the price of capital services in each sector is proportional to a single capital service price for the economy as a whole. The value of capital services is equal to capital income.

Our model of producer behavior includes an equation giving the price of capital services in terms of the price of investment goods at the beginning and end of each period, the rate of return to capital for the economy as a whole, the rate of depreciation, and variables describing the tax structure for income from capital. The current price of investment goods incorporates expectations about all future prices of capital services and all future discount rates.[8] Our model of the U.S. economy includes this forward-looking relationship for the price of investment goods in each time period. The price of capital services determined by the model enters into the price of investment goods through the assumption of perfect foresight or rational expectations. Under this assumption the price of investment goods in every period is based on expectations of future capital services, prices, and discount rates that are fulfilled by the solution of the model.

The final demands for the commodity groups in our model include purchases by the business and household sectors for investment purposes. The final set of behavioral equations in our model of producer behavior is a system of demand functions for investment goods. We have modeled the value shares of all commodities accumulated by the business and household sectors—including producers' and consumers' durables, residential and nonresidential structures, and inventories—as functions of the prices of these commodities. The shares are used to allocate the value of investment goods among commodity groups, as in column I in the use table, figure 3.1.

3.2.2   Consumer Behavior

An important objective of environmental regulation is to induce the substitution of nonpolluting products for polluting ones. This substitution can take place within the household sector as well as the business sector. For example, regulations on exhaust emissions of motor vehicles affect household demands for vehicles and motor fuel. The first problem in modeling consumer behavior is to represent substitution between commodities that are purchased by households. For this purpose, we have constructed an econometric model of the demands for individual commodities by the household sector. As in our models of producer behavior, we have identified purchases of energy and capital services separately, since these commodity groups are directly affected by environmental regulation.[9]

Our model of consumer behavior allocates personal consumption expenditures among the thirty-five commodity groups included in our model of the U.S. economy, capital and labor services, and non-competing imports. The allocation to individual commodities is given in the column labeled C in the use table in figure 3.1. Our model of personal consumption expenditures can be used to represent the behavior of individual households, as in the studies of regulatory policy by Jorgenson and Slesnick (1985). Here, we employ the model to represent aggregate consumer behavior in simulations of the U.S. economy under alternative policies for environmental regulation. For this purpose, we have imbedded this model of personal consumption expenditures into a higher-level model that determines consumer choices between labor and leisure and between consumption and saving.

The second stage of our model of the household sector is based on the concept of full consumption, which is composed of goods and services and leisure time. We have simplified the representation of household preferences between goods and leisure by introducing the notion of a representative consumer. In each time period, the representative consumer allocates the value of full consumption between personal consumption expenditures and leisure time.[10] This produces an allocation of the exogenously given time endowment between leisure time and the labor market. Labor market time is allocated between the thirty-five industries represented in the model and final demands for personal consumption expenditures and government consumption. We have assumed that labor is perfectly mobile among sectors, so that the price of labor services in each sector is proportional to a single wage rate for the economy as a whole. The value of time allocated to the labor market is equal to labor income.

The third and final stage of our model of the household sector is a model of intertemporal consumer behavior. We have described intertemporal preferences by means of a utility function for a representative consumer that depends on levels of full consumption in current and future time periods. The representative consumer maximizes this utility function subject to an intertemporal budget constraint. The budget constraint gives full wealth as the discounted value of current and future full consumption. The necessary conditions for a maximum of the utility function subject to the budget constraint can be expressed in the form of an Euler equation, giving the rate of growth of full consumption as a function of the discount rate and the rate of growth of the price of full consumption.[11]

The Euler equation for full consumption is forward-looking, so the current level of full consumption incorporates expectations about future prices of full consumption and future discount rates. The solution of our model includes this forward-looking relationship for full consumption in each time period. The price of full consumption determined by the model enters full consumption through the assumption of perfect foresight or rational expectations. Under this assumption, full consumption in every period is based on expectations about future prices of full consumption and discount rates that are fulfilled by the solution of the model.

3.2.3 The Solution of the Model

We conclude this overview by outlining the solution of our model of the U.S. economy. An intertemporal submodel incorporates backward-looking and forward-looking equations that determine the time paths of the capital stock and full consumption. Given the values of these variables, an intratemporal submodel determines the prices that balance demand and supply in each time period for the thirty-five commodity groups included in the model, capital services, and labor services. These two submodels must be solved simultaneously to obtain a complete solution of the model.

The dynamics of adjustment to changes in environmental policy are determined by the intertemporal features of our model. For example, investment in equipment for pollution abatement was a very substantial proportion of investment in producers' durable equipment during parts of our sample period, 1947–1985. This type of mandated investment increased the price of investment goods, requiring adjustments of capital service prices and discount rates over the whole future time path of the economy. Reductions in investment in capital accumulation reduced the capital available for production in subsequent time periods.

Given the prices of capital and labor services and noncompeting imports, the first step in the solution of the intratemporal model is to determine prices for the outputs of the thirty-five industries represented in the model. Given these prices, the next step is to determine the domestic supply prices for the corresponding commodities. Finally, the domestic supply price for each commodity is combined with the price of imports to determine the total supply price. These commodity prices enter the determination of intermediate demands by industries and final demands by the household, business, government, and rest-of-the-world sectors.

We have described the determination of supply prices for the thirty-five commodity groups included in our model, given the prices of capital and labor services and the prices of competing and noncompeting imports. The prices of imports are given exogenously in every time period. The prices of capital and labor services are determined by balancing demand and supply for these services. The supply of capital is determined by previous investments and is taken as given in every period. The exogenously given time endowment of the household sector is allocated between the labor market and leisure time by our model of consumer behavior.

The demand side of the intratemporal model is divided between intermediate and final demands for the thirty-five commodity groups, capital and labor services, and noncompeting imports as presented in the use table in figure 3.1. Our models of producer behavior include value shares for inputs of commodities, primary factors of production, and noncompeting imports into each industry. These value shares incorporate income-expenditure identities for the industry, since the total value of output must be equal to the value of total inputs. The value shares determine inputs per unit of output for each industry as functions of the input and output prices. The endogenously determined input-output coefficients in each industry are multiplied by the output of the industry to obtain the input quantities. These quantities are then summed over the thirty-five industries to obtain total intermediate demands.

In our intratemporal model, final demands are divided among personal consumption expenditures, purchases by the business and household sectors for investment purposes, expenditures by the government for public consumption, and exports to the rest of the world. To determine the quantities of the thirty-five commodities for of each these final demand categories, our model of consumer behavior allocates the value of full consumption between the aggregate expenditure on goods and services that make up personal consumption expenditures and the value of leisure time. Given aggregate expenditure, its distribution among households, and commodity prices, this model also allocates personal consumption expenditures among commodity groups, including capital and labor services and noncompeting imports. This allocation determines the quantity of each commodity included in final demand for personal consumption. These quantities are included in column C in the use table in figure 3.1.

While the value of personal consumption expenditures is determined within our model of consumer behavior, the value of gross private domestic investment is driven by private savings. First, the income of the household sector is the sum of incomes from the supply of labor and capital services, interest payments from the government and rest-of-the-world sectors, all net of taxes, and transfers from the government. Savings are equal to income minus personal consumption expenditure, minus personal transfers to foreigners and nontax payments to the government. This is the income-expenditure identity of the household sector.

The balance sheet identity of the household sector sets private wealth equal to the sum of the value of capital stock in the private sector, claims on the government, and claims on the rest of the world. The change in the value of private wealth from period to period is the sum of private savings and the revaluation of wealth as a result of inflation. Private savings plus government savings equal the current account balance of the rest-of-the-world sector plus gross private domestic investment. Within our intratemporal model, the level of investment is determined by savings, since the government deficit and the current account balance are taken to be exogenous. Our model of producer behavior allocates gross private domestic investment among commodity groups. Given the commodity prices, this allocation determines the quantity of each group included in final demand for investment purposes. These quantities are included in column I in the use table in figure 3.1.

In order to complete the determination of final demands in our model, we considered purchases by the government and rest-of-the-world sectors. Wherever possible, we have assigned government enterprises to the corresponding industry. For example, we have assigned the Tennessee Valley Authority to electric utilities and municipal transportation systems to transportation services. A separate industrial sector includes the remaining government enterprises, such as the U.S. Postal Service. Demands for commodities by government enterprises have been incorporated into intermediate demands. Purchases by the government sector for public consumption are part of final demands. Similarly, demands for competing and noncompeting imports are determined by our econometric models of producer behavior. Exports to the rest-of-the-world sector are part of final demands.

The final demands for public consumption are determined by the income-expenditure identity for the government sector. Government revenues are generated by exogenously given tax rates applied to appropriate transactions in the business and household sectors. For example, sales tax rates are applied to the values of outputs of the thirty-five industries to generate sales tax revenues, tariff rates are applied to imports to generate tariff revenues, and income tax rates are applied to incomes from capital and labor services to generate income tax revenues. In addition, property and wealth tax rates are applied to property employed in the business and household sectors and to household sector wealth to generate revenues from property and wealth taxes.

The model of the government sector adds the capital income of government enterprises, determined endogenously, and nontax receipts, given exogenously, to tax revenues to obtain total revenues of the government sector. The model subtracts the government budget surplus (or adds the government budget deficit) from (or to) these revenues to obtain government expenditures. The key assumption here is that the government budget surplus (or deficit) is given exogenously. To arrive at government purchases of goods and services, we subtract interest paid to domestic and foreign holders of government bonds, together with government transfer payments to domestic and foreign recipients. The shares of individual commodity groups in government purchases are taken to be exogenous. The model determines the quantities of all commodities included in the final demand of the government sector by dividing values of government purchases by the corresponding commodity price. The resulting quantities are given in the column denoted G in the use table in figure 3.1.

Our intratemporal model incorporates the income-expenditure identity of the rest-of-the-world sector. The current account surplus of the rest of the world equals the value of exports minus the value of imports plus interest received on domestic holdings of foreign bonds minus private and government transfers abroad minus the interest on government bonds paid to foreigners. The key assumption of our model of the rest-of-the-world sector is that the current account balance is exogenous, so the exchange rate is endogenous. Exports to the rest of the world are determined by demand equations that depend on world income and ratios of commodity prices in U.S. currency to the exchange rate. The quantities of exports of all commodities are included in column X in the use table in figure 3.1. Exogenously given prices of competing and noncompeting imports in foreign currency are expressed in U.S. currency by multiplying these prices by the exchange rate.

To construct a solution of our model of the U.S. economy, we first require values of all the exogenous variables. These variables have been set equal to their historical values for the sample period, 1947–1985. We have projected all the exogenous variables for the post-sample period, 1986–2050, and taken these variables to be constant at their 2050 values through the year 2100. The exogenous variables are held constant for the period 2050–2100 to allow sufficient time for the endogenous variables determined by the model to converge to their steady-state values.

We require projections of the exogenous components of the income-expenditure identities for government and rest-of-the-world sectors in order to project final demands for public consumption and exports. We have projected a gradual decline in the government deficit to the year 2025. For all later years, this deficit has been set to four percent of the nominal value of the government debt. This has the effect of maintaining a constant ratio of the value of the government debt to the value of the national product at a four percent inflation rate in a steady-state solution to our model.

We have set future prices of imports and exports in foreign currency equal to prices in 1985, the last year of our sample period. Projections of prices in U.S. domestic currency depend on the endogenously determined exchange rate. We have projected that the exogenous current account balance for the rest-of-the-world sector will fall gradually to zero by the year 2000. For later years, we have projected a current account surplus sufficient to produce a stock of net claims on foreigners by the year 2050 that equals the same proportion of national wealth as it did in 1982.

The most important exogenous variables in our model of the U.S. economy are those associated with the U.S. population and the corresponding time endowment. We have projected population by individual year of age, individual year of educational attainment, and sex to the year 2050, using demographic assumptions that result in a maximum population in that year.[12] In projecting future levels of educational attainment, we have assumed that future demographic cohorts will have the same level of attainment as the cohort that reached age thirty-five in the year 1985. We have transformed our population projection into a projection of the time endowment used in our model of the labor market by assuming that the relative wages have been constant at 1985 levels.

The size of the economy corresponding to the steady state of our model is effectively determined by the time endowment. The capital stock adjusts to this time endowment, while the rate of return depends only on the intertemporal preferences of the household sector. In this sense, the supply of capital is perfectly elastic in the long run. It is useful to contrast the behavior of our model with that of a neo-classical growth model of the Cass-Koopmans type.[13] For example, the rate of return in the stationary solution of our model is independent of environmental policy, just as in a one-sector neoclassical growth model. However, different policies result in different levels of capital intensity—all corresponding to the same rate of return. This is impossible in a one-sector model.

In the short run, the supply of capital in our model is perfectly inelastic, since it is completely determined by past investment. Under our assumption of perfect mobility of capital and labor, changes in environmental policy can affect the distribution of capital and labor supplies among sectors, even in the short run. The transition path for the economy depends on environmental policy. It also depends on the time path of variables that are exogenous to the model. If the initial wealth of the economy is low relative to the time endowment, the rate of return will exceed the stationary rate of return. This will induce the representative consumer to postpone consumption of goods and leisure into the future, so that the rate of capital accumulation will be positive. Conversely, if the initial wealth of the economy is sufficiently high relative to the time endowment, the rate of capital accumulation will be negative.

3.3   The Impact of Environmental Regulation

Our next objective is to assess the impact of environmental regulation by projecting the growth of the U.S. economy with and without regulation. The base case for our simulations is a regime with pollution controls in effect. To determine the impact of environmental restrictions on economic activity, we simulate U.S. economic growth in the absence of regulation. We perform separate simulations to assess the impact of pollution control in industry and controls ón motor vehicle emissions, which also affect the consumption behavior of households. We then estimate the overall impact of environmental regulation by eliminating both types of pollution control.

Simulations of the U.S. economy in which pollution controls are removed differ from the base case in the steady state, the initial equilibrium, and the transition path between the two. Since capital stock is endogenous in our model, the new steady state corresponds to the long-run impact of environmental regulation on the U.S. economy. The initial equilibrium with a fixed capital stock gives the short-run impact of a change in environmental policy. Since agents in the model are endowed with perfect foresight, this initial equilibrium reflects changes along the entire time path of future regulatory policy. Finally, the transition path between the initial equilibrium and the steady state traces out the dynamics of the adjustment of the economy to a new policy for environmental regulation.

In presenting the results of our simulations of U.S. economic growth, we begin by quantifying the impact of pollution controls on production costs. We then incorporate the changes in costs into our model of the U.S. economy. We first consider the impact of environmental regulations on the steady state of the economy. For this purpose, we focus attention on a few key variables. Capital stock determines the production capacity of the economy, since the time endowment is given exogenously. Full consumption is a measure of the goods and services and leisure time available to the household sector. The level of the gross national product is an overall measure of the output of the economy, including private and public consumption, investment, and net exports to the rest of the world. Finally, the exchange rate is an indicator of the international competitiveness of the U.S. economy.

The second step in our analysis of the impact of environmental regulation is to analyze the transition path of the U.S. economy from the initial equilibrium to the new steady state. The time path of capital stock is the most important indicator of the process of economic adjustment to a change in environmental policy. The price of investment goods is an important determinant of the time path of capital stock, since it incorporates expectations about future prices of capital services and discount rates. The rental price of capital services also reflects the rate of return, which is critical to the allocation of the national income between consumption and savings. We employ the time paths of capital stock, the price of investment goods, the price of capital services, and the level of GNP in describing the adjustment process.

3.3.1   Operating Costs

We have used data collected by the Bureau of the Census (Bureau of the Census, various issues, 1973–1983) to estimate investment in pollution abatement equipment and operating costs of pollution control activities for manufacturing industries.[14] The investment data give capital expenditures on pollution abatement equipment in current prices, while the data on operating costs give current outlays attributable to pollution control. These are the actual costs reported by the business sector and do not include taxes levied as part of the Superfund program. Taxes amounting to more than a billion dollars a year were placed on the petroleum-refining and chemicals industries in 1981 and the primary metals industry in 1986. These may have had a substantial impact on U.S. economic growth, but we do not examine their consequences in this article.

Figure 3.3 summarizes the share of pollution abatement in industry costs, the share of individual industries in total abatement costs, and the share of abatement devices in industry investment for the manufacturing industries. Inspection of the first panel shows that pollution control expenses have formed only a small part of total costs for individual industries. The largest share is for the primary metals industry, at slightly more than two percent. The second panel shows that the expenses for pollution abatement have been concentrated in a relatively small number of industries. Three sectors—chemicals, petroleum refining, and primary metals—account for 55% of total spending. The third panel shows that investment in pollution abatement equipment has consumed more than 20% of total investment for paper and pulp, petroleum refining, and primary metals industries.

The first step in eliminating the operating costs of pollution control is to estimate the share of pollution abatement in the total costs of each industry. The 1983 cost shares are a maximum for the period 1973–1983, since pollution controls have increased steadily over the period. We have assumed that shares for the later years have been constant at the 1983 values. Data for industries outside manufacturing were available only for electric utilities and wastewater treatment,

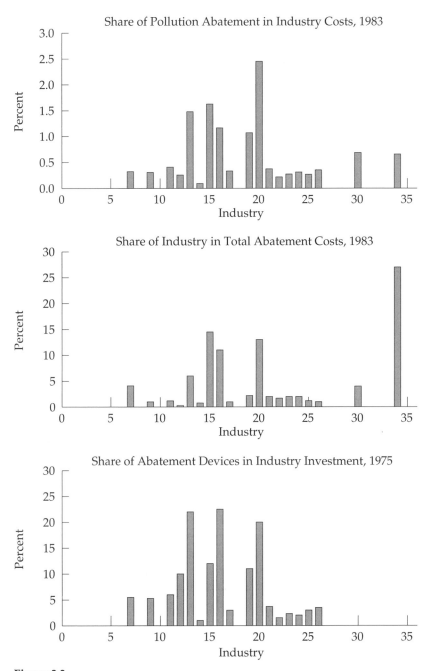

Figure 3.3
The impact of environmental regulation.

which is part of the services industry. For both industries, data on operating costs and investment expenditures for pollution abatement have been compiled by the Bureau of Economic Analysis. We have estimated the proportion of operating costs devoted to pollution abatement for these industries.[15]

Additional information on the impact of environmental regulation on costs is available for electric utilities, namely, the extra costs of burning low-sulfur fuels. Switching from high-sulfur to low-sulfur coal changes the relative proportions of the two products in the output of the coal industry. Since low-sulfur coal is more expensive, this increases the price of coal. Eliminating regulations on sulfur emissions would lower the price of coal by permitting substitution to high-sulfur grades. We have modeled the impact of lifting these emissions controls by subtracting the differential between high-cost and low-cost coal from the costs of coal production.[16] Including the coal industry, twenty industries are subject to pollution abatement regulations.

The long-run impact of eliminating the operating costs of pollution abatement is summarized in the column labeled ENV in table 3.2. The output of the economy, as measured by the real gross national product, is raised by 0.728%. The capital stock rises by 0.544%. Since our model has a perfectly elastic supply of savings in the long run, the rate of return is unaffected by regulation. However, the price of investment goods, which also reflects capital service prices, falls by 0.897%. The price of capital services declines by 0.907%, almost the same as the price of investment goods. The resulting decrease in the prices of goods and services produces a rise in full consumption of 0.278%. This increase is less than that of the gross national product, since full consumption includes leisure time as well as personal consumption expenditures. Finally, the exchange rate, which gives the domestic

Table 3.2
The effects of removing environmental regulations

Variable	Percentage change in steady state			
	ENV	INV	MV	ALL
Capital stock	0.544	2.266	1.118	3.792
Price of investment goods	−0.897	−2.652	−1.323	−4.520
Full consumption	0.278	0.489	0.282	0.975
Real GNP	0.728	1.290	0.752	2.592
Rental price of capital	−0.907	−2.730	−1.358	−4.635
Exchange rate	−0.703	−0.462	−0.392	−1.298

cost of foreign goods, falls slightly, indicating an increase in the international competitiveness of the U.S. economy.[17]

The long-run effects of eliminating operating costs associated with pollution abatement on the prices and outputs of individual industries are shown in figure 3.4. The bars in the first panel indicate the percentage change in the steady-state output price of the corresponding industry. The bars in the second panel give percentage changes in industry output levels. Not surprisingly, the principal beneficiaries of the elimination of operating costs are the most heavily regulated industries. The greatest expansion of output occurs in coal production, since the fuel cost differential between low-sulfur and high-sulfur coal is large relative to the total costs of the coal industry. Turning to manufacturing industries, the primary metals, paper, and chemicals industries have the largest gains in output from the elimination of operating costs for pollution abatement. Several other sectors benefit from the removal of operating costs of pollution abatement, but the impact is fairly modest.

We have now summarized the long-run impact of eliminating operating costs associated with pollution controls in industry. Figure 3.5 presents the dynamics of the process of adjustment to lower costs. After 1973, the price of investment goods falls slowly, reflecting the gradual price decline brought about by the elimination of operating costs associated with increasingly stringent regulations. Lower costs of investment goods tend to increase the rate of return, stimulate savings, and produce more rapid capital accumulation. Additional capital eventually brings down the rental price of capital, lowering costs still further. Finally, the quantity of full consumption rises rapidly to the new steady-state level and remains there.

The transition from the short run to the steady state is relatively slow, requiring almost three decades for capital stock and the price of capital services to adjust fully to the change in environmental policy. The graph of capital stock shows that the process of adjustment is not complete until the year 2000. This reflects the nature of our simulation experiment. The regulations are imposed gradually, so their removal is also gradual. On the other hand, full consumption attains its final value more quickly as a consequence of intertemporal optimization by households under perfect foresight. Since income is permanently higher in the future, current consumption rises in anticipation. However, the rise of consumption is dampened by an increase in the rate of return that produces greater investment.

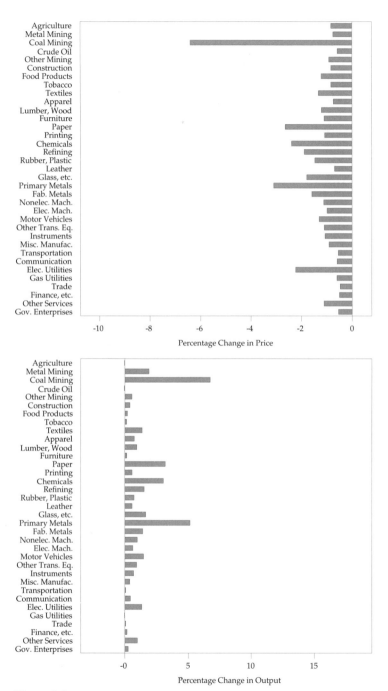

Figure 3.4
The effects of removing abatement costs on industries.

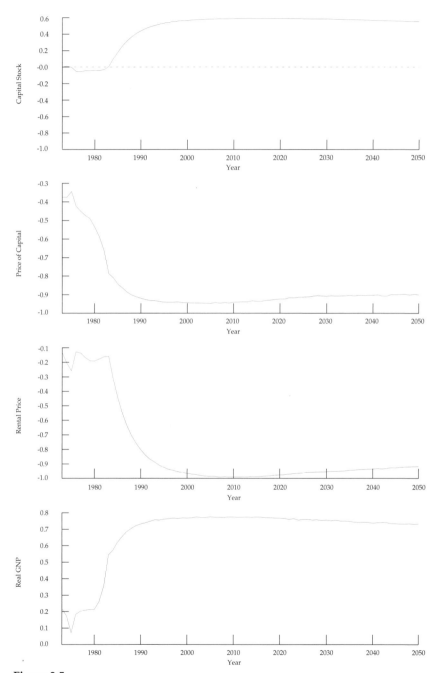

Figure 3.5
The dynamic effects of removing abatement costs.

3.3.2   Investment in Pollution Control Equipment

The most important impact of environmental regulation for some
industries is the imposition of requirements for investment in costly
new equipment for pollution abatement. Investment in pollution control devices crowds out investment for capital accumulation, further
reducing the rate of economic growth. Our second simulation of U.S.
economic growth is designed to assess the impact of investment for
pollution control. An examination of the data on investment presented in figure 3.3 reveals several striking features. First, the paper,
petroleum-refining, and primary metals industries each spent more
than 20% of their total investment on pollution control devices in 1975.
Some other sectors were not far behind, and the overall share of this
investment in total gross private domestic investment was substantial.

The share of investment for pollution abatement rose to a peak in
the early 1970s and then declined substantially. This can be attributed
to the fact that much of the early effort in pollution control was
directed at reducing emissions from existing sources by retrofitting
equipment already in place. The appropriate method for modeling
mandatory investment in pollution control requires a distinction
between achieving environmental standards for existing sources of
emissions and meeting restrictions on new sources of emissions.
Environmental regulations increase the cost of new investments, since
producers are required to purchase pollution abatement equipment
whenever they acquire new investment goods.

We assumed that investment in pollution control equipment provides no benefits to the producer other than satisfying environmental
regulations. Accordingly, we simulated mandated investment as an
increase in the price of investment goods. Unfortunately, the existing
data do not provide a separation between investments required for
new and existing facilities. We have assumed that the backlog of
investment for retrofitting old sources of emissions had been eliminated by 1983. We simulate the impact of removing environmental
regulations on investment by reducing the price of investment goods
by the proportion of total investment attributable to pollution control
for 1983. This captures the effect of requirements for pollution abatement on investment in new capital goods, but does not include the
effect of windfall losses to owners of the capital associated with old
sources of emissions.

Our method for simulating the impact of investment requirements for pollution control has certain limitations that should be pointed out. First, it relies on the assumption that capital is completely malleable and mobile between sectors. An alternative approach would be to incorporate costs of adjustment into our models of producer behavior. However, this approach would lead to considerable additional complexity in modeling and simulating producer behavior. The long-run impact of environmental regulations would be unaffected by costs of adjustment, since these costs would be zero in the steady state of our model.

The steady-state effects of mandated investment in pollution control devices are given in the column labeled INV in table 3.2. The largest change is in the capital stock, which rises by 2.266% as a direct result of the drop in the price of investment goods. In the short run, this price decline pushes up the rate of return, which raises the level of investment. Higher capital accumulation leads to a fall in the rental price of capital services, decreasing the overall price level. The long-run level of full consumption rises by 0.489%, almost double the increase resulting from eliminating operating costs of pollution abatement. The 1.290% rise in GNP is also nearly twice as large as this increase. The exchange rate appreciates by 0.462%, indicating an increase in international competitiveness of the U.S. economy.

The effects of eliminating pollution abatement investment on industry output and price levels are shown in figure 3.6. These effects stem from the drop in the rental price of capital services. The largest gains in output are for communications, electric utilities, and gas utilities, since these are the most capital intensive industries. While most sectors gain from eliminating investment for pollution control, a few sectors are hurt by this change in environmental policy. Outputs of food, apparel, rubber and plastic, and leather all decline noticeably. These sectors are among the least capital intensive, so the fall in the rental price of capital services has little effect on the prices of outputs. Buyers of the commodities produced by these industries face higher prices and substitute other commodities in both intermediate and final demand.

The transition path of the U.S. economy after investment requirements for pollution control have been eliminated is summarized in figure 3.7. The process of adjustment is markedly different from that of the previous simulation. Capital stock grows immediately and rapidly to its new equilibrium value. This comes about as a

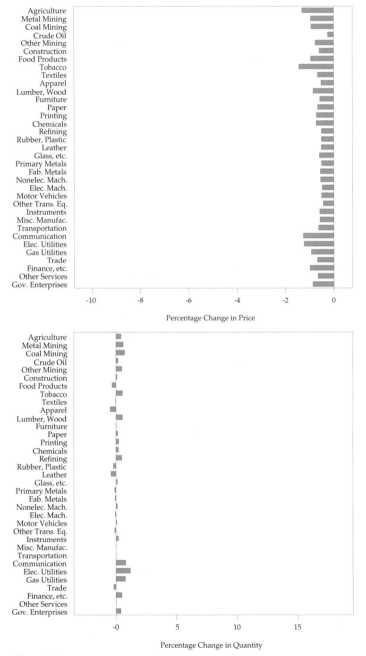

Figure 3.6
The effects of removing abatement investment on industries.

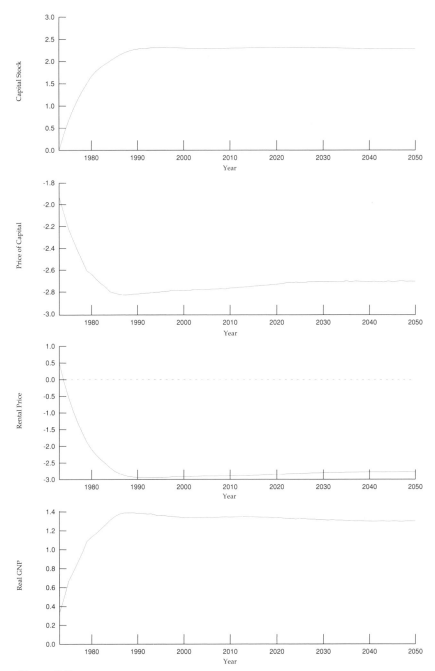

Figure 3.7
The dynamic effects of removing abatement investments.

consequence of the fall in the price of investment goods. As new capital goods become cheaper, beginning in 1973, the rate of return rises, driving up investment and producing a sharp increase in the capital stock. This explanation is further substantiated by the behavior of full consumption. Initially, consumption drops and a larger share of income is diverted to investment. Then, as the capital stock rises, so does consumption. The path of the rental price reflects the behavior of the capital stock and drives output prices downward as more capital is accumulated.

3.3.3   Motor Vehicle Emissions Control

Environmental regulation is not limited to controlling emissions by industries within the business sector. Regulations on motor vehicle emissions affect users of motor vehicles, including households as well as businesses. Motor vehicle regulation is set apart from other forms of environmental control by the fact that the pollution abatement equipment is installed by the manufacturer. Like pollution control in industry, the reduction of motor vehicle exhaust emissions adds to both capital expenditures and operating costs. The catalytic converter is a typical piece of pollution abatement equipment requiring capital expenditures. The premium paid for unleaded gasoline represents an increase in operating costs.

Using data obtained from Kappler and Rutledge (1985), we have estimated the change in motor vehicle prices resulting from emission control regulations. Pollution abatement also imposes additional operating costs on users of motor vehicles. Kappler and Rutledge separated these additional expenses into three components—increased fuel consumption, increased fuel prices, and increased motor vehicle maintenance. We first divided the total cost of pollution abatement equipment between imported and domestic vehicles in proportion to their shares in total supply. We excluded the cost of this equipment from the total cost of domestic production of motor vehicles. Now, we reduce the price of motor vehicles in proportion to the cost of pollution control devices to simulate the impact of eliminating controls on motor vehicle emissions.

The price premium for unleaded motor fuels can be modeled as a change in the cost of output of the petroleum-refining sector. This is similar to the treatment of the fuel cost differential between high-sulfur and low-sulfur coal used in our simulations of the impact of pollution abatement in industry. Only the costs associated with higher fuel prices are removed in our simulation of U.S. economic growth without motor vehicle emissions controls. Consequently, our results understate the impact of these controls. To complete the inputs to our simulation of U.S. economic growth in the absence of controls on motor vehicles emissions, we reduce the price of imported motor vehicles in the same proportion as the price of domestic vehicles.

The economic impact of imposing emissions controls on motor vehicles is similar in magnitude to the impact of pollution controls in industry. These results are summarized in the column labeled MV in table 3.2. The long-run capital stock rises by 1.118% after the elimination of controls on emissions, while full consumption increases by 0.282%. Real GNP increases by 0.752% in the absence of controls. Finally, the exchange rate appreciates by 0.392%. Almost all of the economic impact is due to decreased motor vehicle prices as a consequence of the absence of emissions controls. Changes in the price of investment goods raise the rate of return, leading to large changes in the capital stock. The price of investment goods changes substantially, since motor vehicles make up nearly 15% of new capital goods.

The long-run impact of eliminating motor vehicle emissions controls on the outputs and prices of individual industries is shown in figure 3.8. The principal beneficiary of the elimination of these regulations is the motor vehicles industry. This is partly due to the fact that the demand for motor vehicles is price elastic. A price change of 7% produces an output change of 14%. Two other industries also benefit significantly from the elimination of environmental controls—petroleum refining and electric utilities. Both gain from the reduction in fuel prices associated with elimination of the fuel price premium.

The process of adjustment to a change in controls on motor vehicle emissions is shown for key variables of the model in figure 3.9. The important features of this path are similar to those for the removal of pollution abatement investment in industry.

Vehicles are a large part of investment, so lowering their price brings down the cost of new capital goods substantially. This increases the rate of return, stimulates saving, and leads to a surge in investment. Since the change in vehicle prices is largest in later years, however, the effect is more gradual and the capital stock does not climb as rapidly.

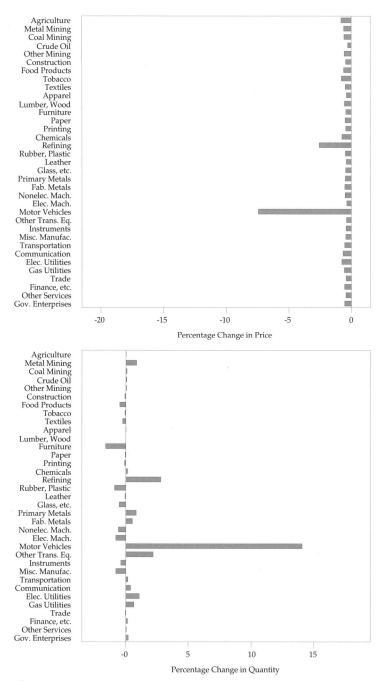

Figure 3.8
The effects of removing vehicle regulation on industries.

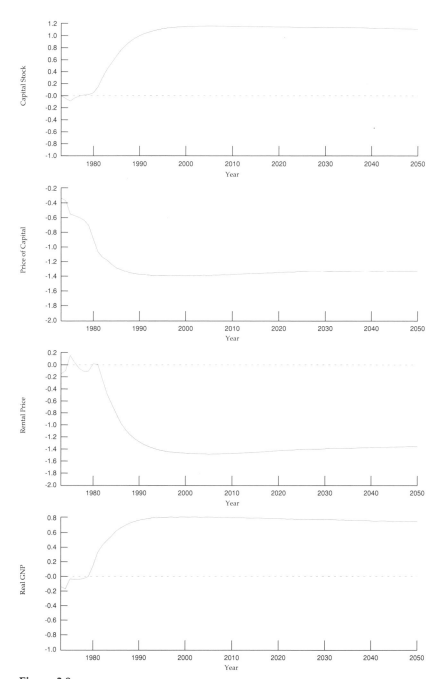

Figure 3.9
The dynamic effects of motor vehicle regulation.

3.3.4   The Impact of Environmental Regulation

To measure the total impact of eliminating all three costs of environmental regulation—operating costs resulting from pollution abatement in industry, costs of investments required by industry to meet environmental standards, and costs of emissions controls on motor vehicles—we perform a final simulation. This simulation is not a simple combination of its three components. Operating costs include capital costs, so combining the reductions in operating costs with the elimination of investment requirements would count the cost reductions associated with capital twice. To solve this problem, the capital component was removed from operating costs in the combined simulation. The results of removing all forms of environmental regulation are summarized in the column labeled ALL in table 3.2.

The long-run consequences of pollution control for different industries are presented in figure 3.10. The sectors hit hardest by environmental regulations are the motor vehicles and coal-mining industries. Primary metals and petroleum refining follow close behind. About half of the remaining industries have increases in output of 1% to 5% after pollution controls are removed. The rest are largely unaffected by environmental regulations. The economy follows the transition path to the new steady state shown in figure 3.11. Driven by large changes in the price of investment goods, the capital stock rises sharply. The quantity of full consumption rises at a similar rate, as does real GNP. The adjustment process is dominated by the rapid accumulation of capital and is largely completed within two decades.

3.4   Conclusions

We can summarize the impact of environmental regulation by analyzing the effects on the growth of GNP over the period 1973–1985. These effects are given in table 3.3. Mandated investment in pollution control equipment has the largest impact, while motor vehicle emissions control is not far behind. The added operating costs due to pollution abatement play a minor role in the growth slowdown. The three types of environmental regulation together are responsible for a drop in GNP growth of 0.191 percentage points.

A number of studies have attempted to measure the effect of pollution control on productivity and economic growth.[18] For example, Denison (1985) found that the growth rate of the U.S. economy was

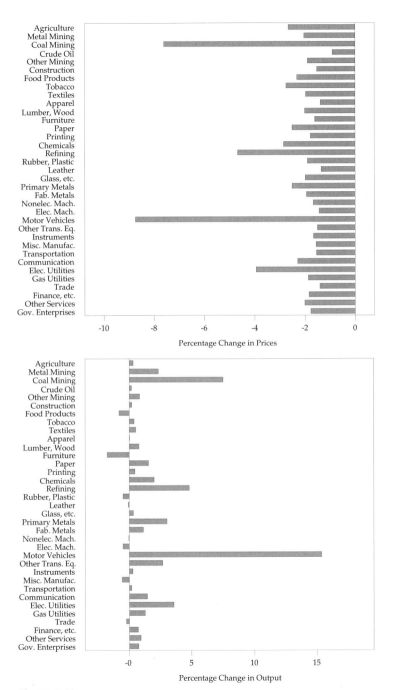

Figure 3.10
The effects of removing all environmental regulation on industries.

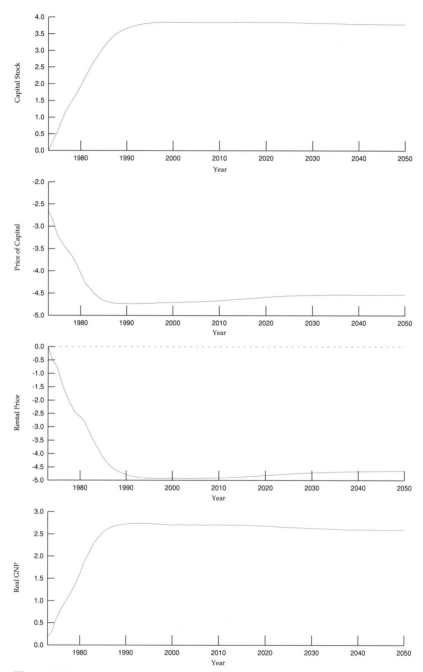

Figure 3.11
The dynamic effects of removing all environmental regulation.

Table 3.3
Summary of the effects on growth over 1974–1985

Simulation	Change in growth rate
Operating costs	0.034
Investment	0.074
Old source investment	0.026
Motor vehicles	0.051
All effects	0.191

reduced by only 0.07 percentage points over the period 1973–1982 due to pollution controls. His estimate is based on an aggregate production function and does not take in account the important differences in environmental restrictions among industries. In addition, Denison does not model the dynamic response of the U.S. economy to pollution controls. Our model incorporates differences among industries in pollution abatement and captures the effect of environmental costs on the rate of capital formation. Accordingly, our estimate of the impact of environmental regulation on U.S. economic growth is several times that reported by Denison.

We can also summarize the impact of higher operating costs associated with environmental regulation on economic growth, using the results given in table 3.3. U.S. economic growth would have been 0.034 percentage points higher during the period 1973–1985 in the absence of the operating costs resulting from environmental regulation. These operating costs had a small but significant effect on long-run output and the rate of growth of the economy in the 1970s and early 1980s. In addition, these costs affected the distribution of economic activity with industries such as primary metals experiencing a considerable drop in output. However, operating costs arising from pollution abatement are not the only effects of environmental regulation.

The impact of pollution abatement investment on the rate of GNP growth during the period 1973–1985 is also given in table 3.3. The growth of GNP would have been 0.074 percentage points higher in the absence of mandated investment in pollution control. Slower productivity growth contributes 0.015 percentage points to this total, while the rest came from slower growth of the primary factors of production. Mandated investment in pollution control has two effects. First, it lowered the long-run capital stock and reduced long-run consumption. Second, it reduced the rate of capital accumulation in the early years of regulation. This reduced the rate of growth of GNP. The impact of eliminating mandated investment in pollution abatement devices was substantially larger than that of eliminating operating costs.

The dampening effect of investment for pollution control on capital accumulation is exacerbated by the investment required to bring existing sources of emissions into compliance with environmental standards. We have taken the share of investment attributable to new investment goods as the 1983 share. The difference between the actual shares in earlier years and the 1983 share gives the proportion devoted to existing sources of emissions. The data presented in figure 3.6 show that this expenditure reached as much as 3 percent of total investment during the mid-1970s.

We have modified our simulation of U.S. economic growth to assess the importance of mandated investment in pollution abatement equipment for existing sources of emissions. For this purpose, we increased the level of investment expenditures for the years 1973 to 1983 by the share attributable to pollution abatement for existing sources. This raises the rate of capital accumulation in the mid-1970s, but there is no long-run effect on economic growth. Eliminating investment in pollution control devices for both new and existing sources raises the average rate of growth for the period 1973–1985 by 0.100 percentage points. We estimated an increase in the growth rate of 0.074 percentage points for the investment required for new sources alone, so that we can attribute an increase of 0.026 points to the investment required to bring existing sources into compliance.

Finally, the rate of growth of the U.S. national product over the period 1973–1985 would have been 0.051 percentage points higher in the absence of motor vehicle emissions controls. This is a surprisingly large effect. It is nearly twice as large as the gain from eliminating mandatory investments for bringing existing sources of emissions into compliance with environmental standards and about half as large as removing all operating costs and all investment requirements for pollution control in industry.

Notes

1. The evaluation of environmental benefits is discussed, for example, in Freeman (1985) and Maler (1985).
2. A detailed survey of U.S. environmental policy is presented in Christiansen and Tietenberg (1985).

3. The data on inter-industry transactions are based on input-output tables for the U.S. constructed by the Bureau of Economic Analysis (1984). The income data came from the U.S. national income and product accounts also developed by the Bureau of Economic Analysis (1986). The data on capital and labor services are based on those of Jorgenson, Gollop, and Fraumeni (1987). Our data are organized according to an accounting system based on the United Nations (1968) in system of national accounts. The details are given in Appendix C in Wilcoxen (1988).

4. The calibration approach is discussed by Mansur and Whalley (1984). This approach is employed by Borges and Goulder (1984) in a model for analyzing the impact of energy prices on U.S. economic growth. The model is based on data for the year 1973. The econometric approach to this problem is reviewed by Jorgenson (1982). Further details on the econometric methodology are presented by Jorgenson (1984a).

5. Forsund and Strom (1976) employ the specification of substitution between commodities introduced by Johansen (1960). The materials balance approach introduced by Kneese, Ayres, and d'Arge (1970) is considered in a general equilibrium setting in Maler (1974). A detailed survey of fixed coefficient input-output models employed in environmental economics is given by Forsund (1985).

6. Our approach to endogenous productivity growth was originated by Jorgenson and Fraumeni (1981). The implementation of a general equilibrium model of production that incorporates both substitution among inputs and endogenous productivity growth is discussed by Jorgenson (1984a, 1986). This model has been analyzed in detail by Hogan and Jorgenson (1991).

7. This approach was originated by Armington (1969).

8. Further details are given by Jorgenson (1989).

9. The econometric methodology employed in our study was originated by Jorgenson, Lau, and Stoker (1982). The econometric model we have employed was constructed by Jorgenson and Slesnick (1987a). Further details on the econometric methodology are given by Jorgenson (1984a, 1990a).

10. The price of leisure time is equal to the market wage rate, reduced by the marginal tax rate on labor income, which is the opportunity cost of foregone labor income. The price of personal consumption expenditures is a cost of living index, generated from the first stage of our model of consumer behavior. This cost of living index is discussed by Jorgenson and Slesnick (1983).

11. The Euler equation approach to modeling intertemporal consumer behavior was originated by Hall (1978). Our application of this approach to full consumption follows Jorgenson and Yun (1986).

12. Our breakdown of the U.S. population by age, educational attainment, and sex is based on the system of demographic accounts compiled by Jorgenson and Fraumeni (1989). The population projections are discussed in detail by Wilcoxen (1988), Appendix B.

13. This model was originated by Cass (1965) and Koopmans (1967). The Cass–Koopmans model has recently been discussed by Lucas (1988) and Romer (1989). Neo-classical growth models with pollution abatement have been presented by Maler (1975) and Uzawa (1975).

14. A detailed description of the data is given by Wilcoxen (1988), Appendix D.

15. The details are given by Wilcoxen (1988), Appendix D.

16. The details of our methodology for estimating cost differentials between high-sulfur and low-sulfur coal are given by Wilcoxen (1988), Appendix D.

17. An alternative analysis of the impact of environmental regulation on U.S. international competitiveness is given in Kalt (1988).

18. A detailed survey of studies of the impact of environmental regulation on productivity and economic growth in the United States is presented by Christiansen and Tietenberg (1985).

4

Reducing U.S. Carbon Dioxide Emissions: The Cost of Different Goals

Dale W. Jorgenson and
Peter J. Wilcoxen

4.1   Introduction

The possibility that carbon dioxide emissions from fossil fuel combustion might lead to global warming through the greenhouse effect has emerged as a leading international environmental concern. Many nations, including the United States, are considering policies to reduce carbon dioxide emissions. Moreover, multilateral action is being discussed under the auspices of the Intergovernmental Panel on Climate Change. For the most part, however, public debate has focused on a few fairly arbitrary targets, such as holding carbon dioxide emissions constant or reducing emissions by twenty percent. Little attention has been devoted to deciding what the optimal target would be.[1] Finding the optimal target requires an accurate assessment of both the costs and benefits of different policies. In this chapter, we present a detailed model of the U.S. economy and use it to compute the costs of attaining three different emissions goals by imposing taxes on the carbon content of primary fuels.[2] The goals we consider differ considerably in stringency, so our results give a clear picture of the cost curve lying behind different levels of emissions reductions. We find that costs rise very rapidly, so it is imperative that policy makers carefully assess the benefits of carbon dioxide abatement before adopting a particular target.

The greenhouse effect comes about because several trace gases in the atmosphere, often called greenhouse gases, are transparent to visible light but reflect infrared. Sunlight passes through such gases unimpeded and is absorbed by objects on the ground. Later, much of that energy is re-emitted as infrared radiation. Since greenhouse gases reflect infrared, they tend to trap energy in the atmosphere, which results in heating. The concentration of greenhouse gases in the atmosphere determines how much energy is trapped, and thus, how much heating occurs.[3]

Carbon dioxide (CO_2) is the most important contributor to the greenhouse effect, although other gases are also important. These other gases include methane (CH_4), chlorofluorocarbons (CFCs), ozone (O_3), nitrous oxide (N_2O), and other oxides of nitrogen (NO_X). Much of the carbon dioxide in the atmosphere originates as a natural consequence of respiration, but combustion, particularly of fossil fuels, has increased the atmospheric concentration by 25 percent since the industrial revolution (Schneider, 1989). At present rates of emission, carbon dioxide accounts for about half the increase in the concentration of greenhouse gases, while other gases account for the remainder (Houghton and Woodwell, 1989).

That greenhouse gases trap energy and lead to heating of the atmosphere is not controversial; however, a great deal of uncertainty exists about how much heating will be produced by a given increase in greenhouse gases, and when the heating will occur. Current research indicates that the concentration of greenhouse gases is likely to double sometime in the next century, with mean surface temperatures rising by 1.5 to 5.5 degrees centigrade.[4] Historical data indicate that global temperatures have risen by 0.5 degrees centigrade during the past 100 years, and that the rate of increase has been accelerating.[5]

The environmental consequences of global warming could be severe. It might change patterns of precipitation, cause land to be inundated by increases in the sea level, or increase the frequency of violent storms such as hurricanes. As a consequence, a sizable constituency has developed for policy measures to reduce greenhouse gas emissions. For example, the Toronto Conference on the Changing Atmosphere, held in June 1988 and attended by representatives from 48 nations, recommended that world carbon dioxide emissions be reduced to twenty percent below 1988 levels by the year 2005, and eventually to fifty percent of 1988 levels (Natural Resources Defense Council, 1989). In the United States, Senator Timothy Wirth has introduced legislation that would sharply reduce carbon dioxide emissions.[6] In addition, environmental groups such as the Natural Resources Defense Council have called for strong, immediate action to reduce the emission of greenhouse gases.[7]

One of the policies proposed for fighting the greenhouse effect is a tax on the carbon content of fossil fuels.[8] This is known as a "carbon" tax, and it could be an effective way to reduce CO_2 emissions. For example, a carbon tax would lead to substitution of other inputs for fossil fuels, and to an increase in the use of fuels such as natural gas that have lower carbon content and hence contribute less to the greenhouse effect. In this chapter, we examine the costs of a carbon tax in detail, focusing in particular on how those costs change as CO_2 emissions goals become more stringent.

Ours is by no means the first study of greenhouse abatement policies. An important series of studies of the effect of CO_2 restrictions on the U.S. energy sector was initiated by Edmonds and Reilly (1983, 1985).[9] The Edmonds-Reilly approach uses a very detailed model of the energy sector, but it excludes the rest of the economy. Thus, it cannot be used for computing the economy-wide costs of CO_2 abatement, nor can it be used to analyze the impact of restrictions on U.S. economic growth.

Manne and Richels (1990) examined several CO_2 reduction policies using GLOBAL 2100, a five region model of the world economy. GLOBAL 2100 combines a process analysis model of the energy sector with a macroeconomic growth model.[10] The growth model is based on an aggregate production function with inputs of capital, labor, electricity, and nonelectric energy. The production function allows for the possibility that there are "autonomous energy efficiency improvements" which reduce the share of energy in GNP over time. The energy submodel is fairly detailed, including ten electric generation technologies and six sources of nonelectric energy. After examining a number of scenarios combining different assumptions about when various technologies become available, Manne and Richels conclude that a U.S. policy of reducing carbon emissions to the 1985 rate by the year 2000 and subsequently to eighty percent of that rate by 2020 would lower annual GNP by five percent by the year 2030. The carbon tax needed to achieve this drop in emissions is enormous, varying over time between $350 and $800 per ton of carbon.[11]

Nordhaus (1989) has recently assessed several policies for controlling greenhouse emissions using rough estimates of the costs and benefits of each.[12] Estimates of benefits are taken from EPA (1988), which quantifies the cost of global warming. A number of alternative abatement strategies are considered—controlling CFCs, reducing CO_2 emissions, reforestation, and imposing a tax on gasoline. Comparing

estimates of the marginal cost of reducing greenhouse emissions by
the equivalent of one ton of CO_2, Nordhaus argues that the optimal
reduction in emissions of greenhouse gases could be achieved with a
large reduction in CFCs and a comparatively small reduction in carbon dioxide emissions. Reforestation and gasoline taxes are found to
be excessively costly in relation to the amount of carbon removed
from the atmosphere.

Whalley and Wigle (1990) have used a global static general equilibrium model to determine the effects of various carbon taxes. Their
model divides the world into three regions: high-income countries,
low-income countries, and oil exporters. They conducted several
experiments, each designed to achieve a fifty percent decrease in the
production of energy from sources that contribute to the greenhouse
effect. (Underlying this is an implicit assumption that greenhouse
gases and certain forms of energy are produced in fixed proportions.)
Their results show that world welfare would fall by more than $250
billion annually (U.S. dollars). Depending on how the carbon tax was
implemented, the revenue raised could be substantial—from $100 bil-
lion to $300 billion dollars a year in the high-income countries alone.
An interesting feature of the study is the possible distributions of
these revenues among the three regions.

From these studies a great deal of valuable information has been
accumulated about the economic impact of policies to limit the emissions of greenhouse gases. However, the analysis of the impact on
U.S. economic growth of restrictions on these emissions is seriously
incomplete. In order to measure this cost, it is essential to model the
responses of businesses and households at a highly disaggregated
level. Policies such as carbon taxes are intended to reduce fossil fuel
use by inducing producers and households to substitute toward other
inputs, and a detailed model is needed to capture these effects. Moreover, carbon taxes are likely to affect the price of new capital goods,
and thus will affect the rate of capital accumulation. To capture this
effect requires a model with endogenous capital formation. In addition, carbon taxes will increase the price of energy to purchasers,
which may reduce or accelerate technical change. To address these
concerns requires a disaggregated, dynamic general equilibrium of the
U.S. economy in which technical change is endogenous. In the
remainder of this chapter we present such a model and use it to examine the effects of several carbon taxes.

4.2 An Overview of the Model

The results presented in section 4.3 are based on simulations we conducted using a disaggregated, econometrically estimated intertemporal general equilibrium model of the United States. The model itself is an extension of our earlier work on environmental regulation, and is documented in detail in Jorgenson and Wilcoxen (1990a, 1990b). Rather than presenting the entire model again, in this section we will confine ourselves to outlining a few of its key features and discussing how we extended it to calculate carbon emissions.

4.2.1 Producer Behavior

Several of the model's most important features are closely connected to our submodel of producer behavior. For example, production is moderately disaggregated: total output is divided into 35 separate commodities, each of which is produced by one or more of 35 industries. The industries correspond roughly to two-digit SIC classifications, and are shown in table 4.1. This level of detail allows us to measure the effect of shocks on fairly narrow segments of the economy. Since carbon dioxide emissions are concentrated in energy production—a small part of the overall economy—a disaggregated model is essential for examining the sectoral effects of global warming policies.

Each of the 35 industries is represented by an econometrically estimated nested translog unit cost function. At the function's top level, output is produced using capital, labor, energy and materials (KLEM). Capital and labor are both primary factors purchased directly from households. Energy and materials, on the other hand, are translog aggregates of intermediate goods. The energy aggregate is composed of inputs of coal, crude petroleum, refined petroleum, electricity, and natural gas,[13] while the materials aggregate is composed of inputs of all other intermediate goods. Minimizing costs subject to this specification allows us to derive factor demands for capital, labor and intermediate inputs of the 35 commodities. When fully parameterized, these demands completely describe producer behavior.

To parameterize the producer submodel (and, indeed, the rest of the model), we constructed a special data set of consistent input-output tables running from 1947 through 1985.[14] This data set allowed us to estimate all parameters in all of the model's behavioral

Table 4.1
Industry classifications

Number	Description
1	Agriculture, forestry, and fisheries
2	Metal mining
3	Coal mining
4	Crude petroleum and natural gas
5	Nonmetallic mineral mining
6	Construction
7	Food and kindred products
8	Tobacco manufacturers
9	Textile mill products
10	Apparel and other textile products
11	Lumber and wood products
12	Furniture and fixtures
13	Paper and allied products
14	Printing and publishing
15	Chemicals and allied products
16	Petroleum refining
17	Rubber and plastic products
18	Leather and leather products
19	Stone, clay, and glass products
20	Primary metals
21	Fabricated metal products
22	Machinery, except electrical
23	Electrical machinery
24	Motor vehicles
25	Other transportation equipment
26	Instruments
27	Miscellaneous manufacturing
28	Transportation and warehousing
29	Communication
30	Electric utilities
31	Gas utilities
32	Trade
33	Finance, insurance, and real estate
34	Other services
35	Government enterprises

equations, a feature which most clearly distinguishes our model from others. This method of parameterization, known as the econometric approach, stands in marked contrast to the calibration method used for most general equilibrium models. Calibration involves choosing the model's parameters so that the model will replicate a particular year.[15] Because it requires fairly little data, calibration has been widely applied in general equilibrium modeling.

By taking the econometric approach, however, we gained several advantages over calibration. First, by using a long time series of data (rather than a single point), we are able to estimate more flexible functional forms. Thus, our approach imposes less structure on the data than the simple functional forms used for calibration. We do not, for example, need to assume that production is Cobb-Douglas or CES. A second advantage is that estimated parameters based on a long time series are less likely to be corrupted by noise. Calibrated parameters, on the other hand, are forced by construction to absorb all noise present in the data. This poses a severe problem when the benchmark year is unusual in some respect because calibrated parameters will build that distortion into the model. Estimation avoids this problem by reducing the influence of any particular year's data on the parameters. Most importantly, however, by estimating each industry's cost function on a consistent set of time series data, our model implicitly incorporates elasticities of substitution consistent with historical observations.[16]

The third important feature of the producer submodel is our treatment of technical change. As part of each industry's cost function, we include several terms to allow for technical change.[17] Most other models used to study global warming, such as Manne and Richels (1990), assume a constant exogenous rate of technical change. In our model, however, technical change is endogenous. Moreover, it is determined at the industry level, which allows different sectors to grow at different rates. In addition, each industry's technical change may be biased toward some inputs and away from others. Differing rates of biased technical change are a common feature of historical data, but are necessarily absent from aggregated models. By including endogenous industry-level technical change, our model is able to capture the medium-run evolution of individual sectors much more accurately.

In sum, the salient features of the production submodel are that it is disaggregated and econometrically estimated, and that it allows for industry-level biased technical change. In addition, it fully captures substitution among intermediate inputs. We now turn briefly to a discussion of the model's final demands: consumption, investment, government spending, and foreign trade.

4.2.2 Consumption

Our final demand vector giving household consumption by commodity is the end result of a three-stage intertemporal optimization problem. At the first stage, each household allocates full wealth (the sum of financial wealth, discounted future labor earnings, and an imputed value of leisure time) across different time periods according to its rate of time preference and its intertemporal elasticity of substitution. We formalize this decision using a representative agent who maximizes an intertemporal utility function subject to an intertemporal budget constraint. The agent's optimal allocation must satisfy a set of necessary conditions which can be summarized in the form of an Euler equation.[18] The Euler equation is forward-looking, so current consumption, and hence the rate of saving, will depend on expectations about future prices and interest rates. Because capital formation is an important contributor to economic growth, this formulation of the savings decision plays a significant role in the model. We will return to this point in the section on investment.

Once households have allocated full wealth across periods, they begin the second stage of their optimization: deciding on the mix of leisure and goods to consume in each period. As in the intertemporal allocation, we simplify the representation of household preferences between goods and leisure by the use of a representative consumer. The representative consumer has a translog intraperiod indirect utility function which depends on the prices of leisure and an aggregate consumption good. (We take the price of leisure to be the after-tax wage rate and the price of the aggregate consumption good to be a price index based on the commodities consumed.) From this, we derive the consumer's demands for leisure and goods in each period as a function of prices and the amount of full wealth allocated to the period. This produces an allocation of the household's time endowment, which is given exogenously, between leisure time and the labor market. Thus, the second stage of the consumer model determines labor supply.

The third stage of the household optimization problem is the allocation of consumption expenditures among capital, labor and the 35 commodities. At this stage, we abandon the representative consumer assumption and instead follow the methodology of Jorgenson, Lau and Stoker (1982) by formulating a system of individual household demand systems which can be aggregated. We then distinguish between 672 household types based attributes such as the number of household members and the geographic region in which the household is located. For each of these households, we follow the approach of Jorgenson and Slesnick (1987a) by using a nested translog tier structure to represent demands for individual commodities.[19]

As with production, all behavioral equations in all stages of the consumer model are econometrically estimated. This includes the Euler equation, the allocation equations for leisure and personal consumption, and the equations governing the allocation of consumption among commodities.[20] Thus, our household model incorporates historical substitution shown by consumers. Moreover, an important feature of our specification is that we do not require household demands to be homothetic. Thus, as incomes rise the pattern of consumption will shift, even in the absence of price changes. This captures an important and often noted feature of historical data which is usually ignored in general equilibrium modeling.

4.2.3   Investment and Capital Accumulation

As noted above, an important feature of the model is that it is based on intertemporal optimization by households, which is the source of our savings supply function. In addition, we also assume intertemporal behavior on the part of investors. Both types of intertemporal behavior are very important for greenhouse abatement simulations as much of the impact of regulation occurs far in the future. Since many of these effects will be anticipated by households and firms, future events will have consequences for current decisions. Saving, for example, depends on households' expectations of future earnings and interest rates, while investment depends on firms' expectations of future wages and prices. Changes in saving and investment affect the rate of capital accumulation, and hence the rate of economic growth.

Our investment model is based on perfect foresight or national expectations. In particular, we require that the price of new investment goods always be equal to the present discounted value of the returns expected on an extra unit of capital.[21] For tractability, we assume there is a single capital stock in the economy which is perfectly malleable and can be reallocated between industries at zero cost.[22] The total supply of capital, however, is fixed at any time by past investment behavior. This implies that the return on a unit of capital in a given period is precisely equal to the economy-wide rental price of capital goods. In addition, we assume that new capital goods are produced out of individual commodities according to a production function estimated from historical data, so the price of new capital will depend on commodity prices. Thus, the price of capital goods and the discounted value of future rental prices must be brought into equilibrium by adjustments in the term structure of interest rates. Finally, the quantity of investment done in each period is determined by the amount of savings made available by households.

The production function for new capital goods was estimated using final demand data for investment over the period 1947–1985. Thus, our model incorporates substitution between different inputs in the composition of the aggregate capital good. This feature sometimes plays an important role. In our earlier work on environmental regulation, for example, we found that a substantial drop in the price of automobiles would shift investment toward motor vehicles and away from other durable goods.

In sum, capital accumulation is the outcome of intertemporal behavior on the part of households and firms. Households determine the amount of savings available in each period through intertemporal utility maximization. Firms, for their part, invest until the returns on additional investment are driven to the cost of new capital goods. Finally, savings and investment are equilibrated by the interest rate.

4.2.4   Government and Foreign Trade

The two remaining final demand categories are the government and the foreign sector. Beginning with the government, we determine final demands for government consumption from the income-expenditure identity for the government sector. The first step is to compute total tax revenue by applying exogenous tax rates to appropriate transactions in the business and household sectors. We then add the capital income of government enterprises (determined endogenously) and nontax receipts (exogenous) to tax revenue to obtain total government revenue.

Next, we make an important assumption about the government budget deficit; namely that it can be specified exogenously.[23] We add the deficit to total revenue to obtain total government spending. To arrive at government purchases of goods and services, we subtract interest paid to domestic and foreign holders of government bonds together with government transfer payments to domestic and foreign recipients. We allocate the remainder among commodity groups according to fixed shares constructed from historical data. Finally, we determine the quantity of each commodity by dividing the value of government spending on the good by its price.

Foreign trade, on the other hand, has two components: imports and exports. Imports are handled by assuming that they are imperfect substitutes for similar domestic commodities.[24] To implement this, we assume the goods actually purchased by households and firms are translog aggregates of domestic and imported products, where parameters of the aggregation function are determined by estimation. Thus, each commodity is governed by a separate elasticity of substitution between foreign and domestic goods. The result is that intermediate and final demands implicitly determine imports of each commodity. The prices of imports are given exogenously in each period.

Exports, on the other hand, are modeled by a set of explicit foreign demand equations, one for each commodity, which depend on foreign income (given exogenously) and the foreign price of U.S. exports. Foreign prices are computed from domestic prices by adjusting for subsidies and the exchange rate. The demand elasticities appearing in these equations were estimated from historical data.[25]

The final important part of the foreign trade submodel is our treatment of the current account and the exchange rate. Without an elaborate model of international trade (far beyond the scope of this study), it is impossible to determine both the current account and the exchange rate endogenously. Thus, in the simulations reported below, we take the current account balance to be exogenous and the exchange rate to be endogenous.

4.2.5 Computing Carbon Emissions

The most important remaining feature of the model is the way in which carbon dioxide emissions are calculated. For tractability, we assume CO_2 is emitted in fixed proportion to fossil fuel use. This implicitly assumes that nothing can be done to reduce the CO_2 produced by any given combustion process, but in practice that is largely the case.[26] For comparability with other studies, we measure CO_2 emissions in tons of contained carbon.[27]

We calculated the carbon content of each fossil fuel in the following way. From the Department of Energy we obtained the average heat

Table 4.2
Carbon emissions data for 1987

Item	Fuel		
	Coal	Oil	Gas
Unit of measure	ton	bbl	kcf
Heat content (10^6 Btu per unit)	21.94	5.80	1.03
Emissions rate (kg per 10^6 Btu)	26.9	21.4	14.5
(kg per unit)	590.2	124.1	14.9
Total domestic output 10^9 units	0.9169	0.3033	17.8
Total carbon emissions 10^6 tons	595.3	414.1	268.6

content of each fuel in millions of Btu per quantity unit (Department of Energy, 1990). Next, we obtained data from the Environmental Protection Agency on the amount of carbon emitted per million Btu produced from each fuel.[28] Multiplying EPA's figures by the heating value of the different fuels gives the carbon content of a unit of each fuel. Total carbon emissions can then be calculated using figures on total fuel production. Table 4.2 shows data for each fuel in 1987.

Our simulation model, however, is normalized so that all prices are equal to one in 1982. Thus, its quantities do not correspond directly to physical units. Moreover, the model has a single aggregate sector for oil and gas. To convert the figures above into a form appropriate for the model's quantity units, we summed carbon production for oil and gas and divided by the model's output for Industry 4 (oil and gas extraction) in 1987. This gave the carbon coefficient for that industry. Similarly, the coefficient for coal was computed by dividing total carbon production from coal by the model's 1987 value for coal output. These coefficients were then used to compute carbon emissions in each simulation. We now turn to a brief discussion of the model's base case.

4.2.6   The Base Case

In order to solve the model, we must provide values for all exogenous variables in all periods. We accomplish this in two steps. First, we develop a set of default assumptions about the values each exogenous variable will have over time in the absence of changes in government policy. This is used to generate a simulation called the "base case." The second step is to change certain exogenous variables to reflect a proposed policy and then solve the model again to produce a "revised case." We can then compare the two simulations to assess the effects of the policy. Thus, the assumptions underlying the base case are of some importance in understanding the model's results.

Because the model includes agents with perfect foresight, we must solve it far into the future. In order to do that, we project values for all exogenous variables over the period 1990–2050. After 2050, we assume the variables will remain constant at their 2050 values, which allows the model to converge to a steady state by the year 2100. Some of the most important or interesting projections are noted briefly below; a more detailed discussion appears in Jorgenson and Wilcoxen (1990b).

First, we set all tax rates to their values in 1985, the last year in our sample period. Next, we assume that foreign prices of imports (in foreign currency and before tariffs) remain constant in real terms at 1985 levels. Third, we project a gradual decline in the government deficit through the year 2025, after which the deficit is held at four percent of the nominal value of the government debt. This has the effect of maintaining a constant ratio of the value of the government debt to the value of the national product when the inflation rate is four percent (as it is in our steady state). Fourth, we project that the current account deficit will fall gradually to zero by the year 2000. After that, we project a small current account surplus sufficient to produce a stock of net claims on foreigners by the year 2050 equal to the same proportion of national wealth as in 1982.

Finally, the most important exogenous variables are those associated with U.S. population growth and the corresponding change in the economy's time endowment. We project population by age, sex, and educational attainment through the year 2050, using demographic assumptions consistent with Social Security Administration forecasts.[29] After 2050, we hold population constant, which is roughly consistent with Social Security projections. In addition, we project educational attainment by assuming that future demographic cohorts will have the same level of attainment as the cohort reaching age 35 in the year 1985. We then transform our population projection into a projection of the time endowment used in our model of the labor market by assuming that relative wages across occupations are constant at 1985 levels. Since capital accumulation is endogenous, these population projections effectively determine the size of the economy in the more distant future.

4.3   The Impact of Different Emissions Targets

We now turn to our results on the effects of using a carbon tax to achieve different CO_2 emissions goals. All together, we ran three simulations in addition to the base case, one for each of the following policies:

1. Stabilizing carbon emissions at the 1990 base level beginning immediately.

2. Decreasing carbon emissions gradually over 1990–2005 until they are twenty percent below the 1990 base level.

3. Doing nothing until 2000, then gradually increasing the carbon tax over 2000–2010 to stabilize emissions at the year 2000 base level.

These policies vary considerably in stringency. In 1990, base-case fossil fuel use produced 1,576 million tons of carbon. Policy 1 would keep that level constant forever, even in the face of rapid GNP growth. Policy 2, however, is even more restrictive: it requires emissions to drop to 1,261 million tons by 2,005 and remain at that level forever. Policy 3, on the other hand, is the least restrictive: it allows emissions to rise to the base case year 2000 level of 1,675 million tons.

In each simulation, we constrained total carbon emissions and allowed the level of the carbon tax to be determined endogenously. The tax was applied to primary fuels (industries 3 and 4) in proportion to carbon content. Because even the least stringent policy produces substantial tax revenue, it was also necessary to make an assumption about how the revenue would be used. In these simulations, we held the real value of government spending constant at its base-case level and allowed the average tax on labor to adjust to keep the difference between government spending and government revenue equal to the exogenous budget deficit. At the same time, we held the *marginal* tax on labor constant, so adjustments in the average rate reflect changes in the implicit zero-tax threshold.

4.3.1   Long-Run Effects

The principal direct consequence of all three carbon control strategies is to increase purchasers' prices of coal and crude oil. This can be seen most clearly by examining the model's results for each simulation at a particular point in time, so in this section we present detailed results for the year 2020. Our model is most suitable for medium run analysis (periods of 20–30 years), so for our purposes 2020 is the long run.

We begin with results for the first experiment: holding emissions at 1990 levels. By the year 2020, maintaining 1990 emissions will require a tax of $16.96 per ton of carbon contained in primary fuels.[30] Using the data in table 4.2, it can be shown that this amounts to a tax of about $11.01 per ton of coal, $2.32 per barrel of oil, or $0.28 per thousand cubic feet of gas. The tax would generate revenue of $26.7 billion annually.

The rising price of fossil fuels provokes substitution toward other energy sources and away from energy in general. Total Btu consumption falls by twelve percent to about 68 quads. This substitution away from energy, and hence toward more expensive production techniques, results in a drop of 0.7 percent in the capital stock and 0.5 in real GNP. These figures are fairly small because they measure, in a loose sense, the welfare losses from introducing a small distortionary tax. Because revenue from the tax is returned to households through essentially lump-sum adjustments in the income tax, social welfare falls purely due to the inefficiency of the tax.

At the commodity level the impact of the tax varies considerably. Figure 4.1 shows changes in the supply price of the 35 commodities measured as percentage changes relative to the base case. The largest change occurs in the price of coal (commodity 3), which rises by forty percent. This, in turn, increases the price of electricity (commodity 30) by about five percent. Electricity prices rise considerably less than coal prices because coal accounts for only about thirteen percent of total utility costs. Other prices showing significant effects are those for crude and refined petroleum (goods 4 and 16) and gas utilities (good 31). These rise, directly or indirectly, because of the tax on oil.

These changes in prices affect demands for the commodities, which in turn determine how industry outputs are affected. Figure 4.2 shows percentage changes in quantities produced by the thirty-five industries. Most of the sectors show only small changes in output. Coal mining (sector 3) is the exception: its output falls by twenty-six percent.

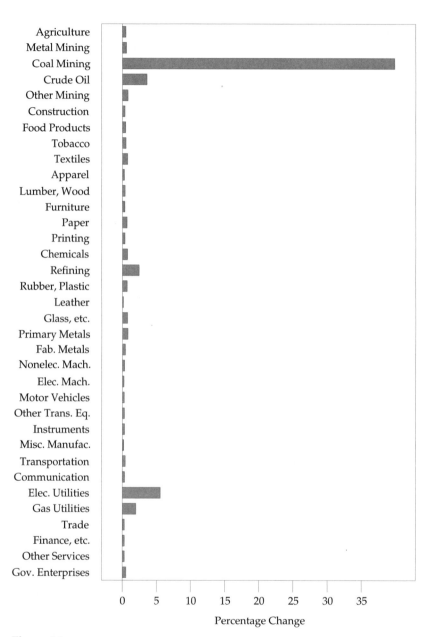

Figure 4.1
Carbon Tax (1990)—Effect on Prices.

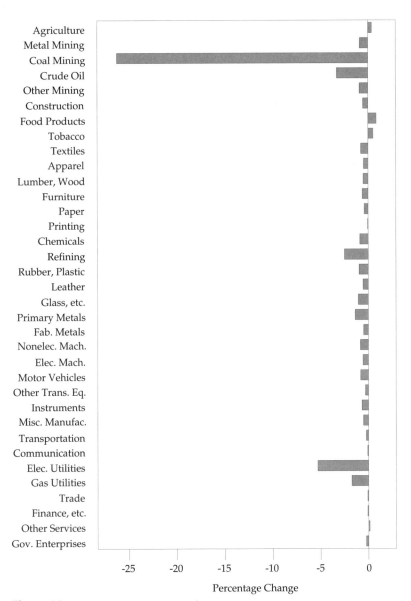

Figure 4.2
Carbon Tax (1990)—Effect on Output.

Coal is affected strongly because the demand for it is somewhat elastic. Most coal is purchased by electric utilities, which in our model can substitute toward other fuels when the price of coal rises. Moreover, the utilities also have some ability to substitute other inputs, such as labor and capital, for energy, further reducing the demand for coal. Since electric utilities play such an important role in determining how a carbon tax affects coal mining, we now digress briefly to discuss how the utilities are represented in the model.

Electric utilities, like all other sectors, are represented by a nested translog unit cost function. The top tier of the function gives cost in terms of the prices of four inputs: capital, labor, an energy aggregate, and a materials aggregate. Substitution between energy and other inputs takes place at this level. The price of the energy aggregate itself is formed at a lower tier by translog aggregation of the prices of five inputs: coal, crude petroleum, refined petroleum, electricity, and natural gas from gas utilities. Substitution between fuels takes place at that level.

Estimated parameters govern the ease of substitution at both the KLEM and energy tiers of the cost function. At the KLEM level, substitution between energy and capital is very inelastic (an elasticity of -0.15), substitution between energy and labor is moderately inelastic (-0.64), and substitution between energy and materials is slightly elastic (-1.16). Thus, increases in the relative price of energy will, for the most part, induce substitution toward materials. In addition, substitution possibilities also exist at the energy tier. The elasticity of substitution between coal and refined petroleum is -0.7, although between coal and natural gas it is only -0.1. Thus, an increase in the relative price of coal will produce some substitution toward other fuels. Overall, the parameters appearing in the cost function for electric utilities imply that an increase in the relative price of coal will lead to substitution toward other fuels and toward non-energy inputs.

The second policy we considered was a twenty percent reduction below 1990 emission rates, to be phased in gradually over fifteen years. By 2020, this would amount to a drop of thirty-two percent below base case emissions, and would require a tax of $60.09 per ton of carbon. Using the data in table 4.2, this is equivalent to a tax of $39.01 per ton of coal, $8.20 per barrel of oil, or $0.98 per thousand cubic feet of gas. The tax would produce $75.8 billion in revenues. Comparing these results to those for maintaining 1990 emissions shows that the tax would more than triple, from $17 to $60. At equilibrium, the tax gives the marginal cost of reducing emissions by an additional ton of carbon, so it is clear that further reductions are becoming significantly more difficult.

Tighter carbon regulations also lead to a reduction in total fossil fuel Btu production to 57 quads, a drop of twenty-seven percent from the base case. This, in turn, reduces the capital stock by 2.2 percent and real GNP by 1.6 percent. These figures are about triple the values obtained for holding emissions at 1990 levels. Although the changes in capital and GNP appear small, recall that they are measures of deadweight loss associated with fairly large marginal changes in the energy sector.

At the commodity and industry level, results for this experiment are qualitatively similar to those for maintaining 1990 emissions, although they are numerically somewhat different. Figure 4.3 shows percentage changes in commodity prices relative to the base case. The price of coal more than doubles, rising by 137 percent from its base-case value. The price of oil rises by thirteen percent, while that of electricity rises by about eighteen percent. The prices of refined petroleum and natural gas also rise, but by somewhat less. Comparing figures 4.3 and 4.1 shows how this simulation compares with the previous one. In particular, commodity prices rise roughly in proportion to the increase in the carbon tax: the tax rises by a factor of 3.5, and so do most of the percentage changs in commodity prices.

The quantity results, shown in figure 4.4, display a similar pattern except that they scale up in proportion to the change in carbon reductions rather than the change in taxes. That is, reducing emissions to twenty percent below 1990 levels requires a cut of about twice the size needed to reach 1990 levels. Thus, percentage changes in quantities from the base case are about twice those of the previous experiment. The most important results are the 53% drop in coal production and the fifteen percent drop in electricity produced.

In contrast, the looser restrictions implied by maintaining emissions at year 2000 levels produce much smaller effects on the economy. The tax required is only $8.55 per ton of carbon, which implies charges of $5.55 per ton of coal, $1.17 per barrel of oil, or $0.14 per thousand cubic feet of gas. The tax would produce $14.4 billion annually in revenue. Aggregate effects are also considerably smaller than in the two previous scenarios. The capital stock will fall by 0.4%, and GNP will drop by 0.3%, about half the value obtained in the 1990 simulation. This is quite reasonable since the cut in emissions is about half as

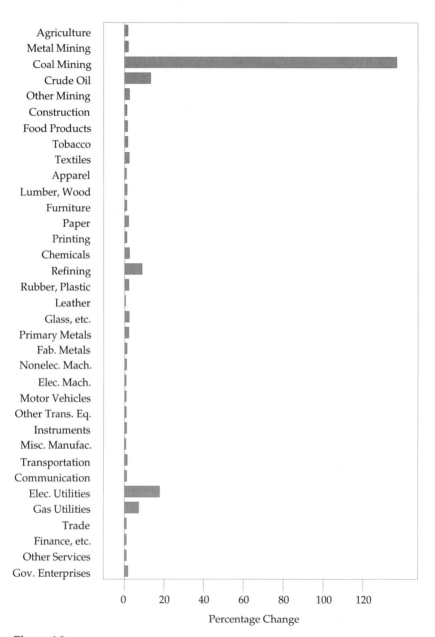

Figure 4.3
Carbon tax (80%, 1990)—Effect on Prices.

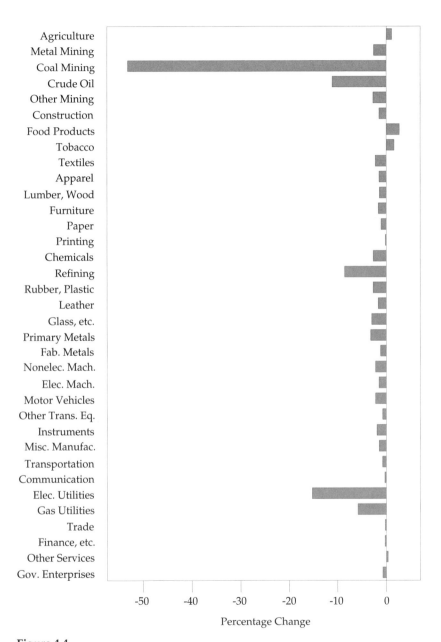

Figure 4.4
Carbon tax (80%, 1990)—Effect on Output.

Table 4.3
Summary of long-run carbon tax simulations

		Emissions target		
Variable	Unit	2000 Level	1990 Level	80% of 1990
Carbon emission	%Δ	−8.4	−14.4	−31.6
Carbon tax	$/ton	8.55	16.96	60.09
Tax on coal	$/ton	5.55	11.01	39.01
Tax on oil	$/bbl	1.17	2.32	8.20
Tax on gas	$/kfc	0.14	0.28	0.98
Labor tax rate	Δ	−0.25	−0.45	−1.22
Tax revenue	Bill.$	14.4	26.7	75.8
Btu production	%Δ	−7.1	−12.2	−27.4
Capital stock	%Δ	−0.4	−0.7	−2.2
Real GNP	%Δ	−0.3	−0.5	−1.6
Price of coal	%Δ	20.3	40.0	137.4
Quantity of coal	%Δ	−15.6	−26.3	−53.2
Price of electricity	%Δ	2.9	5.6	17.9
Quantity of electricity	%Δ	−2.9	−5.3	−15.3
Price of oil	%Δ	1.8	3.6	13.3

deep. The industry results look qualitatively so similar to those of the previous experiments that we omit the graphs. The principal numerical result is that coal prices rise by twenty percent while coal output shrinks by about 16 percent.

The results of all three carbon tax simulations are summarized in table 4.3, in which the policies are listed in order of increasing stringency. From these results it appears that maintaining emissions at the year 2000 base-case level can be accomplished with a very low carbon tax and minimal disturbance of the economy. The strongest effect would be felt by the coal mining industry, which would see its demand fall as electric utilities substituted toward other fuels. More stringent regulations, however, would lead to markedly higher energy prices and greater disruption of the economy. Under any scenario, however, coal mining would bear the brunt of the changes brought about by the tax. Of the remaining sectors, electric utilities would be affected most strongly.

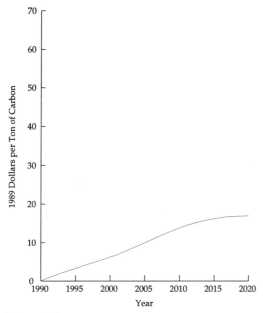

Figure 4.5
Carbon tax to maintain 1990 emissions.

4.3.2   Intertemporal Results

Carbon restrictions adopted today will have effects far into the future. At the same time, anticipated future restrictions will have effects today. To assess the intertemporal consequences of carbon taxes, we now turn to the model's dynamic results. As with the long run results, we begin by discussing a carbon tax designed to maintain emissions at 1990 levels. Following that, we examine the dynamic behavior of other experiments.

The path of the carbon tax needed to maintain 1990 emissions is shown in figure 4.5. Base-case emissions increase over time, so the tax grows gradually, about $0.70 per year, over the next few decades. It reaches a peak around the year 2020 when our forecast of the U.S. population crests.[31] The tax produces significant reductions in carbon emissions which are shown in figure 4.6 as percentage changes from the base case. Emissions begin dropping immediately and by 2020 are about fourteen percent below their unconstrained level.

As suggested by the long-run results, the principal effect of the tax is to reduce coal mining. This is shown clearly in figure 4.7, which

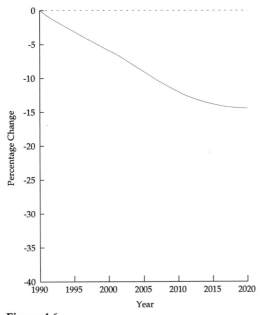

Figure 4.6
Carbon emissions under a carbon tax.

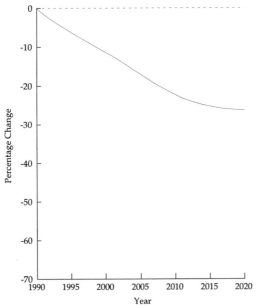

Figure 4.7
Coal production under a carbon tax.

gives percentage changes in coal output from the base case. Production gradually slows as the tax is introduced. It does not, however, fall all the way back to its 1990 level—some of the reduction in emissions comes about through reductions in oil consumption. This can be seen in figure 4.8, which gives percentages changes in crude petroleum and natural gas extraction over time.

The increasing price of energy raises costs and reduces household income. This, in turn, changes the rate of capital accumulation. The outcome is shown in figure 4.9, which gives percentage changes in the capital stock from the base case. Unlike variables in the preceding graphs, the capital stock does not start declining immediately; instead, it tends to remain near its base-case level for the first few years. This comes about because of intertemporal optimization by households. From a household's point of view, the effect of the tax is to decrease its real income by an amount related to the tax's deadweight loss.[32] Thus, the household regards carbon taxes as reductions in future earnings, so it reacts by lowering consumption in all periods. In the early years, however, the carbon tax is minimal and household income is largely unaffected. During that period, therefore, the drop in consumption leads to an increase in saving. This helps maintain investment—and thus the capital stock—in the early years of the simulation. Eventually, the income effect of the tax begins to be felt and the capital stock finally starts to decline relative to the base case.

The decline in growth of the capital stock leads to a drop in GNP growth, as shown in figure 4.10. Over time GNP gradually falls by about half a percent relative to the base case. The capital stock, however, is not the only factor contributing to the decline. In addition, higher energy prices reduce the rate of technical change in industries which are energy-using. This leads to slower income growth and helps keep GNP below its base-case level. In fact, under the carbon tax simulation average annual GNP growth over the period 1990–2020 is 0.02 percentage points lower than in the base case.[33] About half of this is due to slowing technical change and half due to slower capital accumulation.

The other two carbon control targets we examined showed dynamic behavior qualitatively similar to that described above. These results can best be displayed by plotting each variable's values for all three simulations on a single graph.[34] Figure 4.11, for example, shows the paths of the carbon tax needed to achieve each of the targets. The highest path is the tax required to reduce emissions to twenty percent

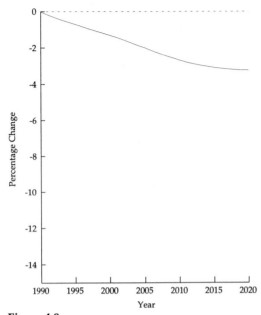

Figure 4.8
Crude oil extraction under a carbon tax.

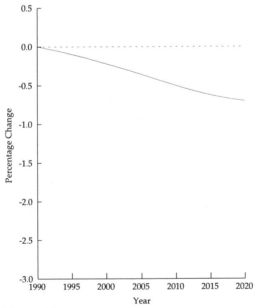

Figure 4.9
Capital stock under a carbon tax.

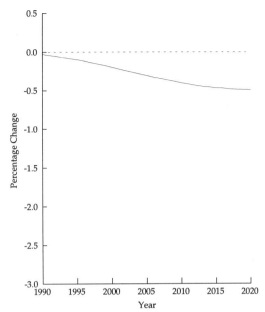

Figure 4.10
Real GNP under a carbon tax.

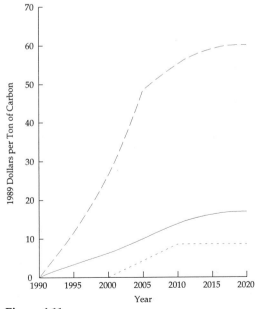

Figure 4.11
Carbon taxes for different targets.

below their 1990 levels; the central path is that for maintaining 1990 emissions; and the lowest path is the tax needed to stabilize emissions at year 2000 levels. Similarly, figure 4.12 shows the carbon reductions achieved under each of the policies.[35] Plotting three curves on each figure makes it easy to compare different targets. For example, many figures show that as the target becomes more stringent, the variable of interest is pushed further away from the base case. However, some of the figures show much more interesting behavior, and we will focus on these for the remainder of this section.

The first feature to note, which is apparent from figure 4.12, is that the three targets require carbon reductions of roughly 8, 14, and 32 percent. (This was also noted in the section on long-run results.) Keeping these reductions in mind, figure 4.13 is quite interesting because it shows that coal production does not fall in proportion to the drop in emissions. This occurs because it becomes increasingly costly to drive coal production toward zero. Coal users, notably electric utilities, find it increasingly difficult to substitute away from coal as the amount they use of it decreases. This is reflected in figure 4.14, which shows that oil extraction consequently more sharply as regulations become more stringent.

One of the most interesting results of our study is shown in figure 4.15, a graph of the capital stock under the three policies. Figure 4.15 is a very clear example of the effects of intertemporal optimization by households. For the policy which has least effect and occurs furthest in the future (maintaining emissions at year 2000 levels), the early reduction in consumption actually leads to a temporary increase in the capital stock. As explained above, this comes about because households reduce consumption in anticipation of lower future earnings. Only in under the most stringent policy (reducing emissions by twenty percent from 1990 levels) does the capital stock begin to fall immediately. Finally, the results for GNP, shown in figure 4.16, echo those for the capital stock. As mentioned above, GNP falls in part because of the drop in capital accumulation and in part because higher energy prices reduce the rate of technical change.

4.4 Conclusion

Several important observations can be made about the carbon tax simulations presented in this chapter. First, the principal effects of a carbon tax will be felt at the industry level. Coal mining, in particular,

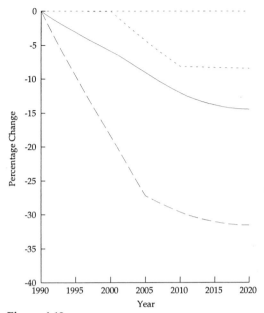

Figure 4.12
Carbon emissions under a carbon tax.

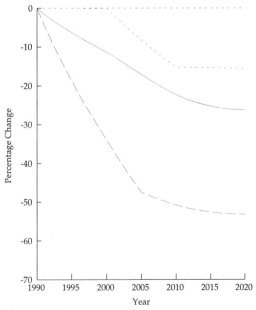

Figure 4.13
Coal production under a carbon tax.

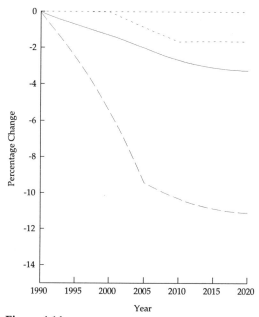

Figure 4.14
Crude oil extraction under a carbon tax.

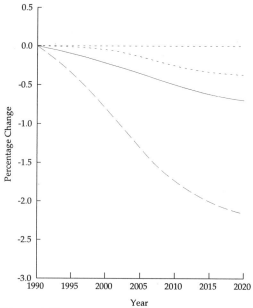

Figure 4.15
Capital stock under a carbon tax.

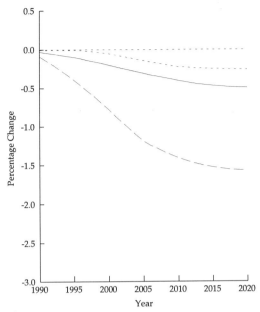

Figure 4.16
Real GNP under a carbon tax.

will be strongly affected. Even under the least restricive policy, coal output will fall sixteen percent from its base-case value; more restrictive policies could lead to reductions of fifty percent or more. Electric utilities will also be affected, with output falling by as much as fifteen percent under tighter emissions restrictions. At more aggregate levels, however, our results also show that the economy-wide effects of a carbon tax would be fairly modest. Thus, the effects of a tax would be concentrated in coal mining, although a handful of other sectors such as oil extraction would also be affected.

A second but no less important observation about these simulations is that the stringency and timing of the tax will determine how strongly the tax affects the economy. Comparing long-run results of the three simulations considered here shows that increasingly stringent targets are increasingly costly. Thus it is essential that any serious national or international goal on carbon dioxide emissions be chosen by carefully comparing costs and benefits. Setting goals arbitrarily risks seriously under or over emphasizing carbon dioxide reductions. Since our model does not compute benefits, we cannot say which policy is most appropriate. We do urge, however, that

careful consideration of benefits be given before any national or international policy is adopted.

Notes

1. The most notable exception is the work of Nordhaus (1989, 1990b) who has devoted a
great deal of effort to measuring the benefits of reducing global warming in order to be
able to calculate the optimal reduction. Preliminary work on benefits has also been
done by Peck and Teisberg (1990).
2. In Jorgenson and Wilcoxen (1990b) we also examined the effect of reducing carbon
dioxide emissions by imposing taxes on the energy content of primary fuels or by
imposing ad valorem fuel taxes.
3. A very thorough discussion of the greenhouse effect and numerous references to the
literature are given by EPA (1989).
4. Schneider (1989, p. 774). However, there is a wide spectrum of scientific opinion, as
described by Stevens (1989).
5. Schneider (1989, p. 772). This is also subject to dispute, as pointed out by Stevens
(1989). For example, Solow (1990) presents a strong case against the position that a
rapid acceleration global warming has already been observed.
6. Schneider (1989, p. 771). A detailed analysis of the potential economic impact of the
legislation introduced by Senator Wirth is presented by the Congressional Budget Office
(1990).
7. See, for example, Natural Resources Defense Council (1989).
8. Many other policies have been suggested; see EPA (1989). These options are discussed from an economic point of view by Lave (1990), Goulder (1990), North (1990)
and Wood (1990).
9. The Edmonds-Reilly model has subsequently been used by Reilly, Edmonds, Garner
and Brenkert (1987), Cline (1992), the Environmental Protection Agency (1989), the Congressional Budget Office (1990), and others.
10. It is a descendant of Manne's earlier work on ETA-MACRO. See Manne (1981).
11. A nontechnical description of the results of Manne and Richels is presented by Passell (1989).
12. Nordhaus (1989) is one of a series of studies beginning with Nordhaus (1977). Additional references are given by Nordhaus (1979, 1982), Nordhaus and Ausubel (1983),
and Nordhaus and Yohe (1983).
13. Sectors 3, 4, 16, 30, and 31 in table 4.1.
14. Data on inter-industry transactions are based on input-output tables for the U.S. constructed by the Bureau of Economic Analysis (1984). Income data are from the U.S.
national income and product accounts, also developed by the Bureau of Economic Analysis (1986). The data on capital and labor services are discussed by Jorgenson (1990b).
Additional details are given by Wilcoxen (1988), Appendix C, and Ho (1989).
15. See Mansur and Whalley (1984) for more detail. An example of the calibration
approach is Borges and Goulder (1984).
16. For a more complete discussion of the econometric approach see Jorgenson (1982,
1984).
17. Our approach to endogenous productivity growth was originated by Jorgenson and
Fraumeni (1981). The implementation of a general equilibrium model of production
that incorporates both substitution among inputs and endogenous productivity growth
was discussed by Jorgenson (1984a). This model has been analyzed in detail by Hogan
and Jorgenson (1991). Further details on the econometric methodology are presented by
Jorgenson (1986).

18. The Euler equation approach to modeling intertemporal consumer behavior was originated by Hall (1978). Our application of this approach to full consumption follows Jorgenson and Yun (1986).

19. This allows our model of personal consumption to be used to represent the behavior of individual households as in Jorgenson and Slesnick (1985). Further details on the econometric methodology are given by Jorgenson (1984a, 1990a,b).

20. See Wilcoxen (1988) and Ho (1989) for more details.

21. The relationship between the price of investment goods and the price of capital services is discussed in more detail by Jorgenson (1989).

22. More accurately, between the industries themselves and between industries and final demand categories. Households, in particular, purchase a considerably amount of capital services.

23. Without a model of Congressional decision-making, we must take either the level of government expenditures or the size of the budget deficit to be exogenous.

24. This is the Armington (1969) approach.

25. See Wilcoxen (1988) or Ho (1989) for more details.

26. Unlike ordinary pollutants, carbon dioxide is one of the natural products of combustion. Little can be done to change the amount of it produced when burning any particular fuel.

27. To convert to tons of carbon dioxide, multiply by 3.67.

28. Environmental Protection Agency (1990) internal memoranda.

29. Our breakdown of the U.S. population by age, educational attainment, and sex is based on the system of demographic accounts compiled by Jorgenson and Fraumeni (1989). The population projections are discussed in detail by Wilcoxen (1988), Appendix B.

30. All dollar amounts are in 1989 prices.

31. As noted in section 4.2, our population forecast is based on work done by the Social Security Administration. Two notable features are that the U.S. population stabilizes early in the next century, and that educational attainment (and hence labor quality) stabilizes as well.

32. Since revenue earned by the tax is given back to households through a vertical shift in the labor tax schedule, the simulation is essentially the replacement of a lump sum tax (the labor tax) by a distorting one (the carbon tax).

33. The difference in two variables growing at rates differing by 0.02 percentage points is about 2% after a hundred years.

34. Recall that the targets were (1) maintaining 1990 emissions, (2) reducing emissions by twenty percent below 1990 levels, and (3) gradually introducing taxes to stabilize at year 2000 emissions.

35. Notice that target policies are drawn using the same line type in each graph. Maintaining 1990 emissions is always a solid line, reducing emissions to twenty percent below 1990 is always dashed, and maintaining emissions at 2000 levels is alternating dots and dashes. Also, variables are plotted on the same scale across different tax instruments for easier comparison.

5

The Economic Impact of the Clean Air Act Amendments of 1990

Dale W. Jorgenson and Peter J. Wilcoxen

5.1 Introduction

The Clean Air Act Amendments of 1990 have inaugurated a new era in environmental legislation in the United States. This landmark legislation includes new regulations in the following five areas:

1. *Nonattainment areas.* Title I of the legislation extends deadlines and specifies control technologies for areas that have failed to comply with existing regulations on ozone, carbon monoxide, oxides of nitrogen, and particulates.

2. *Mobile sources.* Title II requires the reformulation of gasoline, mandates the introduction of special oxygenated fuels in certain areas, and changes emissions regulations.

3. *Air toxics.* Title III regulates the emission of toxic substances into the atmosphere. Most of these substances have not been subject to previous environmental regulations.

4. *Acid rain.* Title IV provides market permits for the emission of sulfur dioxide and provides regulation of emissions of oxides of nitrogen.

5. *Stratospheric ozone.* Title VI implements the Montreal Protocol, an international agreement that provides for the elimination of CFC's (chloro-fluoro-hydrocarbons).

Pollution control legislation began in earnest in the United States in 1965, when amendments to the Clean Air Act set national automobile emissions standards for the first time. The extent of regulation increased dramatically in 1970 with the passage of the National Environmental Policy Act and amendments to the Clean Air Act. In 1972 the Clean Water Act was passed and revisions to this Act and the Clean Air Act were adopted in 1977.[1] The consequence of this legislation was a large and abrupt shift of economic resources toward pollution abatement.

The purpose of this chapter is to quantify the impact of the Clean Air Act Amendments of 1990 and compare this with the impact of previous environmental legislation at the federal level. We analyze the impact of environmental regulation by simulating the long-term growth of the U.S. economy with and without regulation. For this purpose, we have constructed a detailed model of the economy that includes the determinants of long-run growth. Before considering the impact of specific pollution controls we present an overview of the model in section 5.2.

In section 5.3, we show that pollution abatement had emerged as a major claimant on the resources of the U.S. economy well before the Clean Air Act Amendments of 1990. The long-run cost of environmental regulations enacted prior to 1990 was a reduction of 2.59 percent in the level of the U.S. gross national product. This is more than ten percent of the share of total government purchases of goods and services in the national product during the period 1973–1985. Over this period the annual growth rate of the U.S. economy has been reduced by 0.191 percent. This is several times the reduction in growth estimated in previous studies.

Since the stringency of pollution control differs substantially among industries, we have also assessed the impact of environmental regulations on individual industries. We have analyzed the interactions among industries in order to quantify the full repercussions of these regulations. We find that pollution controls have had their most pronounced effects on chemicals, coal mining, motor vehicles, and primary processing industries—such as petroleum refining, primary metals, and pulp and paper. For example, we find that the long-run output of the automobile industry has been reduced by fifteen percent, mainly as a consequence of motor vehicle emissions controls.

In section 5.4, we turn our attention to the economic impact of the Clean Air Act Amendments of 1990. Our analysis of the impact of earlier legislation incorporates detailed data from the Bureau of the Census on costs of compliance by businesses and households. To assess these costs for the 1990 Act, we employ a preliminary set of estimates of costs for the year 2005 prepared by the Environmental Protection Agency (1991). The new legislation will be phased in gradually over fifteen years, so that these estimates reflect the costs of compliance after the new regulations are fully effective.

We estimate that the level of the U.S. gross national product will be reduced by an additional four-tenths of a percentage point by the year 2005 as a consequence of the burden on the economy imposed by the 1990 legislation. This burden will rise to almost half a percent of the national product by the year 2020, when the impact of the legislation on the growth of the U.S. economy will be complete. Although our estimates of impacts on individual industries are necessarily imprecise, it is already apparent that electric utilities and primary metals industries will be hard hit by the new legislation and that many other industries will bear a substantial additional burden as a consequence of the 1990 Act.

5.2   An Overview of the Model

We analyze the impact of changes in environmental policy by simulating long-term growth of the U.S. economy with and without regulation. Our simulations are based on an intertemporal general equilibrium model of the U.S. economy described in detail by Jorgenson and Wilcoxen (1993d). Jorgenson and Wilcoxen (1990b) have employed this model to assess the impact of environmental regulations in the United States.

5.2.1   Producer Behavior

Since environmental regulations differ substantially among industries, a disaggregated model is essential for modeling differences in the response to alternative policies. Our submodel of producer behavior is disaggregated into thirty-five industrial sectors, listed in table 5.1. The model determines levels of output for thirty-five separate commodities, each produced by one or more industries. The industries correspond, roughly, to two-digit industry groups in the Standard Industrial Classification (SIC). This level of industrial detail makes it possible to measure the effect of changes in tax policy on relatively narrow segments of the economy.

We represent the technology of each of the thirty-five industries in our model by means of a hierarchical tier structure of econometric models of producer behavior. At the highest level the price of output in each industry is represented as a function of prices of energy, materials, and capital and labor services. Similarly, the price of energy

Table 5.1
Industry classifications

Number	Description
1	Agriculture, forestry, and fisheries
2	Metal mining
3	Coal mining
4	Crude petroleum and natural gas
5	Nonmetallic mineral mining
6	Construction
7	Food and kindred products
8	Tobacco manufacturers
9	Textile mill products
10	Apparel and other textile products
11	Lumber and wood products
12	Furniture and fixtures
13	Paper and allied products
14	Printing and publishing
15	Chemicals and allied products
16	Petroleum refining
17	Rubber and plastic products
18	Leather and leather products
19	Stone, clay, and glass products
20	Primary metals
21	Fabricated metal products
22	Machinery, except electrical
23	Electrical machinery
24	Motor vehicles
25	Other transportation equipment
26	Instruments
27	Miscellaneous manufacturing
28	Transportation and warehousing
29	Communication
30	Electric utilities
31	Gas utilities
32	Trade
33	Finance, insurance, and real estate
34	Other services
35	Government enterprises

is a function of prices of coal, crude petroleum, refined petroleum, electricity, and natural gas; the price of materials is a function of the prices of all other intermediate goods. We derive demands for inputs of capital and labor services and inputs of the thirty-five intermediate goods into each industry from the price function for that industry.

We have estimated the parameters of production models for the thirty-five industries econometrically. For this purpose, we have constructed a set of consistent interindustry transactions tables for the U.S. economy for the period 1947 through 1985.[2] Our econometric method for parameterization stands in sharp contrast to the calibration method used in almost all applied general equilibrium models. Calibration involves choosing parameters to replicate the data for a particular year.[3]

The econometric approach to parameterization has several advantages over the calibration approach. First, by using an extensive time series of data rather than a single data point, we are able to derive the response of production patterns to changes in prices from historical experience.[4] This is particularly important for the analysis of alternative policies for environmental regulation, since regulatory policies have varied widely during our sample period. The calibration approach imposes responses to policy changes on the data through the choice of functional forms. For example, elasticities of substitution are set equal to unity by imposing the Cobb-Douglas functional form or zero by imposing the Leontief form.

Empirical evidence on substitutability among inputs is essential in analyzing the impact of alternative environmental policies. If it is easy for industries to substitute among inputs, the effects of these policies will be very different than if substitution were limited. Although calibration avoids the burden of data collection required by econometric estimation, it also specifies the substitutability among inputs by assumption rather than relying on empirical evidence. This can easily lead to substantial distortions in estimating the effects of alternative policies.

A second advantage of the econometric approach is that parameters estimated from time series are much less likely to be affected by the peculiarities of the data for a particular time period. By construction, parameters obtained by calibration are forced to absorb all the random errors present in the data for a single benchmark year. This poses a severe problem when the benchmark year is unusual in some respect. For example, parameters calibrated to data for 1973 would incorporate into the model all the distortions in energy markets that resulted from price controls and rationing of energy during the first oil crisis. Econometric parameterization greatly mitigates this problem by reducing the influence of random errors for any particular time period.

An important feature of our producer submodel is that an industry's productivity growth can be biased toward some inputs and away from others. Biased productivity growth is a common feature of historical data, but is often excluded from models of production. By allowing for biased productivity growth, our model provides a separation between price-induced reductions in energy utilization and those resulting from changes in technology. In addition, the rate of productivity growth for each industry in our model is determined endogenously as a function of relative prices.[5]

5.2.2 Consumption

Alternative environmental policies have very different impacts on different households. For example, restrictions on the use of energy are equivalent to a change in the relative prices faced by consumers. An increase in the price of energy adversely affects those consumers who devote a larger share of total expenditure to energy. To capture these differences among households, we have subdivided the household sector into 672 demographic groups that differ by characteristics such as family size, age of head, region of residence, race, and urban versus rural location. We treat each household as a consuming unit, so that the household behaves like an individual maximizing a utility function.

We represent the preferences of each household by means of an econometric model of consumer behavior. The econometric approach to parameterization enables us to derive the response of household expenditure patterns to changes in prices from historical experience. This approach to modeling consumer behavior has the same advantages over the calibration approach as those we have described for modeling producer behavior. Empirical evidence on substitutability among goods and services is essential in analyzing the impact of alternative environmental policies. If it is easy for households to substitute among commodities, the effects of these policies will be very different than if substitution were limited.

Our model of household behavior is generated by a three-stage optimization process. At the first stage, each household allocates full wealth, defined as the sum of human and nonhuman wealth, across different time periods. We formalize this decision by introducing a representative agent who maximizes an additive intertemporal utility function, subject to an intertemporal budget constraint. The optimal allocation satisfies a sequence of necessary conditions that can be summarized by means of an Euler equation.[6] This allocation is determined by the rate of time preference and the intertemporal elasticity of substitution. The Euler equation is forward-looking, so that the allocation of full wealth incorporates expectations about all future prices and discount rates.

After households have allocated full wealth to the current time period, they proceed to the second stage of the optimization process—choosing the mix of leisure and goods. We represent household preferences between goods and leisure by means of a representative agent with an indirect utility function that depends on the prices of leisure and goods. We derive demands for leisure and goods as functions of these prices and the wealth allocated to the period. This implies an allocation of the household's exogenously given time endowment between leisure time and the labor market, so that this stage of the optimization process determines labor supply.

The third stage of the household optimization problem is the allocation of total expenditure among capital and labor services and the thirty-five commodity groups included in the model. At this stage, we replace the representative consumer approach by the approach of Jorgenson, Lau, and Stoker (1982) for deriving a system of demand functions for each household. We distinguish among household types cross-classified by attributes such as the number of household members and the geographic region in which the household is located. For each type of household we employ a hierarchical tier structure of models of consumer behavior to represent demands for individual commodities.[7]

The parameters of the behavioral equations for all three stages of our consumer model are estimated econometrically.[8] This includes the Euler equation, demand functions for leisure and personal consumption expenditures, and demand functions for individual commodities. Our household model incorporates extensive time series data on the price responsiveness of demand patterns by consumers and detailed cross-section data on demographic effects on consumer behavior. An important feature of our household model is that we do not require that demands are homothetic. As levels of total expenditure increase, patterns of expenditure on individual commodities change, even in the absence of price changes. This captures an important feature of cross-section data on household expenditure patterns that is usually ignored in applied general equilibrium modeling.

5.2.3 Investment and Capital Formation

Our investment model, like our model of saving, is based on perfect foresight or rational expectations. Under this assumption, the price of investment goods in every period is based on expectations of future capital service prices and discount rates that are fulfilled by the solution of the model. In particular, we require that the price of new investment goods is always equal to the present value of future capital services.[9] The price of investment goods and the discounted value of future rental prices are brought into intertemporal equilibrium by adjustments in prices and the term structure of interest rates. This intertemporal equilibrium incorporates the forward-looking dynamics of asset pricing by producers.

For tractability, we assume there is a single capital stock in the economy that is perfectly malleable, so that it can be reallocated among industries and between industries and final demand categories at zero cost. Under this assumption, imposition of alternative tax policies can affect the distribution of capital and labor supplies among sectors, even in the short run. In each time period, the supply of capital in our model is completely inelastic, since the stock of capital is determined by past investment. Investment during the period is determined by the savings made available by households. The relationship between capital stock and past investment incorporates backward-looking dynamics into our model of intertemporal equilibrium.

We assume that new capital goods are produced from individual commodities, so that the price of new capital depends on commodity prices. We have estimated the price function for new capital goods using final demand data for investment over the period 1947–1985. Thus, our model incorporates substitution among inputs in the composition of the capital. This feature can play an important role in the evaluation of alternative environmental policies. Jorgenson and Wilcoxen (1990a) have found, for example, that an increase in the price of automobiles resulting from mandatory installation of pollution control devices shifts investment away from motor vehicles and toward other types of capital.

5.2.4 Government and Foreign Trade

The two remaining final demand categories in our model are the government and foreign sectors. We determine final demands for government consumption from the income-expenditure identity for the government sector. The first step is to compute total tax revenue by applying exogenous tax rates to appropriate transactions in the business and household sectors. We then add the capital income of government enterprises, determined endogenously, and nontax receipts, also determined exogenously, to tax revenue to obtain total government revenue.

We assume the government budget deficit can be specified exogenously. We add the deficit to total revenue to obtain total government spending. To arrive at government purchases of goods and services, we subtract interest paid to domestic and foreign holders of government bonds together with government transfer payments to domestic and foreign recipients. We allocate the remainder among commodity groups according to fixed shares constructed from historical data. Finally, we determine the quantity of each commodity by dividing the value of government spending on the good by its price.

Foreign trade has two components—imports and exports. We assume that imports are imperfect substitutes for similar domestic commodities.[10] The goods actually purchased by households and firms reflect substitution between domestic and imported products. The price responsiveness of these purchases is estimated econometrically from historical data. In effect, each commodity is assigned a separate elasticity of substitution between domestic and imported goods. Since the prices of imports are given exogenously, intermediate and final demands implicitly determine imports of each commodity.

Exports, on the other hand, are determined by a set of export demand equations, one for each commodity, that depend on exogenously given foreign income and the foreign price of U.S. exports. Foreign prices are computed from domestic prices by adjusting for subsidies and the exchange rate. The demand elasticities in these equations are estimated from historical data. Without an elaborate model of international trade, it is impossible to determine both the current account balance and the exchange rate endogenously. In the simulations reported below, we take the current account to be exogenous and the exchange rate to be endogenous.

5.2.5   The Base Case

To simulate the U.S. economy, we must provide values of the exogenous variables for all time periods. We have accomplished this in two steps. First, we have adopted a set of default assumptions about the time path of each exogenous variable in the absence of changes in government policy. These assumptions are used in generating a simulation of U.S. economic growth called the "base case." Our second step is to change certain exogenous variables to reflect the introduction of alternative environmental policies and simulate U.S. economic growth again to produce an "alternative case." We then compare the two simulations to assess the impact of the policy change. Obviously, the assumptions underlying the base case are important in interpreting the results.

Since our model is based on agents with perfect foresight, we must solve the model indefinitely far into the future. To do this we project values for all exogenous variables over the period 1990–2050. After 2050 we assume the variables remain constant at their 2050 values, which allows the model to converge to a steady state by the year 2100.[11] First, we set all tax rates to their values in 1985, the last year in our sample period. Next, we assume that prices of imports in foreign currency remain constant in real terms at 1985 levels before U.S. tariffs are applied.

We project a gradual decline in the government deficit through the year 2025, after which the nominal value of the government debt is maintained at a constant ratio to the value of the national product. Finally, we project the current account deficit by allowing it to fall gradually to zero by the year 2000. After that we project a current account surplus sufficient to produce a stock of net claims on foreigners by the year 2050 equal to the same proportion of national wealth as in 1982.

The most important exogenous variables are those associated with growth of the U.S. population and corresponding changes in the economy's time endowment. We project population by age, sex, and educational attainment through the year 2050, using demographic assumptions consistent with Census Bureau projections.[12] After 2050, we hold population constant, which is approximately in line with these projections. In addition, we project the educational composition of the population by holding the level of educational attainment constant, beginning with the cohort reaching age 35 in the year 1985. We transform our population projection into a projection of the time endowment by taking relative wages across different types of labor input to be constant at 1985 levels. Since capital formation is endogenous in our model, our projections of the time endowment effectively determine the size of the economy in the more distant future.

5.3   The Impact of Environmental Regulation

Our next objective is to assess the impact of environmental regulations introduced in the 1970s and early 1980s. Our approach will be to use the model of section 5.2 to simulate the growth of the U.S. economy with and without regulation. We begin by observing that our base case implicitly includes environmental regulation since it is based on historical data. Thus, to determine the effect of regulation we conduct counterfactual simulations in which regulation is removed from the economy. In addition, we decompose the overall effect of regulation into components associated with both pollution control in industry and controls on motor vehicle emissions.

Removing environmental regulation produces simulations which differ from the base case at the steady state, at the initial (first year) equilibrium, and along the transition path between the two. The difference between the new steady state and the base case shows the long-run impact of environmental regulation after the capital stock has adjusted. The difference between the new initial equilibrium and the base case gives the short-run impact of a change in policy before the capital stock can adjust at all. However, since agents in the model have perfect foresight, this initial equilibrium reflects changes along the entire time path of future regulatory policy. Finally, the transition path between the initial equilibrium and the steady state traces out the economy's adjustment to the new environmental policy.

In presenting the results of our simulations, we begin by quantifying the impact of pollution controls on production costs. We then incorporate these cost changes into the model and run counterfactual simulations. In interpreting the simulation results, we first consider the impact of environmental regulation on the steady state of the economy, concentrating our analysis on a few key variables. Next, we analyze the transition path of economy from the initial equilibrium to the new steady state. We focus particular attention on the path of capital stock, since it is the most important overall measure of the effect on the change in policy. We also discuss a number of other important variables including the price of investment goods, the rental price of capital services, and the level of the gross national product (GNP).

5.3.1 Operating Costs

We employ data collected by the Bureau of the Census to estimate investment in pollution abatement equipment and operating costs of pollution control activities for manufacturing industries.[13] Our first step in eliminating the operating costs of pollution control is to estimate the share of pollution abatement in the total costs of each industry. For years between 1973 and 1985, we have calculated the actual share from historical data. After 1983, we assume that the share remained constant at its 1983 value. Outside manufacturing, data were only available for electric utilities and wastewater treatment (wastewater treatment is part of the services industry). For both of these industries, data on operating costs and investment expenditures for pollution abatement are available from the Bureau of Economic Analysis.[14]

For electric utilities, the Bureau of Economic Analysis also estimates the extra cost of burning low-sulfur fuels to comply with sulfur dioxide regulations. The principal low-sulfur fuel used by utilities is low-sulfur coal. In terms of our model, switching from high-sulfur to low-sulfur coal changes the relative proportions of the two products in the output of the coal industry. Since low-sulfur coal is more expensive when transportation costs are included, this increases the price of coal. Eliminating regulations on sulfur emissions would lower the price of coal by permitting substitution toward high-sulfur grades. We model the impact of lifting these restrictions by subtracting the differential between high cost and low cost coal from the cost of coal production.[15]

Twenty of the thirty-five industries in our model are subject to pollution abatement regulations. We use the share of abatement costs in total costs for each industry to compute the share of total costs excluding pollution abatement. Since our data set on pollution abatement ends in 1983, we assume the shares for later years are constant at their 1983 values. To simulate the effect of eliminating the operating costs associated with pollution abatement we reduce total costs of each industry by the abatement costs. This has the effect of excluding operating costs associated with pollution control from total costs in each industry.

Table 5.2
The effects of removing environmental regulations

Variable	Percentage change in steady state			
	ENV	INV	MV	ALL
Capital stock	0.544	2.266	1.118	3.792
Price of investment goods	−0.897	−2.652	−1.323	−4.520
Full consumption	0.278	0.489	0.282	0.975
Real GNP	0.728	1.290	0.752	2.592
Rental price of capital	−0.907	−2.730	−1.358	−4.635
Exchange rate	−0.703	−0.462	−0.392	−1.298

The long-run impact of eliminating the operating costs of pollution abatement is summarized in the column labeled ENV in table 5.2. The output of the economy, as measured by the GNP, rises by 0.728 percent. Much of this comes from an increase in the capital stock which rises by 0.544 percent. Since the model has a perfectly elastic supply of savings in the long run, the rate of return is unaffected by regulation. However, the price of new investment goods falls by 0.897 percent. This increases capital accumulation and reduces the price of capital services. Cheaper capital services lead to a fall in the prices of goods and services and a rise in full consumption by 0.278 percent. This increase is less than that of gross national product, since full consumption includes leisure time as well as personal consumption expenditures. Finally, the exchange rate, which gives the domestic cost of foreign goods, falls slightly, indicating an increase in the international competitiveness of the U.S. economy.[16]

5.3.2   Investment in Pollution Control Equipment

For some industries, the most important impact of environmental regulation is through mandatory investment in costly pollution abatement equipment. Investment in pollution control devices crowds out investment for ordinary capital accumulation, reducing the rate of economic growth. Our second simulation is designed to assess the impact of this investment. We begin by assuming that investment in pollution control equipment provides no benefits to producers other than satisfying environmental regulations. Accordingly, we simulate mandated investment as an increase in the price of investment goods. Unfortunately, our data set does not distinguish between investments required for new and existing facilities. To separate the two, we assume the backlog of investment for retrofitting old sources was eliminated in 1983. This allows us to infer that the 1983 share of pollution abatement devices in total investment was entirely due to new investment.

We can simulate the impact of removing environmental regulations on new investment by reducing the price of investment goods in that proportion. This captures the effect of requirements for pollution abatement on investment in new capital goods, but does not include the effect of windfall losses to owners of capital associated with old sources of investment. The long-run economic impact of required investment in pollution abatement equipment is given in the column INV of table 5.2. This impact is considerably more substantial than that of increased operating costs resulting from environmental regulation.

The long-run effects of mandated investment in pollution control devices are given in the column labeled INV in table 5.2. The largest change is in the capital stock, which rises by 2.266 percent as a direct result of the drop in the price of investment goods. In the short run this price decline pushes up the rate of return, raising the level of investment. Higher capital accumulation leads to a fall in the rental price of capital services, decreasing the overall price level. The long-run level of full consumption rises by 0.489 percent, almost double the increase resulting from eliminating operating costs of pollution abatement. The 1.290 percent rise in the national product is also nearly twice as large. The exchange rate appreciates by 0.462 percent, indicating an increase in international competitiveness of the U.S. economy.

5.3.3 Motor Vehicle Emissions Control

Environmental regulation is not limited to controlling pollution by industries in the business sector. Restrictions on motor vehicle emissions affect both businesses and households. Like pollution control in industry, the reduction of motor vehicle exhaust emissions requires both capital expenditures and operating costs. A catalytic converter is a typical piece of pollution abatement equipment requiring capital expenditure and the premium paid for unleaded gasoline is an example of an increase in operating costs.

Kappler and Rutledge (1985) present data on capital costs associated with motor vehicle regulation and three types of operating cost—increased fuel consumption, increased fuel prices, and increased

vehicle maintenance. Given the industries in our model, the price premium for unleaded motor fuels can best be modeled as a change in
the cost of output of the petroleum refining sector. This is similar to
the treatment of the fuel cost differential between high-sulfur and low-
sulfur coal. Only the operating costs associated with higher fuel prices
were removed in this simulation; fuel consumption and vehicle maintenance were held constant. Consequently, our results understate the
overall impact of emission controls.

As shown in column MV of table 5.2, the long-run economic impact
of imposing emissions controls on motor vehicles is similar in magnitude to the impact of pollution controls in industry (column ENV).
The capital stock rises by 1.118 percent, full consumption increases by
0.282 percent, real GNP increases by 0.752 percent, and the exchange
rate appreciates by 0.392 percent. Almost all of the impact is due to
the drop in motor vehicle prices resulting from the elimination of
required pollution control equipment. Motor vehicles are one of the
principal inputs into the production of investment goods, so that
changes in their price have a significant effect on the overall price of
investment goods.

5.3.4   The Overall Impact of Environmental Regulation

To measure the total impact of eliminating all three costs of environmental regulation—operating costs resulting from pollution abatement in industry, mandated investments to meet environmental
standards in particular industries, and cost of emission controls on
motor vehicles—we performed a final simulation. However, this
experiment was not a simple combination of the three components.
Operating costs include capital costs, so combining the reductions in
operating costs with the elimination of mandated investment would
count the cost reductions associated with capital twice. To solve this
problem, the capital component was removed from operating costs in
the combined simulation. The results of removing all forms of environmental regulation are summarized in column ALL of table 5.2.

The long-run consequences of pollution control for different commodities and industries are presented in figure 5.1. The sectors hit
hardest by environmental regulations were the motor vehicles and
coal mining industries. Primary metals and petroleum refining followed close behind. About half the remaining industries have
increases in output of one to five percent after pollution controls are

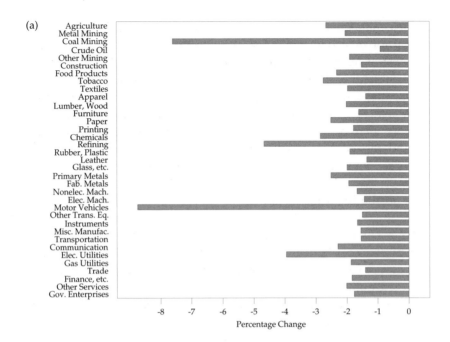

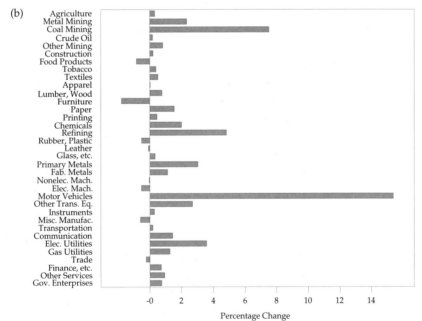

Figure 5.1
(a) Effect of removing regulation on prices at 2020. (b) Effect of removing regulation on output at 2020.

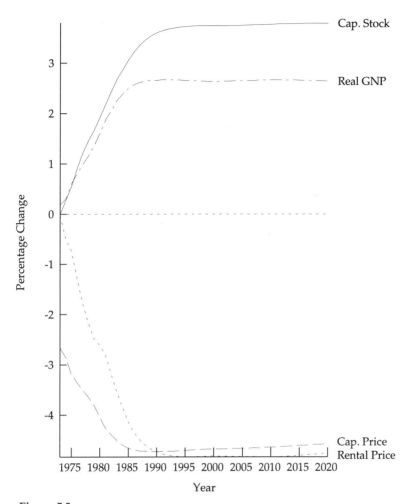

Figure 5.2
Dynamic effects of removing regulation.

removed. The rest is largely unaffected by environmental regulations. The economy follows the transition path to the new steady state shown in figure 5.2. Driven by large changes in the price of invest-ment goods, the capital stock rises sharply. The quantity of full con-sumption rises at a similar rate, as does real GNP. The adjustment process is dominated by the rapid accumulation of capital and is largely completed within two decades.

5.4   The Impact of the Clean Air Act Amendments of 1990

Our final objective is to analyze the impact of the Clean Air Act Amendments of 1990. For this purpose, we proceed, as in section 5.3, by projecting the growth of the U.S. economy with and without the 1990 legislation. The base case is the same as the one we have employed in section 5.3. In this base case all pollution controls resulting from legislation enacted before 1990 are in effect. We project the growth of the U.S. economy without the 1990 legislation. We then incorporate estimates of the costs of compliance with this legislation into our projections. Finally, we compare growth of the U.S. economy with and without the 1990 legislation.

To quantify the impact of the Clean Air Act Amendments of 1990 on U.S. economic growth, we begin with estimates of the cost of compliance with this legislation in the year 2005 prepared by the Environmental Protection Agency (1991). We employ the year 2005 as a point of reference, since the provisions of the 1990 legislation will be phased in gradually over a fifteen-year period. By the end of this period in 2005, the pollution controls embodied in the 1990 legislation are fully effective. The overall costs of compliance for the year 2005 is $24 billions in prices of 1990.

We have already pointed out that the provisions of the Clean Air Act Amendments of 1990 are divided among eleven separate "titles" of the Act. The Environmental Protection Agency (1991) has prepared separate estimates of costs of compliance for five separate programs. About half the costs in the year 2005, $12.2 billions in prices of 1990, are associated with Title I, which extends deadlines and specifies control technologies for areas which have failed to comply with existing regulations on emissions of ozone, carbon monoxide, oxides of nitrogen, and particulates. Since we do not have information on the distribution of these costs by industry, we have allocated them to the manufacturing industries in proportion to costs of compliance in the latest year for which data are available, which is 1988.

Of the remaining titles of the 1990 legislation, Title IV deals with acid rain. We have allocated the estimated costs for the year 2005, $3.6 billions in prices of 1990, to electric utilties. Title V provides for marketable permits for emissions of sulfur dioxide and regulates emissions of oxides of nitrogen. Title III regulates emissions of toxic substances into the atmosphere. Title VIII provides for miscellaneous additional regulations. The corresponding costs are $0.2 billions, $7.9

billions, and $0.1 billions, respectively, all in prices of 1990. We have allocated these costs to manufacturing industries in proportion to their total costs of compliance in 1988.

We have estimated the ratio of costs of compliance for the year 2005 for each industry to the value of the output of that industry in our base case. We have simulated U.S. economic growth with industry costs that include these costs of compliance. To reflect the fact that costs of compliance will increase gradually as the new regulations are implemented, we increase the costs of compliance linearly, beginning with a value of zero in 1990 and rising to the 2005 levels. Obviously the allocation of costs of compliance among programs included in the 1990 legislation, the distribution of these costs among industries, and the time phasing of the introduction of the new pollution controls can be further refined.

We have simulated the growth of the U.S. economy with and without the costs of compliance associated with the Clean Air Act Amendments of 1990. We present the impact of this legislation on individual industries in the year 2005 in figure 5.3. The sectors most affected by the new pollution controls are electric utilities and primary metals. The output of electric utilities is reduced by three percent, while that of primary metals is reduced by 3.5 percent. To provide estimates of a long-run impact, like those presented for earlier legislation in section 5.3, we provide industry impacts in the year 2020 in figure 5.4. Again, primary metals and electric utilities stand out as the industries most heavily affected by the 1990 legislation.

The U.S. economy follows the transition path presented in figure 5.5 in adjusting to a new steady state. The initial impact of the legislation on the gross national product is positive, since there is a short-run surge of investment to take advantage of lower prices of investment goods before the full impact of the legislation works its way through the economy. This surge in investment is over by the year 2000. The capital stock gradually falls as new pollution controls take hold, raising the price of capital goods. The rental price or cost of capital rises, reaching a level about 0.6 percent higher than the base case by the year 2020. The adjustment process reflects the forward-looking character of expectations about future prices of assets and future rates of return.

We find that the Clean Air Act Amendments will impose substantial costs on U.S. industries over the period 1990–2005, as the new pollution controls are implemented. These costs represent a net addition

(a)

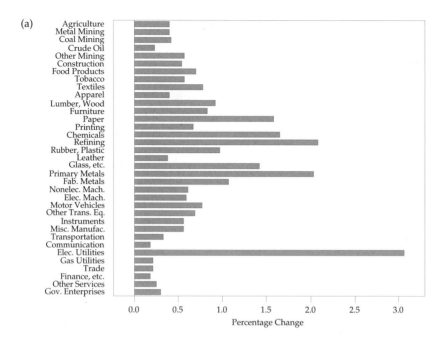

(b)

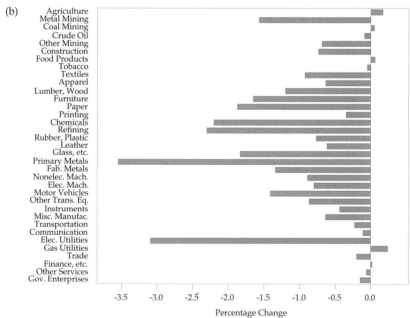

Figure 5.3
(a) Effect of the 1990 CAAA on prices at 2005. (b) Effect of the 1990 CAAA on output at 2005.

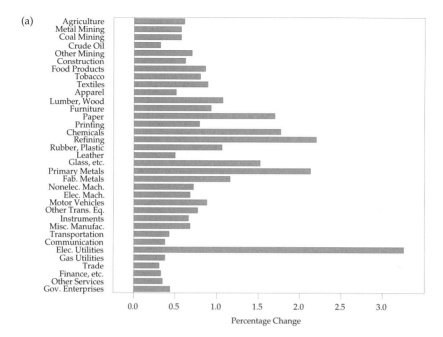

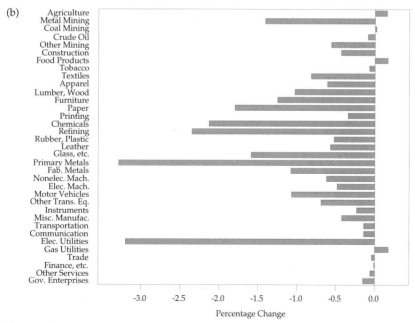

Figure 5.4
(a) Effect of the 1990 CAAA on prices at 2020. (b) Effect of the 1990 CAAA on output at 2020.

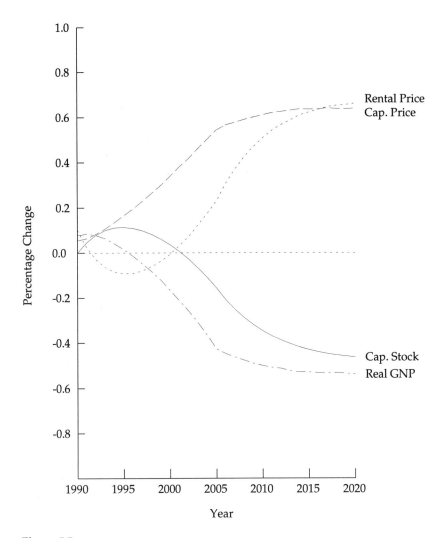

Figure 5.5
Dynamic Effects of the 1990 CAAA.

of about one-fifth to costs of compliance associated with previous legislation. The U.S. economy adapts itself to these costs of compliance
through an upward adjustment in the prices of capital goods. This
increases the rental price or cost of capital and reduces the level of the
capital stock. This generates a reduced rate of capital formation.

Notes

1. Detailed surveys of U.S. environmental policy is presented by Christiansen and Tietenberg (1985) and Portney (1990b). Portney (1990a) presents an analysis of the economic impact of the Clean Air Act Amendments of 1990.

2. Data on interindustry transactions are based on input-output tables for the U.S. constructed by the Bureau of Economic Analysis (1984). Income data are from the U.S. national income and product accounts, also developed by the Bureau of Economic Analysis (1986). The data on capital and labor services are described by Jorgenson (1990b). Additional details are given by Wilcoxen (1988), Appendix C, and Ho (1989).

3. See Mansur and Whalley (1984) for more detail. An example of the calibration approach is Borges and Goulder (1984), who present a model of energy policy calibrated to data for the year 1973. Surveys of applied general equilibrium modeling are given by Bergman (1985, 1990).

4. A detailed discussion of our econometric methodology is presented by Jorgenson (1984a, 1986a). The econometric approach is also employed by the Congressional Budget Office (1990) and Hazilla and Kopp (1990).

5. Our approach to endogenous productivity growth was originated by Jorgenson and Fraumeni (1981). A general equilibrium model of production that incorporates both substitution among inputs and endogenous productivity growth is presented by Jorgenson (1984a). The implications of this model have been analyzed by Hogan and Jorgenson (1991). Further details are given by Jorgenson (1986) and Jorgenson and Wilcoxen (1993d).

6. The Euler equation approach to modeling intertemporal consumer behavior was originated by Hall (1978). Our application of this approach follows Jorgenson and Yun (1986).

7. Our model of personal consumption expenditures can be used to represent the behavior of individual households, as in Jorgenson and Slesnick (1987a), or the behavior of the household sector as a whole, as in Jorgenson (1990a). Jorgenson, Slesnick, and Wilcoxen (1992) have employed the results for individual households to separate the overall impact of a carbon tax into equity and efficiency components.

8. Details on the econometric methodology are given by Jorgenson (1984a, 1990a). Additional details are provided by Wilcoxen (1988), Ho (1989), and Jorgenson and Wilcoxen (1993d).

9. The relationship between the price of investment goods and the rental price of capital services is discussed in greater detail by Jorgenson (1989).

10. This is the Armington (1969) approach. See Wilcoxen (1988), Ho (1989), and Jorgenson and Wilcoxen (1993d) for further details on our implementation of this approach.

11. Some of the most important projections are noted briefly below; a more detailed discussion is given by Jorgenson and Wilcoxen (1993d).

12. Our breakdown of the U.S. population by age, sex, and educational attainment is based on the system of demographic accounts compiled by Jorgenson and Fraumeni (1989). The population projections are discussed in detail by Wilcoxen (1988), Appendix B.

13. The Census data come from various issues of the annual publication, *Pollution Abatement Costs and Expenditures*. A detailed description of our data is given by Wilcoxen (1988), Appendix D. Superfund taxes amounting to more than a billion dollars a year were placed on the petroleum refining and chemicals industries in 1981 and on the primary metals industry in 1986. These may have had a substantial impact on U.S. economic growth, but we do not examine their consequences.

14. Further details are given by Wilcoxen (1988), Appendix D.

15. Details of our methodology for estimating cost differentials between high-sulfur and low-sulfur coal are given by Wilcoxen (1988), Appendix D.

16. An alternative analysis of the impact of environmental regulation on U.S. international competitiveness is given by Kalt (1988).

6

Reducing U.S. Carbon Dioxide Emissions: An Econometric General Equilibrium Assessment

Dale W. Jorgenson and Peter J. Wilcoxen

6.1 Introduction

This work describes research we conducted as part of Energy Modeling Forum 12, a recent study of the costs of limiting carbon dioxide emissions organized by the Energy Modeling Forum at Stanford University.[1] EMF-12 involved more than a dozen models built by research groups from the United States, Europe and Japan. However, our approach had three unusual features which set it apart from the other studies. These features enabled us to explore several questions not addressed by most of the other participants.

First, our results are based on a highly disaggregated intertemporal general equilibrium model of the United States. Using a disaggregated model allowed us to examine the effects of carbon taxes on narrow segments of the economy, such as particular industries or types of household. Second, all parameters in our model were obtained by econometric estimation using a data spanning thirty-nine years. Thus, the response of industries and consumers to changes in prices will be consistent with the historical record. Third, we model productivity growth at the industry level and allow it to be an endogenous function of relative prices. Allowing productivity growth to differ across industries permits the model to reflect a conspicuous feature of historical data.

Together, these features enabled us to reach several important conclusions. First, in the United States the effects of a carbon tax will be very similar to the effects of a tax placed solely on coal. Of all fossil fuels, coal is the least expensive per unit of energy and produces the most carbon dioxide when burned. Thus, a tax levied on carbon emissions will raise the cost of coal-based energy far more in percentage terms than the price of energy derived from oil or natural gas. In response to this price change, the demand for coal will fall substantially. The demands for oil and natural gas will also decline, but by much smaller percentages.

Almost all coal consumed in the U.S. is used to generate electric power. As the price of coal rises, electric utilities will convert some generating capacity to other fuels. However, substitution possibilities are fairly limited, particularly in the short run, so the tax will raise the price of electricity significantly. Consumers and firms will substitute other inputs for electricity, leading to a fall in electricity demand.[2] Higher energy prices will lead to slower productivity growth, reduced capital formation, and a reallocation of labor to lower-wage industries, all of which will cause gross national product to be lower than it would have been in the absence of the tax.

The tax rate needed to achieve a fixed absolute emissions target, such as maintaining emissions at 1990 levels, will depend on how fast emissions grow in the absence of the tax. Baseline emissions growth, in turn, will depend on the rate of productivity growth, the rate of capital accumulation, the rate of growth of the labor force, any energy-saving biases in technical change, and the path of world oil prices. More rapid economic growth will generally lead to higher baseline emissions and will thus require higher tax rates if emissions are to be held at a fixed absolute level. Moreover, deeper absolute cuts in emissions will require sharply increasing tax rates.

A carbon tax large enough to have much effect on emissions will raise tens to hundreds of billions of dollars annually. How this revenue is used will affect the overall economic burden of the tax. By using the revenue to lower highly distortionary taxes elsewhere in the economy, the tax could actually increase output and economic welfare. The remainder of this work presents our model and discusses these findings in more detail.

6.2   An Overview of the Model

Our results are based on a set of simulations we conducted using a detailed model of the United States economy designed specifically for examining the effects of energy and environmental policies. One feature of our approach which distinguishes it from many others is that we use a general equilibrium model. General equilibrium models are constructed by dividing the economy into a collection of interdependent sectors which interact through product and factor markets. The behavior of each sector is represented by an appropriate submodel. Prices and wages adjust until demands and supplies are equated in every market and the economy reaches equilibrium. Our model is composed of thirty-five producing sectors, a consumer sector, an investment sector, a government sector, and a foreign sector. In this section, we present an overview of the model by describing the submodels used to represent each of these sectors. We also discuss our base-case simulation.[3]

6.2.1 Production

Production is disaggregated into the thirty-five industrial sectors listed in table 6.1. Most of these industries match two-digit sectors in the Standard Industrial Classification (SIC). Each industry produces a primary product and may produce one or more secondary products. This level of industrial detail makes it possible to measure the effect of changes in tax policy on relatively narrow segments of the economy. Since most anthropogenic carbon dioxide emissions are generated by fossil fuel combustion, a disaggregated model is essential for capturing differences in the response of each sector to a carbon dioxide control policy.

We derive the behavior of each of the industries from a hierarchical tier-structured transcendental logarithmic cost function. At the highest level, the cost of each industry's output is assumed to be a function of the prices of energy, materials, capital services, and labor. At the second level, we take the price of energy to be a function of prices of coal, crude petroleum, refined petroleum, electricity, and natural gas, and the price of materials to be a function of the prices of all other intermediate goods. Given this structure we derive factor demands for capital services, labor, and intermediate inputs from each of the thirty-five industries.

We estimated the parameters of each industry submodel econometrically, using a set of consistent inter-industry transactions tables constructed for the purpose. The tables describe the U.S. economy for the period 1947 through 1985.[4] Estimating the production parameters over a long time series ensures that each industry's response to changes in prices is consistent with historical evidence.[5]

An unusual feature of our model is that productivity growth is determined endogenously.[6] Other models used to study global warming, for example, Manne and Richels (1992), take productivity growth

Table 6.1
Industry classifications

Number	Description
1	Agriculture, forestry, and fisheries
2	Metal mining
3	Coal mining
4	Crude petroleum and natural gas
5	Nonmetallic mineral mining
6	Construction
7	Food and kindred products
8	Tobacco manufacturers
9	Textile mill products
10	Apparel and other textile products
11	Lumber and wood products
12	Furniture and fixtures
13	Paper and allied products
14	Printing and publishing
15	Chemicals and allied products
16	Petroleum refining
17	Rubber and plastic products
18	Leather and leather products
19	Stone, clay, and glass products
20	Primary metals
21	Fabricated metal products
22	Machinery, except electrical
23	Electrical machinery
24	Motor vehicles
25	Other transportation equipment
26	Instruments
27	Miscellaneous manufacturing
28	Transportation and warehousing
29	Communication
30	Electric utilities
31	Gas utilities
32	Trade
33	Finance, insurance, and real estate
34	Other services
35	Government enterprises

to be exogenous. In our model the rate of productivity growth in each industry is determined endogenously as a function of input prices. In addition, each industry's productivity growth can be biased toward some inputs and away from others. Biased productivity growth is a common feature of historical data but is often ignored when modeling production. By allowing for biased productivity growth, our model is able to capture the evolution of industry input patterns much more accurately.

Although we allow for biased productivity growth, we do not impose that technical change be energy-saving in every industry. Most other participants in EMF-12 introduce energy-saving technical change through an exogenous parameter giving the rate of "Autonomous Energy Efficiency Improvements." The extent to which technical change is energy-saving is a source of considerable controversy. Manne and Richels (1992) suggest that engineering analysis shows technical change to energy-saving, while Hogan and Jorgenson (1991) present econometric evidence that aggregate technical change may be slightly energy-using. However, these positions are not necessarily inconsistent. After the sharp increases in energy prices of the 1970s, the U.S. economy became markedly less energy-intensive as producers and consumers substituted away from energy. To the engineers reported by Manne and Richels, this would have appeared as a shift toward energy-saving technology. Hogan and Jorgenson's study reports biases in technical change *after* accounting for movements induced by substitution. Our model is based on the same data set as Hogan and Jorgenson's work, and so has the technical change properties they describe.

In sum, the salient features of our model of producer behavior are as follows. First, production is disaggregated into thirty-five industries. Second, all parameters of the model are estimated econometrically from an extensive historical data base developed specifically for this purpose. This allows the model to incorporate extensive historical evidence on the price responsiveness of input patterns, including changes in the mix of fossil fuels. Third, the model determines rates of productivity growth endogenously and allows for biased productivity change in each industry.

6.2.2   Consumption

We represent consumer behavior by assuming that households follow a three-stage optimization process. At the first stage, each household allocates full wealth (the sum of financial and human wealth, plus the imputed value of leisure time) across different periods.[7] We formalize this decision by introducing a representative agent who maximizes an additive intertemporal utility function subject to an intertemporal budget constraint. The portion of full wealth allocated to a particular period is called full consumption. At the second stage, households allocate full consumption to goods and leisure in order to maximize an indirect utility function. This allows us to derive demands for leisure and goods as functions of prices and full consumption. The demand for leisure implicitly determines labor supply, while the difference between current income and consumption of goods implicitly determines savings.

The third stage of the household optimization problem is the allocation of total expenditure among capital services, labor services, and the thirty-five commodities. At this stage, we relax the representative consumer assumption in favor of the approach of Jorgenson, Lau, and Stoker (1982) to derive separate systems of demand functions for households of different demographic characteristics. We distinguish among 1,344 household types according to demographic characteristics, such as the number of household members and the geographic region in which the household is located. The spending patterns of each household type are derived from a hierarchial tier-structured indirect utility function. This allows us to derive household demands for individual commodities.

As with production, the parameters of the behavioral equations for all three stages of our consumer model are estimated econometrically.[8] Our household model incorporates extensive time series data on the price responsiveness of demand patterns by consumers and also makes use of detailed cross-section data on the effects of demographic characteristics on consumer behavior. In addition, an important feature of our approach is that we do not impose that household demands be homothetic. As total expenditure increases, spending patterns may change even in the absence of price changes. This captures an important feature of cross-sectional expenditure data which is often ignored.

6.2.3 Investment and Capital Formation

We assume there is a single capital stock in the economy which is in fixed total supply in the short run. However, we also assume that capital is perfectly malleable and can be reallocated among industries, and between industries and final demand categories at zero cost. Thus, the price of a unit of capital services will be equal in every industry and there will be a single economy-wide rate of return on capital.

In the long run, the supply of capital is determined by investment. Our investment model is based on the assumption that investors have rational expectations and that arbitrage occurs until the present value of future capital services is equated to the purchase price of new investment goods. This equilibrium is achieved by adjustments in prices and the term structure of interest rates. New capital goods are produced from individual commodities according to a model identical to those for the industrial sectors so the price of new capital will depend on commodity prices. We estimated the behavioral parameters for new capital goods production using final demand data for investment over the period 1947–1985. Thus, the model incorporates substitution among inputs in the composition of the capital.

6.2.4   Government and Foreign Trade

The two remaining parts of the model are the government and foreign sectors. To specify government behavior, we begin by computing total government spending on goods and services. We apply exogenous tax rates[9] to taxable transactions in the economy and then add the capital income of government enterprises and non-tax receipts to obtain total government revenue.[10] Next, we assume the government budget deficit can be specified exogenously and add the deficit to total revenue to obtain total government spending. To arrive at government purchases of goods and services, we subtract interest paid to holders of government bonds together with transfer payments to domestic and foreign recipients. We then allocate spending among commodity groups according to fixed shares constructed from historical data.

In modeling the foreign sector, we begin by assuming that imports are imperfect substitutes for similar domestic commodities.[11] The mix of goods purchased by households and firms reflects substitution between domestic and imported products. We estimate the price responsiveness of this mixture econometrically from historical data. In effect, each commodity is assigned a separate elasticity of substitution between domestic and imported goods. Since the prices of imports are given exogenously, intermediate and final demands implicitly determine the quantity of imports of each commodity.

Exports are determined by a set of isoelastic export demand equations, one for each commodity, that depend on foreign income and the foreign prices of U.S. exports.[12] Foreign prices are computed from domestic prices by adjusting for subsidies and the exchange rate. The

Table 6.2
Domestic production and heat content of fossil fuels

Fuel	Unit	Domestic production	MBTU per unit	Total QBTU
Coal	ton	916.9×10^6	21.94	20.1
Oil	bbl	3033.2×10^6	5.80	17.6
Gas	kcf	17.8×10^6	1.03	16.8

demand elasticities in these equations are estimated from historical data. Without an elaborate model of international trade it is impossible to determine both the current account balance and the exchange rate endogenously so we take the current account to be exogenous and the exchange rate to be endogenous.

6.2.5   Carbon Dioxide Emissions

For EMF-12, the most important remaining feature of the model is the way in which carbon dioxide emissions are calculated We begin by assuming that carbon dioxide is produced in fixed proportion to fossil fuel use. For each fuel, table 6.2 gives total domestic production, heat content per unit and total heat produced.[13] Heat production is measured in quadrillion Btu.

We calculated the carbon content of each fuel by multiplying the numbers in table 6.2 by figures from the Environmental Protection Agency on the amount of carbon emitted per million Btu produced from each fuel.[14] Total carbon emissions were then calculated using figures on total fuel production. Table 6.3 shows data for each fuel in 1987. For comparability with other studies, we measure CO_2 emissions in tons of contained carbon.[15]

All prices in our model are normalized to unity in 1982, so quantities do not correspond directly to physical units. Moreover, the model has a single sector for oil and gas extraction. To convert the oil and gas data in table 6.3 into a form appropriate for the model, we added carbon production for crude petroleum and natural gas and divided by the industry's output for 1987 to obtain the industry's carbon coefficient. Similarly, the coefficient for coal was obtained by dividing total carbon production from coal by the model's 1987 value for coal mining output. These coefficients were used to estimate carbon emissions in each simulation.

Table 6.3
Carbon emissions data for 1987

Item	Fuel		
	Coal	Oil	Gas
Unit of measure	ton	bbl	kcf
Heat content (10^6 Btu per unit)	21.94	5.80	1.03
Emissions rate			
(kg per 10^6 Btu)	26.9	21.4	14.5
(kg per unit)	590.2	124.1	14.9
Total domestic output (10^9 units)	0.9169	0.3033	17.8
Total carbon emissions (10^6 tons)	595.3	414.1	268.6

6.2.6 The Base Case

To assess the effect of a carbon tax, we must first determine the future path of the U.S. economy in the absence of the tax. To construct such a scenario, which we will call a "base case," we adopted a set of default assumptions about the time path of each exogenous variable in the absence of changes in government policy. Since our model is based on agents with perfect foresight, values must be specified far into the future. Through 1990–2050, we forecast values of the exogenous variables on the basis of their behavior in the sample period. After 2050 we assume the variables remain constant at their 2050 values to allow the model to converge to a steady state by the year 2100.[16]

Our projections for 1990–2050 were made as follows. First, all tax rates are set to their values in 1985, the last year in our sample period. Next, we assume that foreign prices of imports in foreign currency remain constant in real terms at 1985 levels. We then project a gradual decline in the government deficit through the year 2025, after which the nominal value of the government debt is maintained at a constant ratio to the value of the national product. Finally, we project the current account deficit by allowing it to fall gradually to zero by the year 2000. After that, we project a current account surplus sufficient to produce a stock of net claims on foreigners by the year 2050 equal to the same proportion of national wealth as in 1982.

Some of the most important exogenous variables are those associated with growth of the U.S. population and corresponding changes in the economy's time endowment. We project population by age, sex, and educational attainment through the year 2050, using demographic assumptions consistent with Social Security Administration projections.[17] After 2050, we hold population constant, which is roughly consistent with Social Security projections. In addition, we project the educational composition of the population by holding the level of educational attainment constant beginning with the cohort reaching age thirty-five in the year 1985. We transform our population projection into a projection of the time endowment by assuming that the pattern of relative wages across different types of labor remains as it was in 1985. Since capital formation is endogenous in our model, our projections of the time endowment effectively determine the size of the economy in the more distant future.

6.3   A Summary of Results

One policy often proposed for slowing global warming is to stabilize greenhouse gas emissions at 1990 levels. This corresponds to EMF-12 scenario 4, so we begin our discussion there. Subsequent sections will examine the effects of more stringent emissions targets, the consequences of using carbon tax revenue in different ways, and the sensitivity of results to assumptions embodied in the base-case scenario.

6.3.1   Stabilizing Emissions

To implement scenario 4 we introduced a tax on the carbon content of primary fossil fuels. The tax was applied to both domestic and imported sources; domestic fuels were at the mine mouth or well head while imported fuels were taxed at the point of import. The tax rate varied from year to year but was always chosen to be exactly enough to hold U.S. carbon dioxide emissions at their 1990 value of 1,576 million tons. We returned the revenue raised by the tax to households as a lump-sum rebate. The carbon tax we obtained is shown as a function of time in figure 6.1. Base-case emissions increase over time, so the tax grows gradually over the next few decades. By 2020, our forecast of the U.S. population crests and growth begins to slow, reducing the rate of carbon tax growth.[18] The tax produces significant reductions in carbon emissions, as shown in figure 6.2. By 2020 emissions

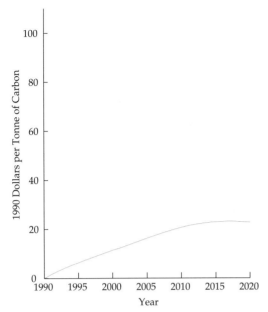

Figure 6.1
Carbon tax under scenario 4.

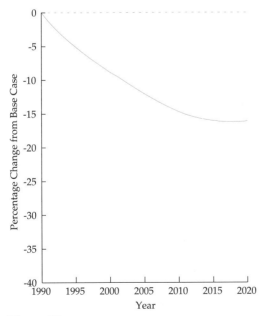

Figure 6.2
Reduction in emissions under scenario 4.

are sixteen percent lower than they would have been without the tax. The tax also produces a significant revenue of $31 billion annually by 2020.[19]

The direct effect of the tax is to increase purchasers' prices of coal and crude oil. By 2020, for example, the tax reaches $22.71 per ton of carbon. This amounts to a tax of $14.75 per ton of coal, $3.10 per barrel of oil, or $0.37 per thousand cubic feet of gas. Figure 6.3 shows the effect of the tax on purchasers' prices of each industry's output in 2020. The price of coal rises by forty-seven percent, the price of electricity rises by almost seven percent (coal accounts for about thirteen percent of the cost of electricity), and the price of crude oil rises by around four percent. Other prices showing significant effects are those for refined petroleum and natural gas utilities. These rise, directly or indirectly, because of the tax on the carbon content of oil and natural gas.

Changes in relative prices affect demands for each good and lead to changes in industry outputs. Figure 6.4 presents percentage changes in industry outputs in 2020 relative to the base case. Most sectors show only small changes in output. Coal mining is an exception—its output falls by almost thirty percent. Coal is affected strongly for three reasons. First, coal emits the more carbon dioxide than oil or natural gas per unit of energy produced. Thus, the absolute level of the tax per unit of energy content is higher on coal than other fuels. Second, the tax is very large relative to the base-case price of coal—at the mine mouth the tax increases coal prices by around fifty percent. Oil is far more expensive per unit of energy; so in percentage terms, its price is less affected by the tax. In fact, the price of crude oil rises only about ten percent. Third, the demand for coal is relatively elastic. Most coal is purchased by electric utilities which can substitute other fuels for coal when the price rises. Moreover, the demand for electricity itself is relatively elastic so when the price of electricity rises, demand for electricity (and hence demand for coal) falls substantially.

For the rest of the economy, the main result of the tax is to increase the prices of electricity, refined petroleum, and natural gas, each by a few percent. This would have two effects. First, higher energy prices would mean that capital goods (which are produced using energy) would become more expensive. To the extent that domestic saving does not rise enough to compensate, higher prices for capital goods mean a slower rate of capital accumulation and lower GNP in the future. Second, higher energy prices discourage technical change in

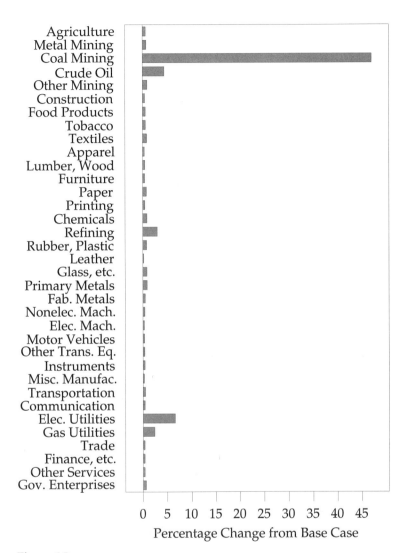

Figure 6.3
Changes in prices at 2020 under scenario 4.

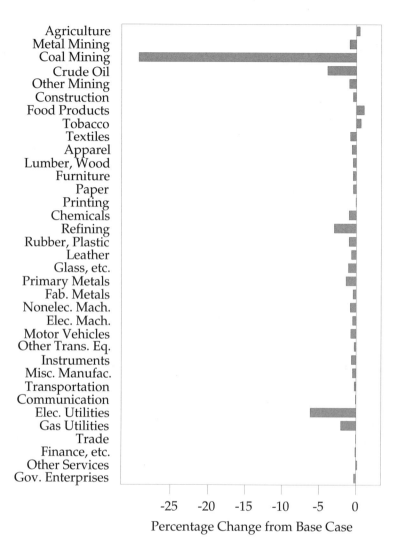

Figure 6.4
Change in output at 2020 under scenario 4.

industries in which technical change is energy-using. Together, these two effects cause the capital stock to drop by 0.7 percent and GNP to fall by 0.5 percent (both relative to the base case) by 2020. Average annual GNP growth over the period 1990–2020 is 0.02 percentage points lower than in the base case. About half of this is due to slower productivity growth and half due to reduced capital formation.

6.3.2 Larger Reductions

EMF-12 scenarios 2 and 3 specify more ambitious goals for carbon dioxide control. In scenario 2, emissions are required to decrease gradually until 2010, when they must be twenty percent below 1990 levels. In scenario 3, emissions must fall by twenty percent in 2010 and then by fifty percent by 2050. Figure 6.5 shows the paths of carbon taxes needed over time in scenarios 2, 3, and 4 while figure 6.6 shows the paths of carbon emissions in each case. Table 6.4 compares key long-run results for these two simulations with results for scenario 4.

Comparing scenarios 2 and 3 with 4 shows that increasing the stringency of the policy rapidly increases its cost. Moving from scenario 4 to 2 doubles the effect of the policy—emissions fall by 32.90% instead

Table 6.4
Selected results for scenarios 2–4 in 2020

Variable	Unit	Scenario		
		2	3	4
Carbon emission	%Δ	−32.90	−39.19	−16.12
Carbon tax	$/t	74.49	108.786	22.71
Price of capital	%Δ	1.10	1.40	0.40
Capital stock	%Δ	−2.35	−2.95	−0.83
Tax revenue	$B	82.52	109.16	31.41
Real GNP	%Δ	−1.71	−2.3	−0.55
Coal price	%Δ	149.86	216.09	46.99
Coal output	%Δ	−55.03	−62.47	−29.28
Electricity price	%Δ	19.46	26.90	6.60
Electricity ouput	%Δ	−16.43	−21.74	−6.17
Oil price	%Δ	15.06	22.37	4.45
Oil output	%Δ	−12.35	−17.63	−3.90

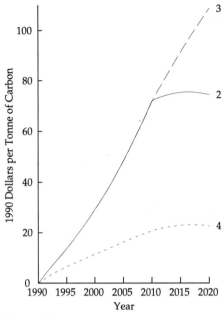

Figure 6.5
Carbon taxes under scenarios 2–4.

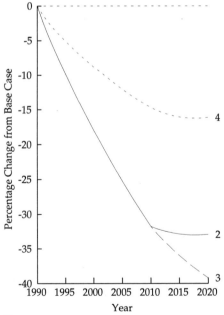

Figure 6.6
Reduction in emissions, scenarios 2–4.

of 16.12%. However, this comes at the cost of tripling the carbon tax and the loss of output. Moving from scenario 4 to scenario 3 raises costs even more sharply—the carbon tax and loss of GNP go up by more than a factor of four while the carbon reduction rises by only a factor of 2.4.

Comparing industry results across each of the scenarios shows that the more stringent policies have progressively larger effects on sectors other than coal mining. Doubling the emissions reduction by moving from scenario 4 to scenario 2 does not cause the reduction in coal output to double. Coal users, particularly electric utilities, find it increasingly difficult to substitute away from coal. Thus, larger reductions in carbon emissions require progressively larger reductions in oil use. From scenario 4 to scenario 2, for example, the drop in oil use more than triples.

6.3.3 Use of Carbon Tax Revenues

Even a modest carbon tax would raise substantial revenue. In the simulations above, we assumed the proceeds were returned to households by a lump-sum rebate. This is probably not the most likely use of the revenue, nor is it likely to be the best use given that the federal budget deficit is large and that other government revenue is raised by distortionary taxes. Using the revenue to reduce a distortionary tax would lower the net cost of the carbon tax by removing inefficiency elsewhere in the economy.

To determine how large this efficiency improvement might be, we constructed three simulations based on EMF-12 scenario 7. In each simulation we impose a carbon tax of $15 per ton in 1990 with the rate rising by five percent annually in subsequent years. The simulations differ in how the revenue was used. In the first simulation, the revenue was returned to households by a lump-sum rebate; in the second it was used to lower taxes on labor, and in the third it was used to lower taxes on capital. Table 6.5 reports results from the three simulations.

The GNP results in table 6.5 show that the disposition of revenue from a carbon tax has a very significant effect on its overall impact. In the lump-sum case, output in 2020 drops by 1.70% relative to the base case. When the revenue is returned by lowering the tax on labor, the loss of GNP is less than half as much—only 0.69%. The improvement is due to an increase in employment brought about by the drop in the

Table 6.5
Selected results revenue experiments in 2020

		Revenue policy		
Variable	Unit	Lump	Labor	Capital
Carbon emission	%Δ	−32.24	−32.09	−31.65
Carbon tax	$/t	64.83	64.83	64.83
Price of capital	%Δ	0.97	−1.86	0.23
Capital stock	%Δ	−2.13	−1.36	−1.89
Tax revenue	$B	79.65	79.82	80.35
Real GNP	%Δ	−1.70	−0.69	−1.10
Coal price	%Δ	143.49	140.57	142.06
Coal output	%Δ	−54.14	−54.19	−53.45
Electricity price	%Δ	18.57	15.97	16.99
Electricity ouput	%Δ	−15.93	−15.37	−14.66
Oil price	%Δ	14.20	12.28	14.55
Oil output	%Δ	−11.92	−11.54	−11.39

wedge between before- and after-tax wages. If the revenue were returned as a reduction in taxes on capital, GNP would actually increase above its base-case level by 1.10%. In this case, the gain is due to accelerated capital formation generated by an increase in the after-tax rate of return on investment. These results suggest that a carbon tax would provide an opportunity for significant tax reform.

6.3.4   Sensitivity to Base-Case Assumptions

Most EMF-12 scenarios required carbon dioxide emissions to be held indefinitely at a specified absolute level, such as that prevailing in 1990. In general, uncontrolled emissions will rise at the overall rate of economic growth less adjustments for increasing fossil fuel prices and energy-saving technical change. Achieving a fixed target in the face of continuously rising baseline emissions will require a growing carbon tax. At each point in time, the magnitude of the tax will depend on the size of the gap between uncontrolled emissions and the target. The more rapid the growth of uncontrolled emissions, the larger will be the gap, and hence, the larger will be the tax needed to keep emissions constant.

The growth of carbon emissions is determined by productivity growth, the rate of capital accumulation, the rate of labor supply growth, any energy-saving biases in technical change, and the path of world oil prices. For most models participating in EMF-12, many of these factors were exogenous. In fact, the EMF-12 study design includes a specified, exogenous GNP growth rate for each region. In our model, however, productivity growth, capital accumulation, and biases in the rate of technical change are all endogenous. Moreover, productivity growth and biased technical change occur at the level of individual industries rather than at the level of the economy as a whole. Thus, GNP growth is fundamentally endogenous in our model.

This difference in the treatment growth makes direct comparisons of our results with those of the other EMF-12 participants difficult. Our base-case estimate of U.S. growth is substantially below the rate specified in the EMF-12 study design. As a result, our base-case path of carbon emissions rises more slowly than it would if growth were faster. Thus, the carbon taxes needed to hold emissions at a fixed absolute level will tend to be lower in our model. To allow our results to be compared more easily with those of the other participants, and to explore the importance of GNP growth in general, EMF-12 scenario 12 was designed. Scenario 12 was identical to scenario 2 (a twenty percent reduction of emissions below 1990 levels), except that the growth rate of the U.S. GNP was set to the value predicted by our base-case simulation. Thus, the results of other participants could be directly compared with ours.

The principle finding of scenario 12 was that the carbon taxes and GNP loss predicted by other participants dropped sharply. Comparing our results for scenario 2 to the scenario 12 results of others, our carbon tax moves from being particularly low to being near the middle of the group. Our prediction for loss of GNP due to the tax moves from the middle of the group to among the highest. This is precisely what might be expected given that our initial growth rate was relatively low. Our model incorporates stronger intertemporal links between current carbon taxes, capital accumulation, and productivity growth than most of the other models. Thus, our model should generate higher GNP losses than the others. Scenario 12 shows that after adjusting for base-case emissions growth, this is *in fact* the case. More generally, scenario 12 emphasizes that overall economic growth will have a profound effect on the cost of controlling carbon dioxide emissions.

6.4   Conclusion

In summary, our approach to EMF-12 has three features that distinguish it from others: our model is disaggregated to the level of individual industries, our behavioral parameters are obtained by econometric estimation, and productivity growth and biased technical change are endogenous in our model. These features allow us to investigate several aspects of carbon taxes that other EMF-12 participants were unable to examine. In particular, we find that a carbon tax will have sharply differing effects in different industries. The tax will fall most heavily on coal mining, leading to a substantial drop in coal use by electric utilities and other industries. Outside the coal industry, the main effect of the tax will be to increase the price of electricity. This will reduce productivity growth and slow the rate of capital formation, leading to slower growth of U.S. output.

The tax needed to attain any particular emissions target will depend heavily on how fast carbon dioxide emissions would have grown in the absence of the tax. Higher rates of GNP growth will lead to higher baseline emissions, and thus will require higher carbon taxes. In addition, to achieve larger reductions in carbon emissions will require sharply increasing carbon taxes and will produce markedly higher losses of output.

Finally, a carbon tax large enough to have much effect on carbon emissions will raise considerable revenue. How this revenue is used will affect the overall economic burden of the tax. If the revenue were used to reduce distortionary taxes elsewhere in the economy, the impact of the tax on GNP would be reduced. In fact, it is possible that GNP would actually increase if the revenue were used to reduce taxes on capital.

Notes

1. A complete description of all findings of EMF–12 is contained in Gaskins and Weyant, *Reducing Carbon Emissions from the Energy Sector: Cost and Policy Options.*
2. In other words consumers and firms will conserve energy as it becomes more expensive.
3. For more detail on the specification of the model or the base-case simulation, see Jorgenson and Wilcoxen (1990b).
4. Data on inter-industry transactions are based on input-output tables for the U.S. constructed by the Bureau of Economic Analysis (1984). Income data are from the U.S. national income and product accounts, also developed by the Bureau of Economic

Analysis (1986). The data on capital and labor services are described by Jorgenson (1990b). Additional details are given by Wilcoxen (1988, Appendix C), and Ho (1989).

5. A detailed discussion of our econometric methodology is presented by Jorgenson (1984a, 1986a).

6. Our approach to endogenous productivity growth was originated by Jorgenson and Fraumeni (1981).

7. Full wealth is defined to be the sum of financial wealth, the present value of future labor earnings, and the imputed value of leisure time.

8. Details on the econometric methodology are given by Jorgenson (1984a). Additional details are provided by Wilcoxen (1988) and Ho (1989).

9. These tax rates are based on data extending through 1985 and hence predate the 1986 tax reform. We are in the process of updating our description of the tax code.

10. The capital income of government enterprises is endogenous while non-tax receipts are exogenous.

11. This is the Armington (1969) approach. See Wilcoxen (1988) and Ho (1989) for further details on our implementation of this approach.

12. We take foreign income to be exogenous.

13. The data are taken from Department of Energy (1990).

14. Environmental Protection Agency (1990) internal memorandum.

15. To convert to tons of carbon dioxide, multiply by 3.67.

16. A more detailed discussion of the base case is given by Jorgenson and Wilcoxen (1992b).

17. Our breakdown of the U.S. population by age, sex, and educational attainment is based on the system of demographic accounts compiled by Jorgenson and Fraumeni (1989).

18. As noted above, our population projection is based on forecasts made by the Social Security Administration in which population growth approaches zero early in the next century.

19. All dollar amounts are in 1990 prices.

7

Reducing U.S. Carbon Dioxide Emissions: An Assessment of Different Instruments

Dale W. Jorgenson and Peter J. Wilcoxen

The possibility that carbon dioxide emissions from fossil fuel use might lead to global warming has become a leading environmental concern. Many scientific and environmental organizations have called for immediate action to limit carbon dioxide production. For the most part, however, public debate has focused on a single policy instrument: a carbon tax applied to fossil fuels in proportion to their carbon content. We present a detailed model of the U.S. economy and use it to compare carbon taxes with two other instruments that could achieve the same reduction in carbon dioxide emissions: a tax on the energy content of fossil fuels (a Btu tax) and an *ad valorem* tax on fuel use. We find that carbon taxes can achieve a given reduction with the least overall effect on the economy, but with a large effect on coal mining. Energy taxes are fairly similar to carbon taxes but with slightly less impact on coal mining and slightly greater overall cost. In contrast, *ad valorem* taxes fall much more lightly on coal mining but have a substantial greater effect on the economy as a whole.

7.1 Introduction

The possibility that carbon dioxide emissions from fossil fuel combustion might lead to global warming has emerged as an international environmental issue.[1] Multilateral action to reduce emissions was discussed under the U.N. Framework Convention on Climate Change in 1992 at the U.N. Conference on Environment and Development in Rio de Janeiro. The U.N. Framework Convention calls for stabilization of carbon dioxide emissions at 1990 levels, but leaves the choice of policy instruments to be used for this purpose to each of the signatory nations.

The policy instrument for reducing carbon dioxide emissions in the United States most often recommended by economists is a carbon tax,[2] a tax on the carbon content of fossil fuels. A carbon tax would lead to substitution away from these fuels and toward other inputs, such as capital, labor, and materials. In addition, a carbon tax would result in less intensive use of coal, which has a high carbon content, and more intensive use of natural gas, which has a low carbon content. The European Community has proposed an energy tax, levied on primary fuels in proportion to their energy (Btu) content. Finally, taxes proportional to the value of individual fuels, such as an *ad valorem* tax on gasoline, have also been discussed.

A great deal of valuable information has been accumulated about the economic impact of policies to limit the emissions of greenhouse gases.[3] However, the analysis of the impact on U.S. economic growth of restrictions on these emissions is seriously incomplete. Alternative tax instruments, such as carbon, energy, and *ad valorem* taxes are intended to reduce fossil fuel use by inducing producers and households to use other fuels. To capture these effects, it is essential to model the responses of businesses and households at a highly disaggregated level. A disaggregated model of producer behavior is required to incorporate differences among sectors in response to energy taxes. A disaggregated model of the household sector is necessary to include differences in responses among households.

Taxes on fossil fuels affect carbon dioxide emissions by changing relative prices. These price changes affect capital formation and the rate of economic growth, so that assessment of the impact of alternative tax instruments requires a model with endogenous capital formation. In addition, these taxes will increase the price of energy to purchasers, which may reduce or accelerate the rate of productivity growth. We present a detailed model of the U.S. economy with endogenous economic growth. We use this model to compare the economic impact of alternative tax instruments for stabilizing U.S. carbon dioxide emissions at 1990 levels, as stipulated in the U.N. Framework Convention.

In section 7.2, we describe the model of the U.S. economy used in our evaluation of the economic impact of alternative tax instruments for stabilizing carbon dioxide emissions. In section 7.3, we compare these alternative instruments and find that a carbon tax will achieve the objective of stabilizing emissions with the least overall impact on the U.S. economy. However, such a tax will have a severe negative impact on coal production. An energy tax is fairly similar to a carbon tax in its economic impact, but has less effect on coal mining and greater overall cost. By contrast, an *ad valorem* tax on fossil fuels has a smaller impact on coal mining, but a much greater negative impact on the growth of the U.S. economy. In section 7.4, we assess the alternative tax instruments and summarize our conclusions.

7.2   An Overview of the Model

Our analysis of the incidence of carbon, energy, and *ad valorem* taxes is based on simulations of U.S. economic growth; we used an intertemporal general equilibrium model of the U.S. economy described in detail by Jorgenson and Wilcoxen (1993). Jorgenson and Wilcoxen (1990b) used this model to assess the impact of environmental regulations in the United States. In this section, we outline the key features of the model and describe its application to alternative tax instruments for the control of carbon dioxide emissions.

7.2.1   Producer Behavior

Because carbon dioxide emissions are generated by fossil fuel combustion, a disaggregated model is essential for modeling differences in the response to alternative policies for controlling these emissions. Our submodel of producer behavior is disaggregated into 35 industrial sectors, listed in table 7.1. The model determines levels of output for 35 separate commodities, each produced by one or more industries. The industries correspond, roughly, to two-digit industry groups in the Standard Industrial Classification (SIC). This level of industrial detail makes it possible to measure the effect of changes in tax policy on relatively narrow segments of the economy.

We represent the technology of each of the 35 industries in our model by means of a hierarchical tier structure of econometric models of producer behavior. At the highest level, the price of output in each industry is represented as a function of prices of energy, materials, and capital and labor services. Similarly, the price of energy is a function of prices of coal, crude petroleum, refined petroleum, electricity, and natural gas; the price of materials is a function of the prices of all other intermediate goods. We derive demands for inputs of capital and labor services and inputs of the 35 intermediate goods into each industry from the price function for that industry.

We have econometrically estimated the parameters of production models for the 35 industries. For this purpose, we have constructed a

Table 7.1
Industry classifications

Number	Description
1	Agriculture, forestry, and fisheries
2	Metal mining
3	Coal mining
4	Crude petroleum and natural gas
5	Nonmetallic mineral mining
6	Construction
7	Food and kindred products
8	Tobacco manufacturers
9	Textile mill products
10	Apparel and other textile products
11	Lumber and wood products
12	Furniture and fixtures
13	Paper and allied products
14	Printing and publishing
15	Chemicals and allied products
16	Petroleum refining
17	Rubber and plastic products
18	Leather and leather products
19	Stone, clay, and glass products
20	Primary metals
21	Fabricated metal products
22	Machinery, except electrical
23	Electrical machinery
24	Motor vehicles
25	Other transportation equipment
26	Instruments
27	Miscellaneous manufacturing
28	Transportation and warehousing
29	Communication
30	Electric utilities
31	Gas utilities
32	Trade
33	Finance, insurance, and real estate
34	Other services
35	Government enterprises

set of consistent inter-industry transactions tables for the U.S. economy for the period 1947 through 1985.[4] Our econometric method for parameterization stands in sharp contrast to the calibration method used in almost all applied general equilibrium models. Calibration involves choosing parameters to replicate the data for a particular year.[5]

The econometric approach to parameterization has several advantages over the calibration approach. First, by using an extensive time series of data rather than a single data point, we are able to derive the response of production patterns to changes in prices from historical experience.[6] This is particularly important for the analysis of alternative tax policies to control carbon dioxide emissions, because energy prices varied widely during our sample period. The calibration approach imposes responses to price changes on the data through the choice of functional forms. For example, elasticities of substitution are set equal to unity by imposing the Cobb-Douglas functional form or zero by imposing the Leontief form. Similarly, all elasticities of substitution are set equal to each other by imposing the constant elasticity of substitution functional form.

Empirical evidence on substitutability among inputs is essential in analyzing the impact of alternative tax policies to control carbon dioxide emissions. If it is easy for industries to substitute among inputs, the effects of these policies will be very different than if substitution were limited. Although calibration avoids the burden of data collection required by econometric estimation, it also specifies the substitutability of inputs by assumption rather than relying on empirical evidence. This can easily lead to substantial distortions in estimating the effects of alternative policies.

A second advantage of the econometric approach is that parameters estimated from time series are much less likely to be affected by the peculiarities of the data for a particular time period. By construction, parameters obtained by calibration are forced to absorb all the random errors present in the data for a single benchmark year. This poses a severe problem when the benchmark year is unusual in some respect. For example, parameters calibrated to data for 1973 would incorporate into the model all the distortions in energy markets that resulted from price controls and rationing of energy during the first oil crisis. Econometric parameterization greatly mitigates this problem by reducing the influence of random errors for any particular time period.

An important feature of our producer submodel is that an industry's productivity growth can be biased toward some inputs and away from others. Biased productivity growth is a common feature of historical data, but is often excluded from models of production. By allowing for biased productivity growth, our model provides a separation between price-induced reductions in energy utilization and those resulting from changes in technology. In addition, the rate of productivity growth for each industry in our model is determined endogenously as a function of relative prices.[7]

In summary, the salient features of our production model are, first, that it is disaggregated into 35 industries. Second, all parameters of the model are estimated econometrically from an extensive historical database developed specifically for this purpose. Third, the model determines rates of productivity growth endogenously and allows for biased productivity change in each industry. Fourth, the model incorporates extensive historical evidence on the price responsiveness of input patterns, including changes in the mix of fossil fuels. We turn next to a brief discussion of our modeling of final demands— consumption, investment, government expenditure, and foreign trade.

7.2.2   Consumption

Alternative tax policies to control carbon dioxide emissions have very different impacts on different households. For example, the imposition of a tax on energy affects the relative prices paid by consumers. An increase in the price of energy resulting from the tax adversely affects those consumers who devote a larger share of total expenditure to energy. To capture these differences among households, we have subdivided the household sector into 672 demographic groups that differ by characteristics such as family size, age of head, region of residence, race, and urban versus rural location. We treat each household as a consuming unit, so that the household behaves like an individual maximizing a utility function.

We represent the preferences of each household by means of an econometric model of consumer behavior. The econometric approach to parameterization enables us to derive the response of household expenditure patterns to changes in prices from historical experience. This approach to modeling consumer behavior has the same advantages over the calibration approach as those we have described for modeling producer behavior. Empirical evidence on substitutability among goods and services is essential in analyzing the impact of alternative tax policies to control carbon dioxide emissions. If it is easy for households to substitute among commodities, the effects of these policies will be very different than if substitution were limited.

Our model of household behavior is generated by a three-stage optimization process. At the first stage, each household allocates full wealth, defined as the sum of human and nonhuman wealth, across different time periods. We formalize this decision by introducing a representative agent who maximizes an additive intertemporal utility function, subject to an intertemporal budget constraint. The optimal allocation satisfies a sequence of necessary conditions that can be summarized by means of an Euler equation.[8] This allocation is determined by the rate of time preference and the intertemporal elasticity of substitution. The Euler equation is forward-looking, so that the allocation of full wealth incorporates expectations about all future prices and discount rates.

After households have allocated full wealth to the current time period, they proceed to the second stage of the optimization process—choosing the mix of leisure and goods. We represent household preferences between goods and leisure by means of a representative agent with an indirect utility function that depends on the prices of leisure and goods. We derive demands for leisure and goods as functions of these prices and the wealth allocated to the period. This implies an allocation of the household's exogenously given time endowment between leisure time and the labor market, so that this stage of the optimization process determines labor supply.

The third stage of the household optimization problem is the allocation of total expenditure among capital and labor services and the 35 commodity groups included in the model. At this stage, we replace the representative consumer approach with the approach of Jorgenson, Lau, and Stoker (1982) for deriving a system of demand functions for each household. We distinguish among household types cross-classified by attributes, such as the number of household members and the geographic region in which the household is located. For each type of household, we use a hierarchical tier structure of models of consumer behavior to represent demands for individual commodities.[9]

The parameters of the behavioral equations for all three stages of our consumer model are estimated econometrically.[10] This includes the Euler equation, demand functions for leisure and personal consumption expenditures, and demand functions for individual commodities. Our household model incorporates extensive time series data on the price responsiveness of demand patterns by consumers and detailed cross-section data on demographic effects on consumer behavior. An important feature of our household model is that we do not require that demands are homothetic. As levels of total expenditure increase, patterns of expenditure on individual commodities change, even in the absence of price changes. This captures an important feature of cross-section data on household expenditure patterns that is usually ignored in applied general equilibrium modeling.

7.2.3   Investment and Capital Formation

Our investment model, like our model of saving, is based on perfect foresight or rational expectations. Under this assumption, the price of investment goods in every period is based on expectations of future capital service prices and discount rates that are fulfilled by the solution of the model. In particular, we require that the price of new investment goods is always equal to the present value of future capital services.[11] The price of investment goods and the discounted value of future rental prices are brought into intertemporal equilibrium by adjustments in prices and the term structure of interest rates. This intertemporal equilibrium incorporates the forward-looking dynamics of asset pricing by producers.

For tractability, we assume there is a single capital stock in the economy that is perfectly malleable, so that it can be reallocated among and between industries and final demand categories at zero cost. Under this assumption, imposition of alternative tax policies can affect the distribution of capital and labor supplies among sectors, even in the short run. In each time period the supply of capital in our model is completely inelastic, because the stock of capital is determined by past investment. Investment during the period is determined by the savings made available by households. The relationship between capital stock and past investment incorporates backward-looking dynamics into our model of intertemporal equilibrium.

We assume that new capital goods are produced from individual commodities, so that the price of new capital depends on commodity prices. We have estimated the price function for new capital goods using final demand data for investment over the period 1947–1985. Thus, our model incorporates substitution among inputs in the composition of the capital. This feature can play an important role in the evaluation of alternative tax policies. Jorgenson and Wilcoxen (1990a) have found, for example, that an increase in the price of automobiles resulting from mandatory installation of pollution control devices shifts investment away from motor vehicles and toward other types of capital.

In summary, capital formation in our model is the outcome of intertemporal optimization by households and firms. Optimization by households is forward-looking and incorporates expectations about future prices, wages and interest rates. Optimization by producers is also forward-looking and depends upon these same expectations. Both types of optimization are very important for modeling the impact of future restrictions on carbon dioxide emissions. The effects of these restrictions will be anticipated by households and firms, so that future policies will have important consequences for current decisions.

7.2.4   Government and Foreign Trade

The two remaining final demand categories in our model are the government and foreign sectors. We determine final demands for government consumption from the income-expenditure identity for the government sector. The first step is to compute total tax revenue by applying exogenous tax rates to appropriate transactions in the business and household sectors. We then add the capital income of government enterprises, determined endogenously, and non-tax receipts, also determined exogenously, to tax revenue to obtain total government revenue.

We assume the government budget deficit can be specified exogenously. We add the deficit to total revenue to obtain total government spending. To arrive at government purchases of goods and services, we subtract interest paid to domestic and foreign holders of government bonds together with government transfer payments to domestic and foreign recipients. We allocate the remainder among commodity groups according to fixed shares constructed from historical data. Finally, we determine the quantity of each commodity by dividing the value of government spending on the good by its price.

Foreign trade has two components—imports and exports. We assume that imports are imperfect substitutes for similar domestic commodities.[12] The goods actually purchased by households and firms reflect substitution between domestic and imported products. The price responsiveness of these purchases is estimated econometrically from historical data. In effect, each commodity is assigned a separate elasticity of substitution between domestic and imported goods. Because the prices of imports are given exogenously, intermediate and final demands implicitly determine imports of each commodity.

Exports, on the other hand, are determined by a set of export demand equations, one for each commodity, that depend on exogenously given foreign income and the foreign price of U.S. exports. Foreign prices are computed from domestic prices by adjusting for subsidies and the exchange rate. The demand elasticities in these equations are estimated from historical data. Without an elaborate model of international trade it is impossible to determine both the current account balance and the exchange rate endogenously. In the simulations reported below, we take the current account to be exogenous and the exchange rate to be endogenous.

7.2.5   Estimating Energy Production and Carbon Emissions

The most important remaining feature of the model is the way in which carbon dioxide emissions and the energy content of fossil fuels are calculated. For tractability, we assume both are produced in fixed proportions to fossil fuel use. This implicitly assumes that nothing can be done to reduce the carbon dioxide emissions or increase the energy produced by a given combustion process.[13] Table 7.2 gives total domestic production, heat content per unit, and total heat produced for each fuel. Heat production is measured in quadrillion Btu (quads or QBtu).

We calculated the carbon content of each fuel by multiplying the heat content of the fuel by the carbon emitted. We obtained the average heat content of each fossil fuel in millions of Btu per quantity unity from the Energy Information Administration (1990). We then obtained data from the Environmental Protection Agency (1988) on the amount of carbon emitted per million Btu generated from each fuel. Multiplying the emissions figures by the heating value gives the

Table 7.2
Domestic production and heat content of fossil fuels

Fuel	Ton	Domestic output	Heat content (MBtu/unit)	Total heat (QBtu)
Coal	ton	916.9×10^6	21.94	20.1
Oil	bbl	3033.2×10^6	5.80	17.6
Gas	kcf	17.8×10^6	1.03	16.8

Table 7.3
Carbon emissions data for 1987

Item	Fuel		
	Coal	Oil	Gas
Unit of measure	ton	bbl	kcf
Heat content (10^6 Btu per unit)	21.94	5.80	1.03
Emissions rate (kg per 10^6 Btu)	26.9	21.4	14.5
(kg per unit)	590.2	124.1	14.9
Total domestic output (10^9 units)	0.9169	0.3033	17.8
Total carbon emissions (10^6 tons)	595.3	414.1	268.6

carbon content of each fuel. Total carbon emissions can then be calculated from fuel production. Table 7.3 gives data for each fuel in 1987.

All prices in our model are normalized to unity in a common base year, so that quantities do not correspond directly to physical units. Moreover, the model has a single sector for oil and gas extraction. To convert the data for this industry into a form appropriate for the model, we added carbon production for crude petroleum and natural gas, and divided by the industry's output for 1987 to obtain the carbon coefficient for this industry. Similarly, the coefficient for coal was obtained by dividing total carbon production from coal by the model's 1987 value for coal mining output. These coefficients were used to estimate carbon emissions in each simulation. We now turn to a brief discussion of the model's base case.

7.2.6 The Base Case

To simulate the U.S. economy we must provide values of the exogenous variables for all time periods. We have accomplished this in two steps. First, we have adopted a set of default assumptions about the time path of each exogenous variable in the absence of changes in government policy. These assumptions are used in generating a simulation of U.S. economic growth called the "base case." Our second step is to change certain exogenous variables to reflect the introduction of alternative tax policies and simulate U.S. economic growth again to produce an "alternative case." We then compare the two simulations to assess the impact of the policy change. Obviously, the assumptions underlying the base case are important in interpreting the results.

Since our model is based on agents with perfect foresight, we must solve the model indefinitely far into the future. To do this, we project values for all exogenous variables over the period 1990–2050. After 2050, we assume the variables remain constant at 2050 values, which allows the model to converge to a steady state by the year 2100.[14] First, we set all tax rates to their values in 1985, the last year in our sample period. Next, we assume that prices of imports in foreign currency remain constant in real terms at 1985 levels before U.S. tariffs are applied.

We project a gradual decline in the government deficit through the year 2025, after which the nominal value of the government debt is maintained at a constant ratio to the value of the national product. Finally, we project the current account deficit by allowing it to fall gradually to zero by the year 2000. After that, we project a current account surplus sufficient to produce a stock of net claims on foreigners by the year 2050 equal to the same proportion of national wealth as in 1982.

The most important exogenous variables are those associated with growth of the U.S. population and corresponding changes in the economy's time endowment. We project population by age, sex, and educational attainment through the year 2050, using demographic assumptions consistent with Social Security Administration projections.[15] After 2050, we hold population constant, which is approximately in line with these projections. In addition, we project the educational composition of the population by holding the level of educational attainment constant, beginning with the cohort reaching age 35 in the year 1985. We transform our population projection into a projection of the time endowment by taking relative wages across different types of labor input to be constant at 1985 levels. Because capital formation is endogenous in our model, our projections of the time endowment effectively determine the size of the economy in the more distant future.

7.3   An Assessment of Different Instruments

A strategy for controlling carbon dioxide emissions consists of a target path of emissions and a tax instrument to be used to attain the target. We compare the economic impacts of three different sequences of tax instruments for holding U.S. carbon dioxide emissions constant at the 1990 level of 1,576 million tons. All three instruments are taxes on fossil fuels. The specific taxes we consider are the following:

(1) A tax on the carbon content of fossil fuels;
(2) A tax on the energy (Btu) content of fossil fuels;
(3) An *ad valorem* tax on fossil fuels.

To measure the impact of adopting sequences of taxes that hold U.S. carbon dioxide emissions constant, we constructed a number of alternative simulations of U.S. economic growth. In the base case, we simulate U.S. economic growth with no limits on emissions. In the alternative case, we simulate growth with emissions of carbon dioxide held constant. To hold the level of emissions constant, we introduced endogenous sequences of taxes applied to fossil fuels in proportion to their carbon content, their energy content, and their monetary value.

Because each of the tax sequences produces substantial revenue, we hold government spending constant at its base-case level. We allow the average tax rate on labor income to adjust to keep the government deficit constant. We hold the marginal tax rate on labor income constant, so that adjustments in the average rate reflect changes in the implicit zero-tax threshold. This tax adjustment is equivalent to a lump-sum transfer to the household sector.

7.3.1   Long-Run Effects

The direct effect of all three tax policies is to increase purchasers' prices of coal, oil, and natural gas. However, the tax bases for these policies are substantially different, so the alternative taxes will produce quantitatively different results. We next present the qualitative results of using a carbon tax to maintain emissions at 1990 levels in the year 2020. We then discuss how the results vary with alternative tax policies.

To achieve 1990 carbon emissions in the year 2020, a 14.4 percent reduction in emissions is required from the base-case level. This requires a tax of $16.96 per ton of carbon contained in fossil fuels.[16] Using the data in table 7.2, this amounts to a tax of $11.01 per ton of coal, $2.31 per barrel of oil, and $0.28 per thousand cubic feet of gas. A carbon tax would generate additional government revenue of $26 billion annually, so that the average labor tax rate could be reduced by 0.45 percent.

The rising price of fossil fuels results in substitution away from these fuels and toward other energy and nonenergy commodities by both firms and households. Total energy consumption falls to about 68 quadrillion Btu. This substitution toward nonenergy inputs results in a drop of 0.7 percent in the capital stock and 0.5 percent in the national product by the year 2020.

The impact of a carbon tax differs considerably among different types of fossil fuels. Figure 7.1(a) shows changes in the supply price of the 35 commodities measured as percentage changes relative to the base case. The largest change occurs in the price of coal, which rises by forty percent. Electricity prices rise considerably less than coal prices because coal accounts for only about thirteen percent of total electric utility costs. Other prices showing significant effects are those for crude and refined petroleum and gas utilities. These rise, directly or indirectly, because of the tax on the carbon content of oil and natural gas.

Changes in relative prices affect demands for energy and nonenergy commodities and lead to a restructuring of industry outputs. Figure 7.1(b) gives percentage changes in quantities produced by the 35 industries by the year 2020. Although most sectors show only small changes in output, the production of coal falls by 26.3 percent. Coal is strongly affected because its demand is elastic. Most coal is purchased by electric utilities. In our model, these utilities can substitute other fuels for coal when the price rises. Moreover, the utilities also have some ability to substitute other inputs, such as labor and capital, for energy, further reducing the demand for coal.

We next consider energy and *ad valorem* tax policies that could be used to control carbon dioxide emissions. Neither of these taxes is as efficient as a carbon tax in controlling emissions. However, both taxes have substantial impacts on fossil fuel use and might be preferable to a carbon tax in achieving other objectives. For example, an energy tax would reduce combustion of fossil fuels, providing environmental benefits other than lower carbon dioxide emissions. An *ad valorem* tax, on the other hand, may be easier to implement. In this section, we

(a)

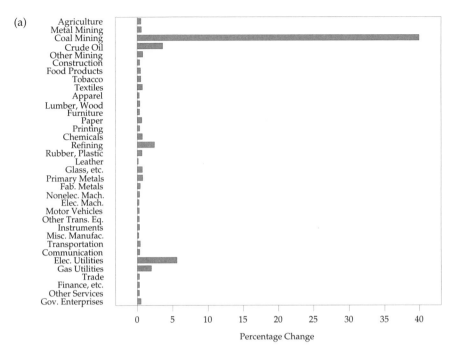

(b)

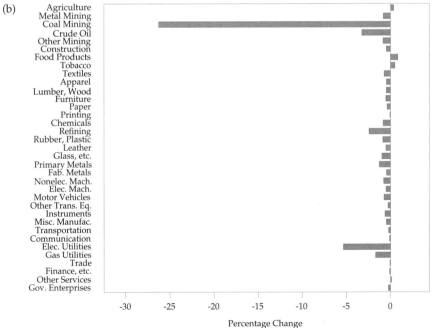

Figure 7.1
Effects of CAR on prices (a) and output (b).

discuss the impact of these alternative taxes in holding emissions at 1990 levels.

For the first alternative tax simulation, we show that limiting carbon dioxide emissions in the year 2020 to 1990 levels would require an energy tax of $0.47 per million Btu. Using data from table 7.2 this can be converted to $10.21 per ton of coal, $2.70 per barrel of oil, and $0.48 per thousand cubic feet of gas. Compared with coal, oil and gas have greater heat content for a given amount of carbon dioxide emissions, so that an energy tax falls more heavily on oil and coal than a carbon tax. The difference between the energy and carbon taxes is −$0.80 per ton of coal, +$0.39 per barrel of oil, and +$0.20 per thousand cubic feet of gas.

Total government revenue from an energy tax that would stabilize carbon dioxide emissions at 1990 levels is $31 billion by the year 2020, allowing the average labor tax rate to be lowered by 0.54 percent. Higher energy prices lead to a decline in the capital stock of 0.8 percent and a fall in the national product of 0.6 percent, relative to the base case. These declines are slightly higher than for the carbon tax simulation, because the energy tax creates greater distortions in the U.S. economy. The impacts on commodity prices and industry outputs are given in figure 7.2. The most important difference between this simulation and the carbon tax simulation given in figure 7.1 is that an energy tax has less effect on coal price and output, and more effect on prices and outputs of petroleum and natural gas. However, the two simulation results are quite similar.

Finally, we consider U.S. economic growth with an *ad valorem* tax on fossil fuels that stabilizes carbon dioxide emissions at 1990 levels. Coal is much less expensive per Btu than petroleum or natural gas. Coal was selling around one dollar per million Btu in 1989, while the price of oil was $2.75 per million Btu.[17] This difference means that an *ad valorem* tax falls much more heavily on oil than carbon or Btu taxes, so that the price of oil rises far more than in the previous simulations. This eliminates much of the interfuel substitution discussed above. In particular, it reduces substitution of oil for coal by electric utilities, so that all energy prices rise substantially.

To achieve 1990 carbon dioxide emissions rates in 2020, an *ad valorem* tax rate of 21.6 percent would be required. This would raise almost $53 billion in tax revenue, which is considerably more than the revenue raised by either carbon or Btu taxes. As a consequence, the average labor tax rate could be lowered by 0.90 percent. An *ad valorem*

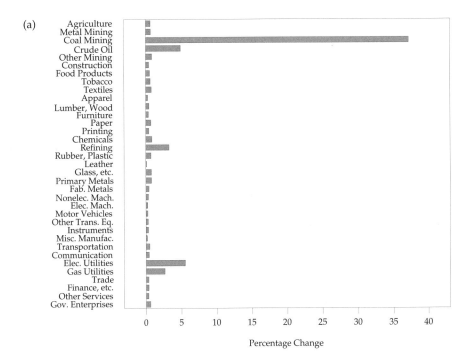

(a)

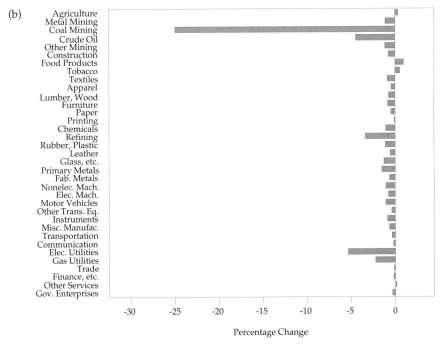

(b)

Figure 7.2
Effect of Btu on prices (a) and output (b).

tax produces much greater economic distortions than either of the alternative taxes, so the capital stock falls by 1.4 percent and the national product drops by one percent, relative to the base case.

Figure 7.3 gives the impacts of an *ad valorem* tax on commodity prices and industry outputs. The increase in coal prices is still substantial, but less drastic than in previous simulations. The price of crude oil, however, rises much more than under carbon or energy taxes. This, in turn, raises prices of refined petroleum, electricity, and natural gas. Figure 7.3 shows that higher energy prices have a marked effect on the outputs of the energy sectors. Both crude and refined petroleum decline by nearly ten percent, while gas and electric utilities fall somewhat less. As in earlier simulations, outputs of a few sectors—notably, food and tobacco—actually increase with restrictions on carbon dioxide emissions. This results from lower personal consumption expenditures and shifting patterns of household consumption.

Table 7.4 summarizes the results of all three simulations. A comparison among alternative tax instruments shows that a carbon tax, as expected, achieves the target reduction in carbon dioxide emissions with a minimum impact on the U.S. economy. However, this tax has a very substantial negative effect on the output of the coal industry. At the other end of the spectrum is the *ad valorem* tax, which produces the

Table 7.4
Long-run effects of different tax instruments

		Instrument		
Variable	Unit	Carbon tax	Btu tax	*Ad valorem*
Carbon emission	%Δ	−14.4	−14.4	−14.4
Carbon tax	$/t	16.96		
Btu tax	$/MBtu		0.47	
Ad valorem tax	%			21.6
Tax on coal	$/ton	11.01	10.21	
Tax on oil	$/bbl	2.31	2.70	
Tax on gas	$/kcf	0.28	0.48	
Labor tax rate	Δ	−0.45	−0.54	−0.90
Tax revenue	$B	26.0	31.0	53.0
Btu production	%Δ	−12.2	−12.4	−13.5
Capital stock	%Δ	−0.7	−0.8	−1.4
Real GNP	%Δ	−0.5	−0.6	−1.0
Price of coal	%Δ	39.9	37.2	26.1
Quantity of coal	%Δ	−26.3	−25.0	−19.5
Price of oil	%Δ	3.6	5.0	12.8

(a)

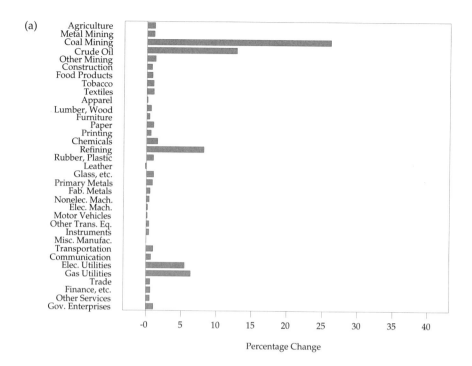

Percentage Change

(b)

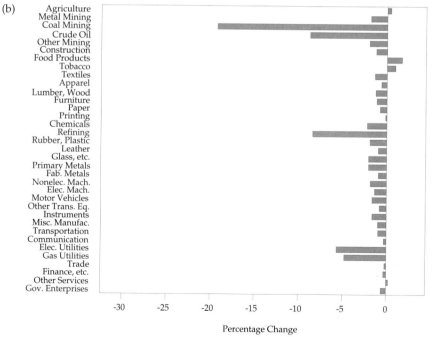

Percentage Change

Figure 7.3
Effect of ADVAL on prices (a) and output (b) ADVAL, *ad valorem* taxes.

greatest distortions in the economy and the least impact on coal mining. The difference arises from the fact that coal is much cheaper than oil for a given heat content. Carbon and energy taxes change the price of coal substantially, but affect the price of oil only a little.

7.3.2   Economic Dynamics

Carbon dioxide restrictions adopted today have effects far into the future. At the same time, anticipated future restrictions will have effects today. To assess the intertemporal effects of alternative tax policies, we now turn to the model's dynamic results. As with the long-run results, we begin by discussing a carbon tax designed to maintain emissions at 1990 levels. Following that, we examine the dynamic response of the U.S. economy to alternative tax policies to lower emissions of carbon dioxide.

The paths of the three taxes needed to maintain 1990 carbon dioxide emissions are shown in figure 7.4. Base-case emissions increase over time, so that each tax rate rises gradually over the next several decades. Because the alternative tax policies stabilize emissions at 1990 levels, they produce identical reductions in emissions, relative to the base case. These reductions are shown in figure 7.5 as annual percentage changes from the base case. Emissions begin dropping immediately and are 14.4 percent below the base-case level by the year 2020.

The principal effect of the alternative tax policies is to reduce the output of the coal industry. This is shown clearly in figure 7.6, which shows percentage reductions in coal production from the base case. The impact of a carbon tax is shown as a solid line, an energy tax as a dashed line, and an *ad valorem* tax as a dotted line.[18] As each tax is phased in, production of coal gradually falls. It does not, however, return to its 1990 level, because some of the reduction in carbon dioxide emissions is caused by reductions in oil consumption. This can be seen in figure 7.7, which gives percentages changes in crude petroleum and natural gas extraction.

The rising price of energy reduces the rate of capital formation, as shown in figure 7.8, giving percentage changes in the capital stock from the base case. The capital stock does not decline immediately; instead, it remains near its base-case level for the first few years. This reflects intertemporal optimization by households. The household treats higher taxes as a reduction in wealth and reacts by lowering consumption in all periods. However, the drop in consumption leads

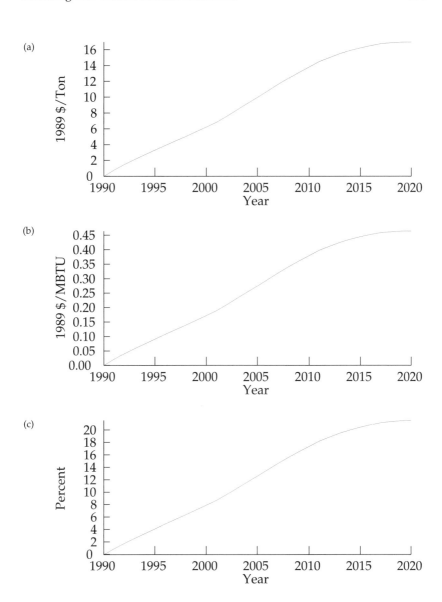

Figure 7.4
Tax required: (a) carbon; (b) Btu; (c) *ad valorem*.

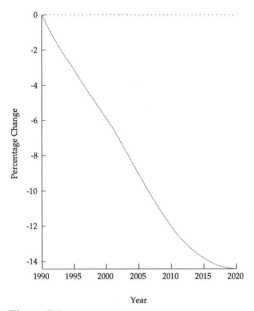

Figure 7.5
Carbon emissions.

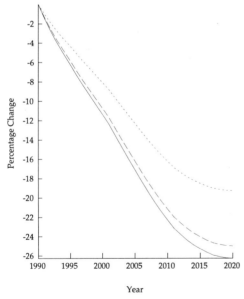

Figure 7.6
Coal production.

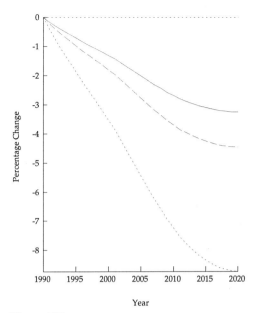

Figure 7.7
Oil and gas extraction.

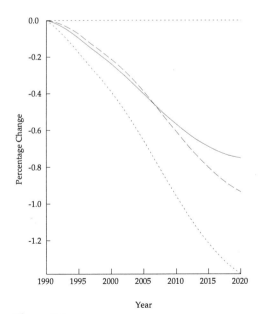

Figure 7.8
Capital stock.

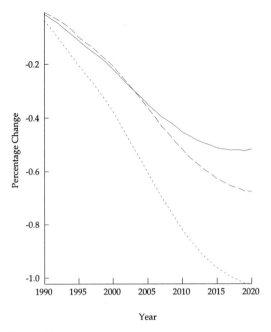

Figure 7.9
Real GNP.

to an increase in saving and helps to maintain capital formation. Eventually, however, the impact of the taxes is to reduce capital stock relative to the base case.

The decline in growth of the capital stock leads to a drop in the growth of the national product, as shown in figure 7.9. Over time the national product gradually falls relative to the base case. Slower capital stock growth is not the only factor contributing to the decline. Higher energy prices reduce the rate of productivity growth, leading to slower growth of output. Under the carbon tax average annual growth of output over the period 1990–2020 is 0.02 percentage points lower than in the base case. About half of this is due to slower productivity growth and half to reduced capital formation. Figure 7.9 shows that the most important difference among the three tax policies is that the *ad valorem* tax produces greater distortions in the U.S. economy.

Our final step in comparing the three alternative tax policies is to estimate the effect of each on the average rate of growth over the period 1990–2020. The results of this calculation are shown in table 7.5.

Table 7.5
Effects of carbon reduction policies on GNP growth (Differences from base-case annual average growth rates over 1990–2020)

Tax	Effect on growth
Carbon	−0.02
Btu	−0.02
Ad valorem	−0.03

An *ad valorem* tax is by far the most expensive in terms of economic growth. None of the tax policies, however, has a substantial impact on the growth rate.

7.4 Conclusion

This section evaluates the usefulness of econometric general equilibrium modeling as a practical guide to assessing the effects of alternative tax policies for controlling emissions of carbon dioxide. The framework for the econometric approach to modeling the impact of alternative tax policies is provided by intertemporal general equilibrium. We have distinguished among 35 industrial sectors of the U.S. economy and identified 35 commodity groups, each one the primary product of one of the industries. In modeling consumer behavior, we distinguished among 672 different household types, broken down by demographic characteristics. Aggregate demand functions for components of consumer expenditures are constructed by summing over individual demand functions.

The econometric method for parameterization used in modeling technology and preferences has important advantages over the calibration approach. The main advantage is that the responses of production and consumption patterns to changes in prices of fossil fuels are derived from historical experience. In section 7.2, we outlined a highly disaggregated model of the U.S. economy suitable to analyzing alternative tax policies for controlling carbon dioxide emissions. An important mechanism for adjusting to changes in tax policy is altering rates of capital formation. A second mechanism is the pricing of capital assets through forward-looking expectations of future prices and discount rates. This illustrates the critical importance of intertemporal equilibrium in modeling the dynamics of the response of the U.S. economy to alternative tax policies.

In section 7.3, we analyzed the economic impact of three alternative tax policies for controlling carbon dioxide emissions—a carbon tax, an energy tax, and an *ad valorem* tax on energy. Each of these taxes results in price-induced energy conservation that has important feedback for would-be to reduce coal production and consumption. Other energy sectors will be significantly affected if a tax policy other than a carbon tax is adopted. The precise form of tax policies to control carbon dioxide emissions will be vitally important to the energy industries that are affected.

The alternative tax policies for controlling carbon dioxide emissions have fairly modest impacts on the U.S. economy. Even though large amounts of government revenue are raised by these taxes, the overall impact on the U.S. economy occurs through introduction of distortions resulting from fossil fuel taxes. This conclusion is supported by the relatively small impact of the alternative policies on growth of the national product. Capital formation and the rate of productivity growth are affected only slightly, so the change in U.S. economic growth is modest. However, there are important differences in economic impact among the alternative tax policies.

Finally, our overall evaluation of three alternative tax policies for controlling carbon dioxide emissions is that a carbon tax has the smallest negative impact on the U.S. economy as a whole. Carbon taxes, do, however, have the most severe effect on coal mining. An energy tax would shift some of the burden to oil extraction but would be more costly to the U.S. economy. The worst policy is clearly an *ad valorem* tax on primary fuels. It would increase energy prices far more than either of the other taxes in achieving the goal of stabilizing emissions.

Notes

1. A thorough discussion of global warming and numerous references to the literature are given in Environmental Protection Agency (1989). For overviews of the economics of global warming, see Nordhaus (1991a) and Schelling (1992).

2. A carbon tax was first analyzed by Nordhaus (1979) and has been discussed by the Congressional Budget Office (1990). Jorgenson and Wilcoxen (1992b) examined the economic impact of using a carbon tax to achieve different restrictions on carbon dioxide emissions. Poterba (1991) and Jorgenson, Slesnick, and Wilcoxen (1992) considered equity and efficiency impacts of a carbon tax.

3. Detailed surveys of estimates of the impact of restrictions on carbon dioxide emissions are given by Cline (1992), Hoeller, Dean, and Nicolaisen (1991), and Nordhaus (1990b).

4. Data on inter-industry transactions are based on input-output tables for the U.S. constructed by the Bureau of Economic Analysis (1984). Income data are from the U.S. national income and product accounts, also developed by the Bureau of Economic Analysis (1986). The data on capital and labor services are described by Jorgenson (1990b). Additional details are given by Wilcoxen (1988), Appendix C, and Ho (1989).

5. See Mansur and Whalley (1984) for more detail. An example of the calibration approach is given by Borges and Goulder (1984), who present a model of energy policy calibrated to data for the year 1973. Surveys of applied general equilibrium modeling are given by Bergman (1985, 1990).

6. A detailed discussion of our econometric methodology is presented by Jorgenson (1984a, 1986a).

7. Our approach to endogenous productivity growth was originated by Jorgenson and Fraumeni (1981). A general equilibrium model of production that incorporates both substitution among inputs and endogenous productivity growth is presented by Jorgenson (1984a). The implications of this model have been analyzed by Hogan and Jorgenson (1991). Further details are given by Jorgenson (1986a) and Jorgenson and Wilcoxen (1993d).

8. The Euler equation approach to modeling intertemporal consumer behavior was originated by Hall (1978). Our application of this approach follows Jorgenson and Yun (1986).

9. Our model of personal consumption expenditures can be used to represent the behavior of individual households, as in Jorgenson and Slesnick (1987a), or the behavior of the household sector as a whole, as in Jorgenson (1990a). Jorgenson, Slesnick, and Wilcoxen (1992) used the results for individual households to separate the overall impact of a carbon tax into equity and efficiency components.

10. Details on the econometric methodology are given by Jorgenson (1984a, 1990a). Additional details are provided by Wilcoxen (1988), Ho (1989), and Jorgenson and Wilcoxen (1993d).

11. The relationship between the price of investment goods and the rental price of capital services is discussed in greater detail by Jorgenson (1989).

12. This is the Armington (1969) approach. See Wilcoxen (1988), Ho (1989), and Jorgenson and Wilcoxen (1993d) for further details on our implementation of this approach.

13. This is largely the case in practice because carbon dioxide is one of the natural products of combustion. Little can be done to change the amount produced when burning any particular fuel. Similarly, the energy content of fossil fuels is largely unaffected by the combustion process, although the useful work that can be performed may be affected by the process. For comparability with other studies, we measure carbon dioxide emissions in tons of contained carbon. To convert to tons of carbon dioxide, multiply by 3.67.

14. Some of the most important projections are noted briefly below; a more detailed discussion is given by Jorgenson and Wilcoxen (1992b).

15. Our breakdown of the U.S. population by age, sex, and educational attainment is based on the system of demographic accounts compiled by Jorgenson and Fraumeni (1989). The population projections are discussed in detail by Wilcoxen (1988, Appendix B).

16. Unless otherwise indicated, all dollar amounts are in 1989 prices.

17. In 1989, the price of coal was $21/ton f.o.b. at the mine mouth. From table 8.2, we see that the heating value of a ton of coal is 21.94 MBtu, so the price per million Btu was $0.96. In the same year, the price of crude petroleum was $15.85/bbl, while its heating value is 5.80 MBtu/bbl, yielding a price of $2.73 per million Btu.

18. We employ this convention in all subsequent figures.

8   Trade Policy and U.S. Economic Growth

Mun S. Ho and
Dale W. Jorgenson

8.1   Introduction

One of the most striking developments in the postwar U.S. economy is the increasing role of international trade. Imports were only 4.4 percent of the national product in 1960, but rose to ten percent of the national product by 1985. There have also been large shifts in the sectoral composition of output. The shares of agriculture and manufacturing in the national product were 4.7 and 31.4 percent, respectively in 1960, but only 2.6 and 22.8 percent in 1985. Finally, the annual growth rate of the national product has declined from 3.7 percent from 1947–1973 to 2.3 percent from 1973–1985.

The purpose of this chapter is to present an intertemporal general equilibrium model for analyzing the impact of changes in trade policy on U.S. economic growth. Traditional approaches to estimate the economic impact of trade restrictions are purely static. The first of these is based on detailed partial equilibrium models, such as that of Hufbauer, Berliner, and Elliot (1986). The second approach uses multicountry general equilibrium models, such as the "Michigan Model" of Deardorff and Stern (1986) and the world trade model of Whalley (1985).[1] Each of these approaches has many desirable features, but both ignore the effects of trade policy on capital formation and productivity growth.

Recently, Jorgenson and Yun (1990) have presented an intertemporal general equilibrium model for analyzing the impact of tax policy on U.S. economic growth. However, this model is too highly aggregated to be useful for analyzing the impact of trade policy. In this work, we combine the intertemporal features of tax modeling with the detailed disaggregation by commodity and industrial sector employed in models of international trade. This enables us to capture the impact of trade policy on U.S. imports and exports, the sectoral composition of output, capital formation, and productivity growth.

If tariffs in the U.S. and rest of the world had been eliminated in 1980, we find that U.S. consumption of goods and services would have risen by only 0.16 percent in the first year. This is similar to the results reported by Deardorff and Stern (1986) and Whalley (1985). However, consumption would have been 0.82 percent higher in the long run. The mechanism underlying this substantial growth in consumption is that trade liberalization reduces the price of capital goods relative to other prices. This leads to an increase in investment and more rapid growth of capital stock, thereby expanding both output and consumption.

Over recent decades the focus of trade policy in the U.S. and the rest of the world has shifted from tariffs to quantitative restrictions. Tariff revenue as a percentage of the value of U.S. commodity imports has declined steadily in the postwar period. However, the scope and stringency of quotas and "voluntary" export restrictions have increased dramatically. We model these restrictions by means of "equivalent" tariffs. If the most significant quotas had been eliminated along with tariffs in 1980, the consumption of goods and services would have been 1.08 percent higher in the long run, compared to a first year increase of only 0.36 percent. Our estimates of the first year effects of trade liberalization are very similar to those obtained from static general equilibrium models. Over time, however, our estimates increase by several times. The difference is due to the impact of trade liberalization on U.S. capital formation and productivity growth.

In section 8.2 we outline the structure of our model and our key assumptions. Jorgenson and Wilcoxen (1990b) have described our models of producer and consumer behavior in considerable detail. We emphasize the features that are critical in capturing dynamic adjustments by households and businesses to changes in trade policy. We then describe our treatment of U.S. demand for imports and rest-of-the-world demand for exports from the U.S. We conclude with a description of the exogenous and endogenous elements in our model of the U.S. current account balance.

In section 8.3 we estimate the impact of trade barriers on U.S. economic growth. We first examine the effects of U.S. trade restrictions still in effect after the Tokyo Round of negotiations under the General Agreement on Trade and Tariffs (GATT). These negotiations were finally concluded in 1979 and have been analyzed by Cline,

Kawanabe, Kronsjo, and Williams (1978). We estimate the effects of a multilateral agreement abolishing all remaining tariffs in the U.S. and the rest of the world. We then estimate the impact of also eliminating quantitative restrictions on trade. Finally, we compare our results with those of Deardorff and Stern (1986) and Whalley (1985). Section 8.4 concludes the chapter.

8.2   The Structure of the Model

We divide the U.S. economy among four sectors: businesses, house-holds, governments, and the rest of the world. Since trade policy differs substantially among industries, we subdivide the business sector into the thirty-five industries listed in table 8.1 below. These industries correspond approximately to two-digit industries in the Standard Industrial Classification. Our model distinguishes the same number of commodities as industries. Each industry produces a primary product; this is the commodity group in which the industry is predominant. Industries also produce secondary products; the primary products of other industries.

8.2.1   Producer Behavior

We represent producer behavior by means of econometric models for each of our thirty-five industries. We first express the output of each industry as a function of inputs of intermediate goods, capital services, and labor services. These production functions are characterized by constant returns to scale. The rate of productivity growth in each industry is endogenous and can be expressed as a function of the input prices.[2] The intermediate inputs include the thirty-five commodities produced within the U.S. business sector. Each commodity group is allocated among intermediate demands by the thirty-five industries and final demands for private and public consumption, investment by households and businesses, and exports to the rest of the world.

To implement our econometric approach to modeling producer behavior we have constructed a consistent time series of inter-industry transactions tables for the U.S. economy, covering the period 1947–1985 on an annual basis. An alternative approach would be to characterize substitution among inputs by calibration from a single data point.[3] For example, Deardorff and Stern (1986) and Whalley (1985) characterize

Table 8.1
Import demand elasticities

Industry	Substitution elasticities			Import price elasticities				
	Stern	Sheills	Ours	Stern	Sheills	Petri	Cline	Ours
Agriculture			0.70				−0.90	−0.68
Metal mining			0.11				−0.22	−0.09
Coal mining							−0.22	
Oil and gas mining							−0.22	
Non-metal mining			0.34				−0.22	−0.34
Construction								
Food and kindred	1.13	0.31	0.65	−1.13	−0.21		−1.13	−0.62
Tobacco	1.13	−16.2	2.60	−1.13	−7.57		−1.13	−2.59
Textile mill	1.15	2.58	1.62	−1.14	−1.41	−1.2	−2.43	−1.54
Apparel	4.27	1.62	1.27	−3.92	−0.52	−1.2	−2.43	−1.01
Lumber and wood	1.76	0.26	1.76	−0.69	−1.32	−1.4	−0.96	−1.60
Furniture	3.10	12.13	1.49	−3.00	−9.56	−1.4	−0.96	−1.36
Paper	1.58	1.80	1.16	−0.55	−1.80	−1.4	−1.44	−1.07
Printing and publishing	3.01	2.72	1.22	−3.00	−1.46	−1.4	−1.44	−1.20
Chemicals	2.61	9.85	1.20	−2.53	−6.82	−0.8	−0.97	−1.10
Petroleum refining	2.36	−0.34	1.09	−1.96	−0.79	−0.8	−0.97	−1.00
Rubber and plastic	5.71	2.67	1.76	−5.26	−1.32	−0.8	−3.57	−1.65
Leather	1.81	4.11	1.86	−1.58	−2.01		−2.46	−1.11
Stone clay and glass	1.63	4.29	1.86	−1.60	−2.86	−0.8	−1.37	−1.72
Primary metal	1.45	3.05	1.48	−1.42	−2.28	−1.6	−1.99	−1.29
Fabricated metal	3.67	1.54	1.13	−3.59	−0.94	−1.1		−1.08
Machinery	1.02	3.34	1.72	−1.02	−0.88	−0.9	−0.87	−1.53
Electrical machine	2.11	7.46	1.45	−1.00	−3.08	−0.6	−0.87	−1.23
Motor vehicles	3.59	2.01	1.52	−3.28	−1.24	−2.5	−2.53	−1.16
Transport. equipment	3.59	2.01	1.35	−3.28	−1.24	−2.5	−1.70	−1.28
Instruments	1.98	0.45	0.86	−1.08	−0.44	−0.9		−0.77
Misc. manufactures	1.98	3.55	1.52	−2.06	−2.37	−0.8	−4.44	−1.14
Transportation								
Communications								
Electric utilities								
Gas utilities								
Trade								
Finance, insurance								
Services								
Government enterprises								

The industrial classification system is different for each study. All entries correspond to the categories used in this study.
Stern: Central tendencies in Stern, Francis and Schumacher (1976), sample period before 1974.
Sheills: Sheills, Stern and Deardorff (1986), sample period 1962–1978.
Petri: Petri (1984), U.S. imports from rest of the world, excluding Japan, 1960–1980.
Cline: Cline et al. (1978), page 58.
Ours: Elasticities evaluated at 1983 shares, sample period 1964–1985.

producer behavior in the U.S. economy by means of fixed "input-output" coefficients for intermediate goods, estimated from a single inter-industry transactions table. The possibility of substitution among intermediate goods, such as energy and materials, is ruled out by assumption.

Empirical evidence on substitutability among inputs is essential in analyzing the impact of trade restrictions. A high degree of substitutability implies that the cost of these restrictions is relatively low, while a low degree of substitutability implies high costs of trade restrictions. Although a calibration approach avoids the burden of estimation, it also specifies the substitutability among inputs by assumption rather than relying on empirical evidence. This defeats one of the major purposes of modeling the impact of trade policy changes.

In our model of the U.S. economy, a single stock of capital is allocated among the thirty-five industries and the household sector. We assume that capital is perfectly malleable and mobile among sectors, so that the price of capital services in each sector is proportional to a single capital service price for the economy as a whole. The supply of capital available in every year is the result of past investment. This relationship is represented by an accumulation equation, giving capital at the end of each year as a function of investment during the year and capital at the beginning of the year. This backward-looking equation incorporates the whole past history of investment and constitutes the first component of our dynamic model of adjustment to changes in trade policy.

Our model of producer behavior also includes an equation giving the price of capital services in terms of the price of investment goods at the beginning and end of each period. The current price of investment goods incorporates expectations about future prices of capital services and discount rates through the assumption of perfect foresight or rational expectations. Under this assumption the price of investment goods is based on expectations that are fulfilled by the solution of the model. This forward-looking equation incorporates expectations about all future prices and is the second component of our dynamic model of adjustment to trade policy changes.

8.2.2   Consumer Behavior

Our model of consumer behavior is based on full consumption, comprised of goods and services and leisure time. Full consumption is allocated over time to maximize an intertemporally additive utility function, subject to an intertemporal budget constraint. The necessary conditions are expressed as an Euler equation, giving the growth rate of full consumption as a function of the discount rate and the growth rate of the price of full consumption.[4] This forward-looking equation embodies the same rational expectations assumption as our model of producer behavior. Current full consumption incorporates expectations about all future prices that are fulfilled by the solution of the model. This is the third component of our dynamic model of adjustment to changes in trade policy.

In our model of the U.S. economy, there is a single, exogenously given time endowment. The U.S. population grew substantially during our sample period, 1947–1985. For later periods, we project the population and transform it into a projection of the time endowment. In each period, this endowment is divided between leisure time and the labor market. Our model of consumer behavior allocates full consumption between goods and services and leisure. Time in the labor market is allocated among the thirty-five industries; labor services are also included in final demands for personal consumption expenditures and public consumption. We assume that labor is perfectly mobile among sectors so that the wage rate in each sector is proportional to a single wage rate for the U.S. economy as a whole.

Finally, total expenditure on goods and services by the household sector includes expenditures on the thirty-five commodities represented in the model, capital services, and labor services. We estimate price and total expenditure elasticities econometrically for each of 672 types of households.[5] An alternative approach would be to assume that preferences for all types of households are homothetic, so that all total expenditure elasticities are set equal to unity. However, this assumption is strongly contradicted by empirical evidence.

Introducing nonhomothetic preferences into a dynamic general equilibrium model of the U.S. economy raises issues not confronted by static models. If productivity growth were to continue indefinitely, equal rates of productivity growth would be required for all industries, at least in the limit. Otherwise, relative prices would not converge to a steady state. Even if productivity growth rates converged to the same limit, total expenditure per capita would rise indefinitely, so that at least one of the expenditure shares for the household sector would become negative. Accordingly, we require that the productivity level in each industry converges to an upper limit. Our projection of the future U.S. population reaches a maximum, so that aggregate expenditure approaches an upper limit in the steady state.[6]

8.2.3 Total Supply and Imports

We next describe the features of the rest-of-the-world sector of our model. The total supply of commodities in the U.S. economy comes from the output of domestic industries and "competitive" imports. Competitive imports are defined in the U.S. national income and product accounts as commodities produced in the U.S. In our model, purchasers of these commodities regard them as imperfect substitutes for the domestically produced counterparts.[7] Noncompetitive imports enter directly into the production functions for each industry in the same way as other inputs. They also enter final demands for consumption by households and governments, and investment by businesses and households.

We model the allocation of total supply of the ith commodity QS_i between domestic production QC_i and competitive imports M_i by means of the translog price function:

$$\ln PS_{it} = \ln p'_{it}\, \alpha_{it} + \frac{1}{2} \ln p'_{it}\, B_i \ln p_{it} , \tag{8.1}$$

where PS_{it} denotes the price of total supply and in period t and:

$$\ln p'_{it} = (\ln PC_{it}, \ln PM_{it})$$

is a vector of logarithms of prices of the domestic commodity, PC_{it}, and competitive imports, PM_{it}.

The shares of the domestic commodity and competitive imports in the value of total supply are denoted v_{it}, where:

$$v_{it} = \begin{bmatrix} PC_{it}\ QC_{it}/PS_{it}\ QS_{it} \\ PM_{it}\ M_{it}/PS_{it}\ QS_{it} \end{bmatrix} .$$

These value shares can be expressed in terms of logarithmic derivatives of the price function with respect to logarithms of the input prices:

$$v_{it} = \alpha_{it} + B_i \ln p_{it} \, , \tag{8.2}$$

where B_i is a matrix of share elasticities, defined as derivatives of the value shares with respect to logarithms of the prices.

A novel feature of our model is that the vector α_{it} in equation (8.2) is treated as a function of time. This permits us to represent the large increases in import penetration experienced by the U.S. economy during the postwar period without resorting to implausible values of the price elasticities. The phenomenon of "unexplained imports" is noted by Petri (1986), who observed that the postwar U.S. demand for imports cannot be explained by price variations alone. According to Petri's estimates, such an explanation would have required a price elasticity of demand for U.S. steel imports of thirty-two. By comparison the Michigan Model's assumed price elasticity is only 1.4.[8]

A common approach to modeling import demands has been to use a measure of aggregate economic activity as an explanatory variable for imports. We have employed a time trend instead, since we concur with Petri's conclusion that the high elasticities of imports with respect to aggregate activity estimated from time series data are probably spurious.[9] The limiting behavior of the time trends α_{it}, presents a potential problem for our model of supply. Unless these functions remain bounded, one of the value shares must eventually become negative. Accordingly, we take these trends to be logistic in form, so that:

$$v_{it} = \alpha_i + \frac{\beta_i}{1 + e^{-\mu_i(t - \tau_i)}} + B_i \ln p_{it} \, , \tag{8.3}$$

where α_i, β_i, μ_i, τ_i are parameters that differ among commodities. We find that these time trends greatly simplify the model and fit the historical data reasonably well.

We model dynamic adjustments by producers to changes in trade policy through the backward-looking accumulation equation for capital and the forward-looking asset pricing equation for the price of investment goods. We estimate the import demand functions (8.2) by applying nonlinear two-stage least squares to annual data for the sample period 1964–1985.[10] We present the implied price elasticities of demand for imports in table 8.1. For comparison, we also present elasticities employed in previous studies. Imports of most manufactured commodities are price elastic, while imports of most primary commodities are price inelastic. For eighteen of our twenty-five commodity groups, the values of R^2 are greater than 0.8.

Our model is limited to the U.S. economy, so that we do not model production by the rest of the world.[11] Accordingly, we take the prices of competitive and noncompetitive imports into the U.S. as exogenously given; during our sample period, 1947–1985, we set these prices equal to the actual data. Since our model determines prices, both domestic and foreign, relative to a numeraire given by the U.S. wage rate, we allow prices of imports from the rest of the world to change through the terms of trade, say e_t, and through tariffs levied on imports by the U.S. government, say θ_{it} and θ_{it}^n:

$$PM_{it} = (1 + \theta_{it})\, e_t\, PM_{it}^*, \quad PNCI_{it} = (1 + \theta_{it}^n)\, e_t\, PNCI_{it}^*, \tag{8.4}$$

where PM_{it} and $PNCI_{it}$ are prices for competitive and noncompetitive imports paid by the U.S., and PM_{it}^* and $PNCI_{it}^*$ are prices received by the rest of the world. The terms of trade e_t is the price of goods in the U.S. relative to the price of goods in the rest of the world.

8.2.4   Exports

Since we do not model production in the rest of the world, we express the demand for U.S. exports, say X_{it}, as a function of rest-of-the-world output Y_t^* and the price of exports PC_{it}:

$$X_{it} = EX_{i0}(Y_t^*)\left[(1 + \theta_{it}^*)\,\frac{PC_{it}}{e_t}\right]^{\eta_i}, \tag{8.5}$$

where $EX_{i0}(Y_t^*)$ represents actual U.S. exports during the sample period, 1947–1985, and projected exports outside this period, θ_{it}^* is the rest-of-the-world tariff rate on U.S. exports, and the term in square brackets is the price for U.S. exports faced by the rest of the world. We do not have the data on rest-of-the-world imports from the U.S. required for estimation of the export price elasticities η_i. We take these elasticities as averages of import price elasticities of major trading partners of the U.S.

A number of alternative estimates of price elasticities of demand for U.S. exports are presented in table 8.2. Petri (1984) has estimated rest-of-the-world demand for U.S. exports. Petri's export elasticities are

Table 8.2
Export price elasticities

Industry	Petri	Stone	Cline
Agriculture		−0.72	−0.61
Metal mining		−0.92	
Coal mining		−0.92	
Oil and gas mining		−0.92	
Non-metal mining		−0.92	
Construction	*		
Food and kindred		−1.975	−0.63
Tobacco		−1.975	−0.63
Textile mill	−1.6	−1.18	−1.57
Apparel	−1.6	−1.18	−1.57
Lumber and wood	−1.0	−1.5	−1.43
Furniture	−1.0	−1.5	−1.43
Paper	−1.0	−1.41	−1.53
Printing and publishing	−1.0	−1.41	−1.53
Chemicals	−0.5	−0.98	−1.47
Petroleum refining	−0.5	−1.72	−1.47
Rubber and plastic	−0.5	−2.10	−2.14
Leather	−1.6	−0.62	−1.49
Stone clay and glass	−0.7	−1.26	−1.56
Primary metal	−1.1	−1.65	−1.97
Fabricated metal	−1.1	−1.06	−1.59
Machinery	−0.9	−1.04	−1.59
Electrical machinery	−1.2	−1.05	−1.59
Motor vehicles	−0.9	−2.49	−1.55
Transport. equipment	−0.9	−2.49	−1.55
Instruments	−0.9	−1.18	−1.85
Misc. manufactures	−1.0	−1.55	−1.62
Transportation	*		
Communications	*		
Electric utilities	*		
Gas utilities	*		
Trade	*		
Finance, insurance	*		
Services	*		
Government enterprises	*		

*Sectors assumed to have zero price elasticities. Trade and transportation exports are margins on exported goods; other service sectors have only negligible exports.

Petri: Petri (1984).

Stone: Stone (1979), average of import elasticities for EEC and Japan.

Cline: Cline *et al.* (1978), average of Canada, EEC, Japan.

remarkably low; however, his sectors are relatively highly aggregated, including only ten manufacturing industries. By contrast, our thirty-five industries include twenty-one manufacturing industries. The remaining estimates are based on imports into a single country with the rest of the world treated as a single supplier. Cline *et al.* (1978), have presented composite elasticities of demand for U.S. exports that are similar to those estimated by Stone (1979), so that we adopt these elasticities.

In projecting the functions $EX(Y_t^*)$, we first estimate the following equation for each commodity from annual data for the period 1947–1985:

$$\ln X_{it} = \gamma_i + \lambda_i \ln Y_t^*, \tag{8.6}$$

where X_{it} is U.S. exports of the ith commodity in year t and Y_t^* is gross world product in that year. We employ the estimated rest-of-the-world output elasticity for U.S. exports λ_i in projecting U.S. exports.[12] Our estimates of these elasticities are reported in table 8.3. These estimates have plausible magnitudes and are consistent with the view that aircraft, computers, and pharmaceuticals are the leading industries in the growth of U.S. exports. In projecting exports after 1985, we assume that the growth rate of world product is initially two percent per year and gradually declines to zero, as required for the existence of a steady state for our model.

8.2.5   Noncommodity Flows

To complete the current account for the U.S. economy, we must determine factor income and payments to the rest of the world. These are interest and dividends on net U.S. private claims on the rest of the world, say BF_t, and net U.S. official liabilities, say BG_t^*. These net factor incomes, denoted by $i_t^* BF_{t-1}$ and $- i_t BG_{t-1}^*$, where i and i^* are domestic and rest-of-the-world rates of return, are set exogenously. The final exogenous flow is net unilateral transfers or foreign aid, denoted *transfers*.

The allocation of savings among domestic capital formation, acquisition of foreign assets, and investment in government bonds is exogenous in our model. This implies that the public sector deficit and current account balance are exogenous. We allow the public sector deficit to decline gradually to a steady-state value in the year 2025,

Table 8.3
Export demand functions—$\log X_{it} = \gamma_i + \lambda_i \log Y_i^*$

Industry	Exports 1982 bil.	α^x	λ^x	R^2
Agriculture	22.03	9.9053	1.1158	0.97
Metal mining	0.70	6.5874	0.3464	0.47
Coal mining	4.98	8.1475	1.0020	0.90
Oil and gas mining	0.79	6.6248	1.6037	0.40
Non-metal mining	0.68	6.4517	0.4769	0.85
Construction	0.06	4.0946	1.0857	0.47
Food and kindred	11.00	9.2225	1.0963	0.99
Tobacco	3.05	7.9161	0.5584	0.98
Textile mill	1.82	7.4994	1.2599	0.92
Apparel	1.33	7.0451	1.3368	0.91
Lumber and wood	2.74	7.9231	1.8252	0.93
Furniture	0.60	5.9395	1.9033	0.84
Paper	4.09	8.3103	1.2732	0.96
Printing and publish	1.37	7.0587	0.9823	0.99
Chemicals	15.64	9.7205	1.5350	0.99
Petroleum refining	8.08	8.8938	0.3972	0.97
Rubber and plastic	7.26	8.8071	1.5698	0.96
Leather	0.52	6.0303	0.90191	0.90
Stone clay and glass	1.82	7.5123	1.0974	0.98
Primary metal	5.68	8.7869	0.7946	0.78
Fabricated metal	6.88	8.6473	1.2608	0.97
Machinery	37.20	10.4400	1.7359	0.99
Electrical machine	18.03	9.6417	2.2744	0.98
Motor vehicles	11.91	9.6537	1.8583	0.97
Transport. equipment	23.34	9.9396	1.9255	0.95
Instruments	8.03	8.9174	1.8918	0.99
Misc. manufactures	2.67	7.5453	1.6481	0.91
Transportation	21.93	9.8604	0.8761	0.98
Communications	1.55	7.2877	1.3805	0.95
Electric utilities	0.21	5.5175	1.5862	0.57
Gas utilities	0.35	6.1484	1.6575	0.36
Trade	24.94	9.8189	1.5746	0.97
Finance, insurance	6.90	8.8025	1.9184	0.91
Services	7.83	8.7675	1.4544	0.96
Government enterprises*	0.25	5.6493		
Travel**	14.10	9.4316	1.5810	0.71

* Most exports in this category are military.

** Travel is expenditures by tourists in the U.S.

equal to the inflationary gain on the stock of outstanding government debt, which has the effect of holding per capita debt constant in real terms. The current account deficit is allowed to fall to zero by the year 2000. These projections are expressed in terms of the numeraire for our model, the U.S. wage rate.

Adding foreign trade and noncommodity flows, we obtain the U.S. current account surplus in year t, say CA_t:

$$CA_t = \sum PC_{it} X_{it} - \sum PM_{it} M_{it} - \sum PNCI_{it} NCI_{it} \tag{8.7}$$
$$+ i_t^* BF_{t-1} - i\, BG_{t-1}^* - \text{transfers} .$$

From equations (8.3)–(8.5), we see that U.S. exports, X_{it}, and imports, M_{it}, are functions of the terms of trade, e_t. This variable is endogenous in our model and adjusts the purchasers' prices of U.S. imports and exports so that the exogenously given current account balance (8.7) is maintained.

8.3 Effects of Trade Barriers

In this section, we estimate the impact of trade policy on U.S. economic growth. We construct a base case for growth of the U.S. economy under actual trade policies, incorporating historical data for all exogenous variables. We then simulate the U.S. economy with a change in trade policy. To evaluate the economic impact of the policy change, we compare the results of the two simulations. We initiate both simulations in 1980, immediately after the conclusion of the Tokyo Round negotiations in 1979. Deardorff and Stern (1986) and Whalley (1986) have provided simulations of the impact of trade policy for the same period, using static general equilibrium models.

8.3.1 Tariff Reductions

We first describe the effects of multilateral reductions in tariffs with no change in quantitative restrictions on trade. In tables 8.4–8.6, we present tariff rates on U.S. imports in 1980, following several rounds of tariff reductions under GATT that culminated in the Tokyo Round. The most highly taxed commodity imports were textiles, apparel, leather (mainly footwear), glass, and primary metals (mainly iron and steel). Total customs duties collected on U.S. imports amounted to $7.2 billions or about 2.9 percent of total commodity imports of $251

Table 8.4
Tariff rates and quota equivalents in 1980

No.	Sector	Tariff rates		Tariff equivalent
		ROW*	U.S.**	
1	Agriculture		0.035	
2	Metal mining		0.000	
3	Coal mining		0.000	
4	Oil and gas mining		0.000	
5	Non-metal mining		0.003	
6	Construction		0.000	
7	Food and kindred		0.027	
8	Tobacco		0.111	
9	Textile mill	0.107	0.108	0.030
10	Apparel	0.207	0.218	0.063
11	Lumber and wood	0.027	0.020	
12	Furniture	0.103	0.035	
13	Paper	0.058	0.005	
14	Printing and publishing	0.029	0.008	
15	Chemicals	0.094	0.041	
16	Petroleum refining		0.000	
17	Rubber and plastic	0.058	0.067	
18	Leather	0.045	0.097	0.056
19	Stone clay and glass	0.105	0.091	
20	Primary metal	0.058	0.030	0.048
21	Fabricated metal	0.090	0.057	
22	Machinery	0.067	0.041	
23	Electrical machinery	0.096	0.055	
24	Motor vehicles	0.077	0.023	0.047***
25	Transport. equipment	0.077	0.026	
26	Instruments	0.078	0.065	
27	Misc. manufactures	0.078	0.058	
28	Transportation			
29	Communications			
30	Electric utilities			
31	Gas Utilities			
32	Trade			
33	Finance, insurance			
34	Services			
35	Government enterprises			

* Rest-of-the-world (ROW) tariff rates are from Deardorf and Stern (1986). See table 8.5 for tariff equivalents of quotas.

** U.S. tariff rates are calculated from International Trade Commission data.

*** 1981 data.

Table 8.5
Tariff equivalents of selected quotas*

	Textiles	Apparel	Leather	Metals	Autos
1973	0	0	0	0.032	0
1974	0.030	0.063	0	0.032	0
1975	0.030	0.063	0	0	0
1976	0.030	0.063	0	0	0
1977	0.030	0.063	0.056	0	0
1978	0.030	0.063	0.056	0.048	0
1979	0.030	0.063	0.056	0.048	0
1980	0.030	0.063	0.056	0.048	0
1981	0.030	0.063	0.056	0.048	0.047
1982	0.071	0.095	0	0.048	0.047
1983	0.071	0.095	0	0.048	0.047
1984	0.071	0.095	0	0.048	0.047
1985	0.071	0.095	0	0.048	0

*Tariff equivalents of "voluntary" export restrictions are calculated from Hufbauer, Berliner, and Elliot (1986) by aggregation to our model's industry classification.

Table 8.6
Tariff equivalents of quotas on U.S. imports from Japan

Sector	1970	1980
Textiles, apparel	3.5	1.3
Primary metal	6.0	7.0
Electrical machinery	–	0.8

Source: Petri (1984), page 138.

billions. For comparison, the U.S. gross national product in 1980 was $2,732 billions in prices of that year.[13]

To evaluate the economic impact of tariffs, we eliminate all domestic and foreign tariffs, beginning in 1980. This is not equivalent to free trade, since quotas and other quantitative restrictions remain in effect. In both the base case and alternative case simulations, we set the U.S. capital stock and all other state variables at the beginning of 1980 equal to their historical values. We then simulate the growth of the U.S. economy from 1980 to the year 2100. This provides ample time for the economy to converge to a steady state. In the base case, the government deficit and tax rates are exogenous, but government spending outside the sample period is endogenous. With all tariffs removed we set government expenditures equal to values from the base case. Government transfers and interest payments are exogenous in both simulations.[14]

The economic impact of eliminating tariffs is summarized diagrammatically in figures 8.1 and 8.2. The vertical axis in these figures gives the percentage change in each variable from the elimination of tariffs. The impact of the tariff cut is to raise consumption of goods and services by 0.16 percent in the first year. From the first panel of figure 8.2, we see that the price of capital goods is lower than in the base case and keeps falling. A falling price of capital goods leads to an increase in investment and boosts the growth of capital stock, as shown in figure 8.2. By the year 2000, the capital stock is 0.49 percent higher than in the base case.

Lower commodity prices and an investment boom induce higher import demands. U.S. exports also increase with reduced tariffs in the rest of the world. From tables 8.4–8.6 we see that these tariffs are generally higher than those in the U.S. Given the elasticities we have employed, the initial impact is greater for exports than for imports. Since the current account balance is exogenous, the terms of trade, e_t, must fall to stimulate higher imports. The required decrease of 0.6 percent in the terms of trade is very substantial. The quantity of exports increases by 6.7 percent while the quantity of imports rises by 7.5 percent.

Over time, the difference between the two simulations increases, due to the growth in capital stock resulting from the elimination of tariffs. By the year 2000 full consumption is 0.17 percent higher; which is comprised of an increase of 0.74 in consumption of goods and services and a decrease of 0.6 percent in leisure. The terms of trade decline over time, since U.S. prices fall but rest-of-the-world prices remain constant, implying an increase in U.S. international competitiveness. As a consequence, the quantity of exports is only 6.5 percent higher in the year 2000, while the quantity of imports is 9.7 percent higher.

Table 8.7 gives the sectoral effects of tariff elimination in the initial year, while table 8.8 shows the effects after twenty years. Raw material industries such as mining have small trade flows; whereas the small decreases in exports are due to the fall in the terms of trade. Agricultural trade is largely governed by quantitative restrictions, including trade embargoes, that we do not explicitly model. The small changes in trade should be interpreted with this in mind. Similarly, the

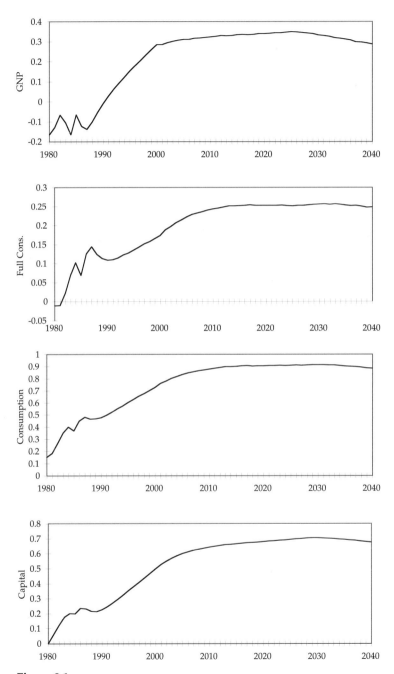

Figure 8.1
Dynamic effects of tariff elimination.

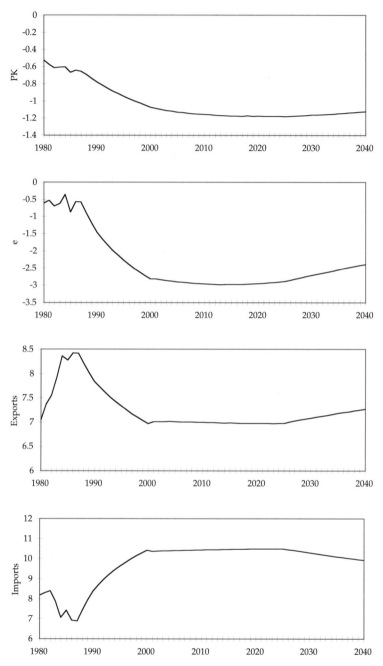

Figure 8.2
Dynamic effects of tariff elimination.

Table 8.7
Sectoral effects of eliminating all tariffs in 1980*

Sector	Output	Capital	Labor	Exports	Imports
Agriculture	−0.32	−0.44	−0.47	−0.34	2.09
Metal mining	2.17	2.08	2.04	−0.43	2.31
Coal mining	0.36	0.26	0.17	−0.44	0.84
Oil and gas mining	0.08	0.00	0.16	−0.56	0.69
Non-metal mining	0.75	0.59	0.35	−0.42	0.97
Construction	0.23	0.05	0.22	−0.14	
Food and kindred	−0.34	−0.45	−0.44	−0.31	1.62
Tobacco	−0.42	−0.47	−0.52	−0.30	20.56
Textile mill	1.42	0.88	0.17	18.94	20.23
Apparel	1.71	−0.26	0.09	29.07	31.06
Lumber and wood	0.25	−0.06	−0.35	3.39	4.59
Furniture	−0.51	−0.66	−0.72	16.25	6.03
Paper	0.85	0.71	0.69	8.64	1.98
Printing and publishing	0.70	0.70	0.57	3.57	2.27
Chemicals	2.47	2.39	2.36	14.58	8.01
Petroleum refining	0.17	0.10	0.12	−0.62	0.75
Rubber and plastic	1.71	1.58	1.45	12.74	15.07
Leather	−1.40	−2.17	−1.75	5.93	16.93
Stone clay and glass	0.37	0.23	0.00	18.04	20.38
Primary metal	2.34	1.74	1.74	11.80	7.48
Fabricated metal	1.63	1.17	1.24	15.56	8.67
Machinery	2.51	1.94	1.87	11.11	10.52
Electrical machinery	2.29	1.84	2.06	16.77	11.17
Motor vehciles	1.84	1.44	0.85	13.08	5.76
Transport equipment	2.93	2.30	2.38	12.65	7.09
Instruments	3.78	3.62	3.50	15.35	9.81
Misc. manufactures	1.44	1.23	1.07	12.94	11.23
Transportation	0.26	0.15	0.15	−0.01	0.78
Communications	0.28	0.26	0.24	−0.05	
Electric utilities	0.22	0.21	0.13	−0.06	0.09
Gas utilities	0.40	0.32	0.34	−0.03	
Trade	0.26	0.22	0.22	−0.02	
Finance, insurance	0.08	0.08	0.07	−0.07	0.65
Services	0.02	−0.01	−0.09	−0.11	0.61
Government enterprises	0.30	0.31	0.27	−0.10	
Household		−0.54	−0.27		
Government		0.00	−0.82		

*Entries are percentage change in the first period from the base case. Output is industry output, not commodity supply. Imports are competitive imports only.

Table 8.8
Sectoral effects of tariff cuts in 2000

	Value $82 billions			Change from base (%)*		
Sector	Output	Exports	Imports	Output	Exports	Imports
Agriculture	296.73	26.75	5.33	−0.52	−1.40	2.53
Metal mining	19.43	1.01	3.16	3.03	−1.62	3.06
Coal mining	31.63	5.75	0.15	0.07	−2.07	2.40
Oil and gas lmining	278.60	0.89	40.23	0.02	−1.52	2.76
Non-metal mining	26.00	0.60	2.11	1.42	−1.75	2.60
Construction	691.57	0.16	0.00	0.25	−0.46	0.00
Food and kindred	290.25	14.88	15.41	−0.70	−1.02	3.23
Tobacco	33.03	3.27	0.22	−0.72	−1.26	18.88
Textile mill	74.28	2.81	2.38	1.21	16.06	26.52
Apparel	125.52	2.92	40.94	2.58	34.46	26.14
Lumber and wood	63.22	4.70	4.82	0.15	1.04	6.86
Furniture	38.44	0.97	4.63	−0.10	13.81	6.93
Paper	148.53	6.81	9.79	1.03	6.02	4.40
Printing and publishing	214.63	2.12	2.06	0.95	1.09	4.39
Chemicals	277.97	35.17	24.56	3.37	12.46	10.05
Petroleum refining	340.84	19.40	16.03	0.54	−2.49	3.28
Rubber and plastic	131.93	19.31	7.50	2.04	9.02	16.33
Leather	18.80	0.97	13.10	−1.47	8.42	16.54
Stone clay and glass	91.21	3.14	7.61	0.61	15.46	15.44
Primary metal	236.17	9.92	32.89	2.72	8.71	10.40
Fabricated metal	165.97	9.13	9.88	1.94	12.62	8.00
Machinery	434.94	96.62	25.92	3.18	8.33	13.59
Electrical machinery	217.47	42.98	43.60	3.38	14.54	12.63
Motor vehicles	213.08	36.81	45.83	2.75	11.25	10.34
Transpoert equipment	202.95	46.70	6.81	3.66	9.51	9.06
Instruments	81.53	20.91	9.81	4.80	12.36	11.23
Misc. manufactures	36.83	3.18	17.55	1.92	12.05	10.26
Transportation	272.90	19.59	3.53	0.46	0.02	2.87
Communications	295.22	1.81	0.00	0.60	−0.12	0.00
Electric utilities	158.29	0.65	1.24	0.74	0.24	1.16
Gas utilities	230.99	0.51	0.00	0.91	0.18	0.00
Trade	908.17	29.95	0.00	0.25	−0.07	0.00
Finance, insurance	689.19	9.43	0.26	0.26	−0.12	2.73
Services	910.16	12.14	0.07	0.05	−0.26	2.62
Government enterprises	150.18	0.51	0.00	0.50	−0.15	0.00

*Entries in the last three columns compare variables in the year 2000. Output is industry output. Imports are competitive imports only.

industries producing nontradables—trade, finance, and services—have have small declines in exports, due mainly to the terms of trade. Commodities with the highest tariff levels—textiles, apparel, rubber, leather, and glass—show the largest gains in imports. Chemicals, electrical machinery (which includes computers), and instruments have the highest rest-of-the-world tariffs and the most substantial increases in exports.

The output and employment effects of tariff reductions largely parallel the shifts in imports and exports. Chemicals, primary metals, machinery, electrical machinery, and instruments show the largest gains in output and employment. Since the capital stock is initially fixed in supply, capital must be drawn from other sectors to these export oriented industries. Import penetration is so high in the food, furniture, and leather industries that domestic output actually falls. Capital and labor shift from these sectors to sectors that are more competitive internationally.

8.3.2   Quantitative Restrictions

With successive reductions in tariff rates, trade policy has shifted away from tariffs to quantitative restrictions, such quotas and "voluntary" export restraints on suppliers of U.S. imports. As a concrete example, world trade in apparel is governed by Multi-Fiber Agreements that allocate quotas to each exporting country. The quotas are highly detailed, covering many categories of apparel. Some countries attain these limits while others are constrained in only a few or even none of the categories. Another example is motor vehicles, where Japanese exports to the U.S. are under "voluntary" export restrictions, while European exports are not.

We have modeled all quantitative restrictions by assuming that the realized import prices reflect the full effects. The primary justification for this approach is simplicity. More specifically, we assume that quotas result in a higher world price of imports PM_{it}^{*}. Hufbauer, Berliner, and Elliott (1986) have provided estimates of the tariff equivalents of quantitative restrictions on U.S. imports. While bearing in mind the many limitations of the concept of a tariff equivalent, these tariff rates are consistent with the assumptions of constant returns to scale and perfect competition employed in our model for all industries.

We next consider the economic impact of eliminating all domestic and foreign tariffs and the tariff equivalents of quantitative restrictions for textiles, apparel, shoes, steel, and automobiles given in tables 8.4–8.6. These are the most significant restrictions, but do not exhaust U.S. quotas. We have ignored restrictions on agricultural products and motor vehicles other than autos. We simulate the elimination of quantitative restrictions by reducing the rest-of-the-world price of U.S. imports PM_{it}^*. Under this change in trade policy, foreigners lose rents that accrue to them under quotas.

As before, we begin our simulation in 1980 and continue through the year 2100. We have combined tariffs with quantitative restrictions to provide an estimate of the impact of eliminating both types of trade barriers. The results given in figures 8.3 and 8.4 are similar but more substantial in magnitude than those for tariff reductions alone. The only exception is the terms of trade, e_t. In our simulations, the elimination of quantitative restrictions is unilateral. Given the exogenous trade balance, the terms of trade must rise in some years to cover the increased U.S. imports of textiles, steel, autos, and shoes. In the initial year the fall in the terms of trade is only 0.53 percent, compared with 0.61 percent for tariffs alone.

By the year 2000, the economic impacts of eliminating all trade barriers are considerably greater than the effects of tariff cuts alone. The percentage changes at the aggregate level are shown in table 8.9. These impacts arise from reductions in import prices for all the five quota items given in table 8.5 and the implied reduction in the price of investment goods. Investment goods industries are large consumers of steel; automobiles are included among these industries.

The sharp drop in the price of investment goods, due to the elimination of auto quotas, raises the U.S. investment level and economic growth rate. These quotas were eliminated in 1985, so that the impact on the growth rate fell. The effects of the elimination of all tariff barriers on growth of the U.S. gross national product is summarized in table 8.10.

The sectoral effects of eliminating all trade barriers are given in table 8.11. This can be compared with table 8.7 for tariff cuts alone. The sectoral effects are quite similar, except for the commodities subject to quotas. Apparel imports, for example, rise by forty-two percent, compared to a gain of only thirty-one percent for tariff cuts alone. For iron and steel, the gain is fifteen percent versus only seven percent; for leather the gain is twenty-eight percent versus seventeen percent. These shifts translate into parallel output changes. The leather industry's output falls by 2.5 percent by comparison with

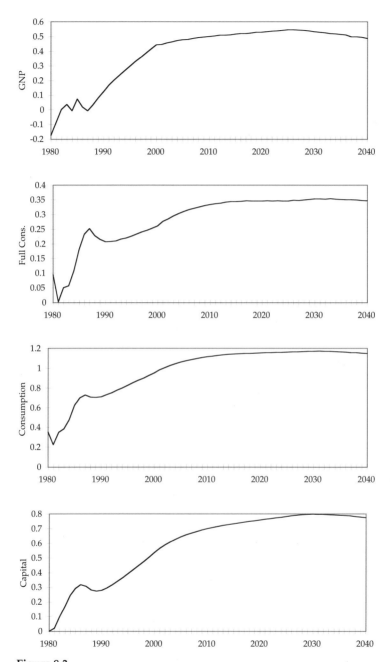

Figure 8.3
Dynamic effects of eliminating tariffs and quotas.

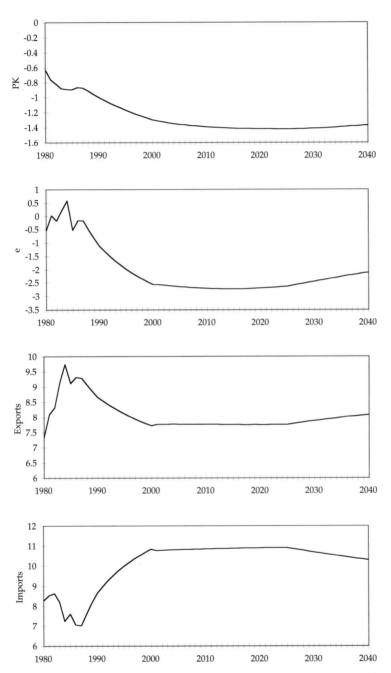

Figure 8.4
Dynamic effects of eliminating tariffs and quotas.

Table 8.9
Elimination of all trade barriers versus tariffs only (% change)

	No tariffs	No barriers
Capital	0.50	0.54
Full consumption	0.17	0.26
Consumption	0.74	0.96
CPI	1.00	1.25
Exports	6.54	7.19
Imports	9.72	10.68
Price of capital	−0.72	−1.30

Table 8.10
Elimination of all trade barriers versus tariffs: effects on GNP

	Annual GNP growth rate %		
	Base case	No tariffs	No barriers
1980–1990	3.47	3.48	3.50
1980–2000	2.34	2.37	2.38

1.4 percent with tariff cuts alone, while textile output rises by only 1.2 percent compared to 1.4 percent. Resources move out of apparel; since textiles, its main intermediate input, also falls in price, the output of apparel actually rises.

In summary, the economic impact of quantitative restrictions is substantial, even though only a few commodities are affected by them. Elimination of these restrictions on the five items we have considered would produce a gain in U.S. consumption that exceeds the gain from abolishing all remaining tariffs. A multilateral reduction of nontariff barriers would probably have had an even greater impact, given the likelihood that quantitative restrictions in the rest of the world are even higher than those in the U.S.

8.3.3   Comparisons with Other Studies

For a multilateral elimination of all tariffs in 1980, Deardorff and Stern (1986) have reported a static gain of 0.1 percent of the U.S. gross national product, based on a 1976 reference year. Whalley (1985)

Table 8.11
Sectoral effects of eliminating all tariffs and selected quotas*

Sector	Output	Capital	Labor	Exports	Imports
Agriculture	−0.34	−0.43	−0.51	−0.14	1.97
Metal mining	2.10	2.09	1.86	−0.18	2.20
Coal mining	0.30	0.24	0.02	−0.27	0.60
Oil and gas mining	0.07	0.00	0.15	−0.32	0.56
Non-metal mining	0.50	0.32	0.03	−0.23	0.68
Construction	−0.15	−0.30	−0.17	−0.21	
Food and kindred	−0.50	−0.56	−0.62	−0.13	1.37
Tobacco	−0.54	−0.54	−0.73	−0.09	20.06
Textile mill	1.19	0.61	−0.24	19.91	25.64
Apparel	2.01	−0.46	−0.09	33.60	42.31
Lumber and wood	−0.12	−0.45	−0.83	3.81	3.91
Furniture	−1.20	−1.35	−1.49	16.81	4.93
Paper	0.81	0.67	0.62	8.94	1.75
Printing and publishing	0.90	0.93	0.72	3.89	2.29
Chemicals	2.45	2.38	2.31	15.13	7.74
Petroleum refining	0.18	0.19	0.09	−0.44	0.62
Rubber and plastic	1.30	1.21	1.01	13.44	14.38
Leather	−2.52	−3.59	−3.04	11.27	27.56
Stone clay and glass	−0.04	−0.16	−0.47	18.83	19.56
Primary metal	2.40	1.33	1.32	13.57	15.09
Fabricated metal	1.66	0.86	0.95	16.42	8.23
Machinery	2.36	1.59	1.45	11.96	9.87
Electrical machinery	2.02	1.46	1.72	17.94	10.52
Motor vehicles	1.58	1.13	0.29	13.95	5.02
Transport. equipment	2.87	2.15	2.10	13.15	6.70
Instruments	3.56	3.40	3.21	16.41	9.42
Misc. manufactures	1.50	1.28	1.02	14.58	10.89
Transportation	0.10	−0.01	−0.03	0.00	0.49
Communications	0.21	0.20	0.14	−0.07	
Electric utilities	0.23	0.25	0.05	−0.02	0.12
Gas utilities	0.35	0.31	0.25	−0.03	
Trade	0.10	0.06	0.05	−0.04	
Finance, Insurance	0.04	0.09	−0.01	−0.09	0.46
Services	−0.01	−0.04	−0.15	−0.15	0.45
Government enterprises	0.23	0.28	0.18	−0.14	
Household		−0.40	−0.50		
Government			−0.99		

*Entries are percentage change from base case in 1980. Imports are competitive imports only.

reports a 0.05 percent gain for a fifty percent multilateral tariff cut, using 1977 as a reference year. By comparison, our model generates a change in consumption equal to 0.16 percent of the U.S. gross national product in 1980, which is closely comparable to previous results.

The sectoral effects of multilateral trade reductions are broadly similar, despite important differences in assumptions among the models. Tariff reductions induce movements of factors of production from the nontradable sectors to manufacturing. Our model allows for an increase in investment, which has a strong positive impact on such industries like primary metals. This counteracts the effects of lower import prices from foreign competitors.[15]

8.4   Conclusion

In this chapter we have implemented an intertemporal general equilibrium model of trade policy and U.S. economic growth. By incorporating the dynamic adjustments of business and households to changes in trade policy, we have successfully captured the impacts on savings and investment ignored by static models. These effects predominate in the long run, so that economic impacts estimated from static models may be substantially understated.

For example, we find that the multilateral elimination of tariffs alone, beginning in 1980, raised long-run consumption by 0.82 percent, compared to an initial gain of only 0.16 percent. When both tariffs and major quotas are lifted, the long-run gain in consumption is estimated to be 1.08 percent. By comparison, the first year gain is only 0.36 percent. These results illustrate the importance of including dynamic adjustments by households and businesses in estimating the impact of changes in trade policy.

In our model, dynamic adjustments are the consequence of intertemporal optimization by households and businesses. With forward-looking consumer behavior, savings and labor supply respond to changes in trade policy. With forward-looking producer behavior, investment is affected by the reduction in the relative price of capital goods. Our model can thus be used to analyze the impact on U.S. economic growth of many other economic policies, such as capital taxation and environmental regulation, as well as exogenous disturbances to the U.S. economy like the oil shocks of the 1970s.

Notes

1. Srinivasan and Whalley (1986) have summarized the features of nine general equilibrium models of world trade.

2. Our methodology for modeling the demand for inputs and productivity growth is discussed by Jorgenson (1984a, 1986a). Additional details on our econometric models of producer behavior are given by Jorgenson and Wilcoxen (1990b).

3. The calibration approach is discussed by Mansur and Whalley (1984).

4. Our application of the Euler equation approach to full consumption follows Jorgenson and Yun (1990).

5. Our methodology for modeling the allocation of total expenditure is discussed by Jorgenson (1984a, 1986a). The model we have employed was constructed by Jorgenson and Slesnick (1987a) and is described in detail by Jorgenson and Wilcoxen (1990b).

6. Additional details are presented by Ho (1989), Appendix C, and Jorgenson and Wilcoxen (1990a, 1990b).

7. This approach was introduced by Armington (1969).

8. Details are given by Ho (1989), chapter 4.

9. Goulder and Eichengreen (1989) present a two-country model with the United States and the rest of the world represented as individual countries. In characterizing the behavior of producers, consumers, and governments in the rest of the world, this approach places heavy reliance on estimates derived from U.S. data.

10. The sign of the bias from omitting export prices is not obvious. If growth of world product were due to productivity growth, then prices in the rest of the world would fall relative to U.S. prices, imparting a downward bias to our estimates of the output elasticities. If growth of world product were due to population growth, the bias would be upward.

11. Tariff rates given in tables 8.4–8.6 were calculated from data generously provided by Andrew Parks of the U.S. International Trade Commission, described in detail by Ho (1989), Appendix H. Tariff rates for the rest of the world are taken from Deardorff and Stern (1986).

12. Further details on our simulation techniques, projections of the exogenous variables, and existence of a steady state are provided by Ho (1989), Appendix F, and Jorgenson and Wilcoxen (1990a, 1990b).

13. More detailed comparisons among results from different models are available from the authors.

9   Environmental Regulation and U.S. Trade

Mun S. Ho and
Dale W. Jorgenson

9.1   Introduction

This chapter examines the relation between U.S. environmental policies and trade patterns. The interaction between environmental policies and trade policies is the focus of much recent research given the heightened concerns about environmental issues among both the general public and economists. The North American Free Trade Area accords, for example, has generated intense interest in whether environmental and trade objectives are in conflict, and if so, how.

This chapter is not concerned with the NAFTA agreement. We examine how environmental regulations introduced in the U.S., beginning in the mid-1960s, affected U.S. competitiveness and patterns of trade. These regulations include pollution abatement from factories as well as motor vehicles. Industry responses to these regulations fall into three categories: process change, input substitution, and end-of-pipe-treatment. The most important response in the period immediately following the promulgation of these regulations was the last category—the development of processes to treat wastes after they have been generated. Such changes obviously affected the supply function of commodities, and since the various industries were affected to very different degrees, pollution control changed the relative prices of goods. This, of course, then affects the trade flows, both the absolute quantity, and composition of total trade.

A theoretical analysis of environmental regulation and trade in the traditional 2×2 Heckscher-Ohlin framework is made in McGuire (1982). He shows how process regulation is equivalent to negative neutral technical progress. We employ such an interpretation in one of the sections below. McGuire also provides Stolper-Samuelson type theorems; these are, however, not directly generalizable to an economy with more than two commodities. Other theoretical discussions

include Pethig (1976) and Siebert (1977). Merrifield (1988) analyzes
the case with capital mobility between countries and shows that unilateral action to reduce pollution may raise net world pollution.

In one of the earlier empirical studies of environmental regulation,
Kalt (1988) used methods employed to test Heckscher-Ohlin theories
on trade. He regressed 1977 net exports of the U.S. (at the 2-digit commodity level) on factor endowments and a measure of pollution abatement costs. He finds a significant negative coefficient on such costs
and concluded that environmental regulation had a small negative
effect on U.S. trade. The environmental cost data at the industry level
used by Kalt come from the U.S. Department of Commerce and the
Environmental Protection Agency. Our study here includes the same
data.

Tobey (1990), using 1975 trade data of highly polluting commodities (at the 3-digit level) from twenty-three countries, ran a similar
H-O test with endowment data from Leamer (1984). He concluded
that environmental regulations introduced by the early 1970s "have
not measurably affected international trade patterns in the most polluting industries." He was also careful to point out factors that may
hide the effects of regulations—the very small size of the effects, the
validity of the H-O equations itself, and the left out variables like
transportation costs and tariffs.

Other studies have focused on specific industries. Some of these are
summarized in Ugelow (1982). They typically find very small effects.
Yet another approach is taken by Robison (1988) who calculates the
pollution content of U.S. trade using data from 1973 and 1982. He concluded that U.S. comparative advantage has shifted away from goods
where the U.S has high abatement costs. (See Dean (1992) for a recent
survey of the literature.)

The partial equilibrium approach taken by these papers only gives
the reduced form effects of the policies, and as Tobey (1990) himself
points out, his tests are weak tests of the H-O hypothesis. Using a
different approach some researchers have used numerical general
equilibrium models to calculate the sectoral and aggregate effects of
reducing pollution. Environmental regulations, like most public policies, affect the economy by changing both the supply function for
products and the demand for factors, and these models are needed to
trace through the linkages. Shortle and Willett (1986) contrasts the
partial versus general equilibrium calculations of water pollution control costs. One of the earlier papers using general equilibrium models

is Richardson and Mutti's (1976) 81-sector model. They find that the industries most affected by pollution taxes are livestock, chemicals, plastic, and utilities.

Much of the more recent research using such numerical models have focused on the effects of reducing carbon dioxide emissions. An example is Whalley and Wigle (1991) which analyze the effects of taxes and CO_2 standards using a five-commodity, three-region world model. They find important differences between national and global taxes, between production and consumption taxes, and between different rules for allocating country targets. In the case of a national consumption tax (to reduce emissions by fifty percent), they find that the developed countries will experience a big reduction in net exports of energy-intensive commodities, while developing and oil exporting countries have a corresponding large increase. For non-energy intensive goods, developing countries have increased net exports while the other regions have lower net exports.

In this chapter, we examine the effects of regulations begining with the 1965 amendments to the Clean Air Act which set automobile emission standards. Subsequent federal legislation include the National Environmental Policy Act (1970), the Clean Water Act (1972) and the 1977 revisions to these main environmental laws. The effects of these laws were essentially which Kalt (1985) and Tobey (1990) were investigating. We are not aware of other studies of these regulations using numerical models.

We analyze the effects of these regulations using a multi-sector dynamic model of the U.S. economy. We find that the environmental regulations reduced the long-run stock of physical capital by about four percent and consumption by one percent. Relative prices of commodities change by some 1–10 percent, with a corresponding change in trade flows. Motor vehicle emission regulations have a large impact on vehicle trade, while exports are hurt by the high costs in the Primary Metal, Chemical and Paper industries.

9.2   A Dynamic Model of the U.S. Economy

The model that we use is described in Jorgenson and Wilcoxen (1990a,b), and Ho and Jorgenson (1992a,b). We shall merely summarize the main features of the model here.

The model is a perfect-foresight multi-sector Cass-Koopmans type growth model where the the optimal path of investment is chosen to maximize discounted returns. The economy is divided into household, business, government, and rest-of-the-world sectors. Since trade and environmental regulations vary substantially across industries, the business sector is further divided into 35 industries. The size of the sectors in the model are illustrated by the 1985 figures in table 9.2.1. Twenty-one of these are manufacturing industries.

These industries produce domestic output using intermediate goods, capital, labor, and noncompetitive imports. We distinguish between industries and commodities following official input-output conventions. Each industry produces a primary commodity and some secondary ones. Thirty-five commodities are represented, each corresponding to the primary product of one of the 35 industries. The input-output structure of the model is illustrated in figures 9.2.1 through 9.2.4. The inputs of industry i may be seen as the ith column of the use table in figure 9.2.1. (The notation of the figures is explained in table 9.2.2.) Matrix U represent the intermediate requirements for production while the rows N, K, and L represent factor inputs.[1]

Each domestic commodity group consist of products from several industries, mostly from the one for which it is the primary commodity. This is represented by the make table in figure 9.2.2. The make up of commodity i is represented by column i of the M matrix, where the biggest element of the column is the M_{ii} element.[2] Total supply of each commodity is the sum of domestic supply and competitive imports (explained below).

9.2.1 Producer Behavior

Output is produced from the two factors (capital and labor), the 35 intermediate commodities, and noncompetitive imports under constant returns to scale technology. We allow for fairly flexible substitution among these inputs unlike the typical Leontief approach. We have constructed econometric models of demands for all inputs by each industry. Inputs of capital, energy, and non-energy intermediates are identified separately since environmental regulations often require abatement equipment or restrictions on certain types of fuels (e.g., high sulfur coal).

Allowing for substitution among inputs is very important, a high degree of substitubility implies that the cost of regulation is low, while rigid production functions imply high costs. To estimate the

Table 9.2.1
Sectoral characteristics of model, 1985 ($billion)

No.	Industry	Value added	Exports	Imports*
1	Agriculture	90.1	16.18	5.57
2	Metal mining	3.5	0.69	1.25
3	Coal mining	15.0	3.56	0.14
4	Oil and gas extraction	87.4	0.54	28.13
5	Non-metal mining	5.9	0.44	0.95
6	Construction	243.7	0.03	0.00
7	Food and kindred products	68.4	10.03	15.46
8	Tobacco	7.5	3.25	0.10
9	Textile mill	14.1	1.51	2.35
10	Apparel	26.1	1.10	21.83
11	Lumber and wood	22.1	2.32	4.59
12	Furniture	13.7	0.52	3.87
13	Paper and allied products	34.4	3.93	8.06
14	Printing and publishing	50.7	1.43	1.27
15	Chemicals	54.1	17.14	16.46
16	Petroleum refining	23.4	7.69	17.49
17	Rubber and plastic	36.3	8.26	9.00
18	Leather	3.5	0.47	6.86
19	Stone clay and glass	24.9	1.76	4.95
20	Primary metal	41.7	4.07	18.74
21	Fabricated metal	63.5	4.91	7.16
22	Machinery	97.4	38.08	37.08
23	Electrical machinery	88.1	21.65	46.26
24	Motor vehicles	51.5	19.03	64.29
25	Transportation equipment	57.1	23.38	6.86
26	Instruments	31.2	9.41	9.34
27	Miscellaneous manufactures	12.1	1.63	13.45
28	Transportation	133.1	20.70	5.00
29	Communications	89.2	1.84	0.00
30	Electric utilities	81.0	0.32	1.11
31	Gas utilities	25.4	0.45	0.00
32	Trade	503.5	22.60	12.27
33	Finance, insurance, and real estate	382.6	7.44	0.09
34	Services	645.6	7.87	0.06
35	Government enterprises	57.8	0.43	0.00

*Competitive imports only.

+ Industry 33, "real estate" excludes owner-occupied housing. This is allocated directly to households.

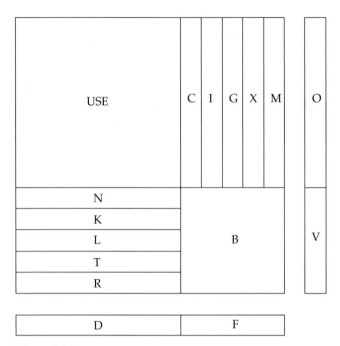

Figure 9.2.1
Organization of the use table.

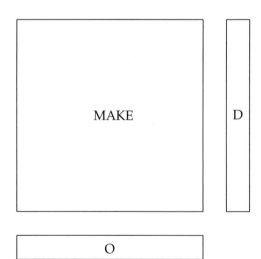

Figure 9.2.2
Organization of the make table.

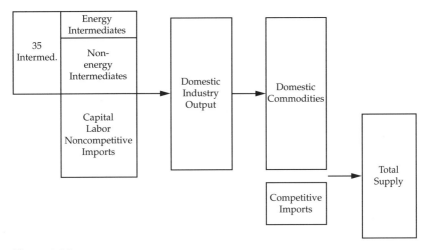

Figure 9.2.3
Supply of commodities.

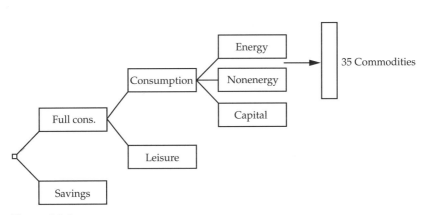

Figure 9.2.4
Consumer demand.

substitution elasticities we have constructed an annual time series of
input-output tables for 1947–1985 corresponding to those outlined in
figures 9.2.1 and 9.2.2. This is in contrast to the more typical calibration approach which derive parameters from a single period's data.

Environmental regulation requires specialized equipment and
causes relative prices to change, inducing substitution among inputs.

Table 9.2.2
Make and use table variables

Category	Variable	Description
Industry-commodity flows:		
	U	Commodities *used* by industries (use table)
	M	Commodities *made* by industries (make table)
Final demand columns:		
	C	Personal consumption
	I	Gross private domestic investment
	G	Government spending
	X	Exports
	M	Imports
Value added rows:		
	N	Noncompeting imports
	K	Capital
	L	Labor
	T	Net taxes
	R	Rest of the world
Commodity and industry output:		
	O	Commodity output
	D	Industry output
Other variables:		
	B	Value added sold directly to final demand
	V	Total value added
	F	Total final demand

This may affect the rate of productivity growth. In our producer model we allow for endogenous technical progress; that is, productivity change depending on the mix of inputs. This approach is discussed in Hogan and Jorgenson (1991).

9.2.2 Capitalist Behavior

There is a single stock of private capital which is rented out to the 35 producers and the household sector. That is, we assume that capital is mobile across sectors in every period. There is essentially only one rental price of capital which is related to its marginal product. This may not be perfectly realistic for short-run analyses, however the model will capture the long-run sectoral effects after the system had adjusted. Allowing for short-run adjustment costs will complicate the model very considerably.

Two dynamic equations characterize the behavior of the owner of the stock. The first is a backward-looking equation which states that the current stock of capital is the sum of past investments less depreciation. The second is a forward-looking equation linking interest rates to capital rental rates and capital gains (in net of tax and net of depreciation terms). Capital gains is made on the price of the capital stock. This price is forward looking in that it incorporates expected future returns and future interest rates. We assume perfect foresight (there is no uncertainty) and these expected future values are realized in the dynamic solution of the model.

The capitalist also decides on the level of aggregate private investment and its composition. Aggregate investment is determined by savings of the household. The allocation of this to the 35 different commodities is determined by relative commodity prices. The investor is allowed to substitute among these commodities, e.g. from machinery to motor vehicles. This constitutes the I column in the input-output table (figure 9.2.1). [Our definition of private capital is wider than most, we include not only industrial stocks but household durables like housing and vehicles as well.] Government capital is ignored in this model.

9.2.3   Consumer Behavior

We represent consumer preferences in three stages (figure 9.2.4). In the first stage, the consumer allocates aggregate consumption to the commodities identified in the model—the 35 goods, noncompetitive imports, and capital. This is the C column in figure 9.2.1, usually referred to as *Personal Consumption Expenditures*. We constructed an econometric model of demands for these commodities allowing for substitution among them. Like the producer model above, we have separate input bundles of capital, energy and non-energy items. This allows the consumer to substitute, say, from energy to capital when the price of electricity rises due to regulations to reduce emissions by electric utilities. This model is described in Jorgenson and Slesnick (1987a).

The consumption model of Jorgenson and Slesnick describes individual household behavior. To use this for our aggregate model we embed this detailed consumption model into a higher-level one via two further stages. In the second stage, we employ the concept of "full consumption," the aggregate of commodities and leisure. An aggregate consumer allocates full consumption, F_t, to leisure and personal consumption expenditures based on the wage rate and the price of the commodity aggregate. The consumer is given an exogenous time endowment which is allocated to leisure and labor supply. This labor supply is perfectly mobile across the 35 industries and government demand, just like the supply of capital. Aggregate time endowment is an index of the population, cross-classified by age, sex, and educational attainment. It should be viewed simply as a time series that adjust for the aging of the U.S. population and the improvement in education attainment in the post-WWII period.[3]

In the third stage, the aggregate consumer makes intertemporal allocations. We view the consumer as maximizing a time separable utility function, a function that sums an infinite stream of full consumption, F_t, discounting at a rate ρ. The consumer is subject to a lifetime budget constraint where the present value of $\{F_t\}_0^\infty$ is equal to the present value of capital and labor income (net of taxes), and government transfers. The maximization of the intertemporal utility function gives an Euler equation that links the growth of F_t between two adjacent periods to the change in the price of full consumption and interest rates. The Euler equation is forward-looking; F_t incorporates expectations about the whole future path of prices and interest rates. Imposing our perfect foresight assumption, the Euler equation is satisfied at all points along the solution path of our model.

9.2.4   Government Behavior

The government plays a passive role in our model. It collects taxes on capital income, labor income, sales receipts, imports, and property. Its purchases includes all 35 commodities and labor. This is represented by column G in figure 9.2.1. The government also makes transfers and pays interest on its debt. These are included only so that tax rates and deficits match the actual data, they play no important role in the simulations of the model here. The government deficit is set exogenously, and cumulated to form the stock of public debt.

9.2.5   The Rest of the World

Ours is a one-country model where the rest of the world is modeled in a simple fashion. Our treatment is comparable to the *Global 2100* model of Manne and Richels (1990). The total supply of commodities to producers and households is the sum of domestic output (Q^C) and competitive imports (M):

$$P_i^S Q_i^S = P_i^C Q_i^C + P_i^M M_i. \tag{9.1}$$

P^S and Q^S denotes, respectively, the price and quantity of total supply of commodities (see figure 9.2.3). The U.S. price of imports (P^M) is the world price (P^{M*}) multiplied by a world relative price variable e, and adjusted for tariffs (θ). For commodity i in period t:

$$P_{it}^M = (1 + \theta_{it}) e_t P_{it}^{M*}. \tag{9.2}$$

We employ the usual Armington assumption that at this level of aggregation, the domestic and imported commodities are imperfect substitutes. For each of the tradeable commodity groups, we express the import share as a function of the price of import relative to the price of the domestic good, and a time trend.

$$\frac{P_{it}^M M_{it}}{P_{it}^S Q_{it}^S} = \alpha + \beta \ln \frac{P_{it}^M}{P_{it}^C} + \gamma f(t). \tag{9.3}$$

The use of time on the right-hand side, instead of income, is a little less typical but is also employed by Petri (1984) and Chipman, Aymann, Ronning, and Tian (1992). These import demands are econometrically estimated on data we constructed for the period 1964–1985. Details of the estimates and the form of the time trend $f(t)$ are given in Ho and Jorgenson (1992a,b). The results are summarized in table 9.2.3, where we also report substitution elasticities from other studies for comparison.[4]

The demand for noncompeting imports are determined by the producer model in a way symmetrical with the other inputs, and depends on import prices defined in a way identical to the one for competitive imports above.

Since we do not have an explicit endogenous model of the rest of the world, the demand for U.S. exports (X) is written simply as a function of world income ($Y*$) and relative prices:

$$X_{it} = f(Y_t^*)[(1 + \theta_{it}^*) P_{it}^C / e_t P_{it}^*]^{\eta_i} \tag{9.4}$$

where $P*$ is the world price, $\theta*$ the world tariff rate, and η gives the degree of elasticity. These commodity exports constitute the column marked "X" in figure 9.2.1.

Table 9.2.3
Import demand elasticities—some comparisons

Industry	Substitution elasticities			Import price elasticities				
	Stern	Sheills	Ours	Stern	Sheills	Petri	Cline	Ours
Agriculture			0.70				−0.90	−0.68
Metal mining			0.11				−0.22	−0.09
Coal mining							−0.22	
Oil and gas mining							−0.22	
Non-metal mining			0.34				−0.22	−0.34
Construction								
Food and kindred	1.13	0.31	0.65	−1.13	−0.21		−1.13	−0.62
Tobacco	1.13	−16.2	2.60	−1.13	−7.57		−1.13	−2.59
Textile mill	1.15	2.58	1.62	−1.14	−1.41	−1.2	−2.43	−1.54
Apparel	4.27	1.62	1.27	−3.92	−0.52	−1.2	−2.43	−1.01
Lumber and wood	1.76	0.26	1.76	−0.69	−1.32	−1.4	−0.96	−1.60
Furniture	3.10	12.13	1.49	−3.00	−9.56	−1.4	−0.96	−1.36
Paper	1.58	1.80	1.16	−0.55	−1.80	−1.4	−1.44	−1.07
Printing and publishing	3.01	2.72	1.22	−3.00	−1.46	−1.4	−1.44	−1.20
Chemicals	2.61	9.85	1.20	−2.53	−6.82	−0.8	−0.97	−1.10
Petroleum refining	2.36	−0.34	1.09	−1.96	−0.79	−0.8	−0.97	−1.00
Rubber and plastic	5.71	2.67	1.76	−5.26	−1.32	−0.8	−3.57	−1.65
Leather	1.81	4.11	1.86	−1.58	−2.01		−2.46	−1.11
Stone clay and glass	1.63	4.29	1.86	−1.60	−2.86	−0.8	−1.37	−1.72
Primary metal	1.45	3.05	1.48	−1.42	−2.28	−1.6	−1.99	−1.29
Fabricated metal	3.67	1.54	1.13	−3.59	−0.94	−1.1		−1.08
Machinery	1.02	3.34	1.72	−1.02	−0.88	−0.9	−0.87	−1.53
Electrical machine	2.11	7.46	1.45	−1.00	−3.08	−0.6	−0.87	−1.23
Motor vehicles	3.59	2.01	1.52	−3.28	−1.24	−2.5	−2.53	−1.16
Transport. equipment	3.59	2.01	1.35	−3.28	−1.24	−2.5	−1.70	−1.28
Instruments	1.98	0.45	0.86	−1.08	−0.44	−0.9		−0.77
Misc. manufactures	1.98	3.55	1.52	−2.06	−2.37	−0.8	−4.44	−1.14
Transportation								
Communications								
Electric utilities								
Gas utilities								
Trade								
Finance, insurance								
Services								
Government enterprises								

The classification system used is different for each source. The entries are listed in categories closest to those used in this study.
Stern: Central tendencies in Stern, Francis and Schumacher. Sample period before 1974.
Sheills: Sheills, Stern and Deardorff. Sample period 1962–1978.
Petri: Petri (1985) U.S. imports from rest of the world excluding Japan, 1960–1980.
Cline: Cline et al., page 58.
Ours: Elasticities evaluated at 1983 shares. Data from 1964–1985.

In the simulations, the foreign prices are set to the historical data for the sample period, and set equal to the 1985 prices for post-sample. Implicitly, the price of foreign goods that competes with U.S. exports are normalized to one. When counterfactual simulations are made we assume that these foreign prices do not change.

For accounting completeness, we take note of the financial flows (interest payments, foreign aid, etc.) but these, like the government interest payments noted above, play no significant role. The current account balance is exports of commodities, less competitive and non-competing imports, plus net financial flows (dividend income, foreign aid, etc.).

$$CA = \sum_i P_i^C X_i - \sum_i P_i^M M_i - \text{noncompeting imports}$$
$$+ \text{net financial flows.} \tag{9.5}$$

The current account is set exogenously and cumulated to form the stock of net U.S. foreign assets.

9.2.6 Static and Dynamic Equilibrium

At the start of every period the economy inherits a stock of capital that is cumulated from past investments. For a given decision on the level of full consumption by the aggregate consumer, all the markets will clear in that period by endogenous prices. The commodities markets are cleared by 35 goods prices, the factor markets are cleared by the rental price and wage rate, the exogenous government deficit is achieved by endogenous government purchases (tax rates are fixed), and finally, the exogenous current account balance is achieved by the endogenous world relative price e. (P_i^M and X_i in equation (9.5) are functions of e.) With the solution of the static equilibrium for that period, we have the level of investment and hence the stock of capital for the following period.

For intertemporal equilibrium, the Euler equation linking adjacent full consumption must be satisfied. Dynamic equilibrium is achieved when the entire path of the economy satisfies both the backward-looking capital accumulation equation and the forward-looking Euler equation. In the language of dynamic optimization, the costate variable—the level of full consumption—in the initial period, must be such that the economy is on the saddle path going towards the steady state where the transversality conditions are satisfied.

To have a well defined steady state, we require that technical progress fall eventually to zero. The size of the economy in the long run is determined by the size of the population. That too rises eventually to a constant. In the steady state, all quantities and relative prices are constant. In that situation, the tax adjusted rate of return on capital is equal to the rate of time preference, and investment exactly covers depreciation. The stock of capital is thus perfectly elastic in the long run, while being completely inelastic in the short run. The steady-state capital stock responds to shocks and policy changes, however, the rate of return is unchanged. This is unlike the original one-sector Cass-Koopmans model.

The final item to be described are the exogenous variables. These are set to the data for the sample period 1947–1985. We project these variables for 1986–2050, after which they are kept constant. We find that the year 2100 is sufficiently far out to be trivially different from the steady state. The exogenous variables are kept constant for 2050–2100 to allow time for the endogenous variables to converge to their steady-state values. The exogenous variables are the population, foreign variables, the budget, and current account deficits.

The population (time endowment) is projected by individual year of age, sex, and educational attainment using the population model of the Social Security Administration. The method of calculating the aggregate index of time endowment follows the system in Jorgenson and Fraumeni (1989). The post-sample import prices are set to the 1985 relative prices. Domestic and foreign tariff rates are also set to the latest available data for the out-of-sample projections. World income for the export function is assumed to grow in a way similar to U.S. income. The long-run government and current account balances are set to historical averages.[5] Our approach is to compare the base-case simulation with counterfactual simulations, the paths by themselves are not of direct interest. How these exogenous variables are set, are therefore of secondary importance. What is important is that they are kept fixed for the different simulations.

9.3   The Trade Impact of Environmental Legislations of 1965–1977

We shall examine the impact of environmental regulations enacted in the 1960s and 1970s by projecting the evolution of the U.S. economy with and without these regulations. The effects on growth and technical change are described in Jorgenson and Wilcoxen (1990a). Here we describe the effects on U.S. exports and imports. We assess the impact of pollution controls on industry and the controls on motor vehicle emissions, each separately and with all regulations together.

Our approach consists of first running a base-case simulation designed to mimic the actual evolution of the post-WWII U.S. economy. The model is estimated on data collected over the period 1947–1985. These data include sectoral output, labor and capital utilization, trade flows, and final demands. The base-case simulation, therefore, is a regime with pollution controls mandated by these environmental laws in place. To assess the impact of these controls, we perform counterfactual simulations where they are removed. That is, we calculate the path of the economy, including how the sectors evolve and how the trade patterns change, had there been no environmental regulation in the U.S. before 1980.[6]

The counterfactual path of the economy is different from the base case at all points; the initial impact, the transition, and the steady state. We shall describe the effects on the steady state in some detail, these are the long-run effects after the economy had adjusted to the new optimal path of investment. In the first year of regulation removal, the capital stock is fixed and the initial equilibrium gives the short-run effect. It should be emphasized that this is not the same as the counterfactual equilibrium in static models. In those models, savings do not change endogenously, but are usually kept fixed. In our perfect foresight model, the rate of consumption and investment change endogenously and immediately.

An important assumption of our model should be repeated at this point. We assume that commodity relative prices (the $P_i *$'s) in the rest of the world remain unchanged even if U.S. policies change. The counterfactual experiment consists of a relaxation of U.S. pollution control rules while the rest of the world maintains its regulations, or lack thereof. A simulation parallel to the multilateral tariff reduction studied in Ho and Jorgenson (1992) is not feasible at present due to the lack of data pertaining to world cost of pollution control.

We have divided the environmental regulations into three separate categories. The first deals with the increase in annual operating costs, the second concerns investment in pollution control equipment, and the third involves motor vehicle emissions. Data on these costs for manufacturing industries are collected by the Bureau of the Census and by the BEA.[7] These data represent actual costs reported by businesses and do not include taxes levied as part of the "Superfund" program. (These taxes amounted to more than one billion dollars annually in the 1980s and probably affected relative prices. We are not, however, going to examine their effects here.) Each of these three categories of regulations is in turn discussed in the sections which follow.[8]

9.3.1   Operating Costs

The increase in direct industry costs is quite substantial. The operating costs of complying to these environmental regulations (exclusive of the purchase of control equipment) were $4.1 billion in 1974, rising to some $20.0 billion in 1983 (in current dollars).[9] How these costs were distributed across the industries in 1983 is given in table 9.3.1.

The first column gives the operating costs for the industries for which data are available.[10] The largest cost was born by water sewage treatment ($5.6 billion) which is part of the Services industry (no. 34)—a non-traded sector. To give an idea of how important these costs are to each industry, the second column (marked λ) gives the percentage of each industry's annual total costs attributable to pollution control activities. These percentages for most part are small. The most affected sectors are Chemicals (1.6%) and Primary Metals (2.5%). These are sectors with high trade shares.

The column marked α gives the sectoral share of the economy's total pollution control operating costs $20.0 billions in 1983. Waste water treatment takes by far the biggest share of the total operating costs. However, since it is part of the huge, largely non-polluting Services sector, the λ share of Services is small. The other major polluting sectors are Chemicals, Petroleum Refining, and Primary Metal (making steel from iron ore and coal).

The Electric Utilities sector (no. 30) is treated somewhat differently since we have information not only on how much was spent on operating special equipment, but also how the industry switched to more expensive low sulphur coal in response to these environmental regulations. We find it most meaningful to divide the effects of regulation here into two parts. The first is the increase in operating cost of the utilities due to the pollution reducing equipment, the second being the increase in the price of the output of the Coal industry (no. 3). The first part is the number reported on line 30 in table 9.3.1. The λ of 4.9% in the Coal sector represents the increase in the price of coal due to the shift to low sulphur types. The experiment of removing the environmental regulations thus includes reducing both operating costs and

Table 9.3.1
Industry environmental costs

No.	Sector	O. Cost %	λ_i %	α_i %	Inv75	Inv83
1	Agriculture	0				
2	Metal mining	0				
3	Coal mining	0	4.94			
4	Oil and gas mining	0				
5	Non-metal mining	0				
6	Construction	0				
7	Food and kindred	924.3	0.32	4.6	5.3	2.8
8	Tobacco	0				
9	Textile mill	164.2	0.31	0.8	5.3	1.2
10	Apparel	+				
11	Lumber and wood	209.0	0.41	1.0	5.9	2.1
12	Furniture	68.1	0.25	0.3	9.6	1.5
13	Paper	1253.1	1.48	6.3	22.3	4.3
14	Printing and publishing	87.5	0.09	0.4	1.2	0.4
15	Chemicals	2984.0	1.63	14.9	12.3	5.7
16	Petroleum refining	2231.0	1.17	11.2	23.0	10.6
17	Rubber and plastic	200.9	0.33	1.0	2.8	1.3
18	Leather	+				
19	Stone clay and glass	522.9	1.07	2.6	11.0	5.6
20	Primary metal	2628.5	2.45	13.1	20.0	5.9
21	Fabricated metal	456.5	0.37	2.3	3.8	2.6
22	Machinery	379.6	0.22	1.9	1.8	0.8
23	Electrical machinery	436.0	0.27	2.2	2.8	1.4
24	Motor vehicles	459.6	0.31	2.3	2.4	2.9
25	Transportation equipment	256.1	0.27	1.3	3.2	1.2
26	Instruments	188.5	0.35	0.9	3.7	1.2
27	Misc. manufactures	+				
28	Transportation	0				
29	Communications	0				
30	Electric utilities	909.7	0.69	4.5	6.3	13.6
31	Gas utilities	0				
32	Trade	0				
33	Finance, insurance	0				
34	Services	5642.0	0.66	28.2	24.0	13.8

Source: Wilcoxen (1988) Appendix D.
O. Cost = Operating cost of pollution abatement in 1983.
λ_i = O. cost as share of industry i's total costs.
α_i = Industry i's O. cost as share of economy's total O. cost.
Inv75 = Investment in pollution abatement equipment as share of industry i's investment in 1975.
Inv83 = Ditto in 1983.
+: Magnitudes insignificant and suppressed by Census Bureau.

the price of coal. That means that in the counterfactual simulation a unit of output of the Coal Industry is cheaper and has a higher proportion of high sulphur coal.

The cost shares (λ_i's) were at their highest in 1983 in our sample period for pollution control data (1973–1983). Environmental controls increased steadily over this period. We assume that the shares for later years remain constant at the 1983 values. In the counterfactual simulation, the cost (and price) of each industry's output is reduced by an amount equal to these environmental cost shares. Algebraically, this has the same effect as neutral technical progress as discussed in Mcguire (1982).

The dynamic effects of removing the operating costs imposed by the environmental laws are summarized in figure 9.3.1. The steady state effects are given in table 9.3.3 and in the column marked "OPER" in table 9.3.2. The second panel of fig. 9.3.1 gives the evolution of full-consumption. Full consumption jumps up immediately and keeps rising until it is 0.3% higher in the steady state. Removing the regulations meant lower prices of goods (relative to the wage numeraire). This is the flip side of requiring less inputs for the same output. This leads to higher consumption and, for the initial periods, lower investment. The evolution of the capital stock is given in the top panel.

Part of the reason for the initial fall in investment is that the higher pollution control operating costs are found in nondurable goods manufacturing industries. These sectors contribute a lot less than the durable goods industries to the Investment Goods Composite (column I of fig. 9.2.1). However, over time and with higher output, both consumption and investment rise. The capital stock is some 0.54 percent higher in the long run.

The world relative price e is given in the last panel of fig. 9.3.1. It falls by 0.7 percent in the steady state. If incomes were unchanged, lower prices of U.S. goods due to removal of these operating costs should lead to higher exports and lower imports. However, the current account deficit is fixed exogenously equal to the base case. Therefore, e must fall (appreciate) to maintain this deficit in the face of lower U.S. goods prices. This does not mean that relative prices do not change (P_i^C relative to P_j^C, and P_i^C, relative to P_i^M). The different sectors enjoy different cuts in their operating costs. Therefore, while the aggregate trade balance must be maintained, the composition of exports and imports are changed. On top of this price effect is the

Capital

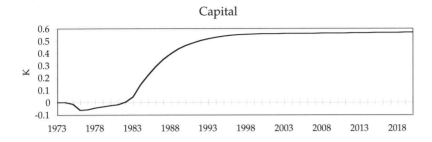

Full consumption

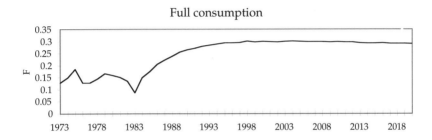

GNP

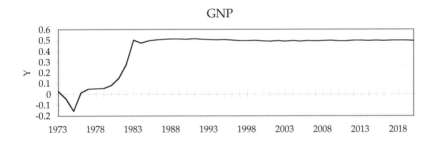

Price of capital

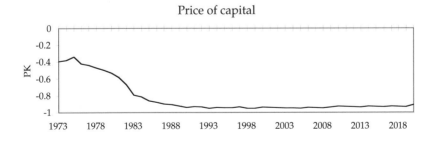

Figure 9.3.1
Effects of removing operating costs. % change from base case.

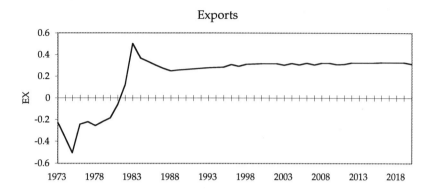

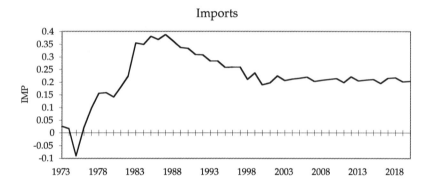

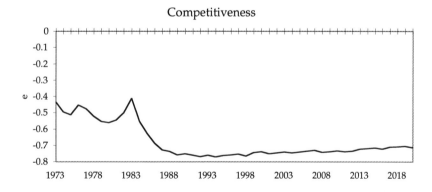

Figure 9.3.1
(continued).

Table 9.3.2
Steady-state effects of removing environmental regulations

	OPER	INV	MV	ALL
Capital stock	0.54	2.31	1.12	3.79
Output	0.48	0.58	0.34	1.16
Full-consumption	0.28	0.50	0.28	0.97
Goods consumption	0.79	1.39	0.79	2.70
Exports	0.28	−0.29	0.44	0.27
Imports	0.21	−1.30	1.11	0.15
Price of capital	−0.89	−2.70	−1.32	−4.52
Consumer prices	−0.92	−1.60	−0.91	−3.12
e	−0.70	−0.47	−0.39	−1.30

higher capital stock and output, i.e., the income effect of a wealthier consumer buying and importing more.

Figure 9.3.2(a) gives the changes in the price of domestic output in the steady state (recall that the numeraire is the wage rate). The biggest change is in the price of Coal, followed by the price of steel (Primary Metals, sector 20), Paper Products, and Chemicals. Prices of the other sectors, while not directly affected by the removal of regulations, enjoy a lower price of capital and intermediate inputs. They therefore also show reductions.

These price changes lead to changes in steady-state trade flows. These are described in figure 9.3.2(b) (we have omitted the services sectors with small trade flows). The first thing to note is that most of the changes in exports and imports are positive. Lower prices encourage exports, while in order to maintain the exogenous current account balance, e falls (appreciates). This increases imports. Added to this price effect is the income effect due to higher lifetime income. The figures are percentage change from the base case, not dollar values (for an idea of the dollar magnitudes, apply the percentages to the data in table 9.2.1). It should be recalled that the magnitude of the quantity changes depends on the size of the price change and the elasticity of substitution. The exporters who gain the most are the expected Primary Metals, Chemicals, Paper, and Coal industries. The appreciation of e is smaller than the fall in domestic goods prices (CPI, for example, falls by 0.92 percent), leading to a small improvement in competitiveness (or fall in the terms of trade). Again, we should point out that foreign goods prices are assumed to be fixed.

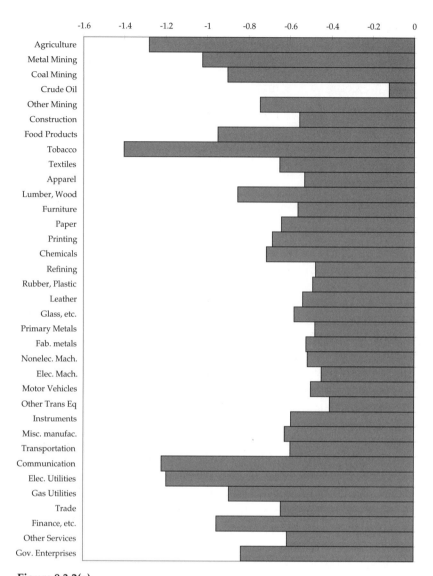

Figure 9.3.2(a)
Steady-state effects of removing operating costs. Price of domestic output:
% change from base case.

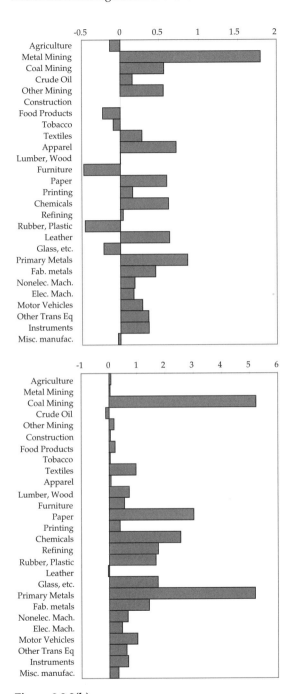

Figure 9.3.2(b)
Top: Competitive imports: % change from base case. Bottom: Exports. %
change from base case.

9.3.2   Investment in Pollution Control Equipment

The second category of environmental regulations is the investment in new equipment for pollution control. An example of this is the use of electrostatic precipitators to reduce emissions of particulates. Such additions to the capital stock do not increase output as conventionally measured. These regulations in effect raise the price of productive capital thus affecting the rate of capital accumulation and economic growth. Investment in such equipment for the business sector amounted to some $10.4 billion in 1975, compared to total business investment of $220 billion. For some industries, this constituted a rather large portion of durables purchases in the 1970s. This can be seen in the last two columns of table 9.3.1. The sectors most affected are the very industries that had high pollution abatement operating costs—Petroleum Refining, Water Utilities (part of Services), Electric Utilities, Paper, Chemicals, and Primary Metal.[11]

These investments peaked in the early 1970s, and have fallen substantially since. Much of the early expenditures went to retrofit equipment already in place. One ought to distinguish between investment made to achieve environmental standards for existing sources of emissions and those made for new sources of emissions. Unfortunately, the data do not allow for such a separation. We assume that the backlog of investment for retrofitting the old sources of emissions had been eliminated by 1983.

We also assume that pollution control equipment provides no benefits to the producer other than that of satisfying the regulations. We therefore regard mandated investment in such equipment as an increase in the price of investment goods. Our counterfactual experiment of eliminating regulations on equipment consists of reducing the price of investment goods by the proportion of total investment attributable to pollution control for 1983. This captures the effect of requirements for abatement on new capital, but ignores the effect of windfall losses to owners of the capital associated with old sources of emissions. It should be pointed out again that our model assumes capital mobility across sectors and that the very short-run movements may be overstated.

The effects of lowering the cost of mandated investment in control equipment are given in figure 9.3.3, figure 9.3.4, and the column labelled "INV" in table 9.3.2. With the lower price of investment goods there is a higher rate of capital formation. In the initial periods, this higher savings investment comes from reduced full consumption—i.e., lower personal consumption expenditures and less leisure. Output jumps up immediately. Over time this greater rate of investment leads to a stock that is some 2.3 percent higher in the steady state. This higher stock of capital allows more output to be produced, which sustains both a higher rate of investment and a higher rate of full consumption. Full consumption is 0.49 percent higher than the base case in the long run.

The general price effects are similar to the previous case although there are no direct sector-specific shocks. The reduction in the price of new capital reduces the rental rate of capital for all sectors. To the extent that different producers use different amounts of capital, and experience different inter-industry effects, their output price responses are different. The variation of price change across the industries is smaller than the operating cost experiment in section 9.3.2 where there was a spectrum of costs. Figure 9.3.4(a) gives the steady-state change in industry output prices. The price of agriculture falls by 1.3 percent while the prices of manufacturing industries fall by about 0.5 percent. The other significant change is in the price of electricity (sector 30), which falls by 1.2 percent. This is a non-traded input used by all industries.

The increased demand for investment goods leads to a higher initial demand for both domestic goods and imports. However, domestic prices fall due to the lower capital costs and the price effect dominates, giving lower aggregate imports. Since the current account balance is fixed, exports also fall. This is accompanied by an initial rise (depreciation) in the world relative price e. Over time, the greater stock of capital and higher output result in lower commodity prices relative to the wage numeraire. The long-run value of e falls relative to the base case but the change is smaller than the fall in domestic prices (U.S. consumer prices fall by 1.6 percent). There is thus a small deterioration in the terms of trade.

The change in trade patterns is rather small, in line with the size of the counterfactual shock and the fact that there is one common capital price. The reduction in the prices of U.S. goods result in a higher proportion of exports from the Lumber, Chemicals, Paper, and Agriculture industries. The size of the sectoral trade flows (table 9.2.1) should be kept in mind. The large percentage change in Construction and Apparel exports translates into trivial absolute changes. Imports are similarly reduced very slightly, with magnitudes depending on the

Capital

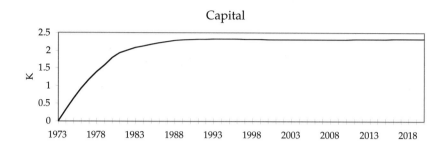

Full consumption

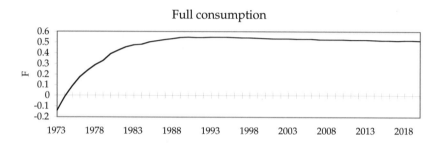

GNP

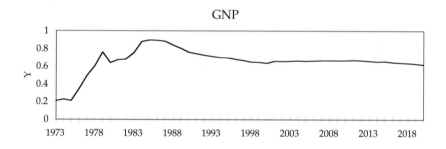

Price of capital

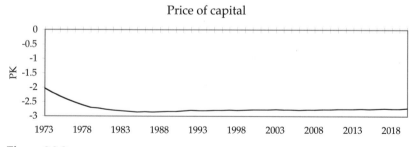

Figure 9.3.3
Effects of lowering mandated investments. % change from base case.

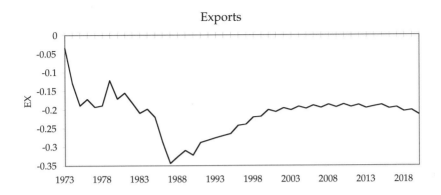

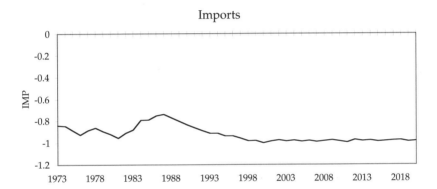

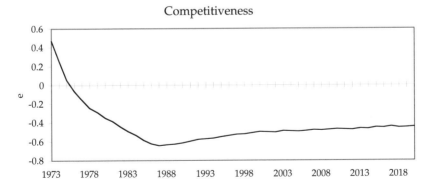

Figure 9.3.3
(continued).

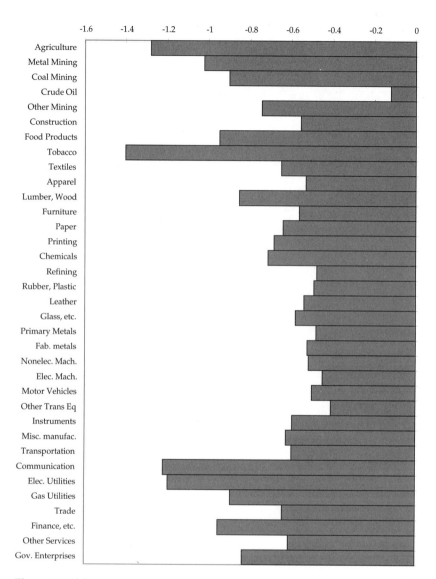

Figure 9.3.4(a)
Steady-state effects of lowering mandated investments. Price of domestic
output: % change from base case.

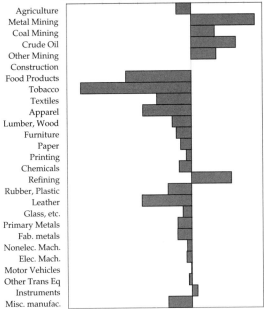

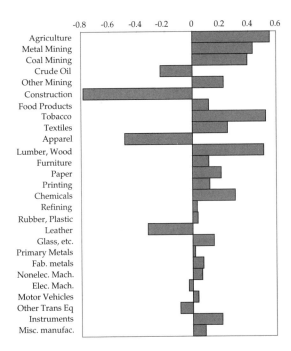

Figure 9.3.4(b)
Top: Competitive imports. % change from base case. Bottom: Exports.
% change from base case.

price elasticity in the face of the change in the common factor e. Food, Apparel and Leather enjoy the largest reductions in import penetration.

9.3.3 Motor Vehicles Emissions Control

While the emission regulations on motor vehicles have only a small overall impact on trade, we report the results briefly for comparison with those discussed in Hogan and Jorgenson (1991). These regulations of course have a large direct impact on trade in vehicles as imports are required to conform to the regulations.

Clean Air Act regulations raise the price of motor vehicles which is part of the capital stock. They also raise operating costs due to higher fuel consumption and the premium paid for unleaded gasoline. The counterfactual experiment of no regulation consists of reducing the price of domestic vehicles by the cost of the abatement equipment. The equipment amounted to some 5.5 percent of the price of vehicles in 1983. A similar proportion is assumed to apply to the price of vehicle imports, which is thus reduced accordingly. Of the three experiments described in this chapter this is the only one where relative import prices are changed (P_i^M relative to P_j^M). The unleaded fuel cost differential is also taken into account by reducing the output price of Industry 16, Petroleum Refining. The fuel price change was 2.2 percent in 1983. We did not take into account the higher fuel requirements.

The differences between the experiment and the base case are summarized in figures 9.3.5, 9.3.6, and the "MV" column in table 9.3.2. Motor vehicles constitute a significant portion of our definition of capital. It was about 16 percent in 1983.[12] Reducing the price of vehicles lowers the price of capital goods, leading to a higher stock and higher total output. There is more trade in motor vehicles in both directions. It should be recalled that there is substantial cross-border vehicle trade between the U.S. and Canada. The overall effects are small, as expected.

The accumulation path of capital here is somewhat different from that in section 9.3.2 where the price of *aggregate* investment is reduced. While Motor Vehicles output is delivered mostly to the investment component of final demand and not to Consumption directly, it is only one of the 35 commodities that make up investment. The price of aggregate investment is changed by much less than the price of Motor

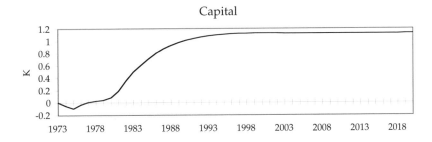

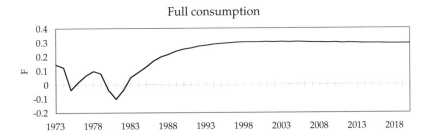

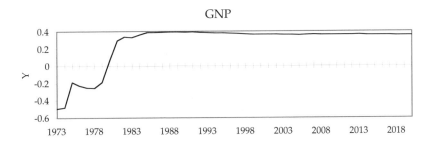

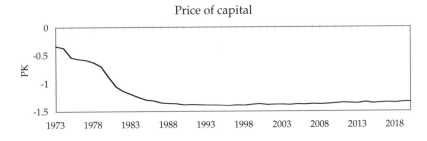

Figure 9.3.5
Effects of removing regulations on motor vehicles. % change from base case.

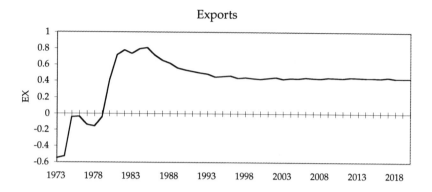

Exports

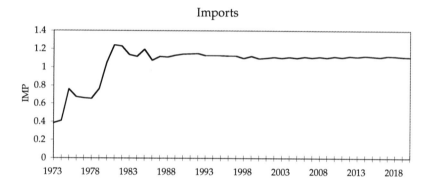

Imports

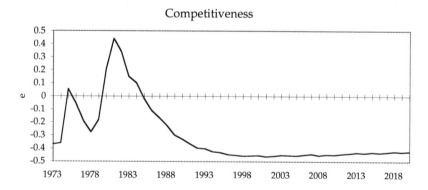

Competitiveness

Figure 9.3.5
(continued).

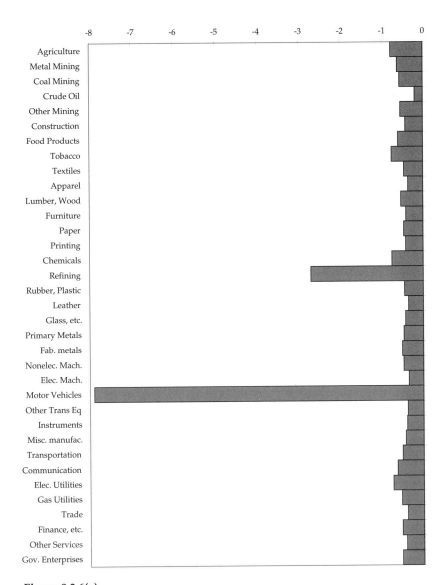

Figure 9.3.6(a)
Steady-state effects of removing regulations on motor vehicles. Price of
domestic output: % change from base case.

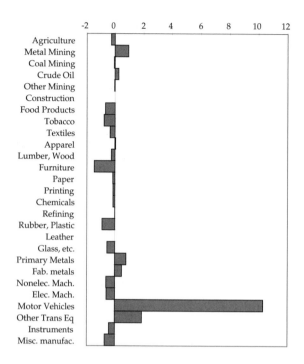

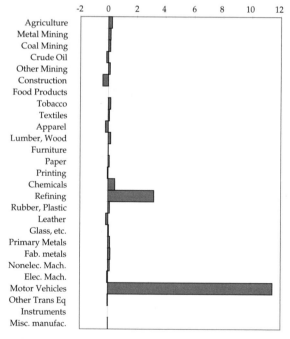

Figure 9.3.6(b)
Top: Competitive imports. % change from base case. Bottom: Exports. %
change from base base.

Vehicles. As is shown in the second panel of figure 9.3.5, full consumption rises immediately, whereas capital falls somewhat initially and rises more slowly in this third experiment. Another difference here is the effect of lower fuel prices. The removal of regulations lowers prices, and thus increases the lifetime wealth of the household, who raise consumption and lower investment initially in response. In section 9.3.2 there is a wealth effect. However, the price effect of the large reduction in the price of aggregate investment dominates and investment rises immediately.

9.3.4   The Overall Impact of Environmental Regulations

Here we perform a final simulation where all the regulations discussed above are removed—abatement equipment requirements, higher operating costs of producers, and motor vehicle regulations. The results above cannot be simply totaled up, in part because the model is nonlinear. Another reason is our accounting procedures. The operating costs in section 9.3.1 include capital charges. There will be a double counting of capital if we simply add them up since there would be no annual capital charges if there were no regulations for equipment. For the combined simulation here, the counterfactual reduction in operating cost excludes the capital charges, while the reduction in the price of investment goods is as in section 9.3.2 above.

Figures 9.3.7, 9.3.8, and the last column of table 9.3.2 report the results. As discussed above, lifting the regulations have opposing effects on initial investment. On one hand, the reduction in the price of investment goods encourages investment. On the other hand, wealth (discounted future incomes) increases which leads to higher consumption demand. Since the current account is fixed, this implies lower savings and investment. The sum of these effects is given in the top panel of figure 9.3.7, capital rises steadily right from the beginning, i.e., the price effect on investment dominates. However, full consumption jumps up too—with the reduction in pollution abatement operating costs, resources can be diverted from reducing emissions to producing more consumption and investment goods.

In the long run, the capital stock is 3.9 percent higher while full consumption is 0.97 percent higher. There is a shift towards goods and away from leisure. Consumption of goods rises by 2.70 percent. All the individual simulations above led to a long-run fall (appreciation) of the world relative price e, which is smaller than the fall in domestic

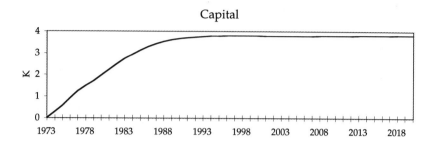

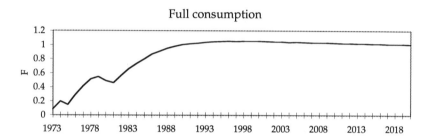

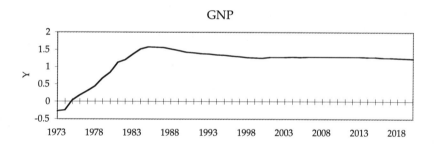

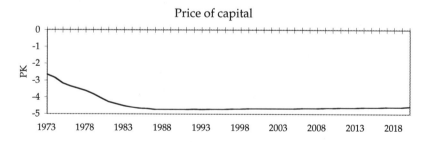

Figure 9.3.7
Effects of removing all environmental regulations. % change from base case.

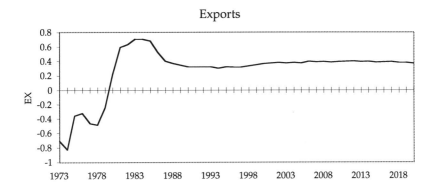

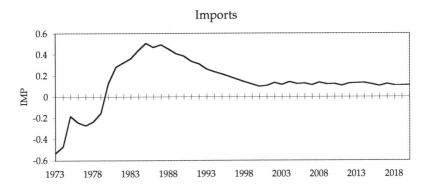

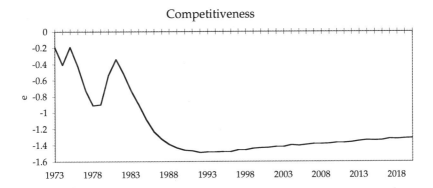

Figure 9.3.7
(continued).

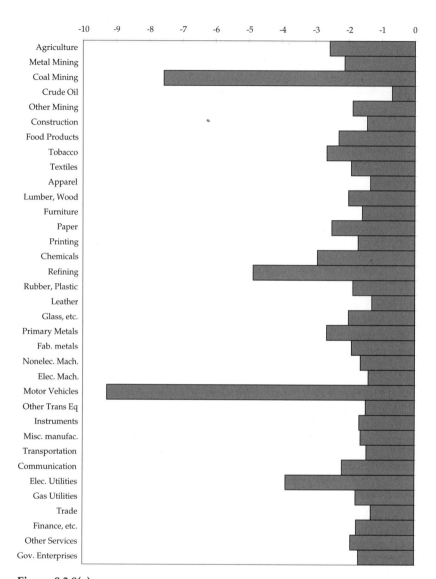

Figure 9.3.8(a)
Steady-state effect of removing all environmental regulations. Price of
domestic output: % change from base case.

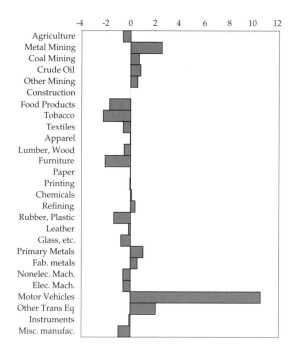

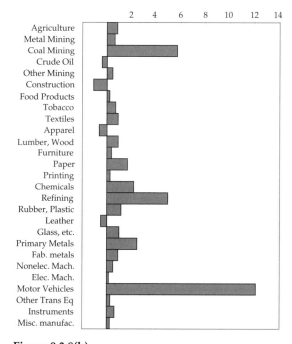

Figure 9.3.8(b)
Top: Competitive imports. % change from base case. Bottom: Exports.
% change from base case.

prices, causing a small deterioration in the terms of trade. In the combined experiment, the steady-state appreciation is some 1.3 percent, while consumer prices fall 3.1 percent. This may be interpreted as the whole world benefitting from the reduction in regulation. U.S. consumers benefit from lower prices and the rest-of-the-world benefits from their improvement in the terms of trade. U.S. aggregate exports rise by 0.27 percent while U.S. imports only increase by 0.15 percent.

The steady-state trade effects are given in figure 9.3.8. While the aggregate effect is very small, there are big sectoral shifts. The sharp drop in the price of motor vehicles provides the biggest change in trade. Both exports and imports of vehicles rise by more than 10 percent. As before, the exports rise most for the highly polluting sectors— Chemicals, Petroleum, and Primary Metals. The sectors that experience higher import penetration are Transportation Equipment (no. 25), and Primary Metals. While the increase in imports of steel (a Primary Metal) may be surprising due to the large reduction in the price of U.S. made steel, it should be recalled that there is a higher capital stock and higher rate of investment. Primary Metal is an important component of Investment, both directly and indirectly.

9.3.5   Sensitivity Analysis

As can be seen in table 9.2.3, the estimates for import price elasticities cover a rather big range. To provide a check on the sensitivity of the results, we used another set of import price elasticities where we doubled the value of our parameter estimates. All other parameters are left unchanged. We first calculated a new base-case path of the economy based on these more elastic parameters. The simulation in section 9.3.4, where all regulations were removed, was next repeated with these new parameters. These two new simulations were then compared just like the original simulations.

The results are very similar. It should be recalled that in the sample period, U.S. imports were only between five percent and twelve percent of GNP. With the more elastic parameters, the increase in steady state capital is 3.85 percent compared to the 3.79 percent reported in the "ALL" column in table 9.3.2. The long-run nominal change in e is bigger, but the change in the terms of trade (e compared to domestic prices) is smaller, 1.5 percent vs. 1.8 percent.

While the aggregate effect of having more elastic parameters are small, the compositional change in trade is more noticeable. The effects on the volume of imports is generally larger than that given in table 9.3.6. The exception is motor vehicles, which now show a less extreme change, 7.5 percent instead of the original 10.5 percent.

9.4 Conclusion

We have examined the trade effects of the environmental regulations of the 1970s and early 1980s using a dynamic growth model. We find that there are substantial effects on long-run output and consumption. Although the effect on aggregate trade flows is small, there are large sectoral effects with the industries experiencing the highest pollution reduction costs having the greatest changes.

While our model does not have an endogenous rest-of-the-world structure, and thus does not take into account the effect of changes in relative U.S. demand on world relative prices, it nevertheless gives important clues for the sectoral responses. The regulations we considered are very U.S.-specific. Other countries are unlikely to change their environmental regulations in response to changes in U.S. policy. The aspect that we have not accounted for is that the world price of import j may change in response to a change in the price of domestic commodity j because the U.S. is a significant world purchaser of that commodity. This leads to an overstatement of the effects on the trade flows of that item. However, unless the elasticities are very different, our ranking of the sectoral shocks would not be affected. The U.S. share of world imports in every commodity has been, and continues to be, falling. Thus over time any such bias will diminish.

We should reiterate what we have and have not shown. The results in Jorgenson and Wilcoxen (1990a,b), and here, show that output and consumption in the U.S. and the rest of the world will be higher in the absence of environmental regulation that requires resources to be devoted to reducing emissions. This does not mean that overall welfare is lower. We have not considered the unmeasured benefits of reduced pollution. What we calculated is the cost side of the ledger. Estimates of the benefit side remain to be made.

Notes

1. Non-competitive imports (N) are those defined by the BEA to be goods that have no close substitutes produced in the U.S. The main items are tropical agricultural products (e.g., natural rubber) and foreign travel. These constituted thirteen percent of non-factor imports in 1985.

2. The term "commodity" is used loosely here to refer to both goods (sectors 1 through 27) and services (sectors 28 through 35). This is to avoid confusion with Services, sector 34.

3. See Ho and Jorgenson (1992b) for detailed definitions.

4. A detailed description of how the trade data is constructed and incorporated into our model is given in Ho (1989) Appendix H.

5. The population projections and the construction of the industry labor inputs are described in Ho (1989) Appendix C. Projections for the other exogenous variables are in Appendix F.

6. The base-case simulation results are described in Ho (1989) Appendix G.

7. A convenient summary of these data may be found in the *Council on Environmental Quality Annual Report*.

8. A detailed description of how these data are incorporated into our model is given in Wilcoxen (1988) Appendix D.

9. These are estimates in Wilcoxen (1988) for industries for which we have published data. These estimates include imputations on capital rental costs. Our data therefore are not identical to the official ones.

10. Sectors marked with a + have been suppressed by the Bureau of the Census because they are trivial, unreliably estimated, or confidential. Data for other years are in Wilcoxen (1988) Appendix D.

11. It should be pointed out again that water utilities ar only a small part of Services. The 24.0 percent of investment in the Services sector devoted to pollution abatement equipment is therefore due to a much larger share of new capital in water utilities. This is a non-traded sector and affects trade flows only through interindustry effects.

12. This share is higher than the one for the usual definition of U.S. capital stock which excludes household assets.

10 Stabilization of Carbon Emissions and International Competitiveness of U.S. Industries

Mun S. Ho and
Dale W. Jorgenson

10.1 Introduction

The relations between environmental policy and international trade, and between trades policy and the environment, have been the focus of much recent debate among both policy makers and the general public. A big portion of environmental concern has focused on the greenhouse effect—the emission of gases (carbon dioxide, methane, oxides of nitrogen, etc.) that trap heat in the atmosphere. There have been various proposals to control the emission of carbon dioxide from the burning of fossil fuels since it is the most important contributor of the greenhouse gases. These proposals, ranging from explicit quotas to taxes on carbon content, have important implications on production and trade patterns. These potentially far-ranging consequences have prompted much current research by economists. Dean (1992) and Nordhaus (1991) give a survey of some of the recent literature. This chapter examines the effects of the various proposed policies to reduce CO_2 emissions on U.S. trade patterns using a growth model of the U.S. economy.

   Much of the recent empirical research on the effects of environmental policies have made use of large-scale applied general equilibrium models to trace through the inter-industry, interregional effects. These models give a wide range of estimates of the effects of carbon taxes and other emissions reducing policies. They focus varying degrees of attention on commodity and energy trade issues. Six of these recent models are compared and summarized in Dean and Hoeller (1992).

   The OECD's GREEN global model (see Burniaux *et al.* (1992)) has twelve regions and eight sectors, of which five are energy related. There are three other sectors that provide "back-stop" energy sources (technologies that are currently not available but is assumed to be ready at some fixed future date at some price). It is a dynamic model with static expectations. The model estimates that, to stablize emissions in the European Community in the year 2000 at 1990 levels using carbon cum energy taxes, GDP would fall by merely half a percent.

Whalley and Wigle (1991) analyse the effects of taxes and CO_2 standards using a five-commodity, three-region world model. They find important differences between national and global taxes, between production and consumption taxes, and between different rules for allocating country targets. In the case of a national consumption tax (to reduce emissions by fifty percent, they find that the developed countries will experience a big reduction in net exports of energy-intensive commodities, while developing and oil exporting countries have a corresponding large increase. For non-energy intensive goods, developing countries have increased net exports while the other regions have lower net exports. Unlike the GREEN model, Whalley and Wigle's is static and assumes that goods from different regions are perfectly substitutable.

Manne and Richels (1990) *Global 2100* model is a five region dynamic perfect foresight model with detailed energy submodels. It also allows for backstop technologies and technological progress in energy use. The model, however, has little industry detail and trade flows are not accounted quite consistently. Manne (1992) reports that policies to hold emissions at 1990 levels beginning in the year 2000, will eventually lead to a loss of more than two percent of GDP for the U.S. He also reports how trade in emission rights would reduce this loss.

McKibbin and Wilcoxen (1998) is the most ambitious multi-region model to date. It has six regions and twelve sectors (five energy and seven non-energy), and consistently accounted for trade and financial flows. The capital stock in each sector adjusts with convex costs and agents have perfect foresight. Unlike the other models, this also provides details on the monetary side of the economy. McKibbin and Wilcoxen show how a unilateral carbon tax differs from a multilateral one; for the U.S. the current account improves more under a unilateral tax because the change in capital flows dominates the change in relative prices. These results are difficult to compare with those from non-monetary models.

Grossman and Krueger (1991) reverse the typical order of asking what the economic impact of environmental regulation is, and instead calculate the environmental impact of trade liberalization under the North American Free Trade Agreement. Using results from the general equilibrium model of Brown, Deardorff, and Stern (1992), they predict that air quality will improve and toxic emissions fall as Mexico shifts towards labor-intensive, cleaner industries.

Another approach in the empirical literature on environmental control costs is the use of one-country models. Such models do not have endogenous world trade and capital flows, but typically have very detailed sectoral and dynamic structures. Conrad and Schröder's (1991) model of the German state of Baden-Württemberg has explicit cost functions for abatement in each industry and for each type of pollutant (CO_2, SO_2, NO_x, particulates). The stocks of capital and consumer durables respond gradually to shocks with adjustment costs and static expectations. The unique feature of their research is that the counterfactual simulations are constrained to reach the same environmental standards as the base case. This allows a more direct welfare comparison of different policy instruments. They conclude that emission taxes are better than abatement subsidies which are superior to command and control policies. They also find, unsurprisingly, that taxes with international cooperation is superior to unilateral taxes. More unexpectedly, the fall in the trade balance is larger under the cooperation regime.

Goulder's (1991) single-country model of the U.S. has perfect foresight and sector specific capital. The model contains a detailed treatment of the long-term supply of oil and gas, and Goulder finds that the exhaustion of these primary fuels affects the time path of carbon taxes. Bergman's (1992) model of the Swedish economy is used to calculate an "environmental quality adjusted NNP" using estimates of willingness to pay for reductions in SO_2.

Jorgenson and Wilcoxen (1992b) used a growth model of the U.S. economy to examine the costs of different CO_2 reduction goals. The model has 35 sectors (five are energy related) and agents have perfect foresight. Producers are allowed to substitute between capital, energy, raw materials, and labor in a flexible manner. If CO_2 emissions are stabilized at 1990 levels right away, they find that national output would be 0.5 percent lower in the long run. If instead, emissions are stabilized at a level twenty percent lower than that of 1990, the fall in output is 1.6 percent. Other calculations are presented to illustrate the steep cost curve of curbing carbon pollution. This model is also used in Jorgenson and Wilcoxen (1990a), and Ho and Jorgenson (1992c), whereby they analyze the effects of actual U.S. environmental regulations of the 1960s and 1970s.

Nordhaus (1992c) extends the typical economic analysis to include equations of a simple climatic model. The side emissions of the production functions turn around and affect the future productivity of the economy. He finds that using the optimal public policy that takes such economic-climatic interactions into account will lead to a 0.04 percent higher value of discounted consumption than a laissez-faire policy. On the other hand, greenhouse gas control policies to limit global temperature increase to 1.5 degrees Celsius will result in a 4.66 percent reduction in consumption.[1]

In this study, we employ the model used in Jorgenson and Wilcoxen (1992b), and Ho and Jorgenson (1992a) to analyze the trade effects of achieving various CO_2 targets. As can be seen in figure 10.1, energy use in the U.S. has changed substantially in the last few decades; annual energy consumption per person has fallen from 350 million Btu in 1979 to 320 in 1991. Energy use per dollar of GDP has fallen even more dramatically. These changes cannot be explained completely by changes in prices. In examining the effects on taxes on fossil fuels it is therefore important to use a dynamic model that allows technology and preferences to be flexible and changeable.

These carbon emission targets that we study here are the same as those in the simulations reported in Jorgenson and Wilcoxen (1992b). We find that the high carbon taxes will reduce oil imports and raise other imports of other commodities. There is an improvement in the terms of trade, or fall in competitiveness; in the policy of medium stringency (stabilizing emissions at 1990 levels), the terms of trade improves by 1.3 percent. This means a reduction in aggregate exports, with exports of energy intensive goods—Primary Metal, Stone and Glass, and Chemicals—falling the most.

10.2 A Dynamic Model of the U.S. Economy

The model that we use, and its solution algorithm, is described in Jorgenson and Wilcoxen (1990a,b), and Ho and Jorgenson (1992b). We shall merely summarize the main features of the model here.

The model is a perfect-foresight, multi-sector Cass-Koopmans type growth model where the the optimal path of investment is chosen to maximize discounted returns. The economy is divided into household, business, government, and rest-of-the-world sectors. Since trade

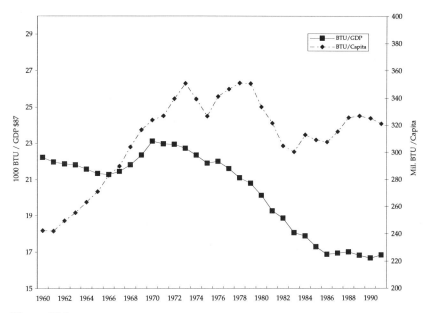

Figure 10.1
Energy use in U.S.

and environmental regulations vary substantially across industries, the business sector is further divided into 35 industries. The size and trade flows of the sectors in the model are illustrated by the 1985 figures in table 10.2.1. Twenty-one of these are manufacturing industries.

These industries produce domestic output using intermediate goods, capital, labor, and noncompetitive imports.[2] We distinguish between industries and commodities following official input-output conventions. Each industry produces a primary commodity and some secondary ones. Thirty-five commodities are represented, each corresponding to the primary product of one of the 35 industries. The term "commodities" refer to all items used in the economy, i.e., both goods and services. The input output structure of the model is illustrated in figures 10.2.1 through 10.2.4. The inputs of industry i may be seen as the ith column of the use table in figure 10.2.1. (The notation of the figures is explained in table 10.2.2. Matrix U represent the intermediate requirements for production while the rows N, K, and L represent factor inputs.)

Each domestic commodity group consist of products from several industries, mostly from the one for which it is the primary commodity.

Table 10.2.1
Sectoral characteristics of model, 1985 ($billion)

No.	Industry	Value added	Exports	Imports*
1	Agriculture	90.1	16.18	5.57
2	Metal mining	3.5	0.69	1.25
3	Coal mining	15.0	3.56	0.14
4	Oil and gas extraction	87.4	0.54	28.13
5	Non-metal mining	5.9	0.44	0.95
6	Construction	243.7	0.03	0.00
7	Food and kindred products	68.4	10.03	15.46
8	Tobacco	7.5	3.25	0.10
9	Textile mill	14.1	1.51	2.35
10	Apparel	26.1	1.10	21.83
11	Lumber and wood	22.1	2.32	4.59
12	Furniture	13.7	0.52	3.87
13	Paper and allied products	34.4	3.93	8.06
14	Printing and publishing	50.7	1.43	1.27
15	Chemicals	54.1	17.14	16.46
16	Petroleum refining	23.4	7.69	17.49
17	Rubber and plastic	36.3	8.26	9.00
18	Leather	3.5	0.47	6.86
19	Stone clay and glass	24.9	1.76	4.95
20	Primary metal	41.7	4.07	18.74
21	Fabricated metal	63.5	4.91	7.16
22	Machinery	97.4	38.08	37.08
23	Electrical machinery	88.1	21.65	46.26
24	Motor vehicles	51.5	19.03	64.29
25	Transportation equipment	57.1	23.38	6.86
26	Instruments	31.2	9.41	9.34
27	Miscellaneous manufactures	12.1	1.63	13.45
28	Transportation	133.1	20.70	5.00
29	Communications	89.2	1.84	0.00
30	Electric utilities	81.0	0.32	1.11
31	Gas utilities	25.4	0.45	0.00
32	Trade	503.5	22.60	12.27
33	Finance, insurance, and real estate	382.6	7.44	0.09
34	Services	645.6	7.87	0.06
35	Government enterprises	57.8	0.43	0.00

*Competitive imports only.

+Industry 33, "real estate" excludes owner-occupied housing. This is allocated directly to households.

This is represented by the "make table" in figure 10.2.2. The make up of commodity i is represented by column i of the M matrix, where the biggest element of the column is the M_{ii} element. Total supply of each commodity is the sum of domestic supply and competitive imports.

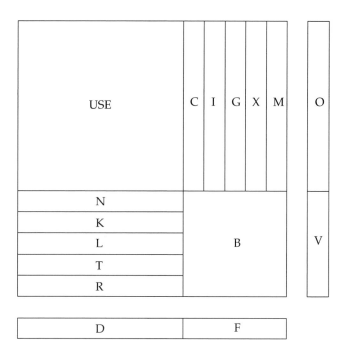

Figure 10.2.1
Organization of the use table.

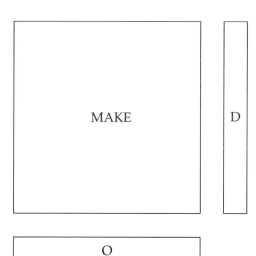

Figure 10.2.2
Organization of the make table.

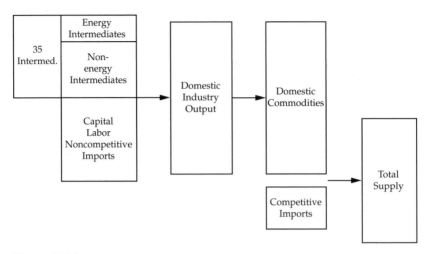

Figure 10.2.3
Supply of commodities.

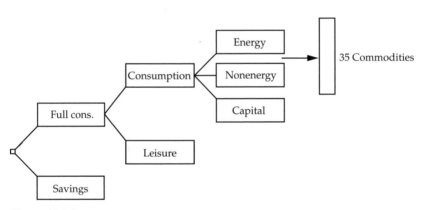

Figure 10.2.4
Consumer demand.

10.2.1 Producer Behavior

Output is produced from the two factors (capital and labor), the 35 intermediate commodities, and noncompetitive imports under constant returns to scale technology. We allow for fairly flexible substitution among these inputs unlike the typical Leontief approach. We have constructed econometric models of demands for all inputs by each industry. Inputs of capital, energy, and non-energy intermediates are identified separately since environmental regulations often require abatement equipment or restrictions on certain types of fuels (e.g.

Table 10.2.2
Make and use table variables

Category	Variable	Description
Industry-commodity flows:		
	U	Commodities *used* by industries (use table)
	M	Commodities *made* by industries (make table)
Final demand columns:		
	C	Personal consumption
	I	Gross private domestic investment
	G	Government spending
	X	Exports
	M	Imports
Value added rows:		
	N	Noncompeting imports
	K	Capital
	L	Labor
	T	Net taxes
	R	Rest of the world
Commodity and industry output:		
	O	Commodity output
	D	Industry output
Other variables:		
	B	Value added sold directly to final demand
	V	Total value added
	F	Total final demand

high sulfur coal). The left-hand column of figure 10.2.3 illustrates the production function,

$$Q = Q(\text{capital, labor, energy, non-energy, technology}).$$

Allowing for substitution among inputs is very important. A high degree of substitutability implies that the cost of regulation is low, while rigid production functions imply high costs. To estimate the substitution elasticities, we have constructed an annual time series of input-output tables for 1947–1985 corresponding to those outlined in figures 10.2.1 and 10.2.2. This is in constrast to the more typical calibration approach which derive parameters from a single period's data.

Environmental regulations may require specialized equipment or impose taxes that differ across commodities. This causes relative prices to change, inducing substitution among inputs. This change in the composition of inputs may affect the rate of productivity growth. In our producer model, we allow for endogenous technical progress where productivity change depends on the mix of inputs. This approach is discussed in Hogan and Jorgenson (1991).

10.2.2   Capitalist Behavior

In this model there is a single stock of private capital which is rented out to the 35 producers and the household sector. That is, we assume that capital is mobile across sectors in every period. There is essentially only one rental price of capital which is related to its marginal product. This may not be perfectly realistic for short-run analyses, however, the model will capture the long-run sectoral effects after the system had adjusted. Allowing for short-run adjustment costs will complicate the model considerably. We also ignore the effects of public capital.

Two dynamic equations characterize the behavior of the owner of the stock. The first is a backward-looking equation which states that the current stock of capital is the sum of past investments less depreciation. The second is a forward-looking equation linking interest rates to capital rental rates and capital gains (in net of tax, net of depreciation terms). Capital gains is made on the price of the capital stock. This stock price is forward-looking in that it incorporates expected future returns and future interest rates. We assume perfect foresight (there is no uncertainty) and these expected future values are realized in the dynamic solution of the model.

The capitalist also decides on the level of aggregate private investment and its composition. Aggregate investment is determined by savings of the household. This aggregate investment is made from all 35 different commodities and the composition is determined by relative commodity prices. The investor is allowed to substitute among these commodities, e.g., from Machinery to Motor Vehicles. This constitutes the *I* column in the input-output table figure 10.2.1. [Our definition of private capital is wider than most, we include not only industrial stocks but household durables like housing and vehicles as well.]

10.2.3   Consumer Behavior

We represent consumer preferences in three stages (figure 10.2.4). In the first stage the consumer allocates aggregate consumption to the commodities identified in the model—the 35 goods, noncompetitive imports, and capital. This is the C column in figure 10.2.1, usually referred to as *Personal Consumption Expenditures*. We constructed an econometric model of demands for these commodities allowing for substitution among them. Like the producer model above, we have separate input bundles of capital, energy, and non-energy items. This allows the consumer to substitute, say, from energy to capital when the price of electricity rises due to regulations to reduce emissions by electric utilities. This model is described in Jorgenson and Slesnick (1987a).

The consumption model of Jorgenson and Slesnick describes individual household demand for commodities. To use this for our aggregate model, we embed this detailed consumption model into a higher-level one via two further stages. In the second stage, we employ the concept of "full consumption," the aggregate of commodities and leisure. An aggregate consumer allocates full consumption, F_t, to leisure and personal consumption expenditures based on the wage rate and the price of the commodity aggregate. The consumer is given an exogenous time endowment which is allocated to leisure and labor supply. This labor supply is perfectly mobile across the 35 industries and government demand, just like the supply of capital. In the database for the model, aggregate time endowment is an index of the population which is cross classified by age, sex, and educational attainment. This should be viewed simply as a time series that adjust the effective labor input for the aging of the U.S. population and the improvement in educational attainment in the sample period (1947–1985). This time series also incorporates detailed projections of the U.S. population for post-sample simulations.[3]

In the third stage, the aggregate consumer makes intertemporal allocations. We view the consumer as maximizing a time separable utility function, a function that sums an infinite stream of full consumption, F_t, discounting at a rate ρ. The consumer is subject to a lifetime budget constraint where the present value of $\{F_t\}_0^\infty$ is equal to the present value of capital and labor income (net of taxes), and government transfers. The maximization of the intertemporal utility function gives an Euler equation that links the growth of F_t between two adjacent periods to the change in the price of full consumption and interest rates. The Euler equation is forward-looking; F_t incorporates expectations about the whole future path of prices and interest rates. Imposing our perfect foresight assumption, the Euler equation is satisfied at all points along the solution path of our model.

10.2.4   Government Behavior

The government plays a passive role in our model. It collects taxes on capital income, labor income, sales receipts, imports, and property. Its purchases includes all 35 commodities and labor. This is represented by column G in figure 10.2.1. The government also makes transfers and pays interest on its debt, which are included exogenously so that tax rates and deficits match the actual data. In the simulations of the model here, they do not play an important role. The government deficit is set exogenously, and cumulated to form the stock of public debt.

10.2.5   The Rest of the World

Ours is a one-country model where the rest of the world is modeled in a simple fashion. Our treatment is comparable to the *Global 2100* model of Manne and Richels (1990). The total supply of commodities to producers and households (the last column of figure 10.2.3) is the sum of domestic output (Q^C) and competitive imports (M):

$$P_i^S Q_i^S = P_i^C Q_i^C + P_i^M M_i \tag{10.1}$$

where P_i^S and Q_i^S denotes, respectively, the price and quantity of total supply of commodity i. The U.S. price of imports (P^M) is the world price ($P^M *$) multiplied by a world relative price variable e, and adjusted for tariffs (θ). For commodity i in period t:

$$P_{it}^M = (1 + \theta_{it})e_t P_{it}^M *. \tag{10.2}$$

We employ the usual Armington assumption that at our level of aggregation, the domestic and imported commodities are imperfect substitutes. For each of the tradeable commodity groups, we express the import share as a function of the price of imports relative to the price of the domestic good, and a time trend:

$$\frac{P_{it}^M M_{it}}{P_{it}^S Q_{it}^S} = \alpha + \beta \ln \frac{P_{it}^M}{P_{it}^C} + \gamma f(t). \tag{10.3}$$

The use of time on the right hand side instead of income is a little less typical but is also employed by Petri (1984) and Chipman *et al.* (1992). These import demands are econometrically estimated on data we constructed for the period 1964–1985. Details of the estimates and the form of the time trend $f(t)$ are given in Ho and Jorgenson (1992a). The results are summarized in table 10.2.3, where we also report substitution elasticities from other studies for comparison.[4]

The demands for noncompeting imports are determined by the producer model in a way symmetrical with the other inputs, and depend on import prices defined in a way identical to the one for competitive imports in equation (10.2).

Since we do not have an explicit endogenous model of the rest of the world, the demand for U.S. exports (X) is written simply as a function of world income $(Y *)$ and relative prices:

$$X_{it} = f(Y_t^*)[(1 + \theta_{it}^*)P_{it}^C/e_t P_{it}^*]^{\eta_i} \tag{10.4}$$

$P *$ is the world price, $\theta *$ the world tariff rate and η gives the degree of elasticity. These commodity exports constitute the column "X" in figure 10.2.1.

In the simulations, the foreign prices are set to the historical data for the sample period, and set equal to the 1985 prices for post-sample. Implicitly, the price of foreign goods that competes with U.S. exports is normalized to one. When counterfactual simulations are made, we assume that these foreign prices do not change.

For accounting completeness we take note of the financial flows (interest payments, foreign aid, etc.) but these, like the government interest payments noted above, play no significant role. The current account balance is exports of commodities, less competitive and noncompeting imports, plus net financial flows:

$$CA = \sum P_i^C X_i - \sum P_i^M M_i - \text{noncompeting imports}$$
$$+ \text{ net financial flows} \tag{10.5}$$

The current account is set exogenously and cumulated to form the stock of net U.S. foreign assets. This exogenous balance is attained with the endogenous e_t which gives a measure of the terms of trade, or aggregate competitiveness.

Table 10.2.3
Import demand elasticities

Industry	Substitution elasticities			Import price elasticities				
	Stern	Sheills	Ours	Stern	Sheills	Petri	Cline	Ours
Agriculture			0.70				-0.90	-0.68
Metal mining			0.11				-0.22	-0.09
Coal mining							-0.22	
Oil and gas mining							-0.22	
Non-metal mining			0.34				-0.22	-0.34
Construction								
Food and kindred	1.13	0.31	0.65	-1.13	-0.21		-1.13	-0.62
Tobacco	1.13	-16.2	2.60	-1.13	-7.57		-1.13	-2.59
Textile mill	1.15	2.58	1.62	-1.14	-1.41	-1.2	-2.43	-1.54
Apparel	4.27	1.62	1.27	-3.92	-0.52	-1.2	-2.43	-1.01
Lumber and wood	1.76	0.26	1.76	-0.69	-1.32	-1.4	-0.96	-1.60
Furniture	3.10	12.13	1.49	-3.00	-9.56	-1.4	-0.96	-1.36
Paper	1.58	1.80	1.16	-0.55	-1.80	-1.4	-1.44	-1.07
Printing and publishing	3.01	2.72	1.22	-3.00	-1.46	-1.4	-1.44	-1.20
Chemicals	2.61	9.85	1.20	-2.53	-6.82	-0.8	-0.97	-1.10
Petroleum refining	2.36	-0.34	1.09	-1.96	-0.79	-0.8	-0.97	-1.00
Rubber and plastic	5.71	2.67	1.76	-5.26	-1.32	-0.8	-3.57	-1.65
Leather	1.81	4.11	1.86	-1.58	-2.01		-2.46	-1.11
Stone clay and glass	1.63	4.29	1.86	-1.60	-2.86	-0.8	-1.37	-1.72
Primary metal	1.45	3.05	1.48	-1.42	-2.28	-1.6	-1.99	-1.29
Fabricated metal	3.67	1.54	1.13	-3.59	-0.94	-1.1		-1.08
Machinery	1.02	3.34	1.72	-1.02	-0.88	-0.9	-0.87	-1.53
Electrical machine	2.11	7.46	1.45	-1.00	-3.08	-0.6	-0.87	-1.23
Motor vehicles	3.59	2.01	1.52	-3.28	-1.24	-2.5	-2.53	-1.16
Transport. equipment	3.59	2.01	1.35	-3.28	-1.24	-2.5	-1.70	-1.28
Instruments	1.98	0.45	0.86	-1.08	-0.44	-0.9		-0.77
Misc. manufactures	1.98	3.55	1.52	-2.06	-2.37	-0.8	-4.44	-1.14
Transportation								
Communications								
Electric utilities								
Gas utilities								
Trade								
Finance, insurance								
Services								
Government enterprises								

The classification system used is different for each source. The entries are listed in categories closest to those used in this study.

Stern: Central tendencies in Stern, Francis and Schumacher (1976). Sample period before 1974.

Sheills: Sheills, Stern, and Deardorff (1986). Sample period 1962–78

Petri: Petri (1984), U.S. imports from rest of the world, excluding Japan. 1960–80.

Cline: Cline et al. (1978), page 58.

Ours: Elasticities evaluated at 1983 shares. Data from 1964–1985.

10.2.6   Carbon Emissions and the Energy Sectors

Using data from the U.S. Department of Energy and the Environmental Protection Agency, we calculated the energy and carbon content of each type of fuel. We assume that these are produced in fixed proportion to the quantity of fuel used, and that CO_2 cannot be removed in a relatively simple way like particulate pollution can be reduced using precipitators.[5] The data on emissions for 1987 are given in table 10.2.4. By convention, carbon dioxide emissions are expressed in tons of contained carbon. (Minor sources of energy, like wood burning, are ignored.)

Our model has a Coal Mining sector, an Oil and Gas Mining sector, and a Petroleum Refining sector (nos. 3, 4, and 16, respectively, in table 10.2.1). Prices in the model are normalized to one, and the quantities therefore are not tons or barrels. The coefficients in table 10.4 are

Table 10.2.4
Carbon emissions data for 1987

Units	Coal s.ton	Oil barrel	Gas 1000 ft^3	Uranium mil. lbs.
Heat Content 10^6 Btu per unit	21.94	5.80	1.03	
Carbon Emissions Rate kg per 10^6 Btu	26.9	21.4	14.5	0
kg per unit	590.2	124.1	14.9	0
Domestic Output 10^9 units	0.9169	3.033	17.8	0.013
Net Imports 10^9 units	−0.080	2.157	0.939	0.014
Energy consumed in U.S. 10^{15} Btu	18.4	32.9	17.7	4.9
Total Carbon Emissions 10^6 s.tons	494	710	307	0*
Use of Fuels (%) Electricity	85.8	3.3	16.5	100
Transportation	0	62.9	3.0	0
Other	14.2	33.8	80.5	0

1000 kg = 1. 102 s.ton (Hydroelectric sources : 3. 1 × 10^{15} Btu)

*Some indirect emissions are produced during processing of nuclear fuel.

Sources: *Annual Energy Review 1990*, DoE Environmental Protection Agency, Internal memo 1990

adjusted for the model's units using the total Btu produced in the combined oil and gas subsectors.

Carbon dioxide is not the only greenhouse gas emitted in the process of generating useful energy. Methane (CH_4), for example, is produced in the use of natural gas through leaks in the distribution system. It has twenty-five times the "greenhouse strength" as carbon dioxide.[6] However, CO_2 is the main source of greenhouse gas. It should also be noted that reducing the use of fossil fuels will not only reduce CO_2 emissions, but also sulphur dioxide, oxides of nitrogen, and other forms of pollution.

10.2.7   Static and Dynamic Equilibrium

At the start of every period, the economy inherits an exogenous population, and a stock of capital that is cumulated from past investments. For a given decision on the level of full consumption/savings by the aggregate consumer, all the markets will clear in that period by endogenous prices—the static equilibrium. The commodities markets are cleared by 35 goods prices, the factor markets are cleared by the rental price and wage rate, the exogenous government deficit is achieved by endogenous government purchases (tax rates are fixed), and finally, the exogenous current account balance is achieved by the endogenous world relative price e. (P_i^M and X_i in equation (10.5) are functions of e.) With the solution of the static equilibrium for that period, we have the level of investment and hence the stock of capital for the following period.

For intertemporal equilibrium, the Euler equation, linking adjacent full consumption, must be satisfied. Dynamic equilibrium is achieved when the entire path of the economy satisfies both the backward-looking capital accumulation equation and the forward-looking Euler equation. In the language of dynamic optimization, the costate variable—in this model, the level of full consumption—in the initial period, must be such that the economy is on the stable manifold going towards the steady state where the transversality conditions are satisfied. In figure 10.2.5 this is represented by the dashed line.

The steady state is characterized by two equations for the costate and state variables, $\dot{F} = 0$ and $\dot{K} = 0$, as drawn in figure 10.2.5. That is, full consumption is constant, the (net) marginal product of capital equals the rate of time preference, and investment exactly covers depreciation.

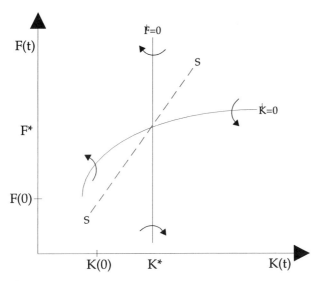

Figure 10.2.5
Saddle path and steady state.

To have a well defined steady state with non-homothetic prefer-ences, we require that technical progress falls eventually to zero. Oth-erwise infinitely rising incomes will drive some relative demands to infinity. The size of the economy in the long run is determined by the size of the population. That too rises eventually to a constant. In the steady state, all quantities and relative prices are constant. In that situ-ation, the tax adjusted rate of return on capital is equal to the rate of time preference, and investment exactly covers depreciation. The stock of capital is thus perfectly elastic in the long run, while being completely inelastic in the short run. The steady-state capital stock responds to shocks and policy changes; however, the rate of return is unchanged. This is unlike the original one-sector Cass-Koopmans model.

10.2.8   Exogenous Variables

The final item to be described are the exogenous variables. These are set to the data for the sample period 1947–1985. We project these vari-ables for 1986–2050 after which they are kept constant. We find that the year 2100 is sufficiently far out to be trivially different from the steady state. The exogenous variables are kept constant for 2050–2100 to allow time for the endogenous variables to converge to their steady-state values. The exogenous variables are the population, foreign variables, the budget, and current account deficits.

The population (time endowment) is projected by individual year of age, sex, and educational attainment using the population model of the Social Security Administration. The method of calculating the aggregate index of time endowment follows the system in Jorgenson and Fraumeni (1989). The post-sample world import prices are set to the 1985 relative prices. Domestic and foreign tariff rates are also set to the latest available data for the out-of-sample projections. World income for the export function is assumed to grow in a way similar to U.S. income. The long-run government and current account balances are set to historical averages.[7] Our approach is to compare the base-case simulation with counterfactual simulations, the paths by themselves are not of direct interest. How these exogenous variables are set, are therefore of secondary importance. What is important is that they are kept fixed for the different simulations.

10.3   Carbon Dioxide Emission Regulation and Trade

Our approach to examining the effects of carbon taxes is to first run a base-case simulation with the existing tax structure. The economy is simulated annually for the saddle path (1990–2100) where all intra- and intertemporal equilibrium conditions are satisfied. This involve computing $F(t = 0)$ given the inherited stock of capital $K(t = 0)$ as in figure 10.2.5. We then run policy simulations where greenhouse gas taxes are imposed. The resulting path of the economy is then compared to the base case. This is illustrated in figure 10.2.6 where SS is the base case saddle path and S'S' is the new path.

In the policy simulations, the level of government purchases is kept equal to the base case so that we can make direct welfare comparisons. The exogenous public deficit is also set to equal the base case; since there are now revenues from the new carbon tax we adjust the average labor income tax to maintain the original deficits. The marginal tax rates on labor, which affects labor supply, are kept unchanged. Changing the average rate but not the marginal one is equivalent to a lump sum transfer. As mentioned, the current account balance is set exogenously, and it is fixed relative to the wage numeraire. The current account in the policy simulations are the same as the base-case value.

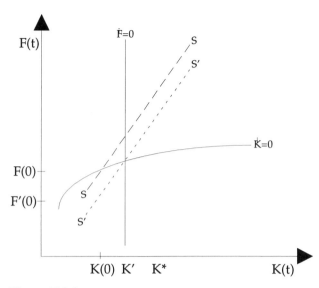

Figure 10.2.6
Effects of CO_2 policy.

We consider three different unilateral U.S. carbon tax policies to reduce carbon dioxide emissions:

C1. Stabilizing carbon emissions at the 1990 base level beginning immediately.

C2. Decreasing carbon emissions gradually over 1990–2005 until they are twenty percent below the 1990 base level.

C3. Doing nothing until 2000, then gradually increasing the carbon tax over 2000–2010 to stabilize emissions at the year 2000 base level.

In the base-case simulation, 1,576 million tons of carbon were produced in 1990 and 1,675 million tons in 2000.[8] Policy C1 will be quite stringent, keeping emissions at 1,576 million tons, in spite of the projected increase in population and incomes (the population is projected to rise by some thirty percent between 1990 and 2100 in our base-case assumptions). Policy C2 is the most restrictive. It requires emissions to fall to 1,261 million tons by 2005 and remain at that level thereafter. Policy C3 is the least stringent, but still requires a fall in *per capita* carbon emission over much of the simulation period. The time paths of the policy targets compared to the base case is given in figure 10.3.1.

We examine two types of tax policies to achieve these CO_2 targets: taxes on the carbon content of fossil fuels and taxes on the energy

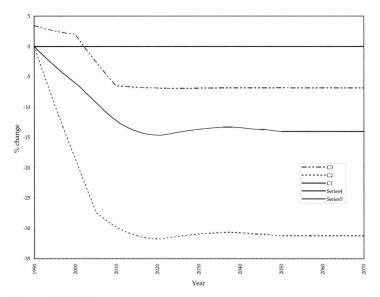

Figure 10.3.1(a)
Carbon emissions under policies 1, 2, and 3.

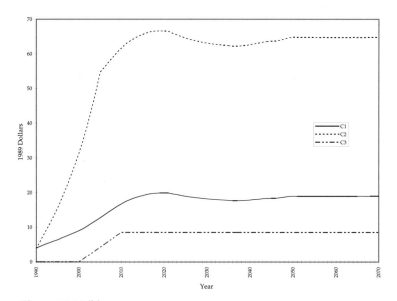

Figure 10.3.1(b)
Carbon taxes.

content. These taxes are applied to coal (output of industry no. 3) and the oil-gas aggregate (industry no. 4) in proportion to their carbon or energy content. Taxes are also placed on imported crude oil and gas (commodity 4), and on imported refined petroleum (16). Exports of coal, which constituted some 8–10% of domestic output in the late 1980s, are not exempt from these taxes for simplicity. The tax rates are determined endogenously given the emission targets. The tax revenue and offsetting changes in the labor tax are of course similarly endogenous.

10.3.1   Taxes on Carbon Content

We first consider taxes based on the carbon content of fossil fuels. The differences in the time paths between the carbon tax policy simulations and the base case are summarized in figures 10.3.2–10.3.4. We first discuss the long-run (steady state) differences.

Long-run effects

As described earlier, the steady state is characterized by the market clearing conditions of the static equilibrium, and two further conditions: (i) equality of net marginal product of capital and the rate of time preference, and (ii) equality of investment and depreciation (so that the capital stock is constant). Also recall that population is constant and that there is no technical progress in the steady state. The base case and "policy" steady states differ by the carbon tax rates required to meet the CO_2 targets. These taxes change prices and induce changes in quantities. Table 10.3.1 summarizes these long-run differences.

Policy C1, which maintains emissions at 1990 levels (first column of numbers in table 10.3.1) would reduce CO_2 output by fourteen percent in the steady state using a tax of $19 per ton of carbon. (Throughout the discussions here we would be using 1989 dollars.) This is equivalent to about $12.3 per ton of coal and should be compared to the price of a ton of "average" coal of $30 in 1989. For crude oil the tax is $2.6 per barrel compared to the 1989 price of about $18 a barrel.[9] The revenue from these taxes amount to some 0.48 percent of GNP and are offset by reducing the labor tax rate from 13.36% to 12.85 percent.

These changes result in higher consumer prices and price of capital (relative to the wage numeraire), and the capital stock is 0.8 percent

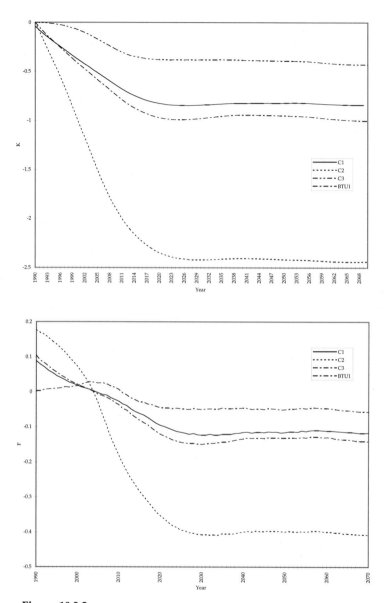

Figure 10.3.2
(a) Capital: % change from base case. (b) Full cons.: % change from base case.

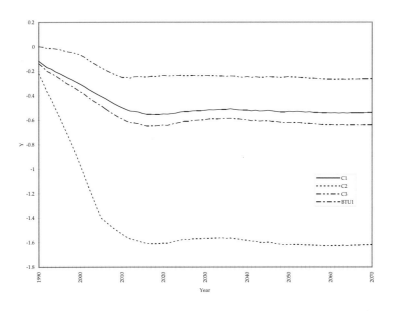

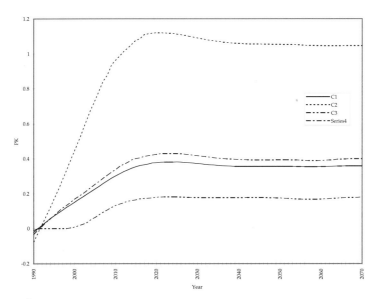

Figure 10.3.3
(a) GNP: % change from base case. (b) Price of K: % change from base case.

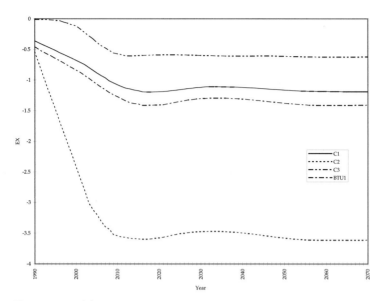

Figure 10.3.4(a)
Exports: % change from base case.

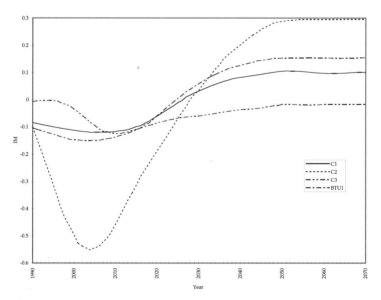

Figure 10.3.4(b)
Imports: % change from base case.

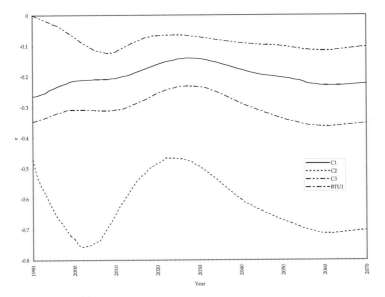

Figure 10.3.4(c)
Competitiveness: % change from base case.

smaller than the base case. Output is smaller by 0.6% and consumption by 0.5 percent. With the higher purchase price of energy, the demand for coal and oil falls. This results in domestic coal output falling by 28.6 percent and crude oil and gas output by 3.7 percent. This reduction in demand for oil reduce imports of oil by 3.6 percent. Given the exogenous trade deficit, which is a fixed value together with the fixed wage numeraire, the fall in demand for oil imports require a decrease in the relative price e (an appreciation) to induce higher imports of other goods and lower exports. This can be seen by writing equation (12.5) conceptually as:

$$\overline{CA} = P^C X(\underset{+}{e}) - P^M_{oil} M_{oil}(\underset{-}{e}) - P^M_{other} M_{other}(\underset{-}{e}).$$

The 0.2% improvement in the terms of trade (fall in competitiveness) is reflected by the fall in aggregate exports of 1.2% and a virtually unchanged total imports.

The sectoral effects are dominated by the huge rise in coal prices. The changes in industry output prices are given in figure 10.3.5(a). The increase in prices of coal and oil (both domestic and imported) result in higher electric and gas bills. The increase in energy costs result in relatively higher prices of energy-intensive industries like

Table 10.3.1
Steady-state effects of imposing carbon taxes (% change from base case unless otherwise indicated)

	Carbon Tax Policies			Btu Tax
	C1 1990 level	C2 80% of 1990	C3 2000 level	1990 level
Capital Stock	−0.8	−2.4	−0.4	−1.0
Output	−0.6	−1.6	−0.3	−0.6
Full–consumption	−0.1	−0.4	−0.0	−0.1
Goods consumption	−0.5	−1.6	−0.2	−0.6
Exports	−1.2	−3.6	−0.6	−1.4
Imports	0.1	0.3	−0.0	0.1
Oil imports*	−3.63	−11.4	−1.67	−4.89
Coal output	−28.6	−55.0	−15.8	−27.1
Crude output+	−3.7	−12.2	−1.7	−5.0
Price of capital	0.3	1.0	0.2	0.4
Consumer prices	0.7	2.1	0.3	0.8
e	−0.2	−0.7	−0.1	−0.4
Carbon emissions	−14	−31	−8	−14
Carbon tax ($/ton)	18.9	64.7	8.6	
Btu tax ($/mBtu)				0.52
Tax on coal ($/ton)	12.3	42.1	5.6	11.3
Tax on oil ($/bbl)	2.6	8.8	1.2	3.0
Tax on labor^ (rate)	12.85%	12.02%	13.11%	12.76%

* This is the sum of Crude oil and gas, and Refined oil imports (Commodity nos. 4 and 16)

+ Output of Oil and Gas Mining (Sector 4).

^ Tax rate on labor in base case = 13.36 percent

** Prices are relative to the wage numeraire.

Chemicals, Primary Metals, and Stone-Glass. These industries suffer a corresponding higher fall in output (not shown in the figures).

These price changes and the fall in e result in a shift of trade patterns drawn in figure 10.3.5(b).[10] Coal exports fall by a huge 37 percent, while Petroleum Refining exports fall by 10 percent. The other big losers in exports are the same energy-intensive industries— Primary Metals, Rubber, and Stone-Glass. For imports, there is a big reduction in the small volume of coal imports (cross-border trade with Canada), and a 4.2 percent fall in crude oil imports. As indicated, the improvement in the terms of trade, given by the fall in e, leads to a small increase in the imports of other commodities. The changes in trade flows in figure 10.3.5(b) should be read with both the changes in domestic prices, as well as the import elasticities (table 10.2.3) in mind.

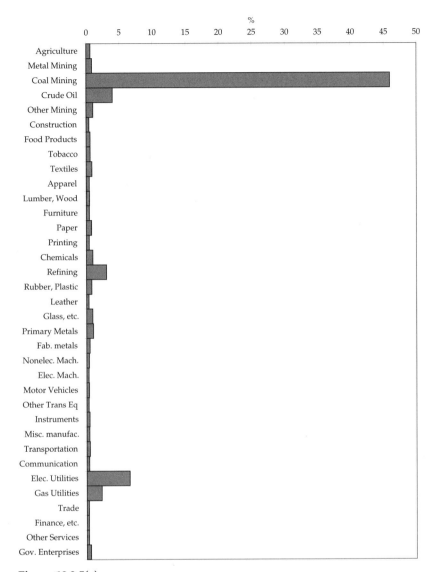

Figure 10.3.5(a)
Price of domestic output: Policy 1. % change.

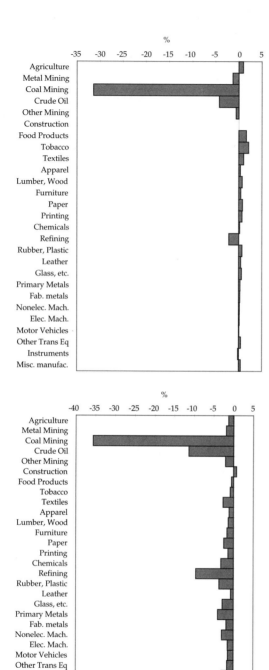

Figure 10.3.5.(b)
Top: Competitive imports: Policy 1. % change. Bottom: Exports: Policy 1. %
change.

(The panel for imports in figure 10.3.5(b) are for competitive imports only. The raw materials in the noncompetitive group are affected in proportion to the change in the output of the various importing industries.)

Policy C2, which is the strictest one examined here, affects the economy in the same direction as the first policy, but in a more exaggerated manner. This can be seen by comparing the first and second columns of table 10.3.1. This restrictive goal is achieved by taxes that raise the price of coal 155 percent above the base case. The revenues from this carbon tax are so substantial that the average labor income tax rate are reduced from 13.36 percent to 12.02 percent, financing the same level of government expenditures.

The long-run capital stock is now 2.4 percent lower than the base case while annual output is 1.6 percent smaller. The terms of trade effect due to the exogenous current account deficit is even bigger, e falls by 0.7 percent, total exports is down 3.6 percent, while total imports rise by 0.3 percent. The energy related sectors are dramatically affected, Coal output falls by more than half while Oil and Gas Mining falls by an eighth. Exports of coal falls by 69 percent while those of Petroleum Refining fall by 30 percent (see figure 10.3.6). Again, the heavily affected industries outside the energy producing sector are the energy-intensive Primary Metals, Rubber, and Chemicals. On the import side, U.S. purchases of coal and crude falls due to the reduction in overall energy demand because of the carbon taxes, while imports rise for most of the other commodities with the overall improvement in the terms of trade.

Policy C3 is the least restrictive and the long-run results are milder compared to the first policy's but very similar in relative effects. The sectoral results are given in figure 10.3.7. The total carbon tax revenue amounts to some 0.23 percent of steady state GNP.

Dynamic path of effects of carbon targets

The restrictiveness over time of the CO_2 targets are illustrated in figure 10.3.1. [All the vertical axes in figures 10.3.1–10.3.4 are percentage changes of the policy paths from the base case, except for the "Carbon Taxes" graph which is in 1989 dollars.] Stabilizing emissions at 1990 levels (Policy C1) eventually means a 14 percent reduction from base-case levels. For this policy, carbon taxes rise steadily between 1990 and 2020, reaching some $19 per ton of carbon. To reach the twenty percent

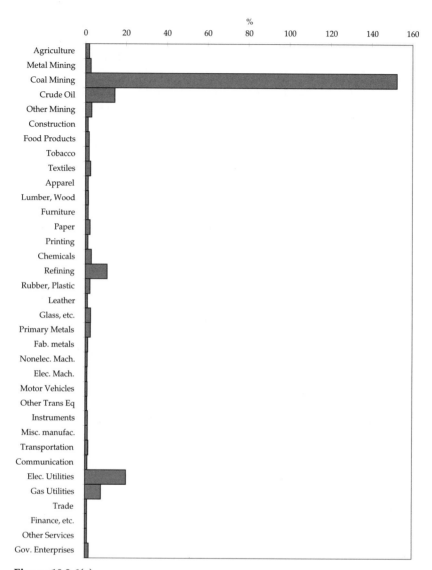

Figure 10.3.6(a)
Price of domestic output: Policy 2. % change.

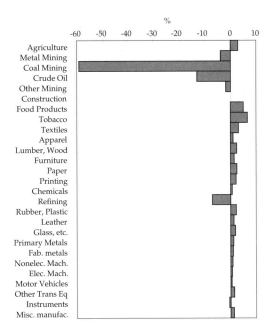

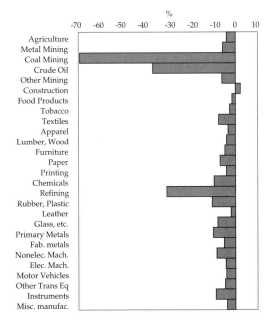

Figure 10.3.6(b)
Top: Competitive imports: Policy 2. % change. Bottom: Exports: Policy 2. % change.

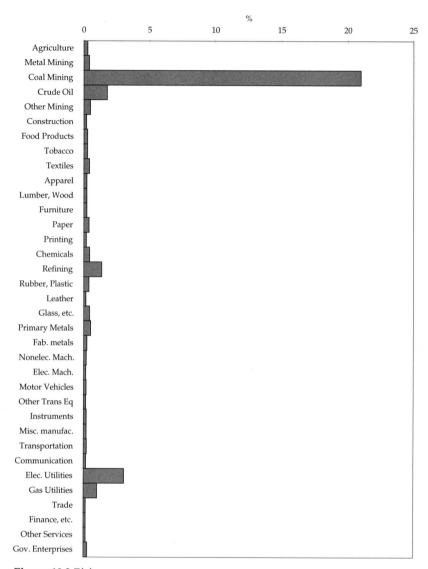

Figure 10.3.7(a)
Price of domestic output: Policy 3. % change.

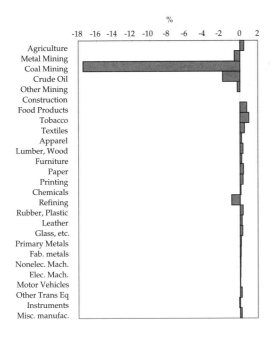

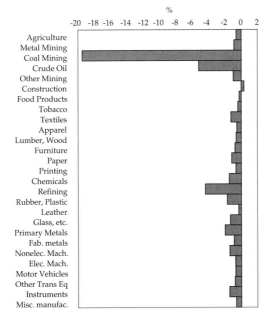

Figure 10.3.7(b)
Top: Competitive imports: Policy 3. % change. Bottom: Exports: Policy 3. % change.

reduction goal of Policy C2, the tax rises eventually to $65 per ton. (To translate this to $ per ton of coal, multiply by 0.6504; to $ per barrel of oil multiply by 0.1368. See the last few lines of table 10.3.1.)

The nonlinear effects of the emissions targeting are obvious when the two panels of figure 10.3.1 are compared. Doubling the percentage reduction in emissions require a tripling of the tax rate.

As taxes are levied on coal and oil, the prices of energy (Petroleum Refining, Electric Utilities, and Gas Utilities) rise. This induces a gradual substitution away from energy towards the other inputs. The net effect on prices is to raise commodity prices relative to the wage numeraire. The effect on the price of capital is typical and shown in figure 10.3.3. These price increases lower the price of leisure and reduce labor supply. The net effect on aggregate quantities is to lower output, consumption of goods, and investment. This results in the lower path of capital accumulation as shown in figure 10.3.2. The effect is cumulative, less initial output and lower investment gives a smaller capital stock which lowers future output even more. In the long run, output is 0.5 percent lower under Policy C1. In the case of Policy C2, output falls substantially more sharply in the first fifteen years when emissions targets are tightened. Again the nonlinear effect on output is clear, it falls by 1.6 percent in the steady state.

With respect to external flows, as prices of domestic goods rises relative to the fixed world prices, the imports of most commodities tend to rise and exports tend to fall. The important exception is coal and oil, imports of these goods are taxed at the same rate as domestic producers and exports are not exempt. Thus, there is no substitution effect between domestic and imported varieties for these two goods that together have a prominent share of U.S. trade. The net effect is substitution away from these energy goods to other inputs; both domestic output and imports of the raw energy materials—Coal (3) and Oil and Gas (4)—are reduced.

The large reduction in imported oil reverses the initial tendency for the imports of the other commodities to rise. This is due to the exogenous current account deficit which is fixed (in terms of the wage numeraire) at equal levels for all simulations. With the large reduction in the imports of crude and refined oil, the world relative price e has to adjust to induce imports of other commodities and reduce exports to reach these exogenous aggregate deficit targets. This means a fall in e as drawn in figure 10.3.3. Another way of looking at this is that a more "protectionist" policy, with respect to oil, improves the overall terms of trade and reduces the competitiveness of output from the manufacturing sectors. This aggregate effect is substantial. For the strictest case, Policy C2, there is a 3.6 percent fall in total exports in the long run and a 0.3 percent rise in total imports. The total exports and imports plotted in figure 10.3.4 are divisia indices aggregated over all the thirty-five commodities.

10.3.2   Comparing Btu Taxes with Carbon Taxes

We now examine the proposal to tax fuels in proportion to the energy content rather than the carbon content. As can be seen from the first three lines of table 10.2.4 the energy proportions of the different units of fuels are closer than the carbon proportions. This means different carbon-energy ratios for the three fuels, with the highest ratio for coal. A tax on carbon content affects coal the most, while an energy tax to reduce CO_2 emissions by the same amount would be less severe on coal and will fall relatively more on oil and gas.

We did another simulation with the same targets as Policy C1: maintaining emissions at 1990 levels immediately, but with a tax applied in proportion to the heat content of the three primary fuels as given in the first line of table 10.2.4. Nuclear and hydroelectric power inputs into the "Electric Utilities (30)" industry are exempt from this "energy tax." The long-run results are given in the last column of table 10.3.1.

The energy tax in the steady state is $0.52 per million Btu which is equivalent to a $11.3 per ton tax on coal and a $3.0 per barrel tax on oil. This is to be compared to the first column in the table which achieves the same emissions using a carbon tax. There the coal tax is $12.3 and the oil tax is only $2.6. With the higher tax rate on oil, which supplies the largest share of Btu in the U.S., the CO_2 tax revenues is higher in this regime (0.57 percent of GNP), and the offsetting labor tax falls to 12.76 percent, instead of 12.85 percent in the carbon tax regime.

This less efficient carbon control instrument results in a long-run capital stock which is one percent lower than the base case, and goods consumption which is 0.6 percent lower. This is more severe than the carbon tax outcome. With the bigger tax on oil, Oil-Gas imports are curbed more compared to Policy C1, falling by 4.89 percent. This forces a bigger adjustment in the world relative price e, which appreciates by 0.4 percent. This improvement in the terms of trade lead to a 1.4 percent fall in total exports and a 0.1 percent increase in total imports.

With a less extreme tax of coal the differences in sectoral changes are smaller as illustrated in figure 10.3.8(a,b). As before, the main export losers are Coal, and the energy intensive manufacturing industries—Primary Metals, Rubber, and Chemicals. The dynamic path under the Btu tax is similar to the path of Policy C1 but with a bigger percentage change from the base path.

The results of this section are unsurprising, given the carbon-energy differences among the various fuels. What needs to be examined for welfare analysis is whether the higher tax revenues from the greater distortion of using this indirect instrument to curb carbon emissions can reduce other pre-existing tax distortions. The results above are essentially lump sum adjustments.

10.4   Conclusion

Carbon taxes to reduce emissions from the main source of greenhouse gases affect the trade flows of the U.S. through three main channels in this model. The first is the usual substitution effect as less oil is imported and production processes shift towards capital, labor, and other materials. Given the different energy intensities in the production of the various goods, the second channel is to shift the composition of trade surplus away from the energy intensive goods. The third channel is the dynamic effects which reduce capital accumulation and change the rate of technical progress. This gives both income and compositional effects on the trade patterns.

Our model is able to trace the first effect by specifying the production functions in a flexible manner with capital, labor, energy, and materials as separate arguments. The detailed disaggregation allows us to trace the compositional effects at the two-digit level. Finally, the dynamic structure of the model allows us to distinguish the short- and long-run effects.

We should finally note here what we have ignored or assumed away. The model does not have an endogenous rest-of-the-world (ROW) structure and therefore have not allowed for changes in world prices of commodities in response to U.S. changes. The compositional effects here would be mitigated if the ROW changes their prices in response to higher U.S. coal and oil prices. For the same reason, we cannot study here the effects on world investment flows, i.e., shifts in current account balances. In addition, we have not considered the possibility that foreign governments may change their tax policies.[11]

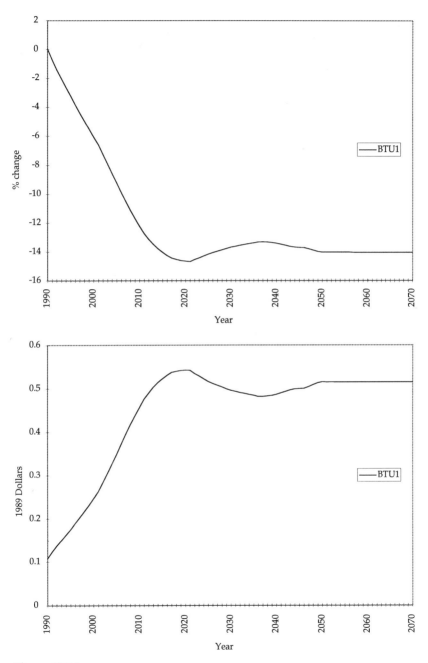

Figure 10.3.8
(a) Carbon emissions: Btu tax policy. (b) Btu taxes.

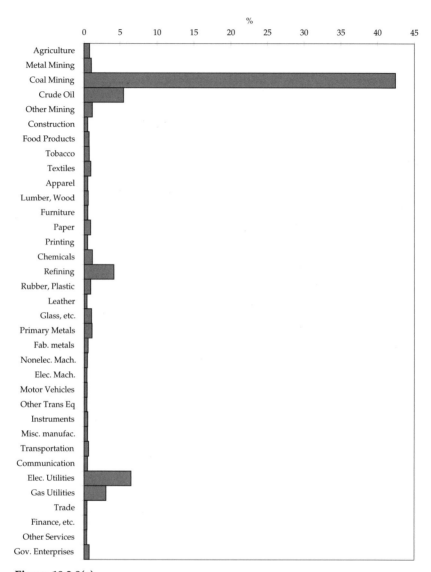

Figure 10.3.9(a)
Price of domestic output: Btu Policy. % Change.

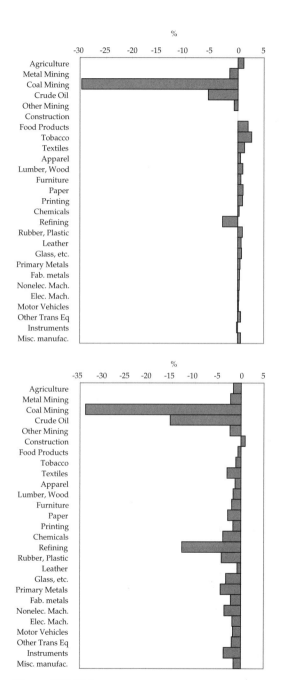

Figure 10.3.9(b)
Top: Competitive imports: Btu Policy. % change. Bottom: Exports: Btu Policy.
% change.

Like most numerical economic models, we have not taken into account backward linkages between climatic change and productivity as done in Nordhaus (1992). This could potentially be important for agricultural products. Additionally, we have not allowed for the possibility of new technologies in the production and consumption of energy.

While our model is highly disaggregated in comparison to other models, it is still not refined enough to address some important issues. As an example, there are two commodities for vehicles identified in our model: Motor Vehicles, and Other Transportation Equipment. Substitution from autos to bicycles, or denser living arrangements, will not be captured at this level of analysis. Finally, we have only considered the costs and tangible effects of CO_2 taxes, the potential benefits of reducing these emissions are not examined.

Notes

1. Simulations of policies in terms of temperature changes are difficult to compare with those using carbon targets. There is a huge range of uncertainty with respect to the temperature effects of carbon dioxide concentrations. Doubling the concentration from 300 to 600 ppm is projected to raise global temperatures anywhere from 1.5 degree C to 5.5 degrees. (See, e.g., Schneider (1989).)

2. Noncompetitive imports (N) are those defined by the BEA to be goods that have no close subsitutes produced in the U.S. The main items are tropical agricultural products (e.g. natural rubber) and foreign travel. These constituted thirteen percent of non-factor imports in 1985.

3. See Ho (1989) Appendix C for detailed definitions.

4. A detailed description of how the trade data is constructed and incorporated into our model is given in Ho (1989) Appendix H.

5. The costs of such methods of pollution control are discussed in Jorgenson and Wilcoxen (1990a,b). The removal of carbon dioxide is estimated to be a very expensive process even if feasible. (See Steinberg, Cheng, and Horn.)

6. See Dean Abrahamson (1989) "Relative Greenhouse Heating from the Use of Fuel Oil and Natural Gas" University of Minnesota.

7. The population projections and the construction of the industry labor inputs are described in Ho (1989) Appendix C; projections for the other exogenous variables are in Appendix F.

8. Throughout the chapter "tons" are short tons.

9. Prices are from *Annual Energy Review* tables.

10. For brevity the table gives only changes in the manufacturing and mining sectors. There is trade in the other "services" sectors which are usually thought of as non-tradables. These trade flows are kept in order to be consistent with the official data, their import demands are set as simple Cobb-Douglas functions.

11. Low and Safadi (1992) discuss the issues of setting environmental and trade policies in a world of sovereign nations, including both cooperative and non-cooperative arrangements. They point out the difficulties of these agreements that may require side payments.

11

Fundamental Tax Reform and Energy Markets

Dale W. Jorgenson and
Peter J. Wilcoxen

11.1 Introduction

Intertemporal general equilibrium modeling provides a natural framework for economic analysis of the impact of taxes.[1] The organizing mechanism of these models is an intertemporal price system balancing demand and supply for products and factors of production. The intertemporal price system links the prices of assets in every time period to the discounted value of future capital services. This forward-looking feature is combined with backward linkages among investment, capital stock, and capital services in modeling the dynamics of economic growth. Alternative time paths of economic growth depend on taxes through their impact on capital accumulation.

In Jorgenson and Wilcoxen (1990a) we have presented a highly disaggregated intertemporal general equilibrium model for analyzing the impact of tax policies. We employ an econometric general equilibrium model of production originated by Jorgenson and Fraumeni (1981). This includes systems of demand functions for inputs and a model of endogenous productivity growth for each of thirty-five sectors of the U.S. economy. Our model also incorporates a model of aggregate consumer behavior based on the exact aggregation approach of Jorgenson, Lau, and Stoker (1982). This dispenses with the notion of a representative consumer employed in previous econometric models of aggregate consumer behavior and includes a system of demand functions for commodity groups.

In this chapter, we present a new intertemporal general equilibrium model for analyzing the economic impact of tax policies for the U.S. We preserve the key features of more highly aggregated intertemporal general equilibrium models. One important dimension for disaggregation is to introduce a distinction between industries and commodities, in order to measure tax impacts for narrower segments of the economy. This also makes it possible to model differences among industries in responses to changes in taxes. A second dimension for disaggregation is to distinguish among households by level of wealth and demographic characteristics. This makes it possible to model differences in responses to tax-induced price changes. It is also useful in examining the distributional effects of taxes. We present the model in more detail in the following section.

To analyze the impact of alternative tax policies, we introduce models of the demand for different types of capital services for each of thirty-five industrial sectors of the U.S. economy and the household sector. These models depend on tax policies through measures of the cost of capital for each type of capital services presented by Jorgenson and Yun (1991b). These measures of the cost of capital incorporate the characteristic features of U.S. tax law. The concept of the cost of capital makes it possible to represent the economically relevant features of highly complex tax statutes in a very succinct form. The cost of capital also summarizes information about the future consequences of investment decisions required for current decisions about capital allocation. We describe the provisions of U.S. tax law that have been incorporated into our model in the third section.

Finally, to illustrate the application of our new model, we consider the impact of fundamental tax reform on energy markets and carbon emissions. For this purpose, we consider the effects of substituting a tax on consumption for income taxes at both federal and state and local levels in the United States. More rapid economic growth resulting from tax reform would result in more energy consumption and greater carbon emissions. However, changes in relative prices could stimulate energy conservation through gains in the efficiency of energy use. Whether more rapid economic growth would outweigh the effects of energy conservation after fundamental tax reform has important implications for U.S. policy-makers. Subsequently, the U.S. negotiated an international agreement on climate policy at the Kyoto meeting of the parties to the 1992 Rio Summit agreement in December 1997.

11.2   An Overview of the Model

In Jorgenson and Wilcoxen (1993d), we describe the econometric implementation of an intertemporal general equilibrium model of the U.S. economy. In this section, we outline the model, emphasizing features that are critical in assessing tax policy impacts. We have constructed submodels for each of four sectors of the U.S. economy—business, household, government, and the rest of the world. Since tax policies affect industries in very different ways, we begin our presentation with the business sector.

11.2.1   Producer Behavior

Modeling the response of producers to changes in tax policies requires distinguishing among industries with different capital intensities. Accordingly, we have subdivided the business sector into the thirty-five industries shown in table 11.1. Each of these corresponds, roughly, to a two-digit industry in the Standard Industrial Classification. This level of industrial disaggregation makes it possible to measure the impact of alternative policies on relatively narrow segments of the U.S. economy. We have also divided the output of the business sector into thirty-five commodities. Each one is the primary product of one of the industries. Many industries produce secondary products as well; for example, the textile industry produces both textiles and apparel, so that we have allowed for joint production. Each commodity is allocated between deliveries to intermediate demands by other industries and deliveries to final demands by households, governments, and the rest of the world.

We represent the technology of each industry by means of an econometric model of producer behavior. In order to estimate the unknown parameters of these production models, we have constructed an annual time series of inter-industry transactions tables for the U.S. economy for the period 1947 through 1985.[2] The data for each year are divided between a use table and a make table. The use table shows the quantities of each commodity—intermediate inputs, primary factors of production, and noncompeting imports—used by each industry and final demand category.[3] The make table gives the amount of each commodity produced by each industry. In the absence of joint production this would be a diagonal array. The organization of the use and make tables is illustrated in figures 11.1 and 11.2; table 11.2 provides definitions of the variables appearing in these figures.

The econometric method for parameterizing our model stands in sharp contrast to the calibration method used in previous general equilibrium modeling of tax policies. Calibration involves choosing

Table 11.1
Industry classifications

Number	Description
1	Agriculture, forestry, and fisheries
2	Metal mining
3	Coal mining
4	Crude petroleum and natural gas
5	Nonmetallic mineral mining
6	Construction
7	Food and kindred products
8	Tobacco manufacturers
9	Textile mill products
10	Apparel and other textile products
11	Lumber and wood products
12	Furniture and fixtures
13	Paper and allied products
14	Printing and publishing
15	Chemicals and allied products
16	Petroleum refining
17	Rubber and plastic products
18	Leather and leather products
19	Stone, clay, and glass products
20	Primary metals
21	Fabricated metal products
22	Machinery, except electrical
23	Electrical machinery
24	Motor vehicles
25	Other transportation equipment
26	Instruments
27	Miscellaneous manufacturing
28	Transportation and warehousing
29	Communication
30	Electric utilities
31	Gas utilities
32	Trade
33	Finance, insurance, and real estate
34	Other services
35	Government enterprises

parameters to replicate the data for a particular year.[4] Almost all general equilibrium models employ the assumption of fixed "input-output" coefficients for intermediate goods, following Johansen (1960). This allows the ratio of the input of each commodity to the output of an industry to be calculated from a single use table like the one presented in figure 11.1; however, it rules out substitution among intermediate goods, such as energy and materials, by assumption. It

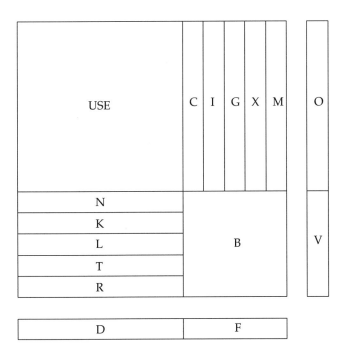

Figure 11.1
Organization of the use table.

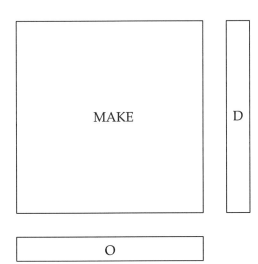

Figure 11.2
Organization of the make table.

Table 11.2
Make and use table variables

Category	Variable	Description
Industry-commodity flows:		
	USE	Commodities *used* by industries (use table)
	MAKE	Commodities *made* by industries (make table)
Final demand columns:		
	C	Personal consumption
	I	Gross private domestic investment
	G	Government spending
	X	Exports
	M	Imports
Value added rows:		
	N	Noncompeting imports
	K	Capital
	L	Labor
	T	Net taxes
	R	Rest of the world
Commodity and industry output:		
	O	Commodity output
	D	Industry output
Other variables:		
	B	Value added sold directly to final demand
	V	Total value added
	F	Total final demand

Note: See figures 11.1 and 11.2 for organizational layout.

also ignores the distinction between industries and commodities and rules out joint production.

The econometric approach to parameterization has several advantages over the calibration approach. First, by using an extensive time series of data rather than a single data point, we can derive the response of production patterns to changes in prices from historical experience. This is particularly important for the analysis of tax policies, since tax policies have changed substantially during our sample period and tax rates have varied widely. The calibration approach imposes responses to these changes through the choice of functional forms rather than econometric analysis of empirical evidence.

A second advantage of the econometric approach is that parameters estimated from time series are much less likely to be affected by the peculiarities of the data for a particular time period. By construction, parameters obtained by calibration are forced to absorb all the random errors present in the data for a single benchmark year. This poses a severe problem when the benchmark year is unusual in some respect. For example, parameters calibrated to the year 1973 would incorporate into the model all the distortions in energy markets that resulted from price controls and the rationing of energy during the first oil crisis. Econometric parameterization greatly mitigates this problem by reducing the influence of disturbances for a particular time period.

Empirical evidence on substitutability among inputs is essential in analyzing the impact of tax policies. If it is easy for industries to substitute among inputs, the effects of these policies will be very different than if substitution were limited. Although calibration avoids the burden of data collection required by econometric estimation, it also specifies the substitutability among inputs by assumption rather than relying on empirical evidence. This can easily lead to substantial distortions in estimating the effects of tax policies.

11.2.2   Consumer Behavior

The substitution of a consumption tax for an income tax would affect relative prices faced by consumers. However, this substitution would have different impacts on different households. To capture these differences among households, we have subdivided the household sector into demographic groups that differ by characteristics such as family size, age of head, region of residence, race, and urban versus rural location. We treat each household as a consuming unit, so that the household behaves like an individual maximizing a utility function.

We represent the preferences of each household by means of an econometric model of consumer behavior. Our models of consumer behavior incorporate time series data on personal consumption expenditures from the annual inter-industry transactions tables for the U.S. economy represented in figure 11.1. The econometric approach for parameterization enables us to derive the response of household expenditure patterns to changes in prices from historical experience. Empirical evidence on substitutability among goods and services by households is essential in analyzing the impact of alternative tax policies. If it is easy for households to substitute among commodities, the effects of these policies will be very different than if substitution were limited.

The econometric approach to modeling consumer behavior has the same advantages over the calibration approach as those we have described for modeling producer behavior. An additional feature of our models of consumer behavior is that they incorporate detailed cross-sectional data on the impact of demographic differences among households and levels of total expenditure on household expenditure patterns. We do not require that consumer demands are homothetic, so that patterns of individual expenditure change as total expenditure varies, even in the absence of price changes. This captures an important characteristic of cross-section observations on household expenditure patterns that is usually ignored in general equilibrium modeling.

Finally, we aggregate over individual demand functions to obtain a system of aggregate demand functions. This makes it possible to dispense with the notion of a representative consumer. The system of aggregate demand functions allocates total expenditure to broad groups of consumer goods and services. Given prices and total expenditure, this system allows us to calculate the elements of personal consumption column in the make table of figure 11.1. We employ the model to represent aggregate consumer behavior in simulations of the U.S. economy under alternative tax policies.

To determine the level of total expenditure, we embed our model of personal consumption expenditures in a higher-level system that represents consumer preferences between goods and leisure and between saving and consumption. At the highest level, each household allocates *full wealth*, defined as the sum of human and nonhuman wealth, across time periods. We formalize this decision by introducing a representative agent who maximizes an additive intertemporal utility function, subject to an intertemporal budget constraint. The allocation of full wealth is determined by the rate of time preference and the intertemporal elasticity of substitution. The representative agent framework requires that intertemporal preferences must be identical for all households.

We model the household allocation decision by assuming that full consumption is an aggregate of goods and leisure. Our model of consumer behavior allocates the value of full consumption between personal consumption expenditures and leisure time. Given aggregate expenditure on goods and services and its distribution among households, this model then allocates personal consumption expenditures among commodity groups, including capital and labor services and noncompeting imports. Finally, the income of the household sector is the sum of incomes from the supply of capital and labor services, interest payments from governments and the rest of the world, all net of taxes, and transfers from the government. Savings are equal to the difference between income and consumption, less personal transfers to foreigners and nontax payments to governments.

11.2.3   Investment and Capital Formation

Our investment model, like our model of saving, is based on perfect foresight or rational expectations. Under this assumption, the price of investment goods in every time period is based on expectations of future capital service prices and discount rates that are fulfilled by the solution of the model. In particular, we require that the price of new investment goods is always equal to the present value of future capital services.[5] The price of investment goods and the discounted value of future rental prices are brought into equilibrium by adjustments in future prices and rates of return. This incorporates the forward-looking dynamics of asset pricing into our model of intertemporal equilibrium.

In each of the thirty-five industrial sectors and the household sector the demand for capital services is first subdivided between corporate and noncorporate subsectors. Within each of these subsectors the demand for capital is further subdivided between short-lived assets or equipment and long-lived assets—structures, inventories, and land. The prices for these different types of capital services reflect provisions of U.S. tax law for taxation of capital income in corporate, noncorporate, and household sectors. These prices also include tax provisions that affect short-lived and long-lived assets differently, such as depreciation allowances and investment tax credits. A detailed description of these tax provisions, based on that developed by Jorgenson and Yun (1991b), is given in the following section.

For tractability, we assume there is a single capital stock in the economy which is perfectly malleable and mobile among sectors, so that it can be reallocated among industries and final demand categories at zero cost. Under this assumption, changes in tax policy can affect the distribution of capital and labor supplies among sectors, even in the short run. However, the total supply of capital in our model in each time period is perfectly inelastic, since the available stock of capital is determined by past investments. An accumulation equation relates capital stock to investments in all past time periods and incorporates the backward-looking dynamics of capital formation into our model of intertemporal equilibrium.

11.2.4   Government and Foreign Trade

The two remaining final demand categories in our model are the government and rest-of-the-world sectors. We determine final demands for government consumption from the income-expenditure identity for the government sector.[6] The first step is to compute total tax revenue by applying exogenous tax rates to all taxable transactions in the economy. We then add the capital income of government enterprises, which is determined endogenously, and nontax receipts, determined exogenously, to tax receipts to obtain total government revenue.

The key assumption of our submodel of the government sector is that the government budget deficit can be specified exogenously. We add the deficit to total revenue to obtain total government spending. To arrive at government purchases of goods and services, we subtract interest paid to domestic and foreign holders of government bonds together with government transfer payments to domestic and foreign recipients. We allocate the remainder among commodity groups according to fixed shares constructed from historical data. Finally, we determine the quantity of each commodity by dividing the value of government spending on that commodity by its price. Government consumption is not included in our representation of the preferences of the household sector.

Foreign trade has two quite different components—imports and exports. We assume that imports are imperfect substitutes for similar domestic commodities.[7] The goods actually purchased by households and firms reflect substitutions between domestic and imported products. The price responsiveness of these purchases is estimated from historical data taken from the import and export columns of the use table, figure 11.1, in our annual inter-industry transactions tables.

Exports, on the other hand, are modeled by a set of explicit foreign demand equations, one for each commodity, that depend on exogenously given foreign income and the foreign price of U.S. exports. Foreign prices are computed from domestic prices by adjusting for subsidies and the exchange rate. The demand elasticities in these equations are estimated from historical data. We assume that U.S. firms are price-takers in foreign markets. The alternative approach of modeling imperfections in international markets would require firm-level data, not only for the U.S., but also for all of its international competitors.

The key assumption of our submodel of the rest-of-the-world sector is that the current account is exogenous and the exchange rate is endogenous. The current account surplus is equal to the value of exports less the value of imports, plus interest received on domestic holdings of foreign bonds, less private and government transfers abroad, and less interest on government bonds paid to foreigners.

11.3 Provisions of U.S. Tax Law

The purpose of this section is to introduce the characteristic features of U.S. tax law into the cost of capital.[8] We distinguish among assets employed in three different legal forms of organization—households and nonprofit institutions, noncorporate businesses, and corporate businesses. Income from capital employed in corporate business is subject to the corporate income tax, while distributions of this income to households are subject to the individual income tax. Income from unincorporated businesses—partnerships and sole proprietorships— is taxed only at the individual level. Income from equity in household assets is not subject to the income tax. Capital utilized in all three forms of organization is subject to property taxation.

Although income from equity in the household sector is not subject to tax, property taxes and interest payments on household debt are deductible from income for tax purposes under the individual income tax. The value of these tax deductions is equivalent to a subsidy to capital employed in the household sector. Interest payments to holders of household debt are taxable to the recipients. Capital gains on household assets are effectively excluded from taxable income at the individual level by generous "roll over" provisions for owner-occupied residential housing. Capital gains on owner-occupied housing are not included in income so long as they are "rolled over" into the same form of investment.

Income from capital employed in noncorporate businesses is taxed at the level of the individual. Income from noncorporate equity is treated as fully distributed to equity holders, whether or not the income is actually paid out. Interest payments to holders of debts on noncorporate businesses are subject to taxation. Property taxes and interest payments are treated as deductions from revenue in defining income from noncorporate businesses for tax purposes. Revenue is also reduced by deductions for capital consumption allowances. Tax liability has been reduced by an investment tax credit that is proportional to investment expenditures. Capital gains on noncorporate assets are subject to favorable treatment as outlined below.

Property taxes and interest payments are treated as deductions from revenue in defining corporate income for tax purposes. Revenue is also reduced by allowances for capital consumption and an investment tax credit has been directly offset against tax liability. At the individual level distributions of corporate income in the form of interest and dividends are subject to taxation as ordinary income. Capital gains realized from the sale of corporate equities are subject to special treatment outlined below. Interest payments to holders of corporate bonds are also taxable.

The special treatment of capital gains arises from three separate features of U.S. tax law. First, capital gains are taxed only when they are realized and not when they are accrued. This feature makes it possible to defer tax liability on capital gains until assets are sold. Second, capital gains have often been given favorable treatment by including only a fraction of these gains in income defined for tax purposes. Finally, capital gains taxes on assets received as part of a bequest are based on their value at the time of the bequest. Capital gains accrued prior to the bequest are not subject to tax.

Under U.S. tax law, income from corporate businesses is taxed at the level of the corporation. Distributions of this income, in the form of dividends and capital gains, are taxed at the level of the individual. Income from equity in noncorporate businesses is treated as if it were fully distributed to equity holders, but this income is taxed only at the individual level. Income from equity in household capital is not subject to income taxation at either corporate or individual levels. However, interest payments to holders of household debt, like interest payments to holders of corporate and noncorporate debt, are taxable to the recipients.

Property taxes and interest payments are treated as deductions from revenue in defining corporate and noncorporate income for tax purposes. While income from equity in household assets is not subject to tax, property taxes and interest payments on household debt are deductible from income for tax purposes at the individual level. This is equivalent to a subsidy to capital employed in the household sector. Revenue is reduced by allowances for capital consumption in defining income from corporate and noncorporate assets for tax purposes. Tax liabilities are reduced directly by a tax credit for investment expenditures.

In this chapter, we have described the characteristic features of U.S. tax law in terms of the cost of capital and the rate of return. We have modeled provisions of U.S. tax law on corporate income taxes, individual income taxes, and property taxes. We have also incorporated the effects of the financial structure of the firm on the taxation of capital income. The financial structure determines the form of distributions of capital income to owners of financial claims. We have distinguished between equity, associated with distributions in the form of dividends and capital gains, and debt, associated with distributions in the form of interest payments.

In order to analyze the impact of changes in taxes, we simulate the growth of the U.S. economy with and without changes in these policies.[9] Our first step is to generate a simulation with no changes in policy that we call the *base case*. The second step is to change the exogenous variables of the model to reflect a proposed policy change. We then produce a simulation that we refer to as the *alternative case*. Finally, we compare the two simulations to assess the effects of the change in policy. Obviously, the assumptions underlying the base case are of considerable importance in interpreting the results of our simulations.

11.4   Fundamental Tax Reform

In this section we consider the impact on U.S. energy markets of substituting a tax on consumption for corporate and individual income taxes at federal, state, and local levels. We limit the analysis to a revenue neutral substitution—one that would leave the government deficit unchanged. We focus on the impact of this fundamental tax reform on economic growth, leaving progressivity of the resulting combination of taxes and government expenditures to be determined on the expenditure side of the government ledger.

11.4.1   Implementation

In *Hearings on Replacing the Federal Income Tax*, held by the Committee on Ways and Means in June 1995, testimony focused on alternative methods for implementing a consumption tax. The consumption tax base can be defined in three alternative and equivalent ways. First, subtracting investment from value added produces consumption as a tax base, where value added is the sum of capital and labor incomes. A second definition is the difference between business receipts and all purchases from other businesses, including purchases of investment goods. A third definition of the tax base is retail sales to consumers.

The three principal methods for implementation of a consumption tax correspond to these three definitions of the tax base:

1. *The subtraction method.* Business purchases from other businesses, including investment goods, would be subtracted from business receipts, including proceeds from the sale of assets. This could be implemented within the framework of the existing tax system by integrating individual and corporate income taxes, as proposed by the U.S. Treasury (1992). In this approach, all businesses would be treated as partnerships or "sub-chapter S" corporations. The second step would be to allow full expensing of investment goods purchases in the year of acquisition. If no business receipts were excluded and no deductions and tax credits were permitted, the tax return could be reduced to the now familiar postcard size, as in the Flat Tax proposal of Majority Leader Dick Armey and Senator Richard Shelby (1995).[10] Enforcement problems could be reduced by drastically simplifying the tax rules, but the principal method of enforcement, auditing of taxpayer records by the Internal Revenue Service, would remain.

2. *The credit method.* Business purchases would produce a credit against tax liabilities for value added taxes paid on goods and services received. This method is used in Canada and all European countries that impose a value added tax. From the point of view of tax administration, the credit method has the advantage that both purchases and sales generate records of all tax credits. The idea of substituting a value added tax for existing income taxes is a novel one. European and Canadian value added taxes were added to pre-existing income taxes. In Canada and many other countries, the value added tax replaced an earlier and more complex system of retail and wholesale sales taxes. The credit method would require substantial modification of collection procedures, but decades of experience in Europe have ironed out many of the bugs.

3. *National retail sales tax.* Like existing state sales taxes, a national retail sales tax would be collected by retail establishments, including service providers and real estate developers. This would also require a new system for tax administration, possibly subcontracting the actual collection to existing state agencies. Enforcement procedures

would be similar to those used by the states, and the Internal Revenue Service could be transformed into an agency that would subcontract collections. Alternatively, a new agency could be created for this purpose and the IRS abolished.

The crucial point is that all three methods for implementing a consumption tax could be based on the same definition of the tax base. This greatly simplifies the tax economist's task, since the economic impact would be the same for all three approaches. This leaves important issues to be resolved by other tax professionals, especially tax lawyers, who would write the legislation and the implementing regulations, and tax accountants, who would translate the laws and regulations into accounting practice, and advise economic decision-makers about their implications.

From the economic point of view, the definition of consumption is straightforward. A useful starting point is Personal Consumption Expenditures (PCE), as defined in the U.S. national income and product accounts. However, the taxation of services poses important administrative problems reviewed in the U.S. Treasury (1984) monograph on the value added tax. First, PCE includes the rental equivalent value of the services of owner-occupied housing, but does not include the services of consumers' durables. Both are substantial in magnitude, but could be taxed by the "prepayment method" described by David Bradford (1986). In this approach, taxes on the consumption of the services would be prepaid by including investment rather than consumption in the definition of the tax base.

The prepayment of taxes on services of owner-occupied housing would remove an important political obstacle to substitution of a consumption tax for existing income taxes. At the time the substitution takes place, all owner-occupiers would be treated as having prepaid all future taxes on the services of their dwellings. This is equivalent to excluding not only mortgage interest from the tax base, but also returns to equity, which might be taxed upon the sale of residence with no corresponding purchase of residential property of equal or greater value. Of course, this argument is vulnerable to the criticism that home owners should be allowed to take the mortgage interest deduction twice—once when the substitution occurs, and again, when consumption tax liabilities are assessed.

Under the prepayment method, purchases of consumers' durables by households for their own use would be subject to tax. This would include automobiles, appliances, home furnishings, and so on. In addition, new construction of owner-occupied housing would be subject to tax, as would sales of existing renter-occupied housing to owner-occupiers. These are politically sensitive issues and it is important to be clear about the implications of prepayment as the debate proceeds. Housing and consumers' durables must be included in the tax base in order to reap the substantial economic benefits of putting household and business capital onto the same footing[11]

Other purchases of services especially problematical under a consumption tax would include services provided by nonprofit institutions, such as schools and colleges, hospitals, and religious and eleemosynary institutions. The traditional, tax-favored status of these forms of consumption would be defended tenaciously by recipients of the services and even more tenaciously by the providers. Elegant, and, in some cases, persuasive arguments could be made that schools and colleges provide services that represent investment in human capital rather than consumption. However, consumption of the resulting enhancements in human capital often takes the form of leisure time, which would remain as the principal untaxed form of consumption. Taxes could, however, be prepaid by including educational services in the tax base.

Finally, any definition of a consumption tax base will have to distinguish between consumption for personal and business purposes. Ongoing disputes over exclusion of home offices, business-provided automobiles, equipment, and clothing, as well as business-related lodging, entertainment and meals would continue to plague tax officials, the entertainment and hospitality industries, and holders of expense accounts. In short, substitution of a consumption tax for the federal income tax system would not eliminate all the practical issues that arise from the necessity of distinguishing between business and personal activities in defining consumption. However, these issues are common to the two tax systems.

The coming debate over tax reform is both a challenge and an opportunity for economists. It is a challenge because the impact of fundamental tax reform will involve almost every aspect of economic life. Economists who have spent their lives pre-occupied by the latest debating points in professional journals read only by other economists will suddenly find themselves swept up in the journalistic maelstrom of American political life. The fine points that dominate scholarly discussions will be subjected to the refiner's fire of public exposure. While translation of professional debating points into sound bites requires considerable talent and experience, a substantial number of economists have acquired the requisite skills.

The debate will be an opportunity for economists, because economic research has generated an enormous amount of valuable information about the impacts of tax policy. Provided that the economic debate can be properly focused, economists and policy makers will learn a great deal about the U.S. economy and its potential for achieving a higher level of performance. Under any one of the three approaches to implementation of a value added tax, substitution of a consumption tax for existing individual and corporate income taxes would be the most drastic change in federal tax policy since the introduction of the income tax in 1913. It should not be surprising that the economic impact could be truly staggering in its dimensions.

The first issue that will surface in the tax reform debate is progressivity or the use of the federal tax system to redistribute resources. Our recommendation is that this issue be set aside at the outset. Fiscal economists of varying persuasions can agree that progressivity or the lack of it, should be used to characterize all of government activity, including both taxes and expenditures. Policies to achieve progressivity could and should be limited to the expenditure side of the government budget. This initial policy stance would immeasurably simplify the debate over the economic impact of fundamental tax reform. We view this radical simplification as essential to intellectual progress, since there is no agreed upon economic methodology for trading off efficiency and equity in tax policy.

The second issue to be debated is fiscal federalism, or the role of state and local governments. Since state and local income taxes usually employ the same tax bases as the corresponding federal taxes, it is reasonable to assume that substitution of consumption for income taxes at the federal level would be followed by similar substitutions at the state and local level. For simplicity, we propose to consider the economic impact of substitution at all levels simultaneously. Since an important advantage of a fundamental tax reform is the possibility, at least at the outset, of radically simplifying tax rules, it does not make much sense to assume that these rules would continue to govern state and local income taxes, even if the federal income tax were abolished.

The third issue in the debate will be the economic impact of the federal deficit. Nearly two decades of economic dispute over this issue has failed to produce resolution. No doubt this dispute could continue well into the next century and preoccupy the next generation of fiscal economists, as it has the previous generation. An effective rhetorical device for insulating the discussion of fundamental tax reform from the budget debate is to limit consideration to deficit neutral proposals. This device was critical to the eventual enactment of the Tax Reform Act of 1986 and is, we believe, essential to progress in the debate over fundamental tax reform.

11.4.2   Simulation Results

We have summarized our conclusions in a series of charts (which appear in the appendix to this chapter).

1. The revenue neutral substitution of a consumption tax for existing income taxes, at both federal and state and local levels, would have an immediate and powerful impact on the level of economic activity. Chart 1 (Base Case GDP) shows the gradual increase of the U.S. gross domestic product (GDP) under the existing tax system. Chart 2 (GDP) shows that substitution of a consumption tax would increase the GDP by about thirteen percent, but this increase would gradually decline to around ten percent.

2. The imposition of a consumption tax would produce a sharply higher tax rate on consumer goods and services, but Chart 3 (Consumption Tax Rate) shows that the consumption tax rate would be under fifteen percent at both federal and state and local levels or only twelve percent at the federal level. This would gradually rise over time, but remain below twenty percent or sixteen percent at the federal level.

3. The implied subsidy to leisure time is equal to the marginal tax rate on labor income and would drop to zero if the tax were abolished. As a consequence of the total transformation of the tax system, individuals would sharply curtail consumption of both goods and leisure. Chart 4 (Capital Stock and Labor Supply) shows that this would produce a dramatic jump in saving and a substantial rise in labor supply. These increases would subside only very gradually over time.

4. Taxation of consumption would induce a radical shift away from consumption toward investment. Chart 5 (Consumption and Investment) shows that real investment would leap upward by a staggering eighty percent! This chart shows that real consumption would initially decline by around five percent, but the level would grow rapidly and overtake that under the income tax within five years.

5. Holding net foreign investment constant, Chart 6 (Imports and Exports) shows that exports would jump to twenty-nine percent, while imports would rise only slightly. The initial export boom would gradually subside, while remaining around fifteen percent higher than under the current tax system.

6. Since producers would no longer pay taxes on profits or other forms of income from capital, and workers would no longer pay taxes on wages, prices received by producers, shown in Chart 7 (Prices 1996) would fall by an average of twenty percent. Chart 8 (Quantities 1996) shows that industry outputs would rise by an average of twenty percent with substantial relative gains for investment goods producers.

7. In the long run, producers' prices, shown in Chart 9 (Prices 2020), would fall by almost twenty-five percent, relative to prices under an income tax. The shift in the composition of economic activity toward investment and away from consumption would drastically redistribute economic activity. Chart 10 (Quantity 2020) shows that production would increase in all industries, but the rise in production of investment goods would be much more dramatic.

8. Changes in relative prices would induce a certain amount of energy conservation, defined as energy consumption per unit of domestic product. However, increased economic growth would outweigh the impact of conservation, resulting in an immediate increase of energy consumption of 7.6 percent, declining to an increase of 7.1 percent in the long run. Chart 11 (Energy Consumption) shows this jump in energy consumption.

9. Energy consumption would be somewhat more carbon intensive due to a rise in consumption of coal, relative to petroleum and natural gas. Chart 12 (Carbon Emissions) shows that carbon emissions would increase immediately by nine percent, but that this would decline gradually to 8.4 percent. Fundamental tax reform would enhance prospects for U.S. economic growth and would result in more energy consumption and greater emissions of carbon.

11.5   Conclusion

Although the intertemporal general equilibrium approach has proved to be useful in modeling the impact of tax policies, much remains to be done to exploit the full potential of this approach. As an illustration, the model of consumer behavior employed by Jorgenson and

Wilcoxen (1990b) successfully dispenses with the notion of a representative consumer. An important feature of this model is that systems of individual demand functions can be recovered from the system of aggregate demand functions. The consumer preferences underlying these individual demand systems can be used to generate measures of individual welfare that are useful in evaluating the distributional consequences of changes in tax policy, as described by Jorgenson (1990a).

We conclude that intertemporal general equilibrium modeling provides a very worthwhile addition to methodologies for modeling the economic impact of taxes. The neo-classical theory of economic growth is essential for understanding the dynamic mechanisms that underly long run and intermediate run growth trends. The econometric implementation of this theory is critical for capitalizing on the drastic changes in energy prices and substantial alterations in environmental policies of the past two decades. This wealth of historical experience, interpreted within an intertemporal framework, can provide valuable guidance in future policy formulation.

Appendix

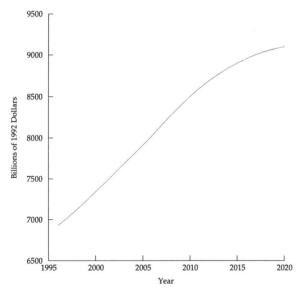

Chart 1
Base Case GDP (in 1992 dollars).

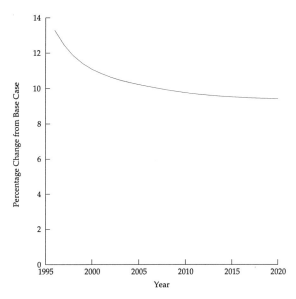

Chart 2
GDP.

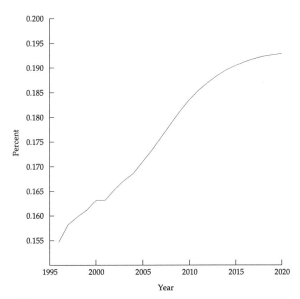

Chart 3
Consumption Tax Rate.

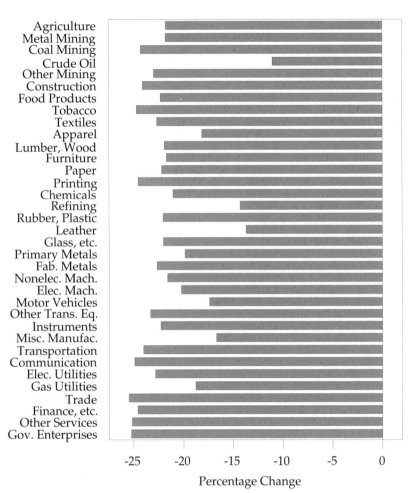

Chart 4
Capital Stock and Labor Supply.

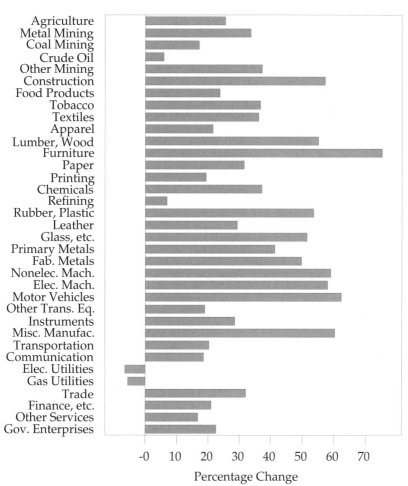

Chart 5
Consumption and Investment.

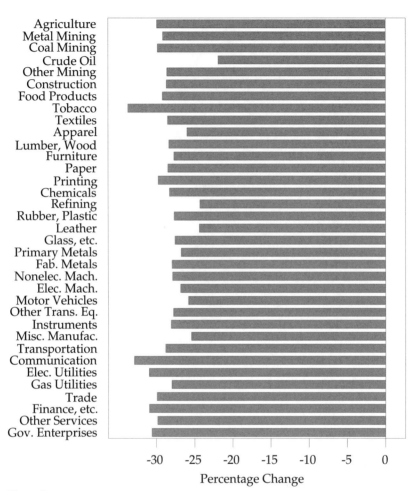

Chart 6
Imports and Exports.

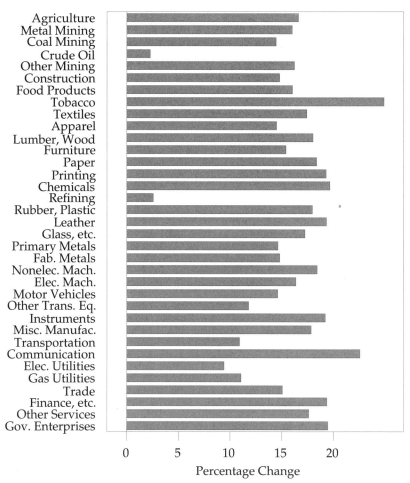

Chart 7
Prices 1996 (percent change).

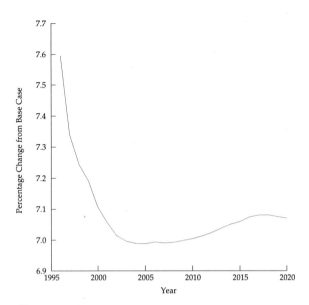

Chart 8
Quantities 1996 (percent change).

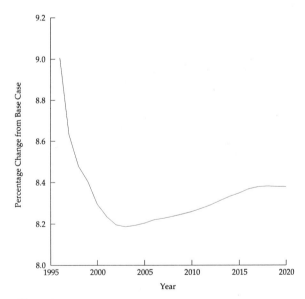

Chart 9
Prices 2020 (percent change).

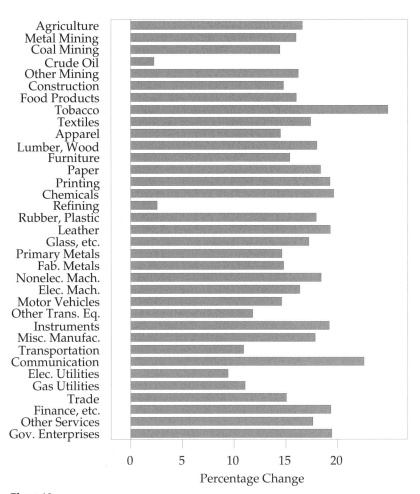

Chart 10
Quantity 2020 (percent change).

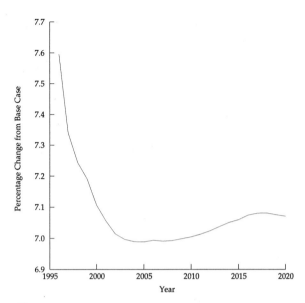

Chart 11
Energy Consumption.

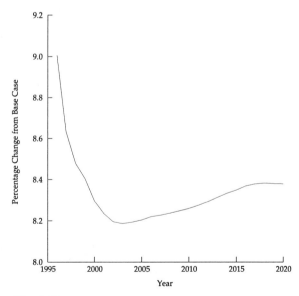

Chart 12
Carbon Emission.

Notes

1. The classic formulation of intertemporal general equilibrium theory is by Lindahl (1970). A detailed survey of this theory is presented by Stokey and Lucas (1989).

2. Our data integrate the capital accounts described by Jorgenson (1990b) with an accounting system based on the United Nations (1993) System of National Accounts. Details are given by Wilcoxen (1988), Appendix C.

3. Noncompeting imports are imported commodities that are not produced domestically.

4. Jorgenson (1986) describes the econometrics of producer behavior. Mansur and Whalley (1984) present the calibration approach.

5. The relationship between the price of investment goods and the rental price of capital services is discussed in greater detail by Jorgenson (1989).

6. Our treatment of government spending differs from the U.S. national accounts in that we have assigned government enterprises to the corresponding industry wherever possible. We include the remaining purchases by the government sector in final demands by governments.

7. This approach was originated by Armington (1969). See Wilcoxen (1988) and Ho (1989) for further details on our implementation of this approach.

8. The incorporation of provisions of U.S. tax law into the cost of capital is based on Jorgenson and Yun (1991b), Chapter 2. Jorgenson and Yun (1990, 1991a) have employed the results in analyzing the impact of the Tax Reform Act of 1986. The cost of capital in nine countries is compared in a volume edited by Jorgenson and Landau (1993).

9. Our solution method is described in Wilcoxen (1988), Appendix E. Methods for solving intertemporal general equilibrium models are surveyed in detail by Wilcoxen (1992).

10. Economists will recognize the Flat Tax proposal as a variant of the consumption-base value added tax proposed by Robert Hall and Alvin Rabushka (1995).

11. See, for example, Jorgenson's testimony before the Committee on Ways and Means of June 6, 1995.

References

Alliance to Save Energy. 1998. *Price It Right*. Washington: Alliance to Save Energy.

Amemiya, Takeshi. 1974. The Nonlinear Two-Stage Least-Squares Estimator. *Journal of Econometrics* 2, no. 2 (July): 105–110.

———. 1977. The Maximum Likelihood Estimator and the Nonlinear Three-Stage Least-Squares Estimator in the General Nonlinear Simultaneous Equation Model. *Econometrica* 45, no. 4 (May): 955–968.

American Iron and Steel Institute *et al.*, 1989. Joint Comments on the U.S. Environmental Protection Agency's *Policy Options for Stabilizing Global Climate*. Draft Report to Congress, February.

Armey, Dick. 1995. The Freedom and Fairness Restoration Act. 104th Congress, First Session. Washington, DC.

Armington, Paul S. 1969. The Geographic Pattern of Trade and the Effects of Price Changes. *IMF Staff Papers* 16, no. 2 (July): 176–199.

Arrow, Kenneth J., Hollis B. Chenery, Bagicha S. Minhas, and Robert M. Solow. 1961. Capital-Labor Substitution and Economic Efficiency. *Review of Economics and Statistics* 43, no. 3 (August): 225–250.

Ayres, Robert U., and Allen V. Kneese. 1969. Production, Consumption, and Externalities. *American Economic Review* 59, no. 3 (June): 282–297.

Ballard, Charles L., and Steven G. Medema. 1989. The Marginal Efficiency Effects of Taxes and Subsidies in the Presence of Externalities: A Computational General Equilibrium Approach. July. Michigan State University: Department of Economics.

Barten, A. P. 1964. Family Composition, Prices and Expenditure Patterns. In *Econometric Analysis for National Economic Planning: 16th Symposium of the Colston Society*, eds. P. Hart, G. Mills, and J. K. Whitaker, 277–292. London, England: Butterworth.

——— 1977. The Systems of Consumer Demand Functions Approach: A Review. In *Frontiers of Quantitative Economics*, vol. 3, ed. Michael D. Intriligator, 23–58. Amsterdam, The Netherlands: North-Holland.

Beaver, Ron. 1993. A Structural Comparison of Models used in EMF 12 to Analyze the Costs of Policies for Reducing Energy-Sector Carbon Dioxide Emissions. In *Reducing Carbon Emissions from the Energy Sector*, eds. D. Gaskins and J. Weyant, Cambridge, MA: MIT Press.

Ben-Zion, Uri, and Vernon W. Ruttan. 1978. Aggregate Demand and the Rate of Technical Change. In *Induced Innovation*, eds. Hans P. Binswanger and Vernon W. Ruttan, 261–275. Baltimore: Johns Hopkins University Press.

Bergman, Lars. 1985. Extensions and Applications of the MSG-Model: A Brief Survey. In *Production, Multi-Sectoral Growth, and Planning: Essays in Memory of Leif Johansen*, eds. Finn R. Forsund, Michael Hoel, and Sven Longva, 127–161. Amsterdam, The Netherlands: North-Holland.

―――. 1990. The Development of Computable General Equilibrium Modeling. In *General Equilibrium Modeling and Economic Policy Analysis*, eds. Lars Bergman, Dale W. Jorgenson, and Erno Zalai, 3-32. Oxford, England: Basil Blackwell.

―――. 1993. General Equilibrium Costs and Benefits of Environmental Policies. Mimeo. Stockholm: School of Economics.

Berndt, Ernst R., and Dale W. Jorgenson. 1973. Production Structure. In *U.S. Energy Resources and Economic Growth*, eds. Dale W. Jorgenson and Hendrik S. Houthakker, chapter 3, Washington, DC: Energy Policy Project.

Berndt, Ernst R., and David O. Wood. 1975. Technology, Prices and the Derived Demand for Energy. *Review of Economics and Statistics* 56, no. 3 (August): 259–268.

―――. 1979. Engineering and Econometric Interpretations of Energy-Capital Complementarity. *American Economic Review* 69, no. 3 (September): 342–354.

Berndt, Ernst R., Masako N. Darrough, and W. Erwin Diewert. 1977. Flexible Functional Forms and Expenditure Distributions: An Application to Canadian Consumer Demand Functions. *International Economic Review* 18, no. 3 (October): 651–676.

Binswanger, Hans P. 1974. The Measurement of Technical Change Biases with Many Factors of Production. *American Economic Review* 64, no. 5 (December): 964–974.

―――. 1978a, Induced Technical Change: Evolution of Thought. In *nduced Innovation*, eds. Hans P. Binswanger and Vernon W. Ruttan, 13– 43. Baltimore, MD: Johns Hopkins University Press.

―――. 1978b. Issues in Modeling Induced Technical Change. In *Induced Innovation*, eds. Hans P. Binswanger and Vernon W. Ruttan, 128–163. Baltimore: Johns Hopkins University Press.

Bjerkholt, Olav, Sven Longva, Oystein Olsen, and Steinar Strom, eds. 1983. Producer Behaviour in the MSG Model. In *Analysis of Supply and Demand of Electricity in the Norwegian Economy*, 52–83. Oslo: Central Bureau of Statistics.

Blackorby, Charles, Richard Boyce, and Robert R. Russell. 1978a. Estimation of Demand Systems Generated by the Gorman Polar Form: A Generalization of the S-Branch Utility Tree. *Econometrica* 46, no. 2 (March): 345–364.

Blackorby, Charles, Daniel Primont, and Robert R. Russell. 1978b. *Duality, Separability, and Functional Structure.* Amsterdam, The Netherlands: North-Holland.

Blundell, Richard. 1986. Consumer Behavior: Theory and Empirical Evidence— A Survey. *Economic Journal* 98, no. 389 (March): 16–65.

Borges, Antonio M., and Lawrence H. Goulder. 1984. Decomposing the Impact of Higher Energy Prices on Long-Term Growth. In *Applied General Equilibrium Analysis*, eds. Herbert E. Scarf and John B. Shoven, 319–362. Cambridge, England: Cambridge University Press.

Bradford, David. 1986. *Untangling the Income Tax.* Cambridge, MA: Harvard University Press.

Brown, Deardorff and Stern. 1992. North American Integration. *Economic Journal*, November.

Bureau of the Census. Various annual issues, 1973–1983. Pollution Abatement Costs and Expenditures. Washington, DC: U.S. Department of Commerce.

————. 1989. Projections of the Population of the United States, by Age, Sex, and Race: 1988–2080. Current Population Reports, ser. P-25, no. 1918. Washington, DC: U.S. Department of Commerce.

————. Various annual issues. *Current Population Reports*, Series P–60, Consumer Income. Washington, DC: U.S. Department of Commerce.

Bureau of Economic Analysis. 1984. The Input-Output Structure of the U.S. Economy, 1977. *Survey of Current Business* 64, no. 5 (May): 42–79.

————. 1986. *The National Income and Product Accounts of the United States, 1929–1982: Statistical Tables.* Washington, DC: U.S. Department of Commerce.

Bureau of Labor Statistics. 1990. *Survey of Consumer Expenditures, 1989.* Washington, DC: U.S. Department of Labor. Magnetic tapes.

Burmeister, Edwin, and A. Rodney Dobell. 1969. Disembodied Technological Change with Several Factors. *Journal of Economic Theory* 1, no. 1 (June): 1– 18.

Burnett, W. M., and S. D. Ban. 1989. Changing Prospects for Natural Gas in the United States. *Science* 244, no. 4902 (April): 305–310.

Burniaux, Jean-Marc, J. Martin, G. Nicoletti, and J. Martins. 1992. GREEN—A Multi-Sector, Multi-Regional, General Equilibrium Model for Quantifying the Costs of Curbing CO_2 Emissions: A Technical Manual, Working Paper no. 116. OECD: Economics Department.

Carlson, Michael D. 1974. The 1972–1973 Consumer Expenditure Survey. *Monthly Labor Review* 97, no. 12 (December): 16–23.

Cass, David. 1965. Optimum Growth in an Aggregative Model of Capital Accumulation. *Review of Economic Studies* 32, no. 3 (July): 233–240.

Center for Strategic and International Studies. 1989. Implications of Global Climate Policies. Mimeo, June.

Chipman, Johns, A. Eymann, G. Ronning and G. Tian. 1992. Estimating Price Reponses of German Imports and Exports. In *European Integration in the World Economy*, ed. H. Vosgerau.

Christiansen, Gregory B., Frank M. Gollop, and Robert Haveman. 1980. *Environmental and Health and Safety Regulations, Productivity Growth, and Economic Performance*, Joint Economic Committee, 96th Congress, 2nd Session. Washington, DC: U.S. Government Printing Office.

Christiansen, Gregory B., and Thomas H. Tietenberg. 1985. Distributional and Macroeconomic Aspects of Environmental Policy. In *Handbook of Natural Resource and Energy Economics* 1, eds. Allen V. Kneese and James L. Sweeney, 345–394, Amsterdam, The Netherlands: North-Holland.

Christensen, Laurits R., and Dale W. Jorgenson. 1973. Measuring Economic Performance in the Private Sector. In *The Measurement of Economic and Social Performance*, ed. Milton Moss, 233–351. NBER Studies in Income and Wealth, vol. 37. New York, NY: Columbia University Press.

Christensen, Laurits R., Dale W. Jorgenson, and Lawrence J. Lau. 1971. Conjugate Duality and the Transcendental Logarithmic Production Function. *Econometrica* 39, no. 4 (July): 255–256.

————. 1973. Transcendental Logarithmic Production Frontiers. *Review of Economics and Statistics* 55, no. 1 (February): 28–45.

————. 1975. Transcendental Logarithmic Utility Functions. *American Economic Review* 65, no. 3 (June): 367–383.

Cline, William, R. 1992. *The Economics of Global Warming.* Washington, DC: Institute for International Economics.

Cline, William R., N. Kawanabe, T. Kronsjo, and T. Williams. 1978. *Trade Negotiations in the Tokyo Round.* Washington, DC: The Brookings Institution.

Committee and Ways and Means. 1996. *Hearings on Replacing the Federal Income Tax.* 104th Congress, First Session. U.S. House of Representatives.

Congressional Budget Office. 1990. *Carbon Charges as a Response to Global Warming: The Effects of Taxing Fossil Fuels*, August. Washington, DC: U.S. Government Printing Office.

Conrad, Klaus, and M. Schroder. 1991. Controlling Air Pollution: The Effects of Alternative Policy Approaches. In *Environmental Scarcity: The International Dimension*, ed. Siebert.

Cottle, R. W., and J. A. Ferland. 1972. Matrix-Theoretic Criteria for the Quasi-Convexity and Pseudo-Convexity of Quadratic Functions. *Linear Algebra and Its Applications* 5: 123–136.

Daly, Thomas, A., N. Goto, Richard F. Kosobud, and William D. Nordhaus. 1984. CO_2 Forecasting and Control: A Mathematical Programming Approach. In *The Energy Industries in Transition*, Part I, ed. John Weyant, 547–561. Washington, DC: International Association of Energy Economists.

d'Arge, Ralph C., William D. Schulze, and Davis S. Brookshire. 1982. Carbon Dioxide and Intergenerational Choice. *American Economic Review* 72, no. 2 (May):251–256.

Darmstadter, Joel, and Jae Edmonst. 1989. Human Development and Carbon Dioxide Emissions: The Current Picture and the Long-Term Prospects. In *Greenhouse Warming: Abatement and Adaptation*, ed. Norman J. Rosenberg. Washington, DC: Resources for the Future.

Dasgupta, Partha S., and Geoffrey M. Heal. 1979. *Economic Theory and Exhaustible Resources.* Cambridge, England: Cambridge University Press.

Dean, Abrahamson. 1989. Relative Greenhouse Heating from the Use of Fuel Oil and Natural Gas. Mimeo. University of Minnesota.

Dean, Judith. 1992. Trade and the Environment: A Survey of the Literature. In *International Trade and the Environment*, World Bank Discussion Papers No. 159.

Dean, Andrew, and Peter Hoeller. 1992. Costs of Reducing Carbon Dioxide Emissions: Evidence from Six Global Models. *OECD Economic Studies* 19 (Winter): 15–49.

Deardorff, A., and R. M. Stern. 1986. *The Michigan Model of World Production and Trade.* Cambridge, MA: The MIT Press.

Deaton, Angus S. 1986. Demand Analysis. In *Handbook of Econometrics*, vol. 3, eds. Zvi Griliches and Michael D. Intriligator, 1767–1840. Amsterdam: North-Holland.

Deaton, Angus S., and John S. Muellbauer. 1980a. An Almost Ideal Demand System. *American Economic Review* 70, no. 3 (June): 312–326.

———. 1980b. *Economics and Consumer Behaviorl.* Cambridge, England: Cambridge University Press.

Denison, Edward F. 1985. *Trends in American Economic Growth, 1929–1982.* Washington, DC: The Brookings Institution.

Diewert, W. Erwin. 1976. Exact and Superlative Index Numbers. *Journal of Econometrics* 4, no. 2 (May): 115–146.

———. 1980. Aggregation Problems in the Measurement of Capital. In *The Measurement of Capital*, ed. Dan Usher, 433–528, Chicago, IL: University of Chicago Press.

Dixon, Peter B., and David T. Johnson. 1989. Estimates of the Macroeconomic Effects on Australia of Attempting to Reduce CO_2 Emissions by Twenty Percent by 2005. Institute for Social and Economic Research, University of Melbourne, November.

Edmonds, James A., and John M. Reilly. 1983. Global Energy and CO_2 to the Year 2050. *The Energy Journal* 4, no. 3 (July): 21–47.

———. 1985. *Global Energy-Assessing the Future*. New York, NY: Oxford University Press.

Energy Information Administration. 1989. *Annual Energy Review 1990*. Washington, DC: U.S. Department of Energy.

Englander, A. Steven, and Axel Mittelstadt. 1988. Total Factor Productivity: Macroeconomic and Structural Aspects of the Slowdown. *OECD Economic Studies* 10 (Spring): 7–56.

Environmental Protection Agency. 1988. The Potential Effects of Global Climate Change in the United States. Draft report to Congress, October.

———. 1989. Policy Options for Stabilizing Global Climate, 3 volumes. Draft report to Congress, February.

———. 1990. Internal memorandum on carbon emissions coefficients.

———. 1991. Estimated Costs of Compliance with the Clean Air Act Amendments of 1990.

———. 1997. The Benefits and Costs of the Clean Air Act, 1970 to 1990. Report to the U.S. Congress, November.

Faucett, Jack, and Associates. 1977. Development of 35 Order Input-Output Tables, 1958–1974, Final Report, October. Washington, DC: Federal Emergency Management Agency.

Fisher, Irving. 1922. *The Making of Index Numbers*. Boston, MA: Houghton Mifflin.

Forsund, Finn R. 1985. Input-Output Models, National Economic Models, and the Environment. In *Handbook of Natural Resource and Energy Economics*, vol. 1, eds. Allen V. Kneese and James L. Sweeney, 325–344. Amsterdam: North-Holland

Forsund, Finn R., and Steinar Strom. 1976. The Generation of Residual Flows In Norway: An Input-Output Approach. *Journal of Environmental Economics and Management* 3, no. 2 (April): 129–141.

Fraumeni, Barbara M., and Dale W. Jorgenson. 1980. The Role of Capital in U.S. Economic Growth, 1948–1976. In *Capital, Efficiency and Growth*, ed. George M. von Furstenberg, 9–250. Cambridge, MA: Ballinger.

Freeman, A. Myrick, III. 1985. Methods for Assessing the Benefits of Environmental Programs. In *Handbook of Natural Resource and Energy Economics*, vol. 1, eds. Allen V. Kneese and James L. Sweeney, 223–270. Amsterdam, The Netherlands: North-Holland.

Frisch, Ragnar. 1959. A Complete Scheme for Computing All Direct Direct and Cross Demand Elasticities in a Model with Many Sectors. *Econometrica* 27, no. 2 (April): 177–196.

Fullerton, Don, Yolanda K. Henderson, and John B. Shoven. 1984. A Comparison of Methodologies in Empirical General Equilibrium Models of Taxation. In *Applied General Equilibrium Analysis*, eds. Herbert E. Scarf and John B. Shoven, 367–409. Cambridge, England: Cambridge University Press.

von Furstenberg, George M., ed. 1980. *Capital, Efficiency and Growth*. Cambridge, MA: Ballinger.

Fuss, Melvin, Daniel L. McFadden, and Yair Mundlak. 1978. A Survey of Functional Forms in the Economic Analysis of Production. *Production Economics*, vol. 1, eds. Melvin Fuss and Daniel L. McFadden, 219–268. Amsterdam, The Netherlands: North-Holland.

Gallant, A. Ronald (1977). Three-Stage Least-Squares Estimation for a System of Simultaneous, Nonlinear, Implicit Equations. *Journal of Econometrics* 5, no. 1 (January): 71–88.

Gallant, A. Ronald, and Dale W. Jorgenson (1979). Statistical Inference for a System of Simultaneous, Nonlinear, Implicit Equations in the Context of Instrumental Variable Estimation, *Journal of Econometrics* 11, nos. 2/3 (October/December): 275–302.

Glomsrud, S., H. Vennemo, and T. Johnsen. 1992. Stabilization of Emissions of Carbon Dioxide: A Computable General Equilibrium Assessment. *Scandinavian Economic Journal* 94, no. 1, 53–69.

Gollop, Frank M., and Mark J. Roberts. 1983. Environmental Regulations and Productivity Growth: The Case of Fossil-Fueled Electric Power Generation. *Journal of Political Economy* 91, no. 4 (August): 654–673.

———. 1985. Cost-Minimizing Regulation of Sulfur Emissions: Regional Gains in Electric Power. *Review of Economics and Statistics* 67, no. 1 (February): 81–90.

Gorman, William M. 1953. Community Preference Fields. *Econometrica* 21, no. 1 (January): 63–80.

———. 1976. Tricks with Utility Functions. In *Essays in Economic Analysis: Proceedings of the 1975 AUTE Conference, Sheffield,* , eds. M. J. Artis and A. R. Nobay, 211–243. Cambridge, England: Cambridge University Press.

———.1981. Some Engel Curves. In *Essays in the Theory and Measurement of Consumer Behavior*, 7–29. New York, NY: Cambridge University Press.

Goulder, Lawrence H. 1990. Using Carbon Charges to Combat Global Climate Change. Mimeo, September.

———. 1991. Effects of Carbon Taxes in an Economy with Prior Tax Distortions: An Intertemporal General Equilibrium Analysis for the U.S., mimeo (June).

———. 1995. Environmental Taxation and the Double Dividend: A Reader's Guide. *International Tax and Public Finance* 2, no. 2 (August): 157–183.

Goulder, Lawrence H., and B. Eichengreen. 1989. Savings Promotion, Investment Promotion, and International Competitiveness. In *Tax Policies for International Competitiveness*, ed. R. Feenstra. Chicago: University of Chicago Press.

Griliches, Zvi, and Michael D. Intriligator. 1983–1985. *Handbook of Econometrics*, 3 vols., Amsterdam, The Netherlands: North-Holland.

Grossman, Gene M., and A. B. Krueger. 1994. Environmental Impacts of a North American Free Trade Agreement. In *Mexico–U.S. Free Trade Agreement*, ed. Peter Garber, 13–56.

Hall, Robert E. 1978. Stochastic Implications of the Life Cycle-Permanent Income Hypothesis: Theory and Evidence. *Journal of Political Economy* 86, no. 6 (December): 971–988.

Hall, Robert E., and Alvin Rabushka. 1995. *The Flat Tax*, 2nd ed. Stanford: The Hoover Institution.

Hazilla, M., and R. J. Kopp. 1986. Systematic Effects of Capital Service Price Definition on Perceptions of Input Substitution. *Journal of Business and Economic Statistics* 4, no. 2 (April): 209–224.

———. 1990. Social Cost of Environmental Quality Regulations: A General Equilibrium Analysis. *Journal of Political Economy* 98, no. 4 (August): 853–873.

Hicks, John R. (1932). *The Theory of Wages*, 2nd ed. 1963. London, England: Macmillan.

Ho, Mun S. 1989. The Effects of External Linkages on U.S. Economic Growth: A Dynamic General Equilibrium Analysis. Ph.D. Dissertation, Cambridge, MA: Harvard University.

Ho, Mun S. and Dale W. Jorgenson. 1993. Trade Policies and U.S. Economic Growth. *Journal of Policy Modeling* 15, no. 2 (June).

———. 1992a. Environmental Policies and U.S. Trade, mimeo. Cambridge, MA: Harvard University.

———. 1992b. Education, Human Capital and U.S. Economic Growth, mimeo. Cambridge, MA: Harvard University.

Hoeller, Peter, Andrew Dean, and John Nicolaisen. 1991. Macroeconomic Implications of Reducing Greenhouse Gas Emissions: A Survey of Empirical Studies. *OECD Economic Studies* 16, 45–78.

Hogan, William W., and Dale W. Jorgenson. 1991. Productivity Trends and the Costs of Reducing Carbon Dioxide Emissions. *Energy Journal* 12, no. 1 (January): 67–85.

Houghton, R. A., and G. M. Woodwell. 1989. Global Climate Change. *Scientific American* 260, no. 4 (April).

Houthakker, Hendrik S. 1957. An International Comparison of Household Expenditure Patterns Commemorating the Centenary of Engel's Law. *Econometrica* 25, no. 4 (October): 532–551.

————. 1960. Additive Preferences. *Econometrica* 28, no. 2 (April): 244–257.

Hudson, Edward A., and Dale W. Jorgenson. 1974. U.S. Energy Policy and Economic Growth, 1975–2000. *Bell Journal of Economics and Management Science* 5, no. 2 (Autumn): 461–514.

Hufbauer, G., D. T. Berliner, and K. A. Elliott. 1986. *Trade Protection in the United States*. Washington, DC: Institute for International Economics.

James, D. E., H. M. A. Jansen, and H. P. Opschoor. 1978. *Economic Approaches to Environmental Problems*. Amsterdam, The Netherlands: North-Holland.

Johansen, Leif. 1960. *A Multi-Sectoral Study of Economic Growth*. Amsterdam, The Netherlands: North-Holland.

Jorgenson, Dale W. 1973. Technology and Decision Rules in the Theory of Investment Behavior. *Quarterly Journal of Economics* 87, no. 4 (November): 523–543.

————. 1980. Accounting for Capital. In *Capital, Efficiency, and Growth*, ed. George M. von Furstenberg, 251–319. Cambridge, MA: Ballinger.

————. 1981. Energy Prices and Productivity Growth. *Scandinavian Journal of Economics* 83, no. 2, 165–179.

————. 1982. Econometric and Process Analysis Models for the Analysis of Energy Policy. In *Perspectives in Resource Policy Modeling: Energy and Minerals*, eds. Rafi Amit and Mordecai Avriel, 9–62. Cambridge, MA: Ballinger.

————. 1984a. Econometric Methods for Applied General Equilibrium Analysis. In *Applied General Equilibrium Analysis*, eds. Herbert E. Scarf and John B. Shoven, 139–203. Cambridge, England: Cambridge University Press.

————. 1984b. The Role of Energy in Productivity Growth. In *International Comparisons of Productivity and Causes of the Slowdown*, ed. John W. Kendrick, 270–323. Cambridge, MA: Ballinger. Earlier, less detailed versions of this material appeared in *American Economic Review* 74, no. 2 (May, 1978): 26–30; and in *The Energy Journal* 5, no. 3 (July, 1984): 11–25.

————. 1986. Econometric Methods for Modelling Producer Behavior. In *Handbook of Econometrics*, vol. 3, eds. Zvi Griliches, and Michael D. Intriligator, 1842–1915. Amsterdam, The Netherlands: North-Holland.

————. 1989. Capital as a Factor of Production. In *Technology and Capital Formation*, eds. Dale W. Jorgenson and Ralph Landau, 1–36. Cambridge, MA: The MIT Press.

————. 1990a. Aggregate Consumer Behavior and the Measurement of Social Welfare. *Econometrica* 58, no. 5 (September): 1007–1040.

————. 1990b. Productivity and Economic Growth. In *Fifty Years of Economic Measurement*, eds. Ernst R. Berndt and J. Triplett, 19–118. Chicago: University of Chicago Press.

————. 1995a. *Productivity, Volume 1: Postwar U.S. Economic Growth*. Cambridge, MA: The MIT Press.

————. 1995b. *Productivity, Volume 2: International Comparisons of Economic Growth*. Cambridge, MA: The MIT Press.

————. 1997a. *Welfare, Volume 1: Aggregate Consumer Behavior*. Cambridge, MA: The MIT Press.

————. 1997b. *Welfare, Volume 2: Measuring Social Welfare*. Cambridge, MA: The MIT Press.

————. 1998. *Econometric General Equilibrium Modeling*. Cambridge, MA: The MIT Press.

————. Forthcoming. *Econometrics and Producer Behavior*. Cambridge, MA: The MIT Press.

Jorgenson, Dale W., and Barbara M. Fraumeni. 1981. Relative Prices and Technical Change. In *Modeling and Measuring Natural Resource Substitution*, eds. Ernst R. Berndt and Barry C. Field, 17–47. Cambridge, MA: MIT Press.

————. 1989. The Accumulation of Human and Nonhuman Capital, 1948–1984. In *The Measurement of Saving, Investment, and Wealth*, eds. Robert E. Lipsey and Helen S. Tice, 227–282. Chicago, IL: University of Chicago Press.

Jorgenson, Dale W., Frank M. Gollop, and Barbara M. Fraumeni. 1987. *Productivity and U.S. Economic Growth*. Cambridge, MA: Harvard University Press.

Jorgenson, Dale W., and Mun S. Ho. 1994. Trade Policy and U.S. Economic Growth. *Journal of Prolific Modeling* 16, no. 2, 119–146.

Jorgenson, Dale W., and Jean-Jacques Laffont. 1974. Efficient Estimation of Nonlinear Simultaneous Equations with Additive Disturbances. *Annals of Social and Economic Measurement* 3, no. 4 (October): 615–640.

Jorgenson, Dale W., and Lawrence J. Lau. 1975. The Structure of Consumer Preferences. *Annals of Economic and Social Measurement* 4, no. 1 (January): 49–101.

————. 1983. *Transcendental Logarithmic Production Functions*. Amsterdam, The Netherlands: North-Holland.

Jorgenson, Dale, W., and Ralph Landau, eds. 1993. Tax Reform and the Cost of Capital: An International Comparison. Washington, DC: Brookings Institution.

Jorgenson, Dale W., Lawrence J. Lau, and Thomas M. Stoker. 1980. Welfare Comparison under Exact Aggregation. *American Economic Review* 70, no. 2 (May): 268–272.

————. 1981. Aggregate Consumer Behavior and Individual Welfare. In *Macroeconomic Analysis*, eds. D. Currie, R. Nobay, and D. Peel, 35–61. London, England: Croom-Helm.

————. 1982. The Transcendental Logarithmic Model of Aggregate Consumer Behavior. In *Advances in Econometrics*, vol. 1, eds. Robert L. Basmann and G. Rhodes, 97–238. Greenwich, CT: JAI Press.

Jorgenson, Dale W. and Daniel T. Slesnick. 1983. Individual and Social Cost of Living Indexes. In *Price Level Measurement*, eds. W. Erwin Diewert and C. Montmarquette, 241–323. Ottawa: Statistics Canada.

————. 1985. General Equilibrium Analysis of Economic Policy. In *New Developments in Applied General Equilibrium Analysis*, eds. John Piggott and John Whalley, 293–370. Cambridge, England: Cambridge University Press.

————. 1987a. Aggregate Consumer Behavior and Household Equivalence Scales. *Journal of Business and Economic Statistics* 5, no. 2 (April): 219–232.

————. 1987b. General Equilibrium Analysis of Natural Gas Price Regulation. In *Public Regulation*, ed. E. E. Bailey, 153–190. Cambridge, MA: MIT Press.

————. 1990. Individual and Social Cost-of-Living Indexes. In *Price Level Measurement*, ed. W. Erwin Diewert, 155–234. Amsterdam, The Netherlands: North-Holland.

Jorgenson, Dale W., Daniel T. Slesnick, and Thomas M. Stoker. 1987. Two-Stage Budgeting and Consumer Demand for Energy. In *Advances in the Economics of Energy and Resources*, vol. 6, ed. J. R. Moroney, 125–162. Greenwich, CT: JAI Press.

————. 1988. Two-Stage Budgeting and Exact Aggregation. *Journal of Business and Economic Statistics* 6, no. 3 (July): 313–326.

Jorgenson, Dale W., Daniel T. Slesnick, and Peter J. Wilcoxen. 1992. Carbon Taxes and Economic Welfare. Papers in Brookings Economic Activities: Microeconomics, 1992, 393–431.

Jorgenson, Dale W., and Thomas M. Stoker. 1984. Aggregate Consumer Expenditures on Energy. In *Advances in the Economics and Energy and Resources*, ed. J. R. Moroney, vol. 5, 1–84. Greenwich, MA: JAI Press.

Jorgenson, Dale W., and Peter J. Wilcoxen. 1990a. Environmental Regulation and U.S. Economic Growth. *The Rand Journal of Economics 21*, no. 2 (Summer): 314–340.

————. 1990b. Intertemporal General Equilibrium Modeling of U.S. Environmental Regulation. *Journal of Policy Modeling 12*, no. 4 (December): 1–30.

————. 1990c. The Cost of Controlling U.S. Carbon Dioxide Emissions. Mimeo, September.

————. 1992a. Global Change, Energy Prices, and U.S. Economic Growth. *Structural Change and Economic Dynamics* 3, no. 1 (March): 135–154.

————. 1992b. Reducing U.S. Carbon Dioxide Emissions: The Cost of Different Goals. In *Advances in the Economics of Energy and Resources*, vol. 7, ed. John R. Moroney, 125–158. Greenwich, CT: JAI Press.

———. 1992c. Reducing U.S. Carbon Dioxide Emissions: The Cost of Different Goals. *Energy, Growth, and the Environment*, no. 7: 125–158.

———. 1993a. The Economic Impact of the Clean Air Act Amendments of 1990. *Energy Journal* 14, no. 1 (January): 159–182.

———. 1993b. Reducing U.S. Carbon Dioxide Emissions: An Assessment of Alternative Instruments. *Journal of Policy Modeling* 15, no. 5 (December): 1–30.

———. 1993c. Reducing U.S. Carbon Dioxide Emissions: An Econometric General Equilibrium Assessment. *Resources and Energy Economics* 15, no. 1 (March): 7–26.

———. 1993d. Energy, the Environment, and Economic Growth. In *Handbook of Natural Resource and Energy Economics*, vol. 3, eds. Allen V. Kneese and James L. Sweeney, 1267–1349. Amsterdam, The Netherlands: North-Holland.

Jorgenson, Dale W., and Kun-Young Yun. 1986. The Efficiency of Capital Accumulation. *Scandinavian Journal of Economics* 88, no. 1: 85–107.

———. 1990. Tax Reform and U.S. Economic Growth. *Journal of Political Economy* 98, no. 5, Part 2 (October): S151–S193.

———. 1991a. The Excess Burden of U.S. Taxation. *Journal of Accounting, Auditing, and Finance* 6, no. 4 (Fall): 487–509.

———. 1991b. *Tax Reform and the Cost of Capital*. New York, NY: Oxford University Press.

Kalt, J. P. 1988. The Impact of Domestic Environmental Regulatory Policies on U.S. International Competitiveness. In International Competitiveness, eds. A. M. Spence and H. A. Hazards, 221–262. Cambridge, MA: Ballinger.

Kappler, F. G., and G. L. Rutledge. 1985. Expenditures for Abating Pollutant Emissions from Motor Vehicles, 1968–1984. *Survey of Current Business* 65, no. 7 (July) 29–35.

Kennedy, Charles. 1964. Induced Bias in Innovation and the Theory of Distribution. *Economic Journal* 74, no. 295 (September): 541–547.

Kirman, A. P. 1992. Whom or What Does the Representative Individual Represent? *Journal of Economic Perspectives* 6, no. 2 (Spring): 117–136.

of the Cost of Living. *Review of Economic Studies* 15, no. 2: 84–87.

Kloek, Tuun. 1966. *Indexcijfers: Enige methodologisch aspecten.* The Hague, The Netherlands: Pasmans.

Kneese, Allen V., Robert U. Ayres, and R. C. d'Arge. 1970. Economics and the Environment: A Materials Balance Approach. Baltimore, MD: Johns Hopkins University Press.

Kneese, Allen V., and James L. Sweeney, eds. 1985. *Handbook of Natural Resource and Energy Economics*, 2 vols., Amsterdam, The Netherlands: North-Holland.

Kolstad, Charles D. 1990. Energy-Economy-Environment Modeling. *The Energy Journal*.

Koopmans, Tjalling Charles. 1967. Objectives, Constraints, and Outcomes in Optimal Growth. *Econometrica* 35, no. 1 (January): 1–15.

Kosobud, Richard, F., Thomas A. Daly, and Yoon I. Chang, 1983. Decentralized CO_2 Abatement Policy and Energy Choices in the Long. Run. In *Government and Energy Policy, International Association of Energy Economists*. Alexandria: Westview Press.

Lau, Lawrence J. 1977a. Complete Systems of Consumer Demand Functions through Duality. In *Frontiers of Quantitative Economics*, vol. 3, eds. Michael D. Intriligator,and David A. Kendrick, 59–86. Amsterdam, The Netherlands: North-Holland.

———. 1977b. Existence Conditions for Aggregate Demand Functions. The Case of Multiple Indexes. Technical Report 248 (October). Stanford, CA: Institute for Mathesmatical Studies in Social Sciences, Stanford Universilty (revised 1980, and 1982).

———. 1978. Testing and Imposing Monotonicity, Convexity, and Quasi-Convexity. In *Production Economics: A Dual Approach to Theory and Applications*, vol. 1, eds. Melvin Fuss and Daniel L. McFadden, 409–453. Amsterdam, The Netherlands: North-Holland.

———. 1982. A Note on the Fundamental Theorem of Exact Aggregation. *Economics Letters* 9, no. 2, 119–126.

———. 1986. Functional Forms in Econometric Model Building. In *Handbook of Econometics*, vol. 3, eds. Zvi Griliches, and Michael D. Intriligator, 1515–1566. Amsterdam, The Netherlands: North-Holland.

Lau, Lawrence J., Wou-Long Lin, and Pan A. Yotopoulos. 1978. The Linear Logarithmic Expenditure System: An Application to Consumption-Leisure Choice. *Econometrica* 46, no. 4 (July): 843–868.

Lave, Lester. 1988. The Greenhouse Effect: What Government Actions are Needed. *Journal of Policy Analysis and Management* 7, no. 3, 460–470.

———. 1990. Modification or Adaptation? *The Energy Journal*.

Leamer, Edward (1984). *Sources of International Comparative Advantage: Theory and Evidence*. Cambridge, MA: MIT Press.

Leontief, Wassily. 1951. *The Structure of the American Economy, 1919–1939*, 2nd ed. (1st ed. 1941), New York, NY: Oxford University Press.

———. 1953, ed. *Studies in the Structure of the American Economy*, New York, NY: Oxford University Press.

———. 1970. Environmental Repercussions and the Economic Structure: An Input-Output Approach. *Review of Economics and Statistics* 52, no. 3 (August): 262–271.

Leontief, Wassily, A. P. Carter, and Peter A. Petri. 1977. *The Future of the World Economy*, Oxford: Oxford University Press.

Leontief, Wassily, and D. Ford. 1972. Air Pollution and the Economic Structure: Empirical Results of Input-Output Computations. In *Input-Output Techniques*, eds. A. Brody, and A. P. Carter, 9–30. Amsterdam, The Netherlands: North-Holland.

Leser, Conrad E. V. 1963. Forms of Engel Functions. *Econometrica* 31, no. 4 (October): 694–703.

Lewbel, Arthur. 1989. Exact Aggregation and the Representative Consumer. *Quarterly Journal of Economics* 104, no. 3 (August): 622–633.

Lindahl, Erik 1970. The Place of Capital in the Theory of Price. In *Studies in the Theory of Money and Capital* (English translation of the Swedish original dating from 1929), London, England: Allen and Unwin, 271–350.

Low, Patrick and R. Safadi. 1992. Trade Policy and Pollution. In *International Trade and the Environment*. World Bank Discussion Paper 159.

Longva, Sven, L. Lorentsen, and Oystein Olsen. 1983. Energy in the Multi-Sectoral Growth Model MSG. In *Analysis of Supply and Demand of Electricity in the Norwegian Economy*, eds. Olav Bjerkholt, Sven Longva, Oystein Olsen, and Steinar Strom, 27–51. Oslo, Norway: Central Bureau of Statistics.

Longva, Sven, and Oystein Olsen. 1983. Producer Behavior in the MSG Model. In *Analysis of Supply land Demand of Electricity in the Norwegian Economy*, eds. Olav Bjerkhold, Sven Longva, Oystein Olsen, and Steinar Strom, 52–83. Oslo, Norway: Central Statistical Bureau.

Lucas, Robert E., Jr. 1967. Tests of a Capital-Theoretic Model of Technological Change. *Review of Economic Studies* 34, no. 98 (April): 175–180.

———. 1988. On the Mechanics of Economic Development. *Journal of Monetary Economics* 22, no. 1 (July): 3–42.

Maler, K.-G. 1974. *Environmental Economics, A Theoretical Inquiry*. Baltimore: Johns Hopkins University Press.

———. 1975. Macroeconomic Aspects of Environmental Policy. In *Economic Analysis of Environmental Problems*, ed. E. S. Mills, 27–56. New York, NY: Columbia University Press.

———. 1985. Welfare Economics and the Environment. In *Handbook of Natural Resource and Energy Economics*, eds. Allen V. Kneese and James L. Sweeney, vol. 1, 3–60. Amsterdam, The Netherlands: North-Holland.

Malinvaud, Edmond. 1980. *Statistical Methods of Econometrics*, 3rd ed. Amsterdam, The Netherlands: North-Holland.

Manne, Alan S. 1981. *ETA-MACRO: A User's Guide*. Palo Alto, Electric Power Research Institute, February.

————. 1992. Global 2100: Alternative Scenarios for Reducing Carbon Emissions. *OECD Economics Department Working Paper* 111.

Manne, Alan S., and Richard G. Richels. 1992. CO_2 Emission Limits: An Economic Analysis for the USA. *The Energy Journal* 11, no. 2 (April): 51–85.

————. 1992. Buying Greenhouse Insurance: The Economic Costs of CO_2 Emissions Limits. Cambridge, MA: The MIT Press.

Mansur, Ahsan, and John Whalley. 1984. Numerical Specification of Applied General Equilibrium Models: Estimation, Calibration, and Data. In *Applied General Equilibrium Analysis*, eds. Herbert E. Scarf and John B. Shoven, 69–127. Cambridge, England: Cambridge University Press.

Martos, Bela. 1969. Subdefinite Matrices and Quadratic Forms. *SIAM Journal of Applied Mathematics* 17: 1215–1223.

McFadden, Daniel L. 1963. Further Results on CES Production Functions. *Review of Economic Studies* 30 (2), no. 83 (June): 73–83.

McGuire, Martin C. 1982. Regulation, Factor Rewards, and International Trade. *Journal of Public Economics* 17:335–354.

McKibbin, W., and P. Wilcoxen. 1998. The Theoretical and Empirical Structure of the *G*-Cubed Model. Economic Modelling (forthcoming).

Meadows, D., J. Randers, and W. W. Behrens, III. 1972. *Limits to Growth*. New York, NY: Universe Books.

Meadows, D., and J. Randers. 1992. *Beyond the Limits*. New York, NY: Chelsea Green.

Merrifield, John. 1988. The Impact of Selected Abatement Strategies on Transnational Pollution, the Terms of Trade, and Factor Rewards: A Genral Equilibrium Approach. *Journal of Environmental Economics and Management* 15:259–284.

Mills, E. S. 1975, ed. *Economic Analysis of Environmental Problems*. New York, NY: Columbia University Press.

Mintzer, Irving M. 1987. A Matter of Degrees: The Potential for Controlling the Greenhouse Effect. Washington, DC: World Resources Institute, April.

Muellbauer, John S. 1975. Aggregation, Income Distribution, and Consumer Demand. *Review of Economic Studies* 42, no. 132 (October): 525–543.

————. 1976a. Community Preferences and the Representative Consumer. *Econometrica* 44, no. 5 (September): 979–999.

————. 1976b. Economics and the Representative Consumer. In *Private and Enlarged Consumption*, eds. L. Solari and J. N. Du Pasquier, 29–54. Amsterdam, The Netherlands: North-Holland.

————. 1977. Testing the Barten Model of Household Composition Effects and the Cost of Children. *Economic Journal* 87, no. 347 (September): 460–487.

National Research Council. 1983. *Changing Climate*. Washington, DC: National Academy Press.

———. 1992. *Policy Implications of Greenhouse Warming*. Washington, DC: National Academy Press.

Natural Resources Defense Council. 1989. Cooling the Greenhouse: Vital First Steps to Combat Global Warming, mimeo.

Nordhaus, William D. 1977. Economic Growth and Climate: the Carbon Dioxide Problem. *American Economic Review* 67, no. 1 (February): 341–346.

———. 1979. *The Efficient Use of Energy Resources*. New Haven, CT: Yale University Press.

———. 1982. How Fast Should We Graze the Global Commons? *American Economic Review* 72, no. 2 (May): 242–246.

———. 1989. A Sketch of the Economics of the Greenhouse Effect. *American Economic Review* 81, no. 2: 146–150.

———. 1990a. An Intertemporal General-Equilibrium Model of Economic Growth and Climate Change, mimeo, October.

———. 1990b. A Survey of the Costs of Reduction of Greenhouse Gases. *The Energy Journal* 11: 37–65.

———. 1991a. To Slow or Not to Slow: The Economics of the Greenhouse Effect. *Economic Journal* 101, no. 407 (July): 920–937.

———. 1991b. A Survey of the Costs of Reduction of Greenhouse Gases. *Energy Journal* 12, no. 1, 920–937.

———. 1991c. The Cost of Slowing Climate Change: A Survey. *Energy Journal* 12, no. 1:37–65.

———. 1992a. Lethal Model 2: The Limits to Growth Revisited. *Brookings Papers on Economic Activity* 2: 1–59.

———. 1992b. An Optimal Transition Path for Controlling Greenhouse Gases. *Science* 258, no. 5086 (November): 1315–1319.

———. 1992c. How Much Should we Invest in Preserving our Current Climate? Mimeo, New Haven, CT: Yale University.

———. 1994. *Managing the Global Commons*. New Haven: Yale University Press.

Nordhaus, William D., and Jesse Ausubel. 1983. A Review of Estimates of Future Carbon Dioxide Emissions. In *Changing Climate*, National Research Council. Washington, DC: National Academy Press.

Nordhaus, William D., and Gary Yohe. 1983. Future Carbon Dioxide Emissions from Fossil Fuels. In *Changing Climate*, National Research Council. Washington, DC: National Academy Press.

North, D. Warner. 1990. Policy Options for the United States. *The Energy Journal*.

Parks, Richard W., and A. P. Barten. 1973. A Cross-Country Comparison of the Effects of Prices, Income, and Population Compensation on Consumption Patterns. *Economic Journal* 83, no. 331 (September): 834–852.

Passell, Peter. 1989. Staggering Cost is Forseen to Curb Warming of Earth. *New York Times*, November 19.

Peck, Stephen C., and Thomas J. Teisberg. 1990. A Framework for Exploring Cost Effective Carbon Dioxide Control Paths. Palo Alto, CA, Electric Power Research Institute, October.

————. 1992. Global Warming Uncertainties and the Value of Information: An Analysis Using CETA. Palo Alto, CA, Electric Power Research Institute, February.

Pethig, Rudiger. 1976. Pollution, Welfare, and Environmental Policy in the Theory of Comparative Advantage. *Journal of Environmental Economics and Management* 2:160–169.

Petri, Peter A. 1984. *Modelling Japanese-American Trade*. Cambridge, MA: Harvard University Press.

————. 1986. Comments, in T. N. Srinivasan and J. Whalley.

Portney, P. R. 1990a. Policy Watch: Economics and the Clean Air Act. *Journal of Economic Perspectives* 4, no. 4 (Fall): 173–182.

————. 1990b, ed. *Public Policies for Environmental Protection*. Washington, DC: Resources for the Future.

Pollak, Robert A., and Terence J. Wales. 1978. Estimation of Complete Demand Systems from Household Budget Data: The Linear and Quadratic Expenditure Systems. *American Economic Review* 68, no. 3 (June): 348–359.

————. 1980. Comparison of the Quadratic Expenditure System and Translog Demand Systems with Alternative Specifications of Demographic Effects. *Econometrica* 48, no. 3 (April): 595–612.

Poterba, James M. 1991. Tax Policy to Combat Global Warming: On Designing a Carbon Tax. In *Global Warming: Economic Policy Responses*, eds. Rudiger Dornbusch and James M. Poterba, 71–97. Cambridge, MA: The MIT Press.

Prais, S. J., and Hendrik S. Houthakker. 1955. *The Analysis of Family Budgets*, 2nd ed., 1971. Cambridge, England: Cambridge University Press.

Reilly, John M., James A. Edmonds, K. H. Gardner, and A. L. Brenkert. 1987. Uncertainty Analysis of the IEA/ORAU CO_2 Emissions Model. *The Energy Journal* 8, no. 3: 1–29.

Richardson, J. D. and Mutti. 1976. Industrial Development through Environmental Controls: the International Competitive Aspect. In *International Environmental Economics*. Wiley.

Robison, H. 1988. Industrial Pollution Abatement: The Impact on the Balance of Trade. *Canadian Journal of Economics* 21(1).

Romer, Paul M. 1989. Capital Accumulation in the Theory of Long-Run Growth. In *Modern Business Cycle Theory*, ed. R. J. Barro, 51–127. Cambridge, MA: Harvard University Press.

Ross, Marc. 1989. Improving the Efficiency of Electricity Use in Manufacturing. *Science* 244, no. 4902 (April): 311–317.

Roy, Rene. 1943. *De l'utilite: Contribution a la theorie des choix.* Paris: Herman and Cie.

Samuelson, Paul A. 1951. Abstract of a Theorem Concerning Substitutability in Open Leontief Models. In *Activity Analysis of Production and Allocation*, ed. Tjalling C. Koopmans, 142–146. New York, NY: Wiley and Sons.

————. 1953. Prices of Factors and Goods in General Equilibrium. *Review of Economic Studies* 21, no. 54 (October): 1–20.

————. 1956. Social Indifference Curves. *Quarterly Journal of Economics* 70, no. 1 (February): 1–22.

————. 1965. A Theory of Induced Innovation along Kennedy-Weizsacker Lines. *Review of Economics and Statistics* 47, no. 3 (November): 343–356.

————. 1973. Relative Shares and Elasticities Simplified Comment. *American Economic Review* 63, no. 4 (September): 770–771.

Scarf, Herbert E., and T. Hansen. 1973. *Computation of Economic Equilibria.* New Haven, CT: Yale University Press.

————. 1984. Computation of Equilibrium Prices. In *Applied General Equilibrium Analysis*, eds. Herbert E. Scarf and John B. Shoven, 1–51, Cambridge, England: Cambridge University Press.

Scarf, Herbert E., and John B. Shoven. 1984, eds. *Applied General Equilibrium Analysis.* Cambridge, England: Cambridge University Press.

Schelling, Thomas C. 1992. Some Economics of Global Warming. *American Economic Review* 82, no. 1 (March): 1–14.

Schipper, L., S. Meyers, Richard Howarth, and Ruth Steiner 1992. *Energy Efficiency and Human Activity: Past Trends, Future Prospects.* Cambridge, England: Cambridge University Press.

Schmookler, Jacob. 1966. Invention and Economic Growth. Cambridge, MA: Harvard University Press.

Schneider, Stephen H. 1989. The Greenhouse Effect: Science and Policy. *Science* 243, no. 4894 (February): 771–781.

Schultz, Henry. 1938. *The Theory and Measurement of Demand.* Chicago: University of Chicago Press.

Schurr, S., B. C. Netschert, V. E. Eliasberg, J. Lerner, and H. H. Landsberg. 1960. *Energy in the American Economy, 1850–1975*. Baltimore, MD: Johns Hopkins University Press.

Schurr, S., C. C. Burwell, W. D. Devine, Jr., and S. Sonenblum 1990. *Electricity in the American Economy: Agent of Technological Progress*. Westport, CT: Greenwood.

Shiells, C., R. M. Stern, and A. Deardorff. 1986. Estimates of the Elasticities of Substitution between Imports and Home Goods for the U.S. *Weltwirtschaftliches Archiv* 3: 497–519.

Shortle, James S., and K. Willett. 1986. The Incidence of Water Pollution Control Costs: Partial vs. General Equilibrium Computations. *Growth and Change* 17(2):32–43

Shoven, John B., and John Whalley. 1992. *Applying General Equilibrium*. Cambridge, England: Cambridge University Press.

Siebert, Horst. 1977. Environmental Quality and the Gains from Trade *Kyklos* 30:657–673.

Solow, Robert M. 1956. A Contribution to the Theory of Economic Growth. *Quarterly Journal of Economics* 70, no. 1 (February): 65–94.

———. 1974a. The Economics of Resources or the Resources of Economics. *American Economic Review* 64, no. 2 (May): 1–14.

———. 1974b. Intergenerational Equity and Exhaustible Resources. *Review of Economic Studies*, Symposium on the Economics of Exhaustible Resources, 29–45.

———. 1988. Growth Theory and After. *American Economic Review* 78, no. 3 (June): 307–317.

———. 1990. Is There a Global Warming Problem? Mimeo.

Srinivasan, T. N., and J. Whalley. 1986. *General Equilibrium Trade Policy Modelling*. Cambridge, MA: The MIT Press.

Steinberg, M., H. Cheng, and F. Horn. 1984. A Systems Study for the Removal, Recovery, and Disposal of Carbon Dioxide from Fossil Fuel Power Plants. *U.S. Department of Energy* CH/00016–2.

Stern, R. M., J. Francis, and B. Schumacher. 1976. *Price Elasticities in International Trade: An Annotated Bibliography*. London, England: Macmillan.

Stevens, William K. 1989. Skeptics Challenging Dire Greenhouse Views. *New York Times*, December 13.

Stokey, N. L., Robert E. Lucas, Jr., and E. C. Prescott. 1989. *Recursive Methods in Economic Dynamics*. Cambridge, MA: Harvard University Press.

Stone, J. A. 1979. Price Elasticities of Demand for Imports and Exports: Industry Estimates for the U.S., the EEC and Japan. *Review of Economics and Statistics* 61(1): 117–123.

Stone, Richard. 1954a. Linear Expenditure Systems and Demand Analysis: An Application to the Pattern of British Demand. *Economic Journal* 64, no. 255 (September): 511–527.

———. 1954b. *Measurement of Consumers' Expenditures and Behavior in the United Kingdom*, vol. 1. Cambridge, England: Cambridge University Press.

Stoker, Thomas M. 1993. Empirical Approaches to the Problem of Aggregation over Individuals. *Journal of Economic Literature* 31, no. 4, (December): 1827–1875.

Stokey, N. L., Robert E. Lucas, Jr., and E. C. Prescott. 1989. *Recursive Methods in Economic Dynamics*. Cambridge, MA: Harvard University Press.

Theil, Henry. 1965. The Information Approach to Demand Analysis. *Econometrica* 33, no. 1 (January): 67–87.

Tobey, James A. 1990. The Effects of Domestic Environmental Policies on Patterns of World Trade: An Empirical Test. *Kyklos* 43(2):191–209.

Tobin, James. 1969. A General Equilibrium Approach to Monetary Theory. *Journal of Money, Credit and Banking* 1 no. 1 (February): 15–29.

Tornqvist, Leo. 1936. The Bank of Findland's Consumption Price Index. *Bank of Finland Monthly Bulletin*, no. 10: 1–8.

Ugelow, J. 1982. A Survey of Recent Studies on Costs of Pollution Control and the Effects on Trade. In *Environment and Trade*, ed. S. Rubin. New Jersey: Allanheld Osmun and Co.

United Nations. 1968. *A System of National Accounts*. New York, NY: United Nations.

———. 1993. *System of National Accounts 1993*. New York: United Nations. U.S. Department of the Treasury.

———. 1984. *Tax Reform for Fairness, Simplicity and Economic Growth*. Washington, DC: U.S. Government Printing Office.

———. 1992. *Taxing Business Income Once*. Washington, DC: U.S. Government Printing Office.

Uzawa, Hirofumi. 1962. Production Functions with Constant Elasticities of Substitution. *Review of Economic Studies* 29 (4), no. 81 (October): 291–299.

———. 1975. Optimal Investment in Social Overhead Capital. In *Economic Analysis of Environmental Problems*, ed. E. S. Mills, 9–22. New York, NY: Columbia University.

———. 1988. *Optimality, Equilibrium, and Growth*. Tokyo: University of Tokyo Press.

von Weizsacker, C. Christian. 1962. *A New Technical Progress Function*. Cambridge, MA: Department of Economics, MIT, unpublished.

Whalley, John. 1985. *Trade Liberalization among Major World Trading Areas*. Cambridge, MA: The MIT Press.

Whalley, John, and Randall Wigle 1990. The International Incidence of Carbon Taxes. In *Global Warming: Economic Policy Responses*, eds. R. Dornbusch and J. M. Poterba, 233–263. Cambridge, MA: The MIT Press.

———. 1991. Cutting CO_2 Emissions: The Effects of Alternative Policy Approaches. *The Energy Journal* 12, no. 1:109–124.

Wilcoxen, Peter J. 1988. The Effects of Environmental Regulation and Energy Prices on U.S. Economic Performance. Ph.D. Dissertation. Cambridge, MA: Harvard University Press.

———. 1992. An Introduction to Intertemporal Modeling. *Notes and Problems in Applied General Equilibrium Economics*, eds. P. R. Dixon, B. R. Parmenter, A. A. Powell, and Peter J. Wilcoxen, 277–284. Amsterdam, The Netherlands: North-Holland.

Wood, David O. 1990. Where Do We Stand? *The Energy Journal*.

Wold, Herman. 1953. *Demand Analysis: A Study in Econometrics*. New York, NY: Wiley and Sons.

World Bank. 1992. *World Development Report*. Washington, DC: World Bank.

World Commission on Environment and Development. 1987. *Our Common Future*. Oxford, England: Oxford University Press.

Index

Acid rain, 229, 246
Ad valorem taxes
    economic dynamics, 294–299
    fossil fuels, 287
    long-term effect, 287–292
    prices and output, 293
Aggregate consumer behavior
    econometric models, 92, 111–119
    equlibrium analysis, 111–119
    model notation, 26
Aggregation. *See also* Exact aggregation
    conditions, 114
    Lau's theory, 113
Agriculture, technical change, 138
Air toxics, 229, 246
Apparel and fabrics, technical change, 139
Arab Oil Embargo, 54
Armey, Dick, 426
Asset prices, 5

Bergman, Lars, xiii
Berndt, Ernst R., xiv
Btu tax. *See* Carbon tax
Bureau of Economic Analysis, 38, 85n
Business sector, 15, 20–22

Canada, value added tax, 426
Capital
    accumulation, 203
    carbon taxes, 394
    discounted value, 5
    intertemporal model, 203
    operating costs, 349
    prices, 100
    services, 5
    translog indexes, 100

Capital formation
    carbon emissions, 282
    environmental regulation, 236
    intertemporal model, 30, 421
    investment, 30–32
    model overview, 236, 258, 282
    tax reform, 421
Capital gains, special treatment, 424
Capitalist behavior, dynamic model, 382, 388
Capital stock
    annual changes, 297
    base model, 35
    carbon tax, 76, 220, 224
    econometric model, 164
    environmental regulation, 43, 53
    higher energy prices, 60
    inelastic supply, 172
    intertemporal results, 81
    oil prices, 62
    pollution abatement, 47
    tax policy, 297
    tax reform, 434
    time path, 173
Carbon dioxide
    abatement costs, 195–198
    alternative tax, xix
    annual emissions, 206
    base case, 206
    calculating emissions, 205, 260
    Edmonds-Reilly model, 197, 226n
    emissions data, 13, 66, 208, 261, 333
    future effects, 217
    Manne-Richels model, 197
    marginal tax, 208
    model overview, 199–207

Carbon dioxide (*cont.*)
  numerical models, 333
  producer behavior, 199–201
  reducing emissions, 195–198
  regulation and trade, 390–393
  restrictions, xxii, 3
  United States, 195–198
Carbon emissions, 56
  annual data, 66, 285, 296, 387
  assumptions, 270
  base case, 261, 270, 285, 391
  climatic model, 376
  computing, 65
  different scenarios, 267
  disaggregated model, 277
  dynamic model, 376–390
  econometric assessment, 253
  economic dynamics, 294–299
  energy sectors, 284, 387
  equilibrium analysis, 253
  estimating, 284
  future impact, 286
  global model, 373
  Grossman-Krueger model, 374
  international trade, 373
  McKibbin-Wilcoxen model, 374
  Manne-Richels model, 374
  model overview, 254–262, 277–286
  multi-region model, 374
  policy instruments, 275, 287–298
  reducing, 267–269
  regulation and trade, 390–393
  simulation model, 65
  single-country models, 375
  stabilizing, 262–267, 373–376
  target paths, 78
  tax policy, 287–298
  United States, 253, 275
  Whalley-Wigle model, 374
Carbon tax
  annual emissions, 218
  vs. Btu tax, 407, 409
  capital stock, 220, 224
  coal production, 218, 223
  commodity prices, 68
  computing emissions, 65
  controlling emissions, 223
  crude oil extraction, 220, 224
  different scenarios, 268
  domestic output, 399, 402
  double dividend, xx

economic dynamics, 294–299
  fossil fuels, 196
  higher energy prices, 54
  impact, 65
  intertemporal results, 73–80, 217–222
  long-term effects, 67, 209, 287, 393
  output and prices, 69, 210, 265, 289
  path and targets, 78, 217, 392, 401
  policy effect, 392–401
  responsibility, 3
  results, 74
  revenue use, 198, 269
  simulation models, 216
  stabilizing emissions, 262–267
  steady-state effects, 398
  trade flows, xxiii
  United States, 275
  Whalley-Wigle model, 198
Cass, David, xii
Chemicals, technical change, 140
Chlorofluorocarbons (CFC), 196, 229
Cholesky factor, consumer behavior, 124
Christensen, Laurits, xv
Clean Air Act, 157, 333
Clean Air Act (1990)
  dynamic effect, 250
  economic impact, 229–231
  future impact, 246–250
  model overview, 231–238
  output and prices, 248
Climate change models, 2
Coal mining
  annual production, 296
  carbon tax, 67, 75, 209, 217, 264
  prices, 67, 264
  production, 75, 218, 223, 296
  tax policy, 296
  technical change, 138
Combustion, fluidized bed technology, 9
Commodities
  defined, 377
  highly polluting, 332
  nonsubstitution theorem, 91
  prices, 17, 91, 118
  supply and demand, 337, 380
  translog model, 118
Commodity groups
  carbon tax, 210
  consumer expenditures, 146
  final demand, 165
  by industry, 160

make and use tables, 162
model overview, 159
pooled estimates, 147–150
types, 146
Communications, technical change, 142
Competitiveness, 350, 397
Conference on Environment and
    Development (1992), 275
Conference on the Changing Environment
    (Toronto), 196
Constant elasticity of substitution (CES),
    9, 91
Construction, technical change, 138
Consumer behavior. *See also* Aggregate
    consumer behavior
    dynamic model, 339, 383
    econometric models, 11, 23, 91, 111, 234,
        420
    economic growth, 165, 308
    economy, 23, 339
    empirical results, 144–151
    environmental regulation, 165–167
    equilibrium analysis, 111–119
    Gorman's model, 113
    integrability, 119–125
    intertemporal model, 23, 166, 308, 419
    model notation, 24, 116, 126
    Muellbauer's model, 113
    stochastic specifications, 125–133
    tax reform, 419–421
    three-stage optimization, 234
    trade policy, 308
    translog model, 115–118
    two-stage allocation, 118
    United States, 23–30
    use table, 17, 23
Consumption
    carbon emissions, 280–282
    environmental regulation, 43, 53, 234
    higher energy prices, 60
    household, 28, 234
    intertemporal model, 202
    Jorgenson-Slesnick model, 339, 383
    model overview, 234, 257, 280
    oil prices, 62
    personal expenditures, 281, 301n
    pollution abatement, 47
    tax reform, 435
Consumption tax
    credit method, 426
    defining, 428

implementing, 425–427
vs. income tax, xxiv
rate, 433
subtraction method, 426
Cost of living index, 166, 193n
Council on Environmental Policy, 372n
Covariance matrix, 127
Crude oil
    carbon tax, 220, 264
    extraction, 224
    prices, 264
    production, 138
    technical change, 138
Current Population Reports (Census
    Bureau), 146

Demand functions, aggregate, 11
Disaggregation models, 5, 13, 80
Double dividend, carbon tax, xx
Dynamic equilibrium, 343, 388
Dynamic integrated climate economy
    (DICE), 2, 5

Econometric models
    aggregate consumer behavior, 111–119
    calibration approach, 161, 193n, 299
    empirical results, 135
    equilibrium analysis, 135
    parameterization, 299
    producer behavior, 95
Economic growth. *See also* Environmental
    regulation
    ad valorem tax, 294–299
    alternative case, 238
    base case, 238, 285
    carbon tax, 294–299
    Cass-Koopman's theory, 1
    Clean Air Act (1990), 229, 246
    consumer behavior, 165–167
    declines, 2
    environment, 1–14
    exogenous variables, 238
    international, xv
    intertemporal model, 305–315
    model overview, 159–161
    neoclassical model, 1
    Norway, 10
    pollution control, 230
    postwar, xv, 157
    producer behavior, 161–165
    solution model, 167–172

Economic growth (*cont.*)
   trade policy, 303–305
   United States, 157, 191, 303
   variables, 34
   world model, 2
Economy
   alternative case, 33–36
   base case, 33–36
   capitalist behavior, 338, 382
   Cass-Koopman's model, 333
   commodity supply, 337
   consumer behavior, 23, 337, 383
   dynamic model, 333, 376–390
   econometric model, 164
   exogenous variables, 389
   future size, 172
   government behavior, 340, 384
   interindustry transactions, 161, 193n
   intertemporal model, 12, 14
   make and use tables, 336, 379
   Manne-Richels model, 340
   model overview, 254–262
   multisector model, 333, 376
   producer behavior, 14, 334, 380
   saddle path, 389
   sectors, 14, 305, 335
   solution model, 167–172
   static equilibrium, 343
   steady-state, 389
   transition path, 173
   United States, 12, 157, 307, 333, 376
Edmonds-Reilly model, carbon dioxide
    emissions, 197, 226n
Education, future levels, 172
Elasticity of substitution, 9
Electrical machinery, 141
Electric utilities
   abatement costs, 38
   carbon tax, 212
   econometric models, 158
   environmental regulation, 176, 240
   Gollop-Roberts model, 9
   operating costs, 240
   technical change, 142
Electrostatic precipitators, 158
Energy
   carbon emissions, 284
   economic growth, 1–14
   efficiency, 257
   environment, 1–14
   policy modeling, 7–9

   production, 284
   tax policy, 276, 287, 294
Energy Information Administration, 284
Energy markets
   consumer behavior, 419–421
   intertemporal model, 413–423
   producer behavior, 415–419
   tax reform, xxiii, 413
Energy Modeling Forum, 253
Energy prices
   carbon tax, 71
   dynamic effects, 59–64
   elasticity of substitution, 69
   higher, 52–56
   natural experiment, 13
   steady-state effects, 57–59
   translog indexes, 100
Energy technology assessment (ETA), 3
Environment
   economic growth, 1–14
   policy modeling, 6–9
   trade policy, 373
Environmental Protection Agency (EPA),
    65, 158, 332
Environmental regulation
   alternative policy, 234
   base case, 238
   consumer behavior, 165–167
   dynamic effects, 190, 245, 333
   economic growth, 157, 229, 239
   equipment investment, 354–360
   Heckscher-Ohlin theory, 331
   industry costs, 347
   legislation, 344, 354, 370
   long-term impact, 241, 244
   model overview, 159, 231
   motor vehicles, 48–50, 360–365
   objectives, 165
   operating costs, 38, 167, 174, 240
   output and prices, 42, 244
   overall impact, 50, 243, 365
   process changes, 158
   producer behavior, 158, 161, 231
   removing, 40
   sensitivity analysis, 370
   solution model, 167–172
   steady-state effects, 351, 358
   trade patterns, 331, 344
   United States, 157–159
Equilibrium, static and dynamic, 343,
    388

Equilibrium analysis
  applied general, 89–95
  calibration models, 90
  commodity substitution, 161, 193n
  computational modeling, 89
  consumer behavior, 111–119
  econometric models, 89–95
  empirical results, 135
  Johansen model, 90
  multicountry model, 303, 310
  world trade model, 303
Exact aggregation
  conditions, 117
  Lau's theory, 12
  translog model, 115
Expenditure shares, aggregate, 117, 127
Exports
  carbon tax, 396, 403
  demand functions, 314
  future prices, 171
  intertemporal model, 311–313
  military, 314
  modeling, 33
  model overview, 283
  operating costs, 350, 353
  price elasticity, 312
  quotas, 304
  tariffs, 311
  tax reform, 436
  trade policy, 311–313
  use table, 17, 32
  voluntary restrictions, 304, 323

Fabricated metals, technical change, 141
Fabrics and apparel, 139
Federal deficit, 207, 429
Federalism, fiscal, 429
Final demands, 168, 170
Finance, technical change, 143
Fisheries, production, 138
Fixed-coefficient analysis, 6–9
Fixed-point models, 10
Flat tax, 426, 441n
Fluidized bed technology, 9, 158
Food products, production, 129
Foreign trade
  Armington approach, 205, 227n, 237
  carbon emissions, 283
  environmental regulation, 237
  government, 32
  imports and exports, 32

  intertemporal model, 32, 204, 422
  model overview, 237, 259, 283
  tax reform, 422
Forestry, technical change, 138
Fossil fuels
  carbon tax, 196
  global warming, 52
  heat content, 260, 284
  production, 260, 264
  tax instruments, 276
Framework Convention on Climate
    Change (1992), 275
Fraumeni, Barbara M., xiv
Frisch, Ragnar, xiii
Fuel prices. See also Fossil fuels
  economic impact, 48
Full consumption, 339
  carbon tax, 394
  operating costs, 349
Full wealth, 273n, 420
Furniture, technical change, 139

Gas utilities, production, 143
General Agreement on Trade and Tariffs
    (GATT), 304, 315
Global warming
  carbon dioxide, 52, 195, 226n
  carbon emissions, 376, 412n
  environmental policy, 13
  international issue, 275, 300n
  Manne-Richels model, 255
  severe consequences, 196
  slowing, 262
Gollop-Roberts model, electric utilities, 9
Gorman, William M., 113
Goulder, Lawrence, xx
Government. See also United States
  behavior, 340, 384
  budget deficit, 32
  carbon emissions, 283
  dynamic model, 340, 384
  enterprises, 143
  environmental regulation, 237
  foreign trade, 32
  intertemporal model, 32, 204, 422
  model overview, 237, 259, 283
  sector model, 170
  spending, 32, 86n
  tax reform, 422
Greenhouse effect, 2
  carbon dioxide, 195

Greenhouse effect (*cont.*)
    chlorofluorocarbons, 196
    controlling, 197
    economic impact, 276
Gross domestic product (GDP), 4, 432
Grossman-Krueger model, carbon
        emissions, 374
Gross national product (GNP)
    annual changes, 298
    carbon tax, 76, 221, 270, 395
    environmental regulation, 43, 53
    higher energy prices, 60
    intertemporal results, 81
    oil prices, 62
    operating costs, 349
    pollution abatement, 47
    tax policy, 298
    trade barriers, 327
Growth. *See* Economic growth

Hearings on Replacing the Federal
        Income Tax (1995), 425
Heckscher-Ohlin framework,
        environmental regulation, 331
Heteroscedasticity, 129
Ho, Mun S., 303, 331, 373
Hogan, William W., 257
Homogeneity, 100, 119
Homothetic preferences, 11
Households
    allocation decisions, 29
    consumption, 27, 234
    demographics, 25, 86n, 146
    expenditure patterns, 23, 169
    income, 169
    model notation, 24–27
    representative models, 29
    three-stage optimization, 234, 257, 280
    translog model, 115
    types, 235
    wealth, 27
Hudson, Edward A., xiv

Imports
    carbon tax, 396, 400, 405
    competitive, 309
    demand elasticity, 306, 342, 386
    economic growth, 309–311
    future prices, 171
    intertemporal model, 309–311
    model overview, 283

operating costs, 350, 353
    postwar demand, 310
    tariffs, xx, 304, 315
    tax reform, 436
    total supply, 309
    trade policy, 309–311
    unexplained, 310
    use table, 17, 32
Indirect utility function, 24
Industry. *See also specific industry*
    classification, 15, 20, 145
    model notation, 20–22
    output prices, 35, 167
    solution model, 167
    technical change, 145
Input-output analysis, xii, 89
Instruments, production, 142
Insurance, technical change, 143
Integrability, 100, 119
Intergovernment Panel on Climate
        Change, 195
Interindustry Transactions Accounts, 136
Intertemporal models
    base case, 33–36
    consumer behavior, 23, 419
    economic growth, 305–315
    energy markets, 413–423
    vs. neoclassical models, 36
Investment
    behavioral equations, 31
    capital formation, 30–32
    carbon emissions, 282
    energy prices, 43, 53, 60
    environmental regulation, 43, 53, 236
    intertemporal model, 30, 203, 421
    model overview, 236, 258, 282
    pollution abatement, 47
    tax reform, 421, 435
    use table, 17, 31

Japan, import quotas, 317
Johansen, Leif, xiii, 8, 90
Joint production, 19
Jorgenson, Dale W., 1, 89, 157, 195, 229,
        253, 275, 303, 331, 373, 413
Jorgenson-Slesnick model, consumption,
        339

Kappler, F. G., 184
Koopmans, Tjalling C., xii
Kronecker product form, 127

Kyoto Agreement (1997), xvii

Labor
    prices, 100
    supply, 434
    tax reform, 434
Lau, Lawrence, xiv, 235, 281
Lau's theory, aggregation, 12, 113
Leather, production, 140
Leisure time, household preferences, 166
Leontief, Wassily W., xii, 6, 89
Limits to Growth (Club of Rome), 7
Lumber, production, 139

Machinery. *See also* Electrical machinery
    technical change, 141
McKibbin-Wilcoxen model, carbon
        emissions, 374
Make and use tables, 17
Manne, Alan S., xviii, 3, 197, 374
Materials balances, 6
Merely positive-subdefinite matrix,
        124
Metals
    fabricated, 141
    mining, 138
    production, 138
Methane, greenhouse effect, 196
Michigan model, multicountry
        equilibrium, 303, 310
Mining. *See* Coal mining
Mobile sources, environmental regulation,
        229
Monotonicity, 102, 123, 137
Motor vehicles
    commodity prices, 49
    economic impact, 41, 48
    emissions control, 48, 184, 242, 360
    environmental regulation, 48, 360
    industry output, 50, 186
    long-term impact, 241
    production, 141
Muellbauer's model, consumer behavior,
        113
Multicountry models, trade policy, 303,
        310
Multisector growth, Johansen's model, 8
Myopic decision rules, 97

National accounts, conventional systems,
        85n

National Environmental Policy Act (1970),
        157, 229, 333
National Income and Product Accounts,
        136
Natural gas, production, 138
Natural Resources Defense Council, 196
Nitrogen oxides, greenhouse effect, 196,
        246
Noncommodity flows, 313–315
Noncompetitive imports, 377, 412n
Nonlinear regression, translog model, 132
Nonlinear three-stage least-squares
        model, 132
Nonnegativity, 102, 122
Nonsubstitution theorem, commodity
        prices, xiii, 10
Nordhaus, William, xviii, 197
Nordhaus model, climate change, 2
North American Free Trade Area
        (NAFTA), 331
Norway, economic growth, 10

Oil and gas extraction
    annual changes, 297
    carbon tax, 75, 79
    tax policy, 297
Oil prices
    carbon tax, 67
    decomposition effects, 64
    industry output, 58
    long-term simulation, 57
    real, 55
    world impact, 64
Our Common Future (World Commission
        on Environment and Development),
        7
Ozone, greenhouse effect, 196, 229

Paper, production, 140
Parameterization, econometric, 16, 82
Personal consumption expenditures, 336,
        427
Petri, Peter A., 310
Petroleum refining. *See also* Oil prices
    motor vehicles, 49
    production, 140
Pollution abatement
    commodity prices, 45
    dynamic effects, 179
    economic growth, 1, 159
    industry cost, 39

Pollution abatement (*cont.*)
  legislation, 157
  operating costs, 38, 240
  output, 46
Pollution Abatement Costs and Expenditures,
    251n
Pollution control
  commodity prices, 51
  dynamic effects, 183
  economic growth, xvi, 230
  equipment investment, 44, 180, 241, 354
  industry output, 52
  long-term effects, 189, 241
  overall impact, 51
  production costs, 173
Population
  demographics, 34, 87n
  forecasts, 207
  model solution, 171
  projections, 34
Precipitators, electrostatic, 158
Price functions
  Cholesky factorizations, 103
  commodity, 17, 19
  sector, 93, 96
  tax reform, 437
  translog, 98, 119
Price It Right (Alliance to Save Energy),
    xxiv
Primary metals, production, 141
Printing and publishing, technical change,
    140
Producer behavior
  capital and labor, 199, 226n
  carbon emissions, 199, 277
  dynamic model, 334, 380
  econometric models, 91, 161, 233, 279
  economic growth, 161, 305
  economy, 14, 334, 380
  empirical results, 136–144
  energy markets, 415–419
  environmental regulation, 161, 231
  equilibrium analysis, 95
  income data, 199, 226n
  integrable systems, 100–104
  intertemporal models, 14, 305, 415
  make and use tables, 417
  model notation, 20, 105
  model overview, 231, 277
  parameterization, 199, 233, 279
  stochastic specifications, 105–109

  tax reform, 415–419
  technical change, 201, 226n
  trade policy, 305–307
  translog model, 97–100
  two-stage allocation, 20
  United States, 14–22
Product exhaustion, 101
Production
  costs, 173
  interindustry transactions, 255
  model overview, 255–257
  parameterization, 138, 255
  pollution controls, 173
  sector models, 138–143
Productivity growth
  biased, 19, 233, 256, 279
  endogenous, 164, 255, 280

Real estate, technical change, 143
*Reducing Carbon Emissions from the Energy
    Sector: Cost and Policy Options*
    (Gaskings and Weyant), 272
Revenues, recycling, xx
Richardson-Mutti model, sector
    equilibrium, 333
Richels, Richard, xviii, 3
Roy's Identity, translog model, 115
Rubber and plastic, production, 140

Sales taxes, state and national, 426
Samuelson, Paul, xiii, 10, 96
Savings, private and government, 169
Scarf, Herbert, xiv
Sector equilibrium, Richardson-Mutti
    model, 333
Sensitivity analysis, environmental
    legislation, 370
Services industry, technical change, 143
Share elasticity, 21
  producer behavior, 137
  price consideration, 98, 153n
Shelby, Richard, 426
Shoven, John, xiii
Slesnick, Daniel T., xviii
Social accounting matrix, xiii
Social Security Administration, 207, 262
Solow, Robert M., 1
Stanford University, 253
Static equilibrium, 343, 388
Stern, Robert, xxi
Stoker, Thomas M., xv, 235, 281

Stolper-Samuelson theorem, trade
    patterns, 331
Stone, clay and glass, production, 141
Sulfur dioxide, environmental legislation,
    246
Summability, consumer behavior, 119
Supply prices, model solution, 168
Survey of Consumer Expenditures
    (1972–1973), 146
Symmetry
    consumer behavior, 120
    producer behavior, 101

Tariffs
    dynamic effects, 319, 325
    elimination, 318–321
    equivalents, 317
    Japan imports, 317
    multilateral, xxi, 327
    vs. quantitative restrictions, 304
    reductions, 315–323
    sector results, 321, 328
    selected quotas, 317
    trade barriers, 315–323
Taxes
    base case, 207
    prepaid, 427
    rates, 207
Tax law
    businesses, 424
    provisions, 423–425
    roll-overs, 423
    United States, 423–425
Tax policy
    alternative, xix, 414
    carbon emissions, 287–298
    comparing, 295
    economic growth, 303
    long-term effects, 287–292
Tax reform
    capital stock, 434
    carbon emissions, 440
    consumer behavior, 419–421
    consumption, 435
    debate, 428–430
    energy markets, 413, 440
    foreign trade, 422
    fundamental, 425–431
    government, 422
    implementation, 425–429
    imports and exports, 436

    intertemporal model, 413–423
    investment, 435
    labor supply, 434
    price changes, 437
    producer behavior, 415–419
    progressive, 429
    simulation results, 430, 432
Technical change
    biases, 99
    econometric models, 96, 153n
    parameter estimates, 138–143
    price indexes, 100
    sector models, 138–143
Technology, econometric modeling, xxiv
Tennessee Valley Authority, 169
Textiles, production, 139
Tobacco, technical change, 139
Toxic air, environmental regulation, 229,
    246
Trade barriers
    effects, 315
    elimination, 327
    quantitative restrictions, 323–327
    tariff reductions, 315–323
    vs. tariffs, 327
Trade patterns. *See also* Foreign trade
    dynamic model, 333
    environmental regulation, 331–333
    Heckscher-Ohlin framework, 331
    Stolper-Samuelson theorems, 331
    United States, 331–333
Trade policy
    economic growth, 303–305
    intertemporal model, 305–315
    producer behavior, 305–307
    United States, 303–305
Transfers, 313
Translog models, 97, 115
Transportation equipment, production,
    142

Unexplained imports, 310
United Nations, 6, 275
United States
    carbon dioxide, 195–198
    carbon emissions, 253, 275
    competitiveness, 373–376
    econometric assessment, 253
    economic growth, 157–159, 303–305
    economy, 333
    energy use, 377

United States (*cont.*)
   environmental regulation, 157–159
   equilibrium analysis, 253
   government, 170
   Postal Service, 169
   tax law, 423–425
   trade patterns, 331–333
   trade policy, 303–305
Use and make tables, commodity groups,
    162
Utilities. *See* Electric utilities
Utility functions, indirect, 94, 125

Value added taxes, 426

Water pollution, equilibrium models, 332
Wealth, household, 27
Whalley, John, xiii, xxi, 198
Wigle, Randall, 198
Wilcoxen, Peter J., 1, 157, 195, 229, 253,
    275, 413
Wirth, Timothy, 196
Wood and lumber, production, 139
World Commission on Environment and
    Development, 7
World economy, five-region model, 197
World trade, equilibrium models, 303

Yun, Kun-Young, xxiii